Performing Artistes in Ancient India

New Vistas in Indian Performing Arts

No. 1 Hindustānī Music and the Aesthetic Concept of Form by Anjali Mittal (ISBN 81-246-0134-8)

No. 2 Hindustani Sangeet and a Philosopher of Art — Music, Rhythm and Kathak Dance — *vis-à-vis* — Aesthetics of Susanne K. Langer by S.K. Saxena (ISBN 81-246-0180-1)

No. 3 Speaking of Dance — The Indian Critique by Mandakranta Bose (ISBN 81-246-0172-0)

New Vistas in Indian Performing Arts, no. 4

Performing Artistes in Ancient India

Iravati

D.K. Printworld (P) Ltd.
New Delhi

Cataloging in Publication Data — DK

Iravati, 1947–

Performing artistes in ancient India.

(New vistas in performing arts; no. 4).

Includes bibliographical references (p.)

Includes Index.

1. Theater — India — History. 2. Entertainers — India — History. I. Title. II. Series: New vistas in performing arts; no. 4.

ISBN 81-246-0207-7

First Published in India in 2003

Published and printed by:

D.K. Printworld (P) Ltd.

Regd. office : *'Sri Kunj'*, F-52, Bali Nagar

New Delhi - 110 015

Phones : (011) 545-3975; 546-6019; *Fax* : (011) 546-5926

E-mail: dkprintworld@vsnl.net

Foreword

Two of my former students chose to work on dramaturgy for their doctoral dissertations. One of them, in the 1960s, was M. Christopher Byrski from Poland (now Professor of Sanskrit at Warsaw and one-time Polish Ambassador to India) and the other is Ms. Iravati, the author of this work (now Reader in Ancient Indian History, Culture and Archaeology at Basant College for Women, Rājghāṭ and a well known Director of theatrical performances at Vārāṇasī). If the former had family background for selecting the topic the latter had personal commitment to it. Both have done splendid work. Byrski's work was published in 1974. I am pleased to find the other one being published now (it deserved to be published much earlier). Byrski focused on the theoretical aspects of theatre in ancient India and discussed its concept, symbolism, etc. Iravati directed her attention to the practising features of the theatre in ancient India and has discussed all the nitty-gritty aspects of it through the ages as known from the primary sources. In my knowledge, Iravati is the first to do such a major study of the theatre as a performing art in ancient India.

The book is indeed a comprehensive treatment of ancient Indian theatre. She has thoroughly examined the genesis of Indian theatre and its phases of development. She concludes convincingly how it arose from folk traditions and was groomed and disciplined by the elites of the society, how the *ācārya*s and the theatre artistes helped the various art forms and disciplines to emerge in a symbiotic relationship and how the *Naṭaśāstra* was transformed into *Nāṭyaśāstra*. This co-existence with mutual appreciation of the folk and classical traditions is significant. Iravati has given a detailed account of the various stages of the symbiotic process involving the *naṭa*s on the one hand and the *naṭācārya*s on the other.

Somehow the identity and individual contribution of artistes in the various branches of arts and crafts have been ignored in studies of ancient history and civilization of India. Iravati has given due recognition not only to the actors and actresses but also to the back-stage workers and the travelling troupes. She has given as well special attention to the various types of female performing artistes and it is interesting to find that there were female counterparts of almost each type of male performing artistes.

Iravati has not forgotten to deal with what she calls 'the love and hate relations' of Indian society with performing artistes for 'people despised their way of life but loved their art' and this leads her to examine the social status and economic conditions of the artistes in ancient India.

Iravati's work is an in-depth study of a little known subject in all its multifaceted features, relations and development. I am sure readers, both the specialists and the general ones, will find this contribution valuable and commendable.

A.K. Narain

Professor Eemeritus
History of South Asian Studies
Dept. of History
University of Wisconsin
Madison, U.S.A.

Preface

FASCINATED by the theatre, primarily as a captivated spectator and later as an artiste and director, I was increasingly drawn to make an indepth study of theatre as an art, as a discipline — in its various aspects like its origin, antiquity, development and atmosphere. I was keen on studying the contributions of those who had helped in creating and later translating the words of drama into action — the actors, actresses, directors, writers, back-stage workers and all those who populated the world of drama in ancient India.

I cannot claim to be an innovator on the subject since much work has been done in the field of drama and poetics. Works in this field are based basically on Bharata's *Nāṭyaśāstra* and Sanskrit dramas but Indian drama has a history dating back much earlier when it was in the form of dance, song and ritualistic impersonation. It seems necessary that students of the history of Indian drama should look into aspects of practice of drama as described in the *Nāṭyaśāstra* and depicted in the sculptures of ancient India. Some scholars like Kapila Vatsyayan and Padma Subrahmanyam have studied the art of dance in the light of ancient Indian sculptures. M.L. Varadpande needs special mention since he, basing his study on archaeological remains, sculptures, folklore and present folk theatre, gave a new direction and a different perspective to the study, though historical chronology is not manifested in a pronounced form in his works. My attempt in the present work is to study the evolution of ancient Indian theatre, particularly its representational aspect — dramatic theory and practice, focusing on the contributions of the performing artistes as actors, actresses and *naṭācārya*s upto 700 AD.

Originating in the form of folk art and enriching itself with several other socio-religious elements, Indian dramatic art was gradually polished and organised by *ācārya*s who made drama a respectable art, rather a discipline. The two traditions of drama folk and classical, co-existed in ancient India, often borrowing elements from each other and finally giving rise to a symbiotic tradition of Indian theatre. I have tried in this work to trace the history of the contributions of the performing artistes to the development of this symbiotic tradition.

As theatrical art developed and became more comprehensive, its different branches — dance, music, narration, acrobatics, impersonation and histrionics — merged into a single art called *nāṭya* and the original distinctive professions of performing artistes like *śailūṣa*, *śailālin*, *śobhanika*, *granthika*, *maṅkha*, *kuśīlava* and *bharata* merged into the single profession of *naṭa*, who originally was a folk artiste but whose art, later, with the intervention of *ācārya*s with sophisticated taste and scientific approach assumed a classical form up to a certain extent. These *naṭācārya*s were originally such *naṭa*s who had been proficient in the art and had gradually become the instructors of novices. When the art became a classical discipline, it attracted scholars from other fields and thus two types of *naṭācārya*s came into being — *ācārya*s of first type were represented by the theoreticians who drew a code for *naṭa*s like *Naṭasūtra* and might have produced '*prayoktā ācārya*s' (producer, director and actor all in one), and the second type, like Bharata, had a perfect knowledge of theory and practice of theatre. The *naṭa*s (actors) on one hand and the *naṭācārya*s on the other contributed to the development of Indian theatre. I have tried to give a detailed account of the various stages of this process.

It seems that due stress has not been laid on the contribution of actresses to drama so far. Much have been written on the position of women in ancient Indian society, but there too, actresses have found only marginal reference. Being an actress and director myself, I felt an urge to explore this field in detail and tried to make an indepth study of various types of female performing artistes such as the professional actress, the professional actress from royal harem the courtesan actress, and the actress of noble birth. There were female counterparts of almost each type of male performing artistes in ancient India like *kuśīlavā* (musician), *gāyanā* (singing and dancing woman), *aditi* (woman practising the art of *maṅkha*, *kauśikī* (a female artiste with the knowledge of music, dance and acting appointed in the harem of the state), *naṭī* or *nāṭakīyā* (an actress), *vaitālikā* (musician), *nepathyapālinī* (the female incharge of *nepathya*) and *sūtradhārī* (the female director of the play) who are mentioned in literature and depicted in sculpture. I have attempted to explore the field of their training and their special field of *abhinaya* and its style.

I have tried to give an account of the back-stage workers, their background and history while describing theatrical troupes. There were travelling troupes also in ancient India and I have attempted to trace their history as well. As several scholars have already studied *abhinaya* (the histrionic expressions) described by Bharata, I did not go in detail regarding the same but tried to explore the reason for the minute description of different modes of expression given by Bharata. Though a large number of books have been devoted to the study of Bharata's *Nāṭyaśāstra*, irrespective of approaches, what is missing in all these is a consideration of Bharata as a *prayoktā* (producer, director who is himself an actor), and as an *ācārya*, pouring his knowledge in every line of his treatise for the benefit of the future active workers of his field. The present work makes an attempt to address this aspect, giving a brief account of the four forms of histrionic art. It also gives a detailed account of various forms of stage and auditorium — open-air stage, cave theatre and pavilion or *maṇḍapa* type of theatre known from ancient Indian literature, sculpture and painting.

Ancient Indian society had a love-and-hate relation with the performing artistes. People despised their way of life but loved their art. I have tried to trace the reason behind their low status in society, giving some glimpses into their everyday life and also an account of their economic status.

This work deals with the genesis of Indian Theatre as an introduction and presents the story of the origin of drama as narrated by Bharata and an account of the spectators and their role in the development of Indian theatre as appendices.

For the original text of Bharata's *Nāṭyaśāstra* I have consulted the Chowkhamba Sanskrit Sansthan's edition (1978) and M. Ghosh's *Nāṭyaśāstra* for translation of the text wherever necessary.

The prefatory remarks would remain incomplete without recording my gratitude to all those who have been kind enough to help me in my intellectual pursuit. An ambitious work like this would have been impossible without the large hearted co-operation and encouragement from various quarters.

I am greatly indebted to my teachers — Prof. A.K. Narain, Professor Emeritus, History and South Asian Studies, Dept. of History, University of Wisconsin, Madison, U.S.A. for his unfailing help, affection and guidance and to Dr. Saroj Bisarya, Ex-Principal, Vasanta College for Women, Krishnamurti Foundation (India), Varanasi, a distinguished playwright, for her constant encouragement and blessings.I express my gratitude to Dr. Mahesh Vikram Singh, Department of History, Mahatma Gandhi Kashi Vidyapith, Varanasi, for his constant interest in this work.

My acknowledgement to Mr. J.S. Yadav, Deputy Director (Library), and staff of the 'American Institute of Indian Studies', whose efficiency I could not help admiring and exploiting. The rare books and plates were made accessible through their courtesy. I offer my thanks to Padmashri Ahalya Chari, Ex-Commissioner, Central Schools and a member of Krishnamurti Foundation (India) for inspiring me to explore this field of study. I wish to record my sincere appreciation to my friend Dr. N. Sharada Iyer, Reader, Department of English, Vasanta College for Women, Krishnamurti Foundation (India), Varanasi, for correcting the language of this work, but thanking her would belittle her affectionate co-operation. I am thankful to Mr. Sanjeev Kumar, Lecturer, Department of History, Vasanta college for women, for directing me to D.K. Printworld for the publication of this book. I also thank Mr. Susheel K. Mittal of D.K. Printworld for his excellent management in shaping the book to its final form.

The inspirational forces behind this work have been many whose blessings have gone into the making of this work. Primarily, my parents to whom I dedicate this work. My revered father, Acharya Sri Krishnananda, First Principal of the D.A.V. Degree College, Varanasi, whose profound wisdom and life, spent in constant academic pursuit, has been a motive and a spirit behind this work. My mother, Smt. Krishnakishori inspired, sustained and supported me in moments of uncertainty during this work. My sister Prof. Vibhawati, Department of Ancient Indian History, Culture & Archaeology, Banaras Hindu University, gave the encouragement I needed most.

Finally I submit my work to the men of learning for their valuable, critical assessment and scholarly opinion which alone could make my endeavour worthwhile.

Iravati

Contents

To
My Beloved Parents

Abbreviations

ASI	:	Archaeological Survey of India
ABORI	:	*Annals of Bhandarkar Oriental Research Institute*
ABI	:	*Annals of Bhandarkar Institute*
BNC	:	*Bhāsa Nāṭaka Cakram*
CSS	:	Chowkhamba Sanskrit Sansthan
EI	:	*Epigraphia Indica*
GOS	:	Gayakwad Oriental Series
HD	:	*History of Dharmaśāstra*
IHQ	:	*Indian Historical Quarterly*
IA	:	*Indian Antiquary*
JOR	:	*Journal of Oriental Research*, Madras
JBBRAS	:	*Journal of Bombay Branch of the Royal Asiatic Society*
JRAS	:	*Journal of Royal Asiatic Society*
JOI	:	*Journal of Oriental Institute*
JAOS	:	*Journal of American Oriental Society*
J&PASB	:	*Journal and Proceedings of Asiatic Society of Bengal*
KA	:	*Kauṭilya Arthaśāstra*

KG	:	*Kālidāsa Granthāvalī*
NŚ	:	*Nāṭyaśāstra*
ŚB	:	*Śatapatha Brāhmaṇa*
TB	:	*Taittirīya Brāhmaṇa*

List of Illustrations

1

Genesis of Indian Theatre

ANCIENT Indian theatre is a very comprehensive art which includes not only histrionics but dance, music — vocal and intrumental, fine arts and various other branches of knowledge. The word used for this art in ancient Indian literature is, *nāṭya*. As an art form, *nāṭya* is both functional and entertaining, making delightful teaching as its end. *Nāṭya* as defined by Bharata is 'the mimicry of the ways of the world, endowed with various emotions and consisting of various situation',[1] and he says 'everyone found in *nāṭya* just what he needed and what was good for him'.[2] In its highest form, *nāṭya* incorporates all branches of learning — literature, art, music, dance, history, philosophy, religion and science, thus appealing to everyone of the spectators. This made Bharata comment, 'There is no knowledge, no fine art, no learning, no skill, no *yoga* and no activity that is not represented in *nāṭya*'.[3] He says, (Here are) all the *śāśtras,* all the fine arts and actions of diverse nature. In *nāṭya* are narrated and represented all the Vedic and all the legendary lore.[4]

The comprehensive nature of ancient Indian theatre is reflected in the story of its origin as narrated by Bharata.

Bharata, while describing the origin of *nāṭya*, combines not only the important elements of the four Vedas and *itihāsa*[5] for creation of the fifth Veda — *Nāṭyaveda* — but also Āryan and non-Āryan elements, symbolically represented as the

1. *NŚ*, I.112.
2. *Ibid.*, I.102-18.
3. *Ibid.*, I.114.
4. *Ibid.*, I.112.
5. *Ibid.*, I.17.

contributions of Śiva[6] and Viṣṇu.[7] This comprehensive nature of Indian theatre has complicated the question of its origin, intriguing the Eastern and Western minds alike. The problem has been approached from various angles basing the study on ancient literature — religious and secular, rituals, popular art styles prevalent then like puppetry, mime and shadow play, and the possible external influences. But one must bear in mind the comprehensive nature of Indian *nāṭya* which has not one but many factors contributing to its origin and development. Hence the myth of the origin of Indian *nāṭya* could be solved only by analysing the Indian *nāṭya* itself. In fact, the constituents of *nāṭya* like dance, music, theme, dialogue and *rāsa* are the real sources of *nāṭya.* Originally they were all separate arts either folk or classical or parts of religious rituals. In the process of historical, social and religious development of the country, these arts and rituals came closer, as shall be seen in the following chapters in detail, and gave rise to Indian *nāṭya*. The example of one of such synchronising factors is festivals — religious and social both, known throughout the history of the country. Dance, drama and music formed the important features of such festivals and their frequency let various arts and rituals come together and thus helped in the genesis of the Indian theatre.

Therefore, it can neither be said that all the theories propagated so far are baseless nor stated that they are absolutely correct. They are true only in relation to the limited range that has been focussed upon in each case. The analogy of the four blind men and the elephant sounds very apt here. Any conclusion arrived at thus would be incomplete and lopsided.

The Genesis

According to the modern line of thinking, drama originated from the primitive man's instinct to imitate the action of people and nature around him. In primitive society dance played an important role, and was the most potent way of conveying thoughts and beliefs. It took the form of magico-religious rites.[8] Drama in its rudimentary form emerged when dance started to express an idea, communicate an experience, relate an episode, or narrate myths with the help of impersonation akin to pantomime.

---

6. *NŚ*, IV.13.
7. *Ibid.*, XXII.2-15.
8. Wankankar and Brook, *Stone Age Painting in India*, p. 80.

It seems that the art of dance and impersonation was known to Indus Valley people too. It is indicated by the bronze figure of a danseuse from Mohenjo-Dāro, (*figs*. 1-2) a male torso of a dancer from Harappā *(figs*. 3-4) and mythical scenes depicted on Indus Valley seals.[9] They suggest ritualistic dance and impersonation, although it is difficult to say if the people used speech or dialogue in their representations.

Such pre-Vedic religious practices with ritualistic dance and music were incorporated in Vedic religion in later Vedic age. One of such rituals was *Mahāvrata* ceremony[10] containing dance, music and dramatic dialogue. Such music, dance and dialogue played an important part in the origin of Indian *nāṭya*. It is known that dance and music have been integral parts of Indian drama throughout its history. Bharata includes dance and music not only as preliminaries[11] but also as device.[12] These arts were so important in *nāṭya* that later dramaturgists thought it essential for an actor to have a proper knowledge of dance and music, too, besides that of acting.[13] Some of the actors were originally ritual dancers (*śailūṣa*)[14] and musicians (*kuśīlava*).[15] This also indicates that dance and music part of drama were originally the contribution of ritualistic dance and music.

Gradually in the nascent form of theatre speech might have been added, though drama proper was yet to be born. The controversial dialogue hymns, too, have their share in the origin of Indian theatre. Whosoever recited these hymns, intentionally or unintentionally, recited them in a dramatic style, i.e., in the style of dialogue delivery, because they are in dialogue form and a good reader unconsciously does so. Thus, even if these hymns did not have the least association with dramatic art in its earliest form, as some scholars believe, they might have inspired the genesis of the art by inspiring the speech part of drama. It is significant that Brahmā took recitation from *R̥gveda*, while creating *nāṭya*,[16] which might mean 'speech'.

---

9. E.J.H. Mackay, *Further Excavations at Mohenjodaro*, p. 334. Seal No. 316.
10. A.B. Keith, *Śāṅkhyāyana Āraṇyaka*, p. 72 H.
11. *NŚ*, V.10-11; V.12-15; V.154-56.
12. *Ibid*., IV.318, 319-20; XXXII.482.
13. *Nāṭyadarpaṇa*, I.4.
14. *gītāya sūtāni nr̥tyāya śailūṣāni* — *TB*, III.4.2.1.
15. *NŚ*, XXV/106; Adya Rangacharya, *Drama in Sanskrit Literature*, pp. 46-48.
16. *NŚ*, I.17.

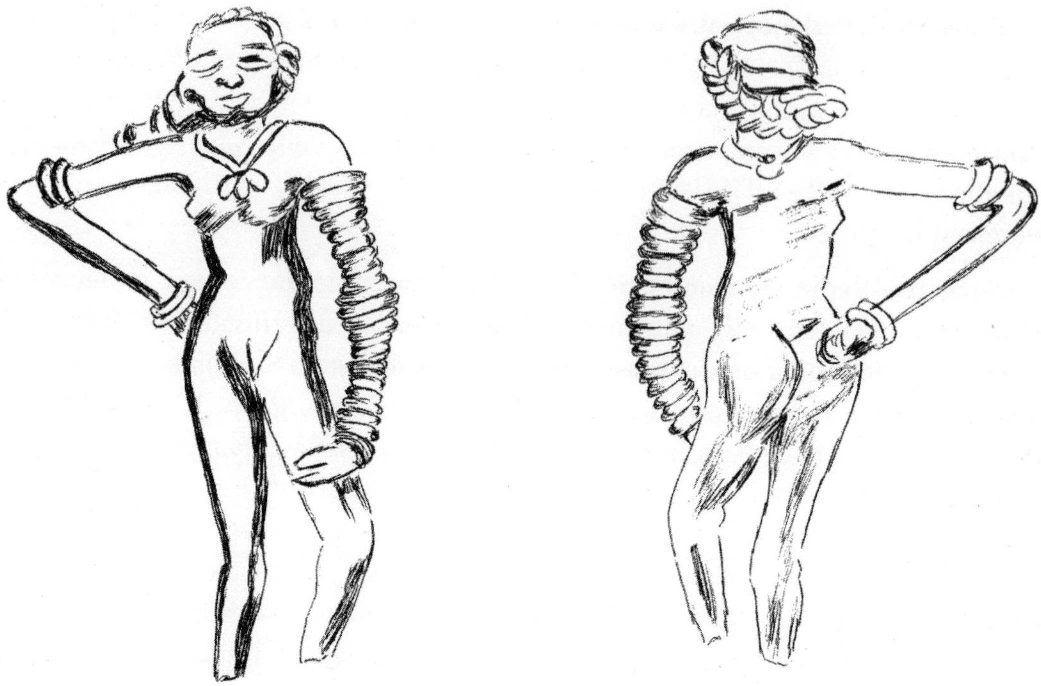

Fig. I & II : Bronze dancer from Mohenjo-Dāro.

Fig. III & IV : Grey slate stone torso of a dancer from Harappā.

The custom of reciting the epics for pious listeners is very old. Gradually an actor or actors were added to the recitation to describe more vividly the events of the story. This type of audio-visual recitation must have contributed the idea of representing a theme in drama embellished with different emotions later known as *rasa*.

Keith is of the opinion that the term *Bharata*, which is used in the sense of an actor, shows the connection of the epic-reciters with the evolution of drama.[17] He thinks that *Bharata*, the rapsodists of *Bharata* tribe, preserved *Mahābhārata*, the great epic of the family. With the passage of time these reciters took upon themselves the newer art of drama.[18] Or is it because the actor represented a theme in the play from the epics with the same appeal as the rapsodists that they came to be called *Bharata*?

We know that earlier Sanskrit plays as those of Bhāsa and Kālidāsa (*Abhijñānaśākuntalam*, *Vikramorvaśīyam*) are based on legends of the epics. This tradition, in fact, continued throughout the history of Sanskrit drama. Almost all of them are based on the stories from epics. The impact of epic themes on *nāṭya*, whether folk or classical, was so strong that the latest and most modern aspects of Indian *nāṭya*, film and television, too, could not resist the temptation of representing them. Hence it is not impossible that epic recitation provided theme and *rasa* to Indian theatre.

A factor significantly subscribing to the development of the theatre in ancient India was 'puppet play'. This, being a very old art, was known to Indians since the Indus Valley period. It was based on imitation and mimicry, a form of drama. This 'play on small scale' was performed by puppets and it may have popularised theatre in ancient India.

The origin of drama as described by Bharata does not seem to be mere fiction. Generally, it is taken by scholars as 'mythical'[19] or 'traditional'[20] legend of dramatic

---

17. A.B. Keith, *The Sanskrit Drama*, p. 30.
18. *Vedic Index*, vol. II, 94A; A.B. Keith, *op. cit.*, p. 30.
19. Sylvain Levi, *The Theatre of India*, p. 12.
20. Adya Rangacharya, *op. cit.*, p. 18.

'genre' or 'legendary stage of drama'.[21] Ghosh[22] and Indushekhara[23] try to discover an undercurrent of 'Āryan' or 'orthodox' opposition to dramatic art in this account. But it seems that Bharata is trying to give an account of the origin and development of Indian *nāṭya* through this story that does contain simple historical truth.

K. Krishnamacharya's[24] opinion in this regard seems most logical and closer to truth. He says that Bharata's statement that God Brahmā took the elements of recitation from *Ṛgveda*, song from *Sāmaveda*, *abhinaya* (action or mimatic art) from *Yajurveda* and the *rasa* or sentiments from *Atharvaveda*, contains historical truth in mythical garb. He explains that *Ṛgveda* is essentially of hymns intended for recitation and thus it is a Veda of recitation; the *Sāmaveda* is of hymns set to music, and therefore, a Veda of song. In *Yajurveda* we find that celebrating certain rituals the priests assumed the role of gods, i.e., they represented gods in certain ceremonies. Thus representation came first into vogue in *Yajurveda*. Even today in *pitṛ-śrāddha* ceremony, which has an unbroken continuity from Vedic age, three brāhmaṇas are invited who represent *pitṛ*s, *viśvadeva*s and Viṣṇu. They assume the character of an individual other than oneself. Similarly *Atharvaveda* consists, to a large extent, of hymns of sorcery, spells and incantations which have directly to do with emotions like love, anger, hatred, disgust and pity. *Rasa*, which partakes of an aesthetic nature, is but an impersonal detachment relished by exhibiting these emotions on the stage. Hence, Krishnamacharya says that perhaps the dramatic *rasa*s can be traced back to *Atharvaveda* as their original source.[25] This tallies to a large extent with what we have tried to trace so far: music (*Sāmaveda*), ritualistic impersonation (*Yajurveda*), recitation (*Ṛgveda*) and emotion (*Atharvaveda*) are among the chief sources of Indian *nāṭya*.

On the basis of Bharata's account of the origin of *nāṭya*, it seems that he had arrived at that stage of the history of Indian drama where drama proper was gradually coming into being with four of its most essential constituents — dialogue, song, action and *rasa*, which were originated from pre-Vedic and Vedic sources. But

---

21. H.N. Dasgupta, *The Indian Stage*, p. 1.
22. M. Ghosh, 'Problems of Nāṭyaśāstra', *IHQ*, vol. VI, p. 53.
23. Indushekhara, *Sanskrit Drama: its Origin and Decline*, pp. 35-36.
24. K. Krishnamacharya, 'On the origin of the Sanskrit Drama', in *Quarterly Journal of Mythic Society*, vol. XXIV, January 1934, pp. 206-7.
25. *Ibid.*, pp. 206-7.

it was Bharata who codified the age-old practical tradition of theatre for posterity. He made drama not only a discipline but also a respectable art encompassing all other disciplines. During his time, it was deprived of a respectable position in society. Bharata's account in *Nāṭyaśāstra* of gods approaching Brahmā to create some form of entertainment for people, who were taking to vulgar ways, indicates Bharata's displeasure at the depraved condition of drama. It was but natural since the performers of *nāṭya* (*śailūṣa, śobhanika, kuśīlava, maṅkha, naṭa, naṭī*, courtesan, etc.) hailed from the common strata, initially entertaining the common mass. The two main sources of ancient Indian theatre — ritual dance, music and dialogue — were drawn from and associated with fertility cult. Bharata by making Brahmā himself as the creator of *nāṭya*, borrowing and developing the art from the four Vedas, raised it to the height of respectability and acceptance by all. Thus, on the one hand providing respectability to *nāṭya*, and on the other, adding literary technique to script-writing, grammar to ordinary spoken language of theatre, technical knowledge to pronunciation, psychological understanding to the portrayal of a character, principles and rules to the art of dance and music, proper direction to back stage workers and actors, actresses and director, he turned the art into a discipline. It was a gradual shift from mass to class. It may be considered as the first conscious, concerted and comprehensive attempt by the aesthetics and guardians of art to gain respectability for the dramatic muse which was 'dear to all muses'.

The two traditions of theatre belonging to mass and class are the by-products of this step. The first was the original crude form of theatre popular among common people and the second was a refined one which was turned into discipline by *ācārya*s like Bharata to match the taste of both classes of the society — lower and upper. There were occasional exchanges between these two traditions but generally mass or folk tradition maintained the traditions of plays having dance and music in abundance with a touch of vulgarity represented by *uparūpaka*s, the minor forms of drama and also by some of the major forms such as *bhāṇa* and *vīthi*. The classical tradition maintained the major forms of play like *nāṭaka*, *prakaraṇa*, etc. *Ācārya*s, who had realised the potentiality of the art (drama) as entertainment and also as the best means to educate people, tried to combine the best of the two traditions, folk and classical. Thus a symbiotic tradition of theatre developed in the country, which had imbibed both the elements — folk and classical.

As the art of drama developed, more and more disciplines were added and they became its integral parts. For example, costume and make-up, required knowledge of painting, cosmetics, hair dressing, making garlands, crown, ornaments, tailoring and sewing. Thus these arts were added to drama. Similarly, for stage setting and preparing the stage properly, technical knowledge was necessary. Thus this, too, was included in drama.

Karma philosophy is the basis of Indian way of life. Drama, which represents life on stage (*lokavṛittānukarṇaṁ*, imitation of the ways of the world), was based on this philosophy. This is the reason why ancient Indian plays depict 'justice deserved'. The wicked is ultimately punished and 'error of judgement' on the part of the hero is always rectified towards the end of the play. The script writer and the artistes who were supposed to portray ways of people on stage had to have a proper knowledge of this philosophy for the success of the play. Thus philosophy, too, was included in this great art, drama. All this enriching of the art of drama was done by *ācārya*s with the help of the performing artistes.

That is why one can say that besides such *ācārya*s, as Bharata, the greatest contribution to the evolution of theatre was also made by performing artistes themselves. In the form of priests, priestesses, *śailūṣa, kṛśāśva, śobhanika, granthika, kuśīlava, maṅkha, naṭa, naṭī*, courtesans, professionals in the garb of *apsaras*es or *devadāsī*s, they kept the flame of the art alive by maintaining the tradition of art on the one hand and adding new techniques and devices to it on the other, throughout the history of the art. Some of them practised the art as their family profession in the form of folk entertainers, while others underwent a systematic training under the *ācārya*s, who were representatives of classical tradition.

The contributions of spectators to drama in its development is also of great importance. Originating from dance, music and pantomimic impersonation and gradually being adorned by speech, song and *rasa*, ancient Indian theatre took its full-fledged form as a most comprehensive art basically catering to the tastes of its spectators having different likings. Without them as an encouraging force, this art would not have attained the glorious height which it has.

Thus, the Indian *nāṭya* or theatre is an art which seems to be the product of the synthesis of various art-forms and disciplines which were brought together by *ācārya*s on the one hand and theatre artistes on the other, during various periods and stages of socio-religious development in the country.

2

Actors and Their Contributions to Theatre in Ancient India

kuśalā ye vidagdhāśca pragalbhāśca jitaśramāḥ ।
teṣvayaṁ nāṭyasaṅgyo hi vedaḥ saṅkrāmyatāṁ tvayā ।।
— NŚ *I/20*

BHARATA observes in his *Nāṭyaśāstra* that after creating the fifth Veda — *nāṭya*, Brahmā offered it to Indra for *prayoga* (representation) with the specific instruction that it should be undertaken with the help of those who are intelligent, sharp, bold, industrious and steadfast, thus meaning one who is endowed with the faculties of reception, retention, absorption, expression, boldness (i.e., neither stage nor audience shy) and is industrious (ready to undergo and withstand the long hours of training) as an actor. These were the natural and acquired qualities expected from an actor or actress. From a study of Bharata's *Nāṭyaśāstra* and works of later dramaturgists, it appears that the inherent talents of theatre artistes were tapped, polished, guided and a few added by the *ācārya*s, the custodians of theatrical arts, both folk and classical.

A study of the history of the actors and their contributions to the captivating art of drama makes an interesting story. There are several terms denoting an actor in ancient Indian literature, the most common being *naṭa*. But we have evidence regarding the existence of the art and artistes much before the prevalence of the term, when they were not a separate class of the community but the community itself.

At the dawn of human history when primitive man was still a hunter, he tried to win the favour of natural powers, for which he invented some magical spells. Since such spells had some ritual dance and enactments as its parts, he significantly dressed himself in masks, wrapped himself in animal skin and accompanied by primitive musical instruments impersonated another being for performing the rite. Each member of the community was an active participant and equally involved in the ceremony. These primitive performers of magical rites became the earliest actors.

Imitation is natural to man and is responsible for the genesis of theatre. Drama is mimicry of actions and conducts of people and nature around one's self. Bharata[1] has defined drama as *lokavṛttānukaraṇaṁ* and that is what the aboriginals were doing to ensure safety from wild animals and natural calamities, to ward of evils and to have a good hunt. At a primitive level, dance is an inevitable outcome of imitation. Since it contained the urge to communicate an emotion and was derived from the urge to imitate, these ancient tribal dancers may correspond to actors. While discussing the origin of drama from primitive dance, Kenneth Macgowan and William Menitz[2] say that due to an aptitude for imitation, primitive man devised magic and rituals, dances and ceremonies. Whatever may be the reason for such ceremonies and ritual dances, this is certain that they contained the rudiments of that art which was later to flourish as the most comprehensive art embracing almost all the aspects of human skill and craft — *nāṭya*. Also, it led Bharata to say that there is no such *jñāna* (knowledge), *śilpa* (craft), *kalā* (art), *yoga* or *karma* (work) which is not found in *nāṭya* (drama).

With the passage of time a small group, which was in some way associated with magical rites, or were gifted dancers and imitators, branched off to form another group with the responsibility of performing the rites (dances). Gradually, the steps of their dance and dress (costume) got codified. A class of ritual dancers came into being that took part in dance and mimicry.

Such ritualistic dance, it seems, was in vogue during Indus Valley period, too. Mackay[3] refers to the 'curious figure' on a seal which from the position of the arms and legs appears to be standing before the animal. He thinks that it 'possibly represents a human figure wearing a mask and false tail for a ceremonial dance before the deified animal'. Possibly there were dancers who depicted myths associated with the cult of the ithyphallic deity with three faces and horn-like headdress. This deity is supposed to be the prototype of later Śiva, in whose cult, dance and music

1. *NŚ*, I.112.
2. Kenneth Macgowan & William Menitz, *The Living Stage*, p. 5.
3. E.J.H. Mackay, *Further excavatins at Mohenjodaro*, p. 334.

was part of the process leading to final deliverance.[4] The posture of a grey slate figure of a male dancer from Harappā[5] reminds of *tāṇḍava* and supports the affinity between the male deity of Harappan culture and later Śiva.

It seems that Indus Valley people were fond of theatrical arts. Dance, whether as a part of ritual or entertainment, was known to them. The bronze statuette of a young danseuse from Mohenjo-Dāro[6] and the above-mentioned figure of the male dancer confirm this. The masks found from different levels of Mohenjo-Dāro[7] suggest the existence of some sort of enactment, mimicry or pantomime. They are hollow at the back with holes at the edges for tying them on. Mackay[8] thinks that they may have served to ornament some wooden structure as did the metal heads on a chariot found at Ur or perhaps they were fastened to the doors or walls of a house to avert ill luck. They may have been used to ornament robes worn on special occasions. S.R. Rao[9] thinks that on festive occasions the dancer used to put them on, which seems closer to truth because the first thought that strikes one's mind on seeing a mask is that of an actor using them for impersonation.

A harp motif engraved on a Mohenjo-Dāro seal and the stringed musical instrument made of shell are referred to by Rao in his book.[10] He thinks that the Harappan dancers had the knowledge of music, too. Probably their performance was accompanied by music.

The above account shows that in all probability dance and mimicry, the natural instinct of man, was performed during Indus Valley period in the form of religious ritual, though they may have been a form of entertainment, too. The figure of a dwarf[11] suggests the same. Keeping dwarfs for entertainment has been customary during later periods of Indian history. *Pramath gaṇas*, the dwarfish attendants of Lord Śiva, were the presiding deity of *hāsya rasa*.[12] If dwarfs used to amuse people,

---

4. R.G. Bhandarkar, *Vaiṣṇavism, Śaivism and Minor Religious Systems*, pp. 122-23.
5. See *figs*. III-IV.
6. See *figs*. I & II.
7. E.J.H. Mackay, *op. cit.*, p. 267, pl. LXXIV, 21, 22, 25; pl. LXXVI, I.
8. *Ibid.*, p. 267.
9. S.R. Rao, *Lothal and Indus Civilisation*, p. 112.
10. *Ibid.*
11. E.J.H. Mackay, *op. cit.*, pl. LXXV, fig. 13.
12. *NŚ*, VI, 45.

it should have been through funny physical gesticulations, since their physical deformity evokes laughter. Besides, Indus Valley people were fond of puppetry, as the terracotta animal and human figures with perforation in the neck, trunk and detachable limbs which moved with the help of strings or wires, suggest.[13] Puppetry itself is imitation of human and animal behaviour in dolls and toys. Hence the basis of puppetry itself is imitation and suggests the existence of an art based on imitation-enactment, which may have inspired puppetry.

Thus, actors in the form of ritual dancers or pantomime and entertainers might have been there during Indus Valley period but whether there was a class of such professional artistes who were given the duty of performing dance or mimicry on special occasions or such rituals were performed by priests and priestesses, cannot be said.

We have veiled reference to actors in Vedic literature. Though Vedic literature is not secular and it is wrong to trace clear references to such artistes in them, it does contain such references which indicate the existence of theatrical arts and their custodians — for example, the dialogue hymns of *Ṛgveda*. We have already discussed in the earlier chapter the importance and contribution of dialogue hymns to drama.

Some Vedic rituals contain within themselves the elements of drama. For example, *Mahāvrata* ceremony, one of the *śrauta* rites, which are described in detail by the authors of the *Śrauta Sūtra*s and are discussed in other Vedic texts as *Sāṅkhyāyana Āraṇyaka*,[14] contain an exchange of abuse between a *brahmacārī* and a hetaera, dance performance by maidens and singing by married women. Dance was performed in *aitareya* and *satrāyaṇa* sacrifices, too.[15] In the horse sacrifice (*aśvamedha*) brāhmaṇas and warriors alike were called to sing.[16] There is a reference to a religious festival in *Aitareya Āraṇyaka*[17] when the priest mounted the temple swing to imitate the course of the sun.

Thus, it seems, that rituals incorporated in their execution song, music, dialogue,

---

13. E.J.H. Mackay, *op. cit.*, p. 557, pls. LXXVIII, 12, LXXXI, 5, 8, 9, 14, etc.
14. A.B. Keith, *Sāṅkhāyana Āraṇyaka*, p. 72.
15. Ludwig, *ṚV*, IV, p. 58.
16. *ŚB*, XIII.5, 3.4; *TB*, III.9.4.4.
17. *Aitareya Āraṇyaka*, I.2.4; IV.3.

symbolic gesture, language, dance and myth — all being essential for drama. Keith[18] was of the opinion that the Vedic rituals contain within themselves germs of drama, yet they are nothing but elements. But it should be borne in mind that describing theatre and theatre artistes was not the purpose of Vedic literature. Hence one has to look for the art and the actor in that literature through such 'elements' only. Konow saw in these ceremonies not only the old popular play, but an imitation of the same in the cult.[19] Keith on the contrary says that the Vedas ignore *naṭa*.

Further, there does not occur any kind of evidence in support of the view that the popular mime is older than the religious practices of the Vedas. But the absence of the term *naṭa* in Vedas may only suggest that the actor during Vedic period was probably not known by that term. There were other terms to denote actors as shall be discussed later. Possibly there were such artistes in Vedic period who had the gift of dance, music and imitation and utilised their talents in religious rituals.

One most important question that comes to mind is that who were these people or artistes who performed rituals containing dramatic elements. First, we find priests reciting Vedic hymns and as Max-Müller[20] believes assuming the character of gods or demons. *Sāmaveda* shows a fully developed stage of music in Vedic period and the priests who recited this Veda would have been well-versed in the art of music. We have noticed that there is a reference to a religious festival in *Aitareya Āraṇyaka* where the priest himself mounted the temple swing. Thus artistes, knowing the art of impersonation and music, existed in the form of priests.

Second, besides priests, there were some other people too who took part in Vedic rituals in the capacity of individual artists. In *aśvamedha* sacrifice, on the day of letting loose of the sacrificial horse, the *vīṇāgāthin*s (i.e., the musicians who sang to the accompaniment of all sorts of lutes as explained by the commentator) were required to sing the praise of the sacrificer along with those of just kings of ancient times. On this day, a brāhmaṇa (other than the priest) lute player had to sing, to the acccompaniment of the *uttaramandrā* (a kind of *vīṇā)*, three stanzas composed by himself. On the same day, a brāhmaṇa lute player sang three *gāthā*s composed by himself that related to the battles fought and the victories won by the sacrificer. Thus, it seems that there already existed in the Vedic period a class of minstrels

18. A.B. Keith, *The Sanskrit Drama*, pp. 23-25.
19. S. Konow, *The Indian Drama*, p. 7.
20. F. Max-Müller, *Ṛ̥V*, I.165.

who composed songs and sang them. This class, however, did not as yet form a closed caste or corporation, for individual brāhmaṇa and kṣatriya musicians could play the same role. Such *vīṇāgāthin*s were later invited to some domestic rites too. On the occasion of *sīmantonnayana* ceremony, which was performed on the expectant mother in the fourth, sixth, seventh or eighth month of pregnancy, the husband had to ask two *vīṇāgāthins* to sing about the king or anybody else who was still more valiant.[21]

Third, there were also minstrels known as *sūta*s and *māgadha*s during later Vedic period. *Sūta,* besides being mentioned as one of the eight *vīras*[22] and even *ratnin*s[23] in Vedic literature, served as royal herald and bard in epics[24] and was the offspring of a kṣatriya father and a brāhmaṇa mother. Similarly, *māgadha*, with some connection with *vrātya*s in *Atharvaveda,*[25] is mentioned as offspring of vaiśya father begotten by a kṣatriya woman. These two in Indian tradition came to be associated with theatre. It seems that as composers and narrators of ancient stories in a dramatic style, *sūta*s and *māgadha*s had developed this relation with theatre artistes and were included in their class. From Bharata we know that poets were included in the troupes of actors.[26] Possibly the brāhmaṇa and kṣatriya composers and singers of *gāthā*s too were later included in the troupe of theatre artistes, like *sūta*s and *māgadha*s, as poets and musicians.

Fourth, it is quite possible that there were such artistes as dancers, musicians and other associated with pantomime in the Vedic age also. Dialogue hymns, festival *sāman* and its nature, and deities addressed as dancers suggests the same. Possibly dancers, musicians or people who were known for their art of impersonation of pantomimic nature were called to perform the rites having dramatic elements. This was the tradition during later Vedic period. We have seen that a hetaera took part in *Mahāvrata* ceremony and exchanged abuses with a *brahmacārī* who was later replaced by a *māgadha*.[27] This is very interesting, as we know that during later

21. *Sāṅkhyāyana Gṛhyasūtra*, I.22.11-12; *Pāraskara Gṛhyasūtra*, I.15.7-8.
22. *PB*, IX.1.4.
23. *Atharvaveda*, III.5.7.
24. Hopkins, *JAOS*, vol. XIII, pp. 254-55; *Mahābhārata*, Anuśāsana Parva, 48/2571-3.
25. *Atharvaveda*, XV.2.1-4.
26. *NŚ*, XXXV.99.
27. J. Gonda, 'Ascetics and Courtesans', *Adyar Library Bulletin*, vol. XXV, Parts, 1-4, 1961, pp. 82-83.

times it was a common practice to appoint a courtesan in a temple as part-time *devadāsī* who served the deity of the temple by dance, music and drama.[28] As for *māgadhas*, even in Vedic period they seem to be associated with theatrical arts. In *Yajurveda*[29] the *māgadha* or man of *Māgadha*, is included among those who were dedicated to *atikruṣṭa* (loud noise) which according to J. Gonda[30] is no doubt explicable from the apotropalic and cathartic function of noice, music, singing, shouting, etc. The association of *māgadha* with theatre artistes is known from *Mahābhārata*[31] also. He is found there as presenting his art on special occasions with other artistes. *Māgadha* was either simply an artiste having the knowledge of music or a minstrel.

Further, besides these artistes, who were associated with religion in some way or the other, there were some pure entertainers even during the Vedic period whose existence is vaguely indicated in the Vedic literature. R.C. Hazara,[32] on the basis of Ṛgvedic verse,[33] says that the term *hasanaṁ upamantriṇaḥ* shows that there were fun-makers who were associated with the crown and recognised as state officers. Not only that, the word *kārī*, mentioned in *Vājasaneyī Saṁhitā*[34] and *Taittirīya Brāhmaṇa*,[35] according to him, denotes such people who practised fun-making as an art for inducing others to laughter. Their mention by the term *kārī* (as distinct from *upamantriṇaḥ*) indicates that they were different from the court jesters and must have earned their livelihood by amusing the common rung of people.[36] Thus possibly, a group of theatre artistes was forming in Vedic period. Though drama may not have evolved, dance, music, recitation of heroic poetry and mimicry were there and these arts are not very far from drama.

In later and post-Vedic literature, we find different names for such artistes.

---

28. Kālidāsa, *Meghadūta*, Pūrvamegha, 39, *KG*, p. 294.
29. *Vājasaneyī Saṁ.*, XXX.5.22; *TB*, III.4.1.1.
30. J. Gonda, *op. cit.*, p. 88.
31. *Mahābhārata*, Virāṭa Parva, 5.72.29.
32. R.C. Hazara, 'The Professional Jesters of the Vedic Age', *IHQ*, vol. XXXVIII, no. 2-3, p. 194.
33. *Ṛgveda*, IX.112.4.
34. *Vājasaneyī Saṁhitā*, XXX.6 and 20.
35. *TB*, III.4;2.
36. R.C. Hazra, *op. cit.*, p. 196.

Their arts had different forms. *Śailūṣa* is often referred to as a dancer. *Śilālin* and *kṛśāśva* were the composers of *Naṭasūtra*. Hence they would have been well aware of that art. *Śobhanika*s were probably pantomimes and *granthika*s were reciters. *Kuśīlava*s and *kathaka*s, though reciters of ancient heroic poetry and musical instruments, were occasionally referred to as actors. *Bhrūkuṅśa*s were actors who played female parts. Bharatas are described as experts in adapting various roles almost same as *naṭa* and *maṅkha* was a picture showman. *Naṭa* was an actor and an embodiment of all these arts in one as detailed later.

As the art developed and became more comprehensive, all these arts performed by various artistes merged into a single one called 'drama' and the artiste who learnt all these arts as various branches of the same great art came to be known as *naṭa*. This was the reason why Bharata[37] said that there is no such art which is not found in drama. An accomplished *naṭa* had a sound knowledge of acting, singing, dancing, speaking, narrating and expressing himself in words and pantomime. Gradually, a tendency to turn the art into a science grew up. Theatre too became a science, and a classical tradition of actors and their style came into being as it is indicated by the literature on dramaturgy. But, as people associated with theatre were common people belonging to the lower strata of the society, the art always had a close affinity with folk tradition, which had its roots in magical dance and impersonation. Its impact was so strong that even after the formation and recognition of a classical tradition of theatre, its popularity and appeal continued. Hence, throughout the history of the theatre in the country these two traditions — classical and folk — influenced each other. The *naṭa*s learned the classical dance, music and art of drama with all its *aṅga*s and *upāṅga*s to please their audiences belonging to the higher class of the society and on the other hand, the classical art impressed by the popularity and appeal of the folk tradition borrowed some characters and techniques from the latter. Theatrical art of India is indebted to both these traditions. Hence, an actor who was well trained by an *ācārya*, eventually grew into a perfect artiste with a deep knowledge of dance, music, acting, costume, stage and various other crafts, language, grammar, poetics, art of public appeal and also human psychology as Bharata's *Nāṭyaśāstra* indicates. We will now study the history of all these theatre artistes and their contribution to drama.

---

37. *NŚ*, I.116.

Śailūṣa

Śailūṣa in Vedic literature is connected with dance and music. According to Keith and Macdonell,[38] by the term *śailūṣa* an 'actor' may be meant. But exact sense of the term depends on the question of how old the drama is in India. Kelakar thinks that *śailūṣa* in *Taittirīya Brāhmaṇa*[39] refers to *naṭa*, i.e., an actor skilled in the four-fold *abhinaya*. It is not certain whether the term *śailūṣa* in *Taittirīya Brāhmaṇa* means an actor, but he was connected with song in *Vājasaneyī Saṁhitā*[40] and with dance in the *Taittirīya Brāhmaṇa*.[41] Mahindra, the commentator, explains the term *śailūṣaṁ* as *naṭaṁ*, though it seems that speech, dress and make-up were lacking in their art in the beginning.

Śailūṣa is included in the list of victims at the *puruṣamedha* sacrifice in the *Yajurveda*.[42] Hazara[43] has pointed out that according to *Vājasaneyī Saṁhitā* and *Taittirīya Brāhmaṇa*, a jester is to be sacrificed to the diety of laughter. Varadpande wonders if *śailūṣa* too was sacrificed to entertain the deities in heaven, because 'things were sacrificed or put into sacrificial fire so that they should reach the deities'.[44] Moreover, Bharata[45] mentions that it is by theatrical performances that the gods are pleased most. *Kārī* was sacrificed to please the 'deity of laughter'. Similarly, the *śailūṣa* who was associated with music and dance may have been sacrificed to please the deity of theatre. Human sacrifice to please the deity of theatre was known to ancient Greeks too. Goat sacrifice was included in the rites connected with the death and dismemberment of Dionysus. Kenneth Macgowan and William Menitz[46] are of the opinion that it seems certain that the goat replaced man not too many years before Thespis, the first actor. In India too, the sacrifice of *śailūṣa* seems significant and might be due to his association with theatrical art.

---

38. *Vedic Index*, Vol. II, p. 395.
39. *TB*, III.4.2.1.
40. *Vājasaneyī Saṁhitā*, XXX.6.
41. *TB*, *op. cit*.
42. *Vājasaneyī Saṁhita.*, *op. cit*.
43. R.C. Hazara, *op. cit.*, p. 194.
44. M.L. Varadpande, *Ancient Indian and Indo-Greek Theatre*, p. 26.
45. *NŚ*, XXXVI.81.
46. Kenneh Macgowan & William Menitz, *The Living Stage*, p. 16.

Śailūṣa, in the sense of an actor, is mentioned in Ayodhyā Kāṇḍa of *Rāmāyaṇa.*[47] Theatre artistes, especially actors, were known for their loose character and for living on the prostitution of their wives. Sītā in *Rāmāyaṇa* says that Rāma is behaving like a *śailūṣa* in leaving her in someone else's hand. *Manu-smṛti*[48] and Kauṭilya[49] express same views regarding a *śailūṣa.*

Manu[50] together with *Viṣṇu Dharmasūtra*[51] and Hārīta quoted by Aparārka[52] distinguished the *śailūṣa* from *Raṅgāvatārī.* While *Brahma Purāṇa*[53] defines him as one who finds employment for *naṭas*, Āpastamba[54] speaks of him in the same breath with *rajak* and *vyādh. Yājñavalkya-smṛti*[55] does the same and the *Mitākṣarā* thereon paraphrases the word by *naṭa*. Thus, it seems that *śailūṣa* was often known either as an actor (*naṭa*) or as an artiste included in that class.

Ruben[56] interprets the word *śailūṣa* as one who camps on the rock and connects him with those rope dancers who belonged to the religion of Śiva. He further refers to *śilālin*, the author of *Naṭasūtra* and *Sūtradhāra*, the rope holder, who in his opinion were associated with the rope dance and the religion of Śiva. Though, while not in total agreement with Ruben, one still wonders if there could have been some sort of connection between *śilā* and *śaila*, since they not only sound phonetically alike but are also similar in meaning. Śiva's association with theatre and mountains is widely known. Hence the possibility of an actor's or dancer's association with mountains cannot be ruled out. This reminds one of ancient cave theatre at

---

47. *svayaṁ tu bhāryāṁ kaumārīṁ ciramadhyuṣitaṁ satīṁ* ।
śailūṣa iva māṁ rāma parebhyo dātumicchasi ।।
— *Rāmāyaṇa*, Ayodhyā Kāṇḍa, 30
48. *Manu-smṛti*, IV.214.
49. *KA*, II.43.3.
50. *Manu-smṛti*, IV.214.
51. *Viṣṇu Dharmasūtra*, 51.13.
52. Aparārka, p. 279. P.V. Kane, *HD*, vol. II, part I, p. 96.
53. *vṛttyāṇveśī naṭānāṁ tu sa tu śailūṣakaḥ smṛtaḥ* — *Brahma Purāṇa* quoted by Aparārka, p. 1178. *HD*, vol. II, part I, p. 96.
54. Āpastamba 9.32 (verse) quoted in *HD*, *op. cit.*, pp. 96-97.
55. *Yājñavalkya-smṛti*, II.48.
56. Ruben, quoted by G.H. Tarlekar, *Studies in the Nāṭyaśāstra*, p. 12.

Sītābeṅgā[57] and Jogimārā, Śilāveśma of Kālidāsa[58] and theatrical activities on Raivatak mountains,[59] and tempts one to associate *śailūṣa* with theatrical activities on mountains.

The word *śailūṣa* was associated with such actors who were well versed in dance because Bāṇa in his *Harṣacarita*[60] refers to Sumitra, the son of Agnimitra, who 'being overfond of drama, was attacked by Mitradeva in the midst of *śailūṣa*s (actors)'. In the same context, he refers to the actors in the wild miracle play (*ārbhaṭī*) with its passionate circular dances.[61] It seems that the word *śailūṣa* gradually came to be associated with such actors who were experts in dance (in Vedic period, *śailūṣa* was a dancer).

Thus, it seems that *śailūṣa*, originally a popular artiste, came to be associated with Vedic ritual in the capacity of a folk artiste who danced, sang and was sacrificed, probably to please the deities. Later he came to be known as an actor with a sound knowledge of dancing and finally became synonymous with *naṭa*.

Śailālin

The term *śailālin* is mentioned in *Aṣṭādhyāyī* of Pāṇini and is derived from the word *śilālin,* which was the name of an *ācārya śilālī*. Pāṇini[62] refers to *Naṭasūtra* aphorism on the science of acting by *śilālin* and *kṛśāśva*. Originally *śailāli* was the name of a ritual teacher in the *Śatapatha Brāhmaṇa*.[63] A *śailāli* brāhmaṇa is mentioned in the *Āpastamba Śrauta-sūtra*[64] and the school of *śailālin* often occurs in the *sūtras*.[65] Kātyāyana calls them *śailālaḥ*. V.S. Agrawala thinks that the students of the Vedic text were known as *śailālaḥ* and those of *Naṭasūtra* as

---

57. *ASI*, *Annual Report*, 1903, pp. 123-31.
58. *Meghadūta*, Pūrvamedgha, 27, *KG*, p. 292.
59. *Mahābhārata*, Ādi Parva, 15.218.8-10.
60. *Śailūṣamadhye* . . . — *Harṣacarita*, p. 192, text, p. 1198.
61. *Ibid*., p. 38, text, p. 51.
62. *pārāśarayaśilālibhyām bhikṣunaṭasūtrayoḥ* ।
    pārāśaryeṇa proktaṁ bhikṣusūtramadhīyate pārāśariṇo bhikṣavaḥ śailālino naṭāḥ ।।
    — *Aṣṭādhyāyī*, IV.3.110, 11
63. *ŚB*, XIII.5.3.3.
64. *Āpastamba Śrauta-sūtra*, VI.4.7.
65. *Anupad Sūtra*, IV.5, etc.

śailālinaḥ. In *Nāṭyaśāstra naṭa*s are called *śailālaka*. Hence it seems that the *naṭa*s who had learnt dramatic art, on the lines of *Naṭasūtra*, probably under the guidance of an *ācārya*, were called *śailālin*. They, thus, represented the classical tradition of the art.

It seems that dramatic art, during Pāṇini's time, was considered as respectable as any other branch of study. Kāśikā says that the *Naṭasūtra* has same place in studies as an *āmnāya* or *chanda*.[66] Agrawala[67] holds that by introducing a secular subject like *Naṭasūtra* a new movement was started in this branch (*caraṇa*) of Vedic studies. In his opinion, most probably Bharata at a later date extended the contents of the earlier *Naṭasūtra* in his *Nāṭyaśāstra*. Sten Konow[68] was also of the same view that at least the essentials of *Naṭasūtra* had been incorporated into the *Nāṭyaśāstra*. Konow has suggested that the word, *naṭa* of Pāṇini, indicates the actors of the pantomimes and *Naṭasūtra* of Śilālin and Kr̥śāśva represents likewise the manuals on the activities and functions of the figures taking part in the mimic performances. But Keith[69] feels that we are in no position to establish the meaning of *naṭa*, which may mean no more than a mere pantomime. Indushekhara[70] is also of the same view and says that at best, the *Naṭasūtra*s signify that the two persons, Śilālin and Kr̥śāśva, were known to have prepared an aphorism on the *naṭa*s who were either dancers or mimes. Though these scholars do not take *Naṭasūtra* as a proof of the existence of a proper drama, they do accept the existence of a kind of theatre artiste (*naṭa*) for whom these *ācārya*s drew a code.

The existence of *Naṭasūtra* and *śailālinaḥ naṭaḥ*[71] shows that *naṭa*s, be they pantomime or dancer, did exist and their art was not far from drama. Drama as a full-fledged art may not have been there during Pāṇini's time, but, theatre artistes, whose existence was there in India since Vedic period (at least in the form of pantomime who entertained people), performed to please others and their art had become so popular that teachers like Śilālin and Kr̥śāśva felt the necessity of writing *Naṭasūtra*s, which were as pious and holy as a Vedic *cāraṇa* itself. The writing of

66. IV.4.114.
67. V.S. Agrawala, *Pāṇini Kālīna Bhāratavarṣa*, p. 327.
68. S. Konow, *The Indian Drama*, tr. S.N. Ghoshal, p. xii.
69. A.B. Keith, *op. cit.*, p. 31.
70. Indushekhara, *Sanskrit Drama — Its Origin and Decline*, p. 50.
71. *Aṣṭādhyāyī*, IV.3.110.

Naṭasūtra itself shows that the art had taken a new turn. This may be called the earliest attempt to codify the folk art and thus turn it into an organised one, i.e., classical art represented by *śailālin*s.

Śobhanika and Granthika

In the course of his discussion on using present tense in describing past events, Patañjali mentions two theatre artistes, *śobhanika* and *granthika* in his *Mahābhāṣya* as performing *kaṁsavadha* and *balibandha*.[72] This could be understood only of a character in a dramatic performance of some kind and the example cited in illustration of the usage is 'Śobhanika causes the death of Kaṁsa', 'He causes the binding of Bali'.

Three modes of the representation of these episodes are described in the passage concerned. In the first, the *śobhanika*s actually carry out the killing of Kaṁsa and the binding of Bali. They represent it by action, like a dumb dramatic spectacle. In the second, it is represented by painters by their painting and in the third, through the words of the *granthika*s, who while relating the fortunes of their subjects from their birth to their death make them real to the imagination of their audience. They divide themselves into two parties: one adhering to Kṛṣṇa and the other to Kaṁsa. Patañjali further says that some are red-faced (*kecidraktamukha*) and some are black-faced (*kālamukhāḥ*). Lüders[73] believed that the *śobhanika*s were persons who supplemented shadow figures with explanation. Their function was to display shadow play. He is supported by Winternitz[74] but Keith[75] rejects his view as erroneous. He says that traditional rendering is recorded by Kaiyaṭa, about a thousand years later, which is quite obscure. He thinks that the passage refers to a pantomimic killing

72. *ye tāvadete śobhankā nāmaite pratyakṣam kaṅsam ghātayanti pratyakṣam ca balim bandhyantī* । *citreṣu kathaṁ* ।

    citreṣvapyudgūrṇā nipatitāśca prahārā dr̥śyante kaṁskarṣaṇyaśca । *granthikeṣu katham yatra śabdagaḍumātram lakṣyate* । *te'api hi teṣāmuttpatti-prabhr̥tyā vināśādridhivyācakṣāṇāḥ sato buddhiviṣayān prakāśayanti* ।

    ātaśca sato vyāmiśrā hi dr̥śyante । *kecit kaṁsabhaktā bhavanti kecid vāsudevabhaktāḥ* । *varṇānyatvaṁ khalu puṣyanti* ।

    kecidraktamukhābhavanti kecit kālamukhāḥ ।

73. Lüders quoted by S. Konow, *The Indian Drama*, p. 14.
74. Winternitz, quoted by A.B. Keith, *op. cit.*, p. 33. fn. 1.
75. *Ibid.*, p. 34.

and binding by *śobhikas* or *śobhanikas*. Levi[76] renders it a meaning that the *śobhanikas* were teachers who trained the actors in the matter of actual acting or demonstrated how Kaṁsa was killed by Kṛṣṇa or Bali was fettered. Dasgupta,[77] accepting the authority of Kaiyaṭa, believes that this demonstration is a visible one given by the instructors while superintending the acting of their disciples. In his book *Pāṇini Kālīna Bhāratavarṣa*, V.S. Agrawala[78] also says that Patañjali refers to *naṭa* teachers of dance initiating novices not through recitation of dramatic texts but by their direct method of taking them to the stage.

Śobhikas are often mentioned in Buddhist literature as belonging to the class of theatre artistes.[79] Buddhaghoṣa explains *śobhanagarakam* (*śobhanakam*) as *naṭānaṁ ambhokiraṇam* (i.e., a troupe of actors). According to Wijesekara,[80] these *naṭas* were either the same persons referred to in *Mahābhāṣya* as *śobhanikas* or at least their precursors in the art. Kauṭilya[81] includes them in the list of theatre artistes. An inscription[82] from Mathurā refers to *gaṇikā* Leṇaśobhikā and her family and faith. Jacobi[83] takes the term to mean a woman who conducts a shadow play. Lüders[84] understands the word as 'cave actress'. Amulya Charan Bidyabhushan[85] also translates the term as 'Actress who performs in a cave'. Tarlekar[86] is also of the same opinion.

In *Kāvyamīmāṁsā* of Rājaśekhara,[87] *śobhika* is included in the list of theatre artistes. If we examine the term *śobhika* or *śobhanika* in this background it would

76. Sylvan Levi, *The Theatre of India*, vol. I, p. 315.
77. H.C. Dasgupta, *A History of Sanskrit Literature: Classical Period*, p. 637.
78. *yadārambhakāḥ raṅgam gacchanti naṭasya śroṣyāmo granthikasya śroṣyāmaḥ* — *Mahābhāṣya*, I.4.29; V.S. Agrawala, *Pāṇini Kālīna Bhāratavarṣa*, p. 327, fn. 2.
79. *Vidhurapandita Jātaka,* V. Fousboll, *The Jātaka*, vol. VI, p. 277.
80. O.H. De.A. Wijesekera, 'Buddhist Evidence of Drama', *IHQ*, June, 1941, pp. 206-7.
81. *etena naṭanartakagāyakavādakavāgjīvanakuṣīlavaplavaka-śaubhikacaraṇastrī vyavahāriṇām striyo gūḍhajīvaśca vyākhyātāḥ.* — *KA*, II.43.3
82. *IA*, vol. XXXIII, p. 152.
83. *Journal of the Greater Indian Society*, vol. VIII, no. 2, pp. 83-93.
84. 'Indian Caves as Pleasure Resorts', *IA*, vol. XXXIV, pp. 199-200.
85. Wilson, Raghavan, Pishroti, *Theatre of the Hindus*, p. 222.
86. G.H. Tarlekar, *op. cit.,* p. 10.
87. *plavakaśaubhikajambhakamallāḥ* — *Kāvyamīmāṁsā*, p. 55, ed. C.D. Dalal, 1924.

seem probable that *śobhanika* of Patañjali was a pantomimic actor. It is not known if they used dialogues; at least there is nothing in the passage to indicate the same.

Patañjali divides the second type of artiste *granthika*s of the same passage into two distinct groups representing the followers of Kr̥ṣṇa and Kaṁsa. Their faces are smeared with red and black colours. Ridgeway[88] thinks that the *granthika*s divide themselves into two parties. Those representing the followers of Kaṁsa have their faces blackened and those of Kr̥ṣṇa have their face red. As Kr̥ṣṇa the black was different from his kinsmen in colour, it is natural that his followers are represented with a red face. Scholars who support this theory believe that the change in colour is in the case of the performers. But there are some scholars who explain that the change in colour should be taken in the case of audience. They think — when the *granthika*s describe effectively in words these incidents, the audiences become one with the episodes. Those partial to Kaṁsa would have their faces darkened when he is killed and those that are devotees of Kr̥ṣṇa would have their faces reddened in anger.[89] But Hillebrandt and Keith[90] refused to believe in the possibility of a Hindu audience containing persons who wished the success of Kaṁsa and maintain that it was performers who had their faces painted.

Indushekhara[91] says that the 'authors of a dramatic stage-play never colour their faces or wear a mask, at best they put on some cosmetics to heighten the effect'. This does not seem correct. The actors in *yakṣagāna* style of play and *kathakalī* dancers paint their faces for the performance according to the nature of the character they play, even today. Similarly, mask is known to have been in vogue during Bharata's time. He ascribes to each sentiment an appropriate colour.[92] Hence, the change in the colour might have been in the case of performers, if we take *granthika*s as performers and not as reciters. But there are some scholars who think that they were reciters.

Lüders derives the term *granthika* from the use of manuscript book in recitation. Keith,[93] though taking the derivation as being too speculative, accepts that there is

---

88. Ridgeway, *The Drama and Dramatic Dances of Non-European Races*, pp. 141-42.
89. G.H. Tarlekar, *op. cit.*, pp. 7-8.
90. A.B. Keith, *op. cit.* p. 35.
91. Indushekhara, *op. cit.*, p. 51.
92. *NŚ*, 23.196.
93. A.B. Keith, *op. cit.*, p. 35.

no doubt that the *granthikas* were reciters. Garola,[94] taking this passage as indicating the existence of a full-fledged play, says that the function of *granthikas* was similar to that of modern promptors. Prabhudayal Agnihotri[95] says that *granthikas* were the people who linked different episodes of a story by reciting the passage between the dialogues. M. Ghosh[96] while writing about drama and the epic says, like Lüders, that *granthika* is mentioned in *Mahābhārata*[97] as 'one who works in connection with a *grantha* — the book,' i.e., recites from it. He further says that the compiler of the *Mahābhārata*, it seems, had in view that kind of primitive drama from the epic, when he described the works of a *granthika*, wherein the reciter had to introduce characters who entered the stage, and he also had to point out the link between their speech, as organised dialogues and co-ordinated scenes where not yet formed — a work similar to that of the *sūtradhāra*.

Kaiyaṭa identifies *granthikas* with the *kathakas* — the story-tellers, in his commentary on *Mahābhāṣya*. It seems that *granthikas* belonged to the class of storytellers like *sūtas* and *kathakas* who recited the heroic deeds of the ancient heroes vividly from the *granthas* (texts or books). Some scholars believe that *kathakas* of the temple at Ayodhyā are their successors. Varadpande[98] says that *kathakas* of Ayodhyā are the individual artistes who recite the story with the help of dancing and some dramatic gestures, while the *granthikas* were a group. But the plural number of *granthika* mentioned in *Mahābhāṣya* does not indicate that they always performed in group as a rule. Possibly Patañjali was referring to the *granthikas* as a class, who in that particular episode performed together as the scene demanded. Hence they may be taken as the ancestors of the modern *kathakas*, who recited stories from epics in a most dramatic style.

Maṅkha

Patañjali's *Mahābhāṣya* describes three modes of presenting the popular episodes of Kaṁsa's killing and Bali's binding. Two modes have already been discussed, viz.,

---

94. Vachaspati Garola, *Bhārtīya Nāṭya Paramaparā aur Abhinayadarpaṇa*, p. 130.
95. Prabhudayal Agnihotri, *Patañjali Kālīna Bhārata*, p. 500.
96. M. Ghosh, *Contributions to the History of the Hindu Drama*, pp. 10, 11.
97. *Mahābhārata*, Āśvamedhika Parva, 70.7.
98. M.L. Varadpande, *Ancient Indian and Indo-Greek Theatre*, pp. 46-47.

actual representing of the episode by *śobhika*s and describing the incidents through words which was done by *granthika*s.

The third, which has not been dealt with, is that of the painters who described the incidents through their painting and brought them alive before the eyes of the onlookers. This reminds one of the art of *maṅkha*s, who used to describe the pictures painted on a board carried by them from one place to another; of *yamapaṭa*, a similar art, wherein the artist described the scenes of the life after death painted on a board or scroll; of heroic deeds of Pabuja described by the *bhopa*s of the present-day Rajasthan; of *behulapaṭa* of Bengal and *citrakathithakura* of Maharashtra. The art of narrating and explaining stories or scenes depicted on a scroll in a sequence, with the help of music or some sort of action, was a popular art in ancient India and the artistes were known as *maṅkha*.

*Maṅkha*s are mentioned in ancient Indian literature, especially in Jain texts. *Aupapātika Sūtra*[99] includes *maṅkha* in the traditional list of theatre artistes who haunted the temple of Yakṣa Pūrṇabhadra. Similar reference is found in the stories of Śramaṇopāsaka and Megha Kumāra Śramaṇa. Maṇiyāra Śreṣṭhī constructed a large *citra-sabhā* with beautiful paintings on cloth decorating the hall. Several threatre artistes, including *maṅkha*s, were appointed there on payment to entertain the people.[100] Similarly when King Śreṇika begot a son, he ordered the city of Rājagṛha to be decorated and theatre artistes to be called to perform on the occasion; one of these artistes was *maṅkha*.[101]

Coomaraswamy[102] has cited a reference from *Bhagavatī Sūtra*[103] which mentions Makkhali Gośāla, whose first name refers to his father's trade of *maṅkha*. The *maṅkha*s are described in the Sanskrit *ṭīkā* of *Bhagavatī Sūtra* as a special class of Indian mendicant vagabondising with picture boards.[104] It appears from the description given in the *sūtra* itself that the picture boards were carried by these beggars in their hands. According to the information provided in the *bhāṣā*, Barua[105]

99. *Aupapātika Sūtra*, 2, pp. 4-5.
100. *Dhammakahāṇuyoga*, Skandha IV, *Śramaṇopāsaka Kathānaka, sūtra* 307, p. 282.
101. *Dhammakahāṇuyoga*, Skandha II, *Śramaṇopāsaka Kathānaka sūtra* 321, p. 158.
102. A.K. Coomaraswamy, 'Picture Showmen', *IHQ*, vol. V, p. 183.
103. *Bhagavatī Sūtra*, XV.1.
104. *Bhagavatī Sūtra*, XV.1, leaf. 1204: *maṅkhāḥ citraphalake vyagrakaro bhikṣuka viseṣaḥ*.
105. B.M. Barua, 'Maskarī Gośala's Early life', *Calcutta Review*, 1927, April-June, p. 364.

thinks that the pictures were drawn upon wooden boards.[106] Gośāla's parents belonged to this class of mendicants according to the Jain accounts. But Barua[107] thinks that the vagrant life of Gośāla's parents which finds mention in the *Bhagavatī Sūtra* is consistent not so much with the mode of ordinary Indian beggars as with that of *parivrājaka*s and *parivrājikā*s of Indian wandering ascetics. He rejects the derivation from *maṅkha*[108] identifying Maṅkhali with Maskarī, with the meaning given for the latter by Pāṇini (viz., *parivrājaka*, who carries a bamboo staff).

But, there is an interesting reference in a Buddhist text *Aśokāvadāna*[109] which goes as follows. A follower of the *Nirgrantha* at Puṇḍravardhan painted a picture, showing Buddha prostrating at the feet of the *nirgrantha*. When Aśoka was informed about it, he ordered all the *ājīvaka*s of Puṇḍravardhan to be killed. A similar incident was cited at Pāṭaliputra where the culprit was burned alive with his family. Sujit Kumar Mukhopadhyay, the editor of the text, says that author of this *avadāna* seems to have confused the *nirgrantha*s (Jain) with *ājīvaka*s. They were two different sects. If so, it would have been the *ajīvaka*s who painted the picture and not a *nirgrantha*. If we study this reference in the background of that of the *Bhagavatī Sūtra* it would appear that there is some truth in Gośāla's father being a *maṅkha*. Since it was a family trade, he himself adopted the same profession as soon as he grew to manhood according to Jain texts.[110] There is a possibility that he might have used this art to propagate his ideas among his disciples and they in their turn used it as a means to propagate their faith, though taking some undue advantage as insulting Buddha in the above-mentioned reference. It was an easy means of communication that could be understood even by the illiterate or a little child. Stella Kramrisch in her *Viṣṇudharmottara Purāṇa*[111] quotes *Sārattha-pakāsinī*[112] of Buddhaghoṣa which says,

106. *Bhagavatī Sūtra*, XV.1, leaf 1204: *maṅkha kāṣṭhacitrāṁ. dekhādato phiraiehavo bhikṣuka viśeṣaḥ.*

107. B.M. Barua, *op. cit.*, p. 359.

108. B.M. Barua, 'Maskarī as an Epithet of Gośāla', *IHQ*, vol. III, 1927, p. 235.

109. *Aśokāvadāna/Vītāśokāvadāna*, pp. 67-68.

110. B.M. Barua, 'Maskarī Gośāla's Early life', *Calcutta Review*, 1927, April-June, p. 359.

111. Stella Kramrisch, *Viṣṇudharmottara Purāṇa*, Part III, p. 7.

112. *nakho nām brāhmaṇo pāsandikā honti te pana koṭṭhakaṁ katvā tattha nānappakāre sugati-duggati-vasena saṁpatti vipattiyo likhāpetvā, idam kammaṁ katvā idaṁ paṭilahhati.* —*Sāratthapakāsinī*, Quoted by Barua, *op. cit.*, p. 364

> There is a class of Brāhmaṇical teachers known by the name of 'Nakha'. They make a (portable) framework upon which they cause to be drawn a variety of pictures, depicting scenes of good and evil destinies of fortunes and misfortunes. . . .

Barua[113] says that there can be no doubt that the *maṅkha*s referred to in the Jain *Bhagavatī Sūtra* and its commentaries and the *nakha brāhmaṇa pāsandika*s referred to in *Sāratthapakāsinī* were representatives of one and the same institution and this folk art (or trade) existed during Buddhaghoṣa's time. Coomaraswamy[114] thinks that the word *nakha* does not sound plausible; he wonders if it is an error for *maṅkha*. But Barua explains that they were called *nakha*s because apart from being painters and picture-expounders, they were skull tappers too. It was their business to tap on skulls with their finger nails to ascertain divine future destinies, in the case of the dead and prediction, in the case of living persons.[115]

V. Raghavan[116] says that there are few Jain Prākr̥t texts which do not mention the *maṅkha*. He adds two more references from the Sanskrit glosses on Jain Prākr̥t texts, which show that *maṅkha*s were known by two other names, *gaurīputraka* and *kedāraka*. The gloss on the *Kalpasūtra* named *sandehaviṣauṣadhi* by Jinaprabhasūri[117] says — *maṅkhaḥ citraphalakahastaḥ bhikṣākā gaurīputrakā iti prasiddhāḥ*. The Jain lexicon Abhidhanarājendra also gives the above passage from the gloss on the *Kalpasūtra* and adds to it a passage from the gloss on the *Piṇḍaniryukti* which says that the *maṅkha* had another name *kedāraka* — *maṅkhaḥ kedārakaḥ yaḥ pīṭhamupadarśya lokamāvarjayati*.

HISTORY AND CONTRIBUTIONS OF MAṄKHAS TO THEATRE

Besides Jain literature, *maṅkha*s are mentioned in Kauṭilya's *Arthaśāstra*[118] too. Kauṭilya while describing the method employed to create split or to do away secretly with unwanted persons, speaks of some men and women engaged in artistic and other pursuits and moving closely with those in power. They could be easily employed

113. Barua, *op. cit.*, pp. 367-68.
114. A.K. Coomaraswamy, *op. cit.*, p. 186.
115. Barua, *op. cit.*, p. 372.
116. V. Raghavan, 'Picture Showmen: Maṅkha', *IHQ*, XII, no. 3, p. 524.
117. *Kalpasūtra*, ed. H. Jacobi, p. 109, fn.
118. *Kauṭilya Arthaśāstra*, XI.1, p. 380, Mysore, 2nd edn.

for such plots. In the Mysore edition, such women are *kauśikastriyo nartakī gāyanā*, but T. Ganapati Shastri reads the text in his edition as *aditikauśikastriyaḥ* and translates *aditistrī* as a woman going about exhibiting pictures of several deities.[119] Madhavayajvan too in his *Nayacandrikā* on *Arthaśāstra* had adopted the reading *aditikauśikastriyaḥ*. He thinks that Aditi and Kauśika both refer to pictures of deities of those names and the women meant here by Kauṭilya are wives of *yogapuruṣa* or secret agents in the guise of beggars carrying these pictures of deities and begging alms.[120]

V. Raghavan takes *aditistrī* of *Arthaśāstra* (XI/1) as incorrect reading of the passage and says that the earlier passage on which this 'wrong repetition' in XI/1 is likely to be based occurs in I/16 (*rājaputrarakṣaṇa*) where, *tena hi dhvajena aditi kauśikavadasyamātr̥bāndhavā bhikṣeraṇa* . . . , is mentioned and the correct reading is *kauśika striyaḥ*. Ganapati Sastri on the basis of *Jayamaṅgalā Ṭīkā* on the text (I/16) says that Aditi was a picture-showing beggar. Thus it seems that during Kauṭilya's time there were women who had adopted the art of 'picture showing' (*maṅkhavidhā*) as their profession, suggesting the existence of female *maṅkha*s too.

This art was so popular that Sanskrit poets could not contain themselves from using it as a dramatic device. In Bhāsa's *Dūtavākyam*,[121] Duryodhana explains the *citrapaṭa* containing Draupadī's picture, like a *maṅkha*. In the seventh act of *Abhijñānaśākuntalam*[122] of Kālidāsa, Mātali, the divine charioteer tells Duṣyanta that gods have composed songs describing his heroic deeds and are writing them on the cloth made of the bark of *kalpavr̥kṣa* with colours. The idea of writing the *carita* (heroic deeds) of Duṣyanta on *Kalpalatāṅśuka* (cloth made of the bark of the *kalpavr̥kṣa*) may have come from the art of *maṅkha*. Besides, the Sanskrit root *likha* denotes both 'writing' and 'drawing' and as the material used for writing or drawing was colour, left by the divine damsels after their make-up, the meaning of the verb *likhanti* as painting seems more suitable and indicates the existence of *maṅkha*s during the Gupta period.

---

119. V. Raghavan, 'On a meaning of the word Kauśika', *Journal of Oriental Research*, Madras, vol. XV, p. 110.

120. *Ibid.*, pp. 1-12.

121. *Dūtavākyam*, Act I, *BNC*, vol. I, pp. 10-14.

122. *Abhijñānaśākuntalam*, Act VII.5, *KG*, p. 91.

These artistes were later known as *yamapaṭṭikā*s because the picture they exhibited represented the reward of good and evil deeds to be experienced in the realm of Yama. Their picture scroll was known as *yamapaṭa*. They existed during Harṣa's time and their art was very popular as we know from Bāṇa's *Harṣacarita*, where it is said:

> In the Bazar street, amid a great crowd of inquisitive children, he observed an 'Inferno showman' (*yamapaṭṭikā*) in whose left hand there was a painted canvas stretched out on a support of upright rods and showing the lord of the dead, mounted on his buffalo, wielding a reed wand in his other hand; he was expounding the features of the next world and chanted.[123]

Mudrārākṣasa[124] too mentions *yamapaṭa* in the form of rolls, which exhibited continuous representation. Such a roll was spread out by a spy of Cāṇakya, before the people, in Candanadāsa's house and was exhibited by him with songs and a characteristic manner of acting. In Bhavabhūti's *Uttara-Rāma-Carita* Lakṣmaṇa takes Rāma and Sītā to a picture gallery (*vīthikā*), which contains pictures drawn by the painter named Arjuna and explains them like a *maṅkha.*[125]

At a later date, *Prabandhacintāmaṇi*[126] mentions 'those who carry picture' and thus, shows the existence of such artistes. This art is still known in Java and Bali and is classed as a dramatic art. Manmohan Ghosh[127] says that the cultural history of these countries shows that the origin of their drama and dramatic art was in India. Such folk artistes are still known in our country, especially in Rajasthan, Bengal and Maharashtra. The *bioscope-vālā*s, of present-day Uttar Pradesh, are also the descendants of *maṅkha*s. They carry a box having a picture scroll, with small holes for looking into it and a wooden stand to place the box on. The box has a small handle on one side at the top, as the picture showman winds it the picture scroll inside the box moves slowly and the pictures become visible. The man sings, while describing the pictures and plays *ghuṅghrū* bells. His art is exactly like that of a *maṅkha*. Children are crazy to see the picture and listen to the man singing in

---

123. *Harṣacarita*, Cowell and Tomas version, p. 136.
124. *Mudrārākṣasa*, I.18, p. 34.
125. *Uttara-Rāma-Carita*, Act I, pp. 15 to 31, ed. M.R. Kale, 1924.
126. *Prabandhacintāmaṇi*, Tawnbeyi's trn., p. 160.
127. M. Ghosh, *Contributions to the History of the Hindu Drama*, p. 47.

a typical style which reminds one of the *yamapṭṭikā* of *Harṣacarita*, who was surrounded by a crowd of inquisitive children.

With the help of this historical study we can derive the following historical data:

1. There were artistes, called *maṅkhas*, in the country, at least since the fifth century BC, who wandered about taking with them portable or movable picture galleries with pictures drawn and exhibited thereupon.

2. The *maṅkhas* referred to in the Jain literature and the *nakha brāhmaṇa pāsaṅdikā* referred to in *Sāratthapakāsinī* were representatives of one and the same institution and their later representatives were known as *yamapaṭṭikā*. The art had some affinities with the picture classed, in *Divyāvadāna*,[128] as *caraṇa* or *karaṇa*.[129]

3. The exhibition of picture by such artistes was accompanied by singing, dancing or dramatic acting and thus, the *maṅkhas* contributed to dramatic art in their own way, as is clear from the description of *yamapaṭṭikā* or *yamapaṭṭikās* in *Harṣacarita* and *Mudrārākṣasa*. This was one of the most important reasons of its popularity.

4. The *maṅkhas* must have used some special costume for the performance because *Bhagavatī Sūtra*[130] informs us that *maṅkha*, the father of Makkhali Gośāla, travelled from one village to another with his wife, dressed in the garb of a *maṅkha*. That would have made the performance still more attractive.

5. The subject-matter of the picture exhibited by them changed according to the time and need. Generally, they had pictures depicting scenes of good and evil destinies and of fortunes and misfortunes. Since, in Bhāsa's *Dūtavākyam* the subject was Draupadī's humiliation by Duḥśāsana and helplessness of her five husbands, and in *Uttara-Rāma-Carita* the subject of delineation was the incidents in the life of Rāma, it seems that deeds of heroes too could have been a popular subject for such pictures. If one could

128. *Divyāvadāna*, pp. 300-3.

129. B.M. Barua, *op. cit.*, p. 357.

130. *Bhagavatī Sūtra*, XV.1.

relate the episode in *Mahābhāṣya* of killing of Kaṁsa and binding of Bali as having some connection with the art of *maṅkha*s, the theme of the painting in that case too would be heroic deeds. This subject, it seems, became more popular than the earlier *yamapaṭa*, because the modern successors of *maṅkha* have heroic deeds of the famous kings (Rajasthan) and Rādhā-Kṛṣṇa story for their subject (Bengal).

6. *Maṅkha*s travelled from village to village exhibiting their picture scroll. This was one of their sources of making money.
7. The art had tremendous effect on the mind of the people — even sophisticated Sanskrit dramas adopted the art as a dramatic device. It indicates the influence of strong folk tradition of theatrical art on the classical one.
8. Probably the tradition of early Buddhist bas-reliefs at Bharhut, Sāñcī and Bodh-Gayā and frescoes of Ajantā were inspired by this art.

Kuśīlava

According to Bharata,[131] *kuśīlava* was an important member of the troupe who arranged various musical instruments properly and was an expert instrumentalist. On the basis of his capability, deep knowledge and unperturbed serenity, he was known as *kuśīlava*.

The term *kuśīlava* denotes an actor in classical Sanskrit literature. It is generally believed that the word *kuśīlava* is derived from Kuśa and Lava of *Rāmāyaṇa*, the twin sons of Rāma who sang *Rāmāyaṇa*.[132] Keith[133] says that the mode of formation of the compound *kuśīlava* is strange, in which the first member represents a woman's name. Probably it was due to the bad morals of such artistes that later, instead of *kuśalava*, they came to be known as *kuśīlava* (*śīla*, meaning manners, with prefix *ku*, denoting bad manners). It seems that the artistes, whose function it was to

131. *nānātodyavidhāne prayogayuktaḥ pravādane kuśalaḥ* ।
kuśalāvadātāvyathitam yasmāttasmāt kuśīlavo jñyeyaḥ ।।
—*NŚ*, XXXV.106

132. S. Konow, *The Indian Drama*, p. 13; A.B. Keith, *The Sanskrit Drama*, p. 31; G.H. Tarlekar, *Studies in Nāṭyaśāstra*, p. 6; S. Dikshit, *Bhārata aur Bhāratīya Nāṭyakalā*, p. 317; H.N. Dasgupta, *The Indian Stage*, p. 28.

133. A.B. Keith, *op. cit.*, p. 31.

recite the heroic deeds of ancient kings in a dramatic style, came to be known as *kuśīlava*s, after the twin brothers of *Rāmāyaṇa*. Formerly they were reciters like later *kathaka*s but gradually their association with drama deepened and they became known as actors. We have several references from ancient texts where they are either classed with actors or themselves called actors.

Kauṭilya[134] includes them amongst traditional theatre artistes. He had laid rules for the *kuśīlava*s, such as, during rainy season they must camp at one place and stop moving. If they are given an excessive reward, far beyond the capacity of the giver, they must not accept it, nor should they entertain excessive praise from the overwhelmed audience; in violation of these rules they will have to pay twelve *paṇa*s as penalty.[135] Kauṭilya allowed *kuśīlava*s to perform at any place in the country and entertain people but also warned them against making adverse comments on some socially sensitive things and hurting people's feelings. They had to avoid making fun of country (*deśa*), caste (*jāti*), family (*gotra*), a certain branch of Vedic studies and representing copulation of men with women.[136] If in spite of all these instructions, the feelings of the people were hurt the magistrate was authorised to impose fine and in case inability of payment was expressed, each *paṇa* was to be matched with lashes.[137] Kauṭilya is against the construction of theatre in the vicinity of a village, because indulgence in pleasure by country people brings about the destruction of the fruits of works of all three times.

Thus, from Kauṭilya, we gather certain important information regarding *kuśīlava*s. During Kauṭilya's time, they were known as actors and were wandering artistes. They were rewarded for their performances and were very popular. While performing they often crossed the limits of decency and taking advantage of their art made undesirable comments on people and country they visited. This was the

---

134. . . . *etena naṭanartakagāyakavādakavāgijīvanakuśilavaplavaka śaubhika* . . .
— *KA*, II.43.3

135. *kuśilavā varṣārātrimekasthā vaseyuḥ* ।
kāmadānamatimātramekasyātivādaṁ ca varṣayeyuḥ ।।
tasyātikrame dvādaśapaṇo daṇḍaḥ ।
kāmadeśajātigotracaraṇamaithunāpahānenarmayeyuḥ ।।
— *Ibid.*, IV.76.1

136. *KA*, IV.76.1.

137. *kuśīlavaiścāraṇabhikṣukāśca vyākhyātaḥ* ।
teṣāmayaśśūlena yāvataḥ paṇānibhavadeyuḥ, tāvantaḥ śiphāprahārā daṇḍāḥ ।।
— *KA*, IV.76.1

reason why Kauṭilya drew a code of conduct for *kuśīlavas*. As such actors could mix freely with general public and move closely with those in power, as part of their retinue, with little moral bindings, Kauṭilya had utilised them for spying. They were employed to watch the character and integrity of villagers, village officers and armed soldiers.[138]

Manu does not have a good impression for *kuśīlavas* either. He lays down that the testimony of a *kuśīlava* is not valid.[139] He further says[140] that the judge would consider the *kuśīlava* as a śūdra and the king should drive him out from the town. This was due to the bad reputation they had since Kauṭilya's time.

In some Sanskrit dramas, *kuśīlavas* are mentioned in the *prastāvanā* as a member of the dramatic troupe responsible for music (*saṅgīta prayoga*) in the play. In *Mr̥cchakaṭikam*,[141] *Mālatī-mādhava*,[142] *Veṇīsaṁhāra*,[143] and *Bālabhārata*[144] he is associated with music and in *Karpūramañjarī*,[145] the Prākr̥t drama, he is an actor in general.

While discussing about Sūta who, according to him, later became *sūtradhāra*, Rangacharya says that in due course as the function of *sūtradhāra* multiplied, it became the duty of *kuśīlava*, musician, to help *sūtradhāra* to open the play with music, to bring the audience into a receptive mood.[146] With the passage of time, a *naṭī* was introduced who had more natural charm and grace than *kuśīlava*. Hence

---

138. *sūdārālikasnāpakasaṁvāhakāstarkakalpakaprāsadha-kodakaparicāra-kārasadāḥ-kubjavāmanakirāta-mūkabadhirajadāṅdhachadmāno naṭanartakagāyan-avādaka-vāgjīvīvanakuśīlavāḥ striyaścābhyantaraṁ cāram vidyuḥ.* —*Ibid.*, I.II

139. *Manu-smr̥ti*, VIII.65.

140. *Ibid.*, VIII.102.

141. *aye, śūnyeyamasmatsangītaśālā kva nu gataḥ kuśīlavāḥ bhaviṣyanti?* — *Mr̥cchakaṭikam*, *Prastāvanā*

142. *tatsarve kuśīlavāḥ sangītaprayogena matsamīhitasam-pādanāya pravartantām* — *Mālatimādhava*, p. 10, ed. M.R. Kale

143. *tatkimiti pāripārśvikanāraṁbhayasi kuśilavaiḥ saha sangītakaṁ* — *Veṇīsaṁhāra*, p. 5, ed. Chhoturam Tiwari

144. *kathamupakrāntameva kuśīlavaiḥ* — *Bālabhāratam*, p. 3, ed. Durgā Prasad

145. *kim uṇa naṭṭapa-aṭṭo viadīsadi amhāṇam kuśīlavāṇam parijaṇo* — *Karpūramañjarī*, p. 5, ed. Durgā Prasad

146. Adya Rangacharya, *Drama in Sanskrit Literature*, pp. 46-48.

with the coming of *naṭī*, *kuśīlava* became rare in the field of drama, if not altogether diasppearing. He thinks that *prastāvanā* of the Sanskrit drama was originally nothing else but music, and singing in praise of the seasonal charm. Music was necessary for *prastāvanā* and it was *kuśīlava* who could change *sthāpanā* into a *prastāvanā*, because he was basically a musician.

It seems that their deep knowledge of music and dramatic style, which made their recitation attractive and melodious to listen to, introduced them to the dramatic troupes. Later, they became permanent musicians of the troupes and because of this association, these folk reciters of heroic deeds of the past came to be known as actors.

Naṭa

Meaning of the root *naṭa* is 'to act'; hence, 'he who acts again and again the stories of men with sentiments (*rasa*), states (*bhāva*) and temperament (*sattva*)' is, according to Bharata,[147] a *naṭa*. He further says that one

> who can apply the music of four kinds of instruments and produce a play according to the meaning of śāstra as well as his own reasoning is called an actor (*naṭa*).[148]

This shows that *naṭa* was a perfect actor who could impersonate other beings, infusing his art with *rasa*, *bhāva* and *sattva*, the three essentials of drama. He was not a mere imitator but qualified the art with his own experience, feelings and knowledge of music, rendering its originality. Bharata often mentions *naṭa* as *nartaka*, which shows that *naṭa* was well versed in the art of dancing too. Bharata[149] says that

> there is nothing that is not comprehended in *nāṭya*, either knowledge, erudition, action, art or craft. It includes all the śāstras or sciences, arts and crafts, hence I created it.

---

147. *naṭayati dhātvartho-ayam bhūyo naṭayati ca lokavr̥ttāntaṁ* ।
rasabhāvasatvyuktaṁ yasmāttasmānnaṭo bhavati ।।
— *NŚ*, XXXV.95

148. *caturātodyavidhānam prayogaśāstrārthaṁ hetuvihitasya* ।
nāṭyasya ca prayoktā sa naṭo nām vijñyeyaḥ ।।
— *Ibid.*, XXV.100

149. *NŚ*, I.117-18.

Bharata's *Nāṭyaśāstra* shows that drama in ancient India was a very comprehensive art, covering various aspects in its fold, and hence, the actors who followed this tradition grew into complete and perfect artistes.

Keith says that the term *naṭa* does not occur in Vedic literature. It is mentioned for the first time in Pāṇini's *Aṣṭādhyāyī*[150] and there it means a pantomime.[151] *Naṭa*s are mentioned in epics with other theatre artistes who were present on various festive occasions to perform. In *Mahābhārata naṭa*s (actors), *vaitālika*s (bards), *sūta*s, *māgadha*s entertained the guests at the marriage of Uttarā and Abhimanyu. *Mahābhārata* says that the king should extend his patronage to *naṭa*s, *nartaka*s, *malla*s (wrestlers) and *māyāvī*s (magicians) because they delight people and intensify the charm of the capital.[152] A compound *naṭa-nartakāḥ* is mentioned in Anuśāsana-Parva of *Mahābhārata*[153] and the commentator, Neelkantha takes the compound to mean 'comedians and dancers'. In Vana-Parva Yudhiṣṭhira says that to earn a good name, he had made occasional payment to the actors and dancers.[154] Varadpande[155] cites a passage from *Mahābhārata*[156] mentioning *naṭa*, referred to by Hillebrandt. It is as follows:

> The king is advised to appropriate the nature of the Kokilā, the boar, the mount Meru, the actor and true friend. Since, the Kokilā gets its young ones reared by other, the boar who draws out the root, destroys the enemy to the very root, the mount Meru remains unshakable and since an empty room remains always ready to receive treasure, in this connection *naṭa* cannot indicate a pantomimic actor, but it should signify a player who sometimes plays this role.

Supporting his view he quotes the commentary which explains the passage according to the sense with the words —

---

150. *Aṣṭādhyāyī*, IV.3.110-11.
151. A.B. Keith, *The Sanskrit Drama*, p. 31.
152. *Mahābhārata*, Śāntī-Parva, 69.60.
153. *Ibid.*, Anuśāsana-Parva, 33.12.
154. *Ibid.*, Vana-Parva, 313.80.
155. M.L. Varadpande, *History of Indian Theatre*, p. 61.
156. *Mahābhārata*, Śāntī-Parva, 143.21.

naṭasya nānārūpatvam iṣṭam
evaṁ rājā snigdhaprasannādīna guṇān bibhrayan

Varadapande says that Hillebrandt wants to suggest that the *naṭa* of the *Mahābhārata* was not just a pantomimic actor but an actor of actual plays. *Yājñavalkya-Saṁhitā*[157] also says:

> As an actor, for exhibiting various characters, paints his body with various colours, so the soul assumes (various) bodies begotten by (multifarious) acts.

*Naṭa*s are mentioned in *Rāmāyaṇa* too as entertainers. Roads were full of *naṭa*s, *nartaka*s and *vādaka*s at the time of Rāma's birth[158] and coronation.[159] These *naṭa*s had their own troupes.[160] In Ayodhyā-kāṇḍa, Sage Mārkaṇḍeya says that in the anarchical state those festivities which contribute to the pleasure of *naṭa*s and *nartaka*s have become rare.[161] *Naṭa*s, *nartaka*s and *talavacāra*s were there to entertain the guests on the occasion of *aśvamedha* sacrifice performed by Rāma. They even accompanied the army to the battlefield.[162]

In these references, from both the epics, the *naṭa* is mentioned with *nartaka*s, *vaitālika*s, *sūta*s, *māgadha*s, *gāyaka*s, *vādaka*s and *talavacāra*s. He cannot be taken as a dancer, musician, reciter or instrumentalist as all of them are mentioned specifically and these terms in their own capacity cannot be taken as denoting an actor exclusively. Hence, the word *naṭa* may mean something different from the above-mentioned artistes. As the art of impersonation, mimicry and fun-making was known in India since pre-Vedic and Vedic period, as we have already noticed, the term *naṭa* may be taken as denoting an actor.

---

157. *Yājñavalkya-Saṁhitā*, III.162.
158. *Rāmāyaṇa*, Bāla-kāṇḍa, 18, 18.
159. *Ibid.*, Ayodhyā-kāṇḍa, 6, 14.
160. *naṭanartakasaṅghānaṁ gāyakānaṁ ca gāyatāṁ* ।
yataḥ karṇasukha vācaḥ suśrāva janatā tataḥ ॥
— *Ibid.*, Ayodhyā-kāṇḍa, 67, 14
161. *Ibid.*, Ayodhyā-kāṇḍa, 67, 15.
162. *naṭanartakasaṅghānaṁ gāyakānaṁ ca gāyatāṁ* ।
yataḥ karṇasukha vācaḥ suśrāva janatā tataḥ ॥
— *Ibid.*, Uttara-kāṇḍa, 64, 3

Keith[163] thinks that the meaning of the term *naṭa* in *Mahābhārata* is not clear, and it may denote a pantomimist. As for *Rāmāyaṇa*, he says,

> Accepting all these references as genuine, which we are not obliged to do, the passages have manifestly no claim to early date, for other reasons than the allusion, and leaves us again without any early evidence. . . .

But, we know that epics contain incidents much older than the time of their compilation. Hence, they may refer to a very old tradition of actors of some sort who were invited to perform on auspicious occasion together with other theatre artistes recorded in them. We have noticed that a community of such artistes was forming in Vedic period itself, and artistes were invited to perform certain ritualistic impersonation, dance and music. It seems that this community was in existence during the age depicted in *Rāmāyaṇa*, which refers to *naṭanartakasaṅghānām*. The way these epics refer to these theatre artistes indicates that they were a community consisting of artistes from both the traditions — classical and folk. This strong symbiotic tradition may have inspired Śilālin and Kṛśāśva to compose *Naṭasūtra*.

*Naṭa*s are mentioned in Buddhist *Nikāya*s as more than mimes or dancers. *Gāmanī Saṁyutta*[164] mentions such *naṭa*s 'who on the stage or in the arena, made people laugh and delight them with truth and falsehood'. Not only this but the *naṭagrāmaṇī* (head of the village of *naṭa*s) and traditional teachers, who were *naṭa*s (*pubbakānāṁ, ācāriyapācariyānaṁ naṭānaṁ* . . .) are mentioned in the above-mentioned passage. In *Jātaka*s too, *naṭa* is not merely a mimetic artiste but also an acrobat, a musician and a reciter. *Vidhura Paṇḍita Jātaka*[165] mentions *naṭa* in the list of entertainers. In *Uccittha Bhaṭṭa Jātaka,*[166] he is an acrobat; in *Labhagaraha Jātaka,*[167] he is described as a tricky person who wins property by relating ill tales but whose art can easily influence the audience. In *Sonaka Jātaka,*[168] *naṭa* is a mime dancer. In *Suruci Jātaka,*[169] *naṭa*s are tumblers and jugglers who divide

163. A.B. Keith, *op. cit.*, pp. 28-29.
164. S. IV, p. 306.
165. V. Fousboll, *The Jātaka*, vol. VI, pp. 276-77.
166. E.B. Cowell, *Jātaka Stories*, vol. II, p. 117.
167. *Ibid.*, vol. III, p. 287.
168. *Ibid.*, vol. V, p. 128.
169. V. Fousboll, *op. cit.*, vol. IV, pp. 324-25.

themselves in seven bands and dance. A *naṭa* makes his half body dance while the other half remains stone still. In *Dubbacha Jātaka,*[170] a *laṅghananaṭa* (acrobat) is mentioned who learned javelin dance under the guidance of another *laṅghananaṭa* who was killed while attempting to jump over five javelins. In *Pādakuśalaka-māṇavaka Jātaka,*[171] *naṭa* is a *vīṇā* player. While *Kaṇavera Jātaka*[172] describes them as wandering actors, musicians and reciters, *naṭa* in Buddhist literature was a professional folk artiste who used to visit public festivals to earn money through his art. Being an entertainer, he was a witty person, a quality which persisted in him even after renouncing the world under Buddhist influence. One such *naṭa* is mentioned in the *Vinaya*. The *Sekhiya* 51 notes a *naṭa* for his jollyness and gives dramatic comment upon an incident or a situation. When a monk drank the milk making a hissing sound, his companion, who was formerly a *naṭa* spoke, 'It seems that this whole order is cooled.'[173]

Kauṭilya[174] also mentions *naṭa*s among other theatre artistes, whose art he utilised for spying and who were required to pay a tax called *durga* to the king. In *Arthaśāstra* too, they are mentioned as a community or a class; their art was their profession, a source of their livelihood. Kauṭilya often mentions *kuśīlava* as actors,[175] and thus it seems that amalgamation of various theatrical arts has already begun.

From second century BC, we find sculptural depictions of the *naṭa*s from Bharhut and Sāñcī. Barua[176] says that *samajjā* formed a part or distinct feature of the *thūpa-maha* (*stūpa* worship) in Bharhut art. The entertainment consisted of not only musical performance and acting but also wrestling and gymnastic feats. He cites examples from Bharhut sculptures depicting gymnastic feats. The gymnastic feats shown consists of riding elephants, horses and *makara*s and in some instances, a

---

170. E.B. Cowell, *op. cit.*, vol. I, p. 259.
171. V. Fousboll, *op. cit.*, vol. III, p. 507.
172. E.B. Cowell, *op. cit.*, vol. III, p. 41.
173. *Vinaya*, Sekhiya 57, p. 266. Quoted by G.S.P. Misra, 'The Vinaya Evidence as the Means of Entertainment in the Age of Buddha', *Ind. Ant.*, vol 1, 1964, p. 194.
174. *KA*, XI.1 (Mysore, II edn.) p. 380.
175. *Ibid.*, IV.76.1. (ed. Gerola).
176. B.N. Barua, *Barhut*, Book III, p. 67.

standing posture,[177] or a man lifting up another standing man on his shoulder[178] and a standing woman on the palm of one's hand.[179] The scene, showing men standing on each others' shoulders, depicts *laṅghananaṭa*s who, according to V.S. Agrawala,[180] are thus forming Mount sumeru. It seems that art of *naṭa*s was so popular that sculptors, too, took delight in depicting these secular scenes even on religious monuments. Besides, the performance of *laṅghananaṭa* might have been a part of *samajjā* festival, held on the occasion of *thūpa-maha*. The *naṭa*s and *naṭī*s performed together as is suggested by a medallion[181] from Bharhut depicting a dancing couple of *kinnara*s in almost identical pose holding their flying sashes. The fluttering plaits of the female figure indicate her movement. There is no need to tell that the sculptor was inspired by the art of contemporary *naṭa*s in depicting this scene.

According to *Mahāparinibbāna Sutta*,[182] on the seventh day after the *mahā-parinibbāna* of Buddha, 'Mallas thought to carry the body of the blessed one outside city to pay honour and reverence, and respect and homage with dance, song and music.' Varadpande thinks that it must have been songs depicting the life of Buddha accompanied by dance, culminating into a kind of spectacle.[183]

According to Marshall, this scene is depicted on the west pillar of the northern gateway of the Sāñcī *stūpa*.[184] The scene depicts *kinnara*s, paying the *stūpa* worship with garlands, in the air, below them, on the ground, worshippers are going round it, in procession as the sort of dance step, a few inside but the greater number outside the first balustrade. Some are clapping their hands, one is waving a standard. In the foreground, an orchestra is seen consisting of a harp, a kettledrum, two sorts of tambourine, double flute and two carved trumpets.[185]

Probably experts in dance and music (*naṭa*s) were called to perform dance and

---

177. *Barhut*, fig. 62, 64, 75-77.
178. *Ibid.*, *op.cit.*, fig. 60.
179. *Ibid.*, fig. 72.
180. V.S. Agrawala, *Bhāratīya Kalā*, fig. 95; also see *Pl.* no. III.
181. See *Pl.* no. IV.
182. *Mahāparinibbāna Sutta*, 251-63, pp. 137-41, ed. Bhikṣu Kittima.
183. M.L. Varadpande, *Religion and Theatre*, p. 108.
184. Marshall & Foucher, *Monuments of Sanchi*, vol. II, pl. 36 (CI).
185. *Monuments of Sāñcī*, vol. II, pl. 36 (CI).

play musical instruments as part of the festivity and *stūpa* worship, as had been the tradition in ancient India. Though the sandals, leggings and capes of the musicians in the foreground, in the above-mentioned panel, resemble those of 'northerners', according to Marshall, the instruments being played by them are Indian and the dance step of the men, in the inner line, is also well-known in later Indian sculptures. These figures probably represent those foreigners who had adopted Indian culture, including Indian religion, having dance and music as part of ritual. Even if it is so, these figures throw important light on contemporary theatrical arts and artistes both.

*Naṭa*s are represented in the Deccan sculptures of second or first century BC. Four episodes of a dance performance by a cavalier dancer with two female partners are depicted in four panels in the *caitya* at Kondane, belonging to the second or first century BC. In first three panels, he is dancing with them by turns and in the fourth, he stands by himself with a smile on his lips, and is inclining his body in a graceful gesture as if to acknowledge the applause which has been showered upon him by the spectators for his successful performance.[186] The cavalier dancer is holding a bow in his right-hand in the first panel, a long club in the second, a sword is seen hanging by his waist in the third and he is holding a shield in the fourth panel. A dancer with weapons suggests two possibilities — either he is a cavalier skilled in the art of dance or he represents a folk dancer (*naṭa*) who dances with weapons. Though the dance, according to Yazdani,[187] is of primitive type comprising only leaping and whirling, the graceful movements of the limbs of the performers and the attractive display of their emotional gesture shows an advanced stage of the art of acting, for example, stretched arm of the male dancer to caress the chin of the female dance partner or coquettishly lowered hand of the woman to finger the fringe of the girdle of her male partner. It seems that the three dancers are performing in accompaniment to a song composed in dialogue form; that is why the whole scene gives a dramatic effect. Such dance can be performed only by a *naṭa* who has a command over the arts of dance, music and acting. One is tempted to think that all these four episodes probably depict four important episodes from a popular folk play with religious leaning, as it is depicted in the *caitya* cave of Kondane. What is important for us is the skilled performer depicted in the panel.

186. G. Yazdani, *The Early History of the Deccan*, pp. 777-78, pl. IV-V.

187. *Ibid.*, p. 777.

The *naṭa*s dancing with their weapons are depicted in the sculptures of Deccan a few centuries later too. At Nāgārjunakoṇḍa a scene,[188] belonging to third century AD, depicts a dancing couple. The male dancer is holding a bow in his stretched left hand and is dancing accompanied by his female partner. Their rythmic movement is indicated by their slightly raised feet. Thus, it seems that there must have been a style of dance known at least in ancient Deccan wherein the dancers performed with their weapons, probably depicting a folk legend and sculptors may have utilised their art as an attractive subject for their carvings as had been done by the sculptors of Bharhut.

*Naṭa*s are mentioned by Patañjali too. His reference to *naṭa* is very significant. He says: *yadārambhakāḥ raṅgaṁ gacchanti naṭasya śrosyāmo granthikasya śrosyāmaḥ*. . . .[189] Interpreting this reference V.S. Agrawala[190] says, 'Patañjali refers to *naṭa* teachers (*ākhyātās*) of *nāṭya*, initiating novices (*ārambhakāḥ*) in the art not through text but by their direct method of stage acting.' We can obtain the following historical data from Patañjali's *Mahābhāṣya*, regarding *naṭa*s:

1. There was a definite style of art to learn before coming into the field.
2. Some experienced *naṭa*s were acting as the instructors of the novices.
3. It was more of a practical than a theoretical discipline.
4. The reference suggests that the art of *naṭa*s was no longer a common folk entertainment but was gradually taking the form of a sophisticated art which needed a proper training and thus was on the path of classicalisation.
5. The instructor trained his pupils on the stage or arena (*raṅga*). People who are in the field of drama or theatre can realise the importance of training on the stage where the show is going to be staged and this was realised by the *naṭa*s of Patañjali's time, too.

But unlike other fields of studies or vedic studies *Upanayan* (initiation) ceremony was not necessary for pupil *naṭa*s to begin thier training.[191]

---

188. R.J. Mehta, *Masterpieces of Female Form in Indian Art*, pl. 14.
189. *Mahābhāṣya*, I.4.29.
190. V.S. Agrawala, *Pāṇini kālīna Bhāratavarṣa*, p. 327, fn. 2.
191. *Ibid.*, pp. 327-28, fn. 2.

In *Manusmṛti*,[192] a particular class has been mentioned in reference to *naṭa*s. They were different from *śailūṣa* and *raṅgāvatārī* in caste but belonged to the same class and status of the society.

In some of the plays of Bhāsa, such as *Avimāraka*, *Pratijñāna Yaugandharāyaṇa*, *Pratimānāṭakam* and *Cārudattam,* a *naṭī* comes with *sūtradhāra* after Nandī. She is often depicted as the wife of *sūtradhāra*. This also shows that *naṭa*s were a community whose profession was drama or theatre and their family partook of their pursuits. Hārīta[193] distinguishes *naṭa* from *śailūṣa*. Aparārka remarks that though not a *naṭa* by caste, *śailūṣa* makes his living by going on the stage. It seems that due to the similarity of their profession, people associated with theatrical arts formed a class, i.e., collectively they made a successful dramatic troupe, where their allied arts gave rise to the greater art drama. One such troupe is mentioned in *Mahāvastu* which was coming from Taxila to Vārāṇasī to earn money by presenting their shows.[194]

Perhaps, such troupes were invited by the Buddhist religious establishments to perform on occasion of religious rituals, such as worship of *bodhi* tree or *stūpa*. In a panel from Gāndhāra[195] region, a *naṭa* is represented in the centre as dancing in accompaniment of flute and drum. The posture of his legs and hands indicates rhythmic movements. Such *naṭa*s needed accompaniment for their performance; hence their group might have gradually developed into theatrical troupe by developing or integrating such talents. The *bodhi* tree on the right shows that the performance is being held on occasion of worship of *bodhi* tree. Inviting such artistes on occasion of *thūpa-maha* (*stūpa* worship) was most probably a tradition known since second century BC as we have already noticed in connection with the representation of the performance of *naṭa*s (*laṅghananaṭa*s) at Bharhut and some dancers worshipping *stūpa* at Sāñcī.

The art of *naṭa*s is specifically mentioned in *Aśokāvadāna* (*c.* second century AD). In its Pāṅśupradānāvadāna, Māra, at the request of Upagupta, agrees to show Buddha in his mortal body. He, 'like an actor clad in a beautiful costume, emerged from the forest in the garb of Buddha'. He acted in such a way that Buddha with his retinue of twelve hundred and fifty *arhat*s came down as if from the heaven and

192. *Manu-smṛti*, 10.22.

193. P.V. Kane, *History of Dharmaśāstra*, vol. II, part I, p. 84.

194. *Mahāvastu*, vol II, p. 169.

195. See *Pl*. XIX.

stood before Upagupta. The scene was so vivid that Upagupta forgot that it was only a make believe and not real.[196] Here we find not merely an imitator but an actor with appropriate costume and make-up at the climax of acting — looking exactly like the character he was playing, which creates illusion. In Buddhist art of Amarāvatī *naṭa*s are represented as dancing and playing musical intruments. A coping stone from Amarāvatī represents Buddha's descent from heaven (see *pl.* XIV); Buddha is represented as an elephant being carried in a palanquin, surround by a crowd dancing and playing lute and flute. Since *naṭa*s are depicted in Buddhist art of Bharhut and Sāñcī and most probably their performance formed a part of the *Samajjā* festival held on occasion of stūpa worship, as discussed earlier, the dancers and musicians represented in this scene, also, may be taken as *naṭa*s invited to perform to celebrate the great occasion — Buddha's descent from heaven.

The ancient tradition of *laṅghananaṭa* was known during the first and the second century AD too, as we infer from some of the Gāndhāra sculptures. A relief from Sahari Bahlol[197] probably depicts the story of Ugrasena, a youth, who for love of an acrobat broke with his family and became an acrobat himself like his wife. One day Buddha saw him performing and converted him on the spot. (*Dhammapada Commentary*, XXIV: 6:226-29) The scene depicts Ugrasena kneeling before the Buddha on the right, while on the left, behind him, two members of his troupe are depicted. One of them is playing a drum. This relief, like the one from Bharhut mentioned earlier, shows *laṅghananaṭa* presenting his show.

Another example is again from Gāndhāra, showing three acrobats.[198] This sculptured fragment depicts:

> Two men standing side by side and a third seated on the shoulders of the man on the right, each dressed in what seems to be an athletic undergarment. Both, costume and the position of the third man, speak for identifying them as acrobats.[199]

Besides these representations, there are some depictions of acrobats in Gāndhāra art that give an idea of the style of their performance. Usually, they performed in

---

196. *Aśokāvadāna*, Pāṅśupradānāvadāna, p. 24 (ed. E. Huber).

197. Ingholt Harald, *Gandhara Art in Pakistan*, Pl. 117.

198. See *Pl.* XV.

199. Ingholt Harald, *op. cit.*, notes on Pl. 427.

group or pairs. It seems that the performance began with dance accompanied by drum and flute.[200] Probably some interesting repartee, too, formed the part of the performance as is suggested by the four episodes of a performance represented on an upright slab.[201] The facial expressions of the artistes are quite clear. In first two episodes, the amused expression of the left figure shows that he had succeeded in leaving his partner dumbfounded by his witty answer. In the last episode,[202] the left figure is again saying something with a smiling countenance to the right figure who is waiting for him to finish. The raised feet and identical hand gestures of the acrobats in the third episode shows that probably the acrobats danced between dialogue sessions, too. A similar depiction is found on another slab from the same region.[203] Climbing on one another's shoulders and thus forming a column or any other structure was most probably the grand finale of the show. These *laṅghananaṭa*s, i.e., acrobats wore athletic costume, like briefs or Indian *dhotī* tied high and tight for their show and tied their hair on top of their heads in a knot as the figures of actrobats in above-mentioned sculptures show.

It is generally believed that Bharata flourished in a period between second century BC and second century AD. Since his work is so comprehensive and indicates an advanced stage of drama (*nāṭya*), it seems that a class of actors having a good knowledge of dramatic art did exist much prior to the time of Bharata and he used their knowledge suitably in proper places in his *Nāṭyaśāstra*. Bharata himself was a *prayoktā* (producer, director and actor) as his name suggests and his work speaks of. Hence, he had a keen eye for dramatic art; he knew how to make drama, a real art, acceptable to all. One of his most significant achievements was to combine folk and classical traditions, which finally made drama a most delightful art and gave a definite style to Indian drama. Such attempts may have been made by *ācārya*s before Bharata too, but since their works have not been found, *Nāṭyaśāstra* seems to be the only surviving evidence of such attempts. In his work theatre artistes, who themselves were gradually growing into a community and had developed an attractive style of drama, are called *naṭa*s. Dance and music were current as the means of popular folk entertainment throughout the history of the country. These

200. See *Pl.* XVIII.

201. See *Pl.* XVI.

202. See *Pl.* XVI.

203. See *Pl.* XX.

arts were adopted by Bharata in the classical tradition and were classicalised. A *naṭa* was expected to learn these two arts, too, besides different modes of acting. Hence, *naṭa* of Bharata is a musician, dancer and actor combined — the three basic features of theatrical arts.

Not only in the *Pūrvaraṅga* did Bharata include dance (*nṛtta*) in drama, but he adopted it as a form of *āṅgika abhinaya*[204] (expression through physical movements and gestures) too, and says that 'if during the performance of any part of the play, the heroine is gradually pacified, dance is to be applied till its end',[205] and 'if any part of a play relates to the adoration of the deity, one should perform there a dance'.[206] But he includes dance in the mainstream of drama so long as it is neither boring nor out of place.[207]

Similarly, according to Bharata,[208] a drama without music is a well-built dwelling house without any colour. He says that 'one should first of all bestow care on songs, for songs have been called the resting place (bed) of the drama'.[209] He gives instructions regarding dance, music, instruments and acting in detail, all being a part of *nāṭya* (drama). This shows that by the time of Bharata, *kuśīlava* (musician), *śailāli* or *śailūṣa* (actor), *nartaka* (dancer) and *naṭa* (actor) had become synonyms and the original distinction of their professions was merged into the single profession of the *naṭa* (actor). Following Bharata, later writers on dramaturgy too used the word *naṭa* in the same sense.

This symbiotic tradition of *naṭa*s, pregnant with both the elements — folk and classical — brought some important changes in the attitude of the people towards theatre, as shall be seen later in this chapter.

In successive periods of Indian history, the term *naṭa* has been used in the sense of an actor. Besides *Abhijñānaśākuntalam* of Kālidāsa where *sūtradhāra-naṭi* device is used to open the play and thus, *naṭa* as a *prayoktā* (producer, director and actor) is known, semi-classical tradition of drama, represented by Bhāṇa plays

---

204. *NŚ*, VIII.14-15.
205. *Ibid.*, IV.318.
206. *Ibid.*, IV.319 and 320.
207. *Ibid.*, V.162, 164.
208. *Ibid.*, XXXII.482.
209. *Ibid.*, XXXII.493.

of early Gupta period, too mentions *naṭa* as an actor. *Naṭa*s are mentioned in the Purāṇas.[210] Harṣa thinks that for the success of the play, a skilled actor is one of the essentials.[211]

The art of *naṭa*s (*nāṭya*), it seems, had made a deep impression on other forms of art. *Vidūṣaka* of Sanskrit dramas representing classical tradition was probably borrowed from the folk theatre, as it is generally believed. This was the reason why he acts as a bridge between classical drama and the folk audience: he speaks Prākr̥t and his character is closer to the common man. Sometimes, this character is depicted in sculptures. A terracotta plaque, found from Mathurā, 'represents a scene showing a woman pulling a scarf drawn round the neck of a male figure who on the basis of his quaint cap may be identified as a jester (*vidūṣaka*)', according to V.S. Agrawala.[212]

A male figure similar to *vidūṣaka* is depicted in cave No.7 Auraṅgābād.[213] The panel depicts Buddhist goddess Tārā. One of the goddesses rests her hand on the head of a dwarf. Yazdani in his book *The Early History of the Deccan*[214] describes 'the expression of the dwarf as comical, as though he is feeling the weight of the heavy arm of the goddess'. The crossed legs, the crooked stick and the exposed teeth of the dwarf add to the grotesque effect of the subject. He thinks that in the sixth or beginning of the seventh century AD, to which date the sculpture belongs, Buddhist art was losing its intellectual qualities. Besides, the depiction shows the 'flair of the artist for the quaint and bizarre'. But the figure, at first sight, reminds one of *vidūṣaka*, who according to Bharata should be a dwarf with exposed teeth and a hunch on the back.[215] He easily gets mixed with women.[216] The crooked stick

---

210. *Śrīmadbhāgvata Purāṇa*, I.XI.20-21.

211. *śrīharṣo nipuṇaḥ kaviḥ pariṣadapyeṣā guṇagrāhiṇī* ।
loke hāri ca vatsrājacaritam nāṭye ca dakṣā vayaṁ ।।
vastvedaikamayīha vāñachitaphalaprāpteḥ padaṁ kiṁ punar ।
madbhāgyopacayādayaṁ samuditaḥ sarva guṇānāmgaṇaḥ ।।
— *Ratnāvalī*, I.5, ed. Krishna Rao Joglekar, 1859

212. V.S. Agrawala, *Gupta Art*, fig. 34 description on p. 110. The plaque is housed at Mathura Museum, no. 2795.

213. See *Pl.* XXXVI.

214. Pp. 716-17.

215. *NŚ*, XXV.79.

216. *Ibid.*, XXXV.93.

(*kuṭilaka*) and the crossed legs also remind one of the gaits of *vidūṣaka* described by Bharata.[217] Hence, it is quite obvious that the artist had this popular character, *vidūṣaka* in mind while carving this figure. *Vidūṣaka* was the most accomplished member of the troupe of the *naṭa*s,[218] who could imitate anyone effortlessly and had presence of mind which is often needed on the stage.

The popularity of *naṭa*s and their art is indicated by the close association of *naṭa*s with poets. Bāṇa enumerates in the *Harṣacarita*[219] that among his friends were an actor and an actress. This association continued to exist even after the period under consideration. For instance, the association of Bhavabhūti with *naṭa*s is known from the introduction of his *Mālatī-Mādhava*. Rājaśekhara[220] includes *naṭa*s in the honourable literary *samāja* held by the kings. Not only this, while writing on subjects other than drama, he unconciously uses the term (*naṭa*) to express his thoughts. He writes in his *Kāvyamīmāṁsā*[221] that translating the thoughts of a poet from one language to another is called *naṭanepathya*, probably because *anukaraṇa* (imitation or translating the feelings and thoughts of the poet or dramatist into acting) is the characteristic feature of a *naṭa*.

In *Kuṭṭanīmatam*,[222] the example of a *naṭa* is given to explain the nature of a prostitute whose feelings are always superficial, just like a *naṭa*, who having a deep knowledge of different modes of expression delights the audience, without experiencing the emotion he is displaying. This, also, shows the popularity of *naṭa* and his art in the eighth century AD.

All these facts indicate that there were always two classes in Indian society — the upper or the elite class, speaking Sanskrit and the lower, speaking Prākṛt. These two classes gave rise to two different theatrical traditions. This is true with other aspects of Indian culture too like religion, art, literature and language. The upper class, from the time of the Vedas, did not give much importance to theatrical arts though accepting it as a part of ritual. This tendency persisted throughout the

---

217. *NŚ*, XIII.143-44.
218. *Ibid.*, XXXV.92-93.
219. *Harṣacarita*, pp. 74-75, ed. Jagannath Pathak.
220. *Kāvyamīmāṁsā*, pp. 54-55, ed. Dalal.
221. *Ibid.*, p. 66.
222. *Ibid.*, p. 501.

history of the country, as we have already noticed. The art of drama originated, it seems, in the lower class of the society.

Perhaps in the Vedic period itself there were people whose function it was to entertain, as we know from the reference to *kārī*, *śailūṣa*, brāhmaṇa, kṣatriya and vaiśya lute prayers and singers (of *gāthā*), *māgadha*s, *sūta*s and harlots taking part in Vedic rituals. Most probably they belonged to the lower class of the Āryan society. With the passage of time, their art was enriched by the pre-Āryan tradition of theatrical arts, as had happened with Vedic religion too in later Vedic period when Āryan and non-Āryan cultures intermingled. The combination of these two gave rise to a strong folk tradition. *Naṭa* seems to be the representative of this folk tradition. That is why dance, music, recitation of heroic deeds, mimicry and impersonation are the characteristic features of his art. This folk tradition is best seen in the *Jātaka*s where *naṭa*s are mentioned as actors, dancers, acrobats, drummers, conch blowers, magicians, reciters and pantomime. Later, when scholars (*ācārya*s) with a sophisticated taste and scientific approach intervened, realising the strong appeal of this folk tradition, the art of *naṭa* gradually took the form of a classical art, a discipline. Probably *Naṭasūtra*, as mentioned by Pāṇini, represents this stage of *naṭa*'s art.

Though Kauṭilya was not in favour of the art, his instructions regarding theatre artistes may have helped the classical tradition to grow as, according to him, instructors (*naṭācārya*s) should be appointed by the state to train theatre artites. These instructors might have been training their pupils according to the rules laid by the *ācārya*s. But, even after going through this *saṁskāra* of training and performing sophisticated classical Sanskrit plays written by great poets like Bhāsa, they did not break away from the folk tradition totally. This is the reason why even after following the *śāstra*s, presenting classical Sanskrit plays and popularising them, they never enjoyed a respectable place in society.

A little later, it was realised that drama can become an art and a *śāstra* only if the strong folk tradition and sophisticated classical tradition are combined. This great task was done by Bharata, who took the best of these two traditions and drama became a *śāstra*, *Nāṭyaśāstra*, as is indicated by his treatise, recognised by both, folk artistes and the classical tradition represented by *ācārya*s and poets. This was the symbiotic tradition of drama that flourished in the succeeding periods of Indian history. The bearers of this tradition were again *naṭa*s.

Bharata

Actors are often called *bharata*s. Bharatas were a well-known Vedic tribe.[223] *Śatapatha Brāhmaṇa*[224] and *Aitareya Brāhmaṇa*[225] mention Bharata as the son of Duṣyanta. His descendants, *bharata*s, gave the name Bhāratvarṣa to the country. None of these *bharata*s was associated with drama, but later the term came to be associated with it.

Levi has identified the name 'Bharata' or 'Bhārata' with *bhāṭ*, a caste of genealogical and family bards. Konow[226] is also of the same opinion. Keith[227] also takes Bharata as rhapsodes and says that their tradition has survived in the modern form of *bhāṭ* denoting a class of reciters. According to him, *bharata*s must be the rhapsodes of the Vedic bharata tribe and it was they who preserved the great epic of this family — *Mahābhārata* — with great care. In due course, they adopted the newer art of drama.

Bharatas, according to Rangacharya,[228] belonged to the famous and talented Vedic tribe who for the first time introduced the art of dramatic representation and its members collectively composed *Nāṭyaśāstra*. But, in *Nāṭyaśāstra* the term is often used in a much broader sense than a family or its members. Rangacharya further says that in the list of *bharata*s, given by Bharata,[229] such artistes are mentioned 'who supply (Sanskrit root *bhṛ*) various materials required for a performance', for example, the scene setter, the *vidūṣaka*, the musician, the dancer, the stage manager, the producer, the dresser, the florist, the painter, the washerman, the artisan. Hence, according to him, *bharata* is not so much an actor but more of a manager or worker of the whole show, because *bharata* and his family were not actors but managers and producers.

Bharatas were, probably, general actors taking different roles. There must have been a large number of actors in the troupe playing character roles and the crowd.

---

223. *Vedic Index*, II, pp. 94-95.
224. *ŚB*, XIII.5.4.
225. *AB*, VIII.21, 23.
226. S. Konow, *The Indian Drama*, p. 13.
227. A.B. Keith, *op. cit.*, p. 30.
228. Adya Rangacharya, *Drama in Sanskrit Literature*, p. 27.
229. *NŚ*, XXXV.66-69.

The success of a play depends not only on the main characters but on each actor, however small a role he may be playing. People, associated with dramatic art, know this fact very well. Besides playing roles, *bharata*s probably did various other back-stage jobs, important for the success of the play. This was the reason why Bharata says in *Nāṭyaśāstra* that through him the play was raised up with various types of roles. He was like a leader; his representation was accompanied by instrumental music and he provided many accessories (to the performance).[230]

Nāṭyaśāstra, the first systematised treatise on dramatic art, is known to be the creation of Bharata, who figures both as its author and as stage manager. This also suggests that Bharata was a name associated with those who had an insight and knowledge of dramatic art — practical and theoretical both. There are two possibilities: either this name was given to actors because they followed the tradition of Bharata (the author of *Nāṭyaśāstra*) or the author of *Nāṭyaśāstra* was named as Bharata, because he belonged to the class of *bharata*s, following their tradition. *Bharata*s are often mentioned in Sanskrit plays as actors.[231]

Actors of Noble Birth

Apart from the above-mentioned artistes who were directly associated with drama, we have references to such people of noble birth in ancient Indian literature and inscriptions, who, though not being directly associated with drama, were well-versed in the art, as it was an accomplishment. *Mahābhārata*[232] tells that Arjuna had mastery over the art and he taught *nāṭya* to Princess Uttarā, disguised as Bṛhannalā. Rāma had a sound knowledge of drama of mixed language (*miśrita bhāṣā*), Sanskrit and Prākṛt.[233] When Bharata, his brother, had a bad dream and was disturbed, his friends presented song, dance and comedies to amuse him.[234] They must have had some knowledge of the art. Rāvaṇa,[235] the king of Laṅkā, was a renowned scholar and master of theatrical arts, especially music and drama, and a great patron of

230. *NŚ*, XXXV.91.

231. *Mālatīmādhava*, p. 5, ed. Kale.

232. *Mahābhārata*, Virāṭa-Parva, II.17, 28-29.

233. *Rāmāyaṇa*, Ayodhyā-kāṇḍa, 1, 7.

234. *Ibid.*, 69, 4.

235. *Rāmāyaṇa*, Uttara-kāṇḍa, 31.44.

ācāryas of various arts. He sang and danced mirthfully in adoration of God Śiva on the banks of Narmadā.[236]

Jain literature also refers to people of noble birth being interested in drama. Meghakumāra, the son of Śreṇika, the king of Rājagṛha, was properly trained by *kalācāryas* (the masters of arts) in various branches of art, including drama, dance, music — vocal and instrumental, and *rūpa* (changing *rūpa* or form).[237]

It seems that not only the members of royal family and noble class but monks also adopted the art as the most appealing method of propagating the teachings of the master. *Piṇḍa Niryukti*,[238] a Jain text, refers to the *Raṭṭhavāla* drama, which was staged at Pāṭaliputra by the monk Āsāḍhabhūi. The play depicted the life of Bharata, the universal monarch. It is stated that

> since a large number of kings and princes retired from the worldly life and joined the ascetic order, after witnessing the play, it was destroyed as it would have done great harm to the world and the earth might have been devoid of kṣatriya, if it continued to be staged.

Buddhism, in its earlier days, was against theatre, but *Lalitavistara*[239] says that Buddha was well versed in various arts including *nāṭya*.

From Bhāsa's play *Pratijñāyaugandharāyaṇa*,[240] we infer that theatrical arts continued to be an accomplishment for the kings. Udayana, the hero of the play, is called *gāndharvavittakaḥ* (one who has a sound knolwedge of theatrical arts). *Gāndharvaveda* was in his family as ancestral *vidyā*.[241] Similarly, Khāravela, the king of Kaliṅga, is proudly called *gāndharvavedabudho* in his Hāthigumphā inscription.[242]

In the Gupta period too, kings continued to be interested in theatrical arts. From Allahabad Pillar Inscription of Samudragupta, we infer that he surpassed

236. *Rāmāyaṇa*, Uttara-kāṇḍa.
237. *Dhammakahāṇuyoga*, Skandha II, Meghakumāra Sūtra 325, p. 161.
238. J.C. Jain, *Life in Ancient India as Depicted in Jain Canons*, p. 186.
239. *Lalitavistara*, Śilpasandarśana Parivartaḥ, 14-20, pp. 146-47.
240. *Pratijñāyaugandharāyaṇa*, Act II, *BNC*, II, p. 58.
241. *Ibid.*, p. 63.
242. R.B. Pandey, *Historical and Literary Inscriptions*, p. 46, Line, 5.

Tambaru and Nārada in music.[243] His interest in music is known from his coins too which depict him as playing *vīṇā*.[244] Kālidāsa, in his *Raghuvaṁśa*,[245] tells that King Agnivarṇa often accompanied his female friends in dancing, by playing *mṛdaṅga* and taught them the art of dancing with *āṅgika* (gesture), *sāttvika* (sentiments) and *vācika* (speech) style of *abhinaya* (acting). In the presence of his friends, he used to give a demonstration competing with expert masters.[246] In fact, the Gupta period was an ideal age for theatrical arts to prosper. Gupta emperors had brought peace and prosperity in the country and they themselves were artistic persons. Hence, people of this age, in general, took interest in theatrical arts and excelled themselves.

Vātsyāyana in *Kāmasūtra*[247] describes *goṣṭhī* which was a conclave of citizens of similar age, wealth, learning, intelligence and character, who met either in the house of a courtesan, or of another citizen or in a *paṇḍāl* and engaged in agreeable discussion on topics dealing with poetry, drama and other arts.

Harivaṁśa, the supplement of *Mahābhārata*, composed in the Gupta period, reflects the cultural life of the age, in mythical garb, when princes and kings felt proud of their knowledge of theatrical arts. It describes in detail the performance of the dramatised version of *Rāmāyaṇa* by Yādava heroes. They disguised themselves as actors to penetrate into the abode of demon Vajranābha and presented the play. Their skill prompted Vajranābha to induce them to perform an episode from the legend of Kubera, the rendezvous of Rambhā.[248] Another passage of the same text describes that at the festival performed by Yādavas after the death of Andhaka, Nārada amused the audience by a series of comic turns imitating the gestures, movements and laughter of distinguished persons.[249] Thus, it seems that acting was not confined to the class of *naṭa*s alone and a divine sage like Nārada did not hesitate to entertain people through this art. This reflects the spirit of the age,

243. R.B. Pandey, *op. cit.*, p. 76, line, 27.

244. A.S. Altekar, *The Coinage of Gupta Empire*, *Corpus of Indian Coins*, vol. IV, p. 73, Pl. no. 15-17.

245. *Raghuvaṁśa*, XIX.14, *KG*, p. 161.

246. *Ibid.*, XIX.36. *KG*, p. 163.

247. *Kāmasūtra*, Part I, Chapter IV, Sūtra 35-36, p. 82, ed. S.C. Upādhyāya.

248. *Harivaṁśa*, II.91.20, 93.1.

249. *Ibid.*, II.89.23-26.

known from Kālidāsa's dramas, Vātsyāyana's *Kāmasūtra* and inscriptions of the age.

Mārkaṇḍeya Purāṇa[250] describes Ṛtudhvaja, *alias* Kuvalayāśa, the son of king Satrājit, as fond of dramatic performance and passing his days delightfully in cultivation of poetry, music, drama and dramatic representation.

In seventh century AD, we find Harṣa associated with dramatic art, and if we accept I-tsing's statement, he himself directed the dance and music part of the play *Nāgānanda*, when it was staged.[251] This shows his aquaintance with the art. In his *Priyadarśikā*[252] he adopted 'drama in drama device', wherein Udayana himself goes on the stage instead of Manoramā and plays his own part. Bāṇabhaṭṭa,[253] in his *Kādambarī*, tells that King Śūdraka was well acquainted with dramatic art and describes him as always surrounded by princes who were quite good at *kāvya*, *nāṭaka* and the rest of the branches of literature. The syllabus of Candrāpīḍa included the study of the several varieties of literature including drama.[254] We are told that Candrāpīḍa had learnt the *Nāṭyaśāstra* of Bharata and other writers.[255] Thus, ideas of Harṣa and Bāṇa, expressed in their works, regarding the activities of the royal personage in the field of drama indicate that kings and people of noble birth were still interested in dramatic art, as they were in the Gupta period. Not only kings and the noble class but citizens of Ujjayanī in general also were acquainted with drama and its theoretical part, known from Bharata.[256]

In *Kuṭṭanīmatam*,[257] Kuṭṭanī describes the qualities of Bhaṭṭaputra to Mālatī, a prostitute and says that his skill in drama and music delights the expert masters of *Gāndharva-śāstra*, like Nārada. This reminds one of the life and interests of a Nāgaraka described in *Kāmasūtra*.

---

250. *Mārkaṇḍeya Purāṇa*, chapter 20.
251. S. Levi, *The Theatre of India*, p. 167.
252. *Priyadarśikā*, Act. III, pp. 52-68, ed. A.V.W. Jackson, 1965.
253. *Kādambarī*, p. 14, ed. M.R. Kale, 1928.
254. *Kādambarī*, p. 126.
255. *bharatādipraṇīteṣu Nṛitta Śāstreṣu* . . . . *ibid.*, p. 126.
256. *Ibid.*, pp. 84-85, ed. M.R. Kale.
257. *Kuṭṭanīmatam*, p. 75.

Naṭācārya or Nāṭyācārya

The existence of *Naṭasūtra*, *Nāṭyaśāstra* and highly developed form of drama, mentioned in the latter, clearly indicate that there were such teachers in the field who instructed their pupil in *nāṭya*, which enriched and refined their skill. Such teachers were known as *naṭācārya* or *nāṭyācārya*. They formed a separate class of theatre artistes, having a deep knowledge of histrionic art — theoretical and practical. Bharata has described the qualities and duties of an *ācārya* in detail. We find reference to such teachers even earlier.

In *Mahābhārata*,[258] Arjuna taught dance and music to Uttarā and other ladies of the *antaḥpura*, disguised as Bṛhannalā. This indicates that appointing skilled teachers for training princesses in theatrical arts was in vogue since very early days.

In a passage of *Gāmanī Saṁyutta*, a Buddhist text, Tālapuṭa, the chief of the village of *naṭas*, is mentioned as having asked Buddha about a saying of the traditional teachers who were actors — whether a player comedian who amused people and stirred delightful laughter was born in the company of laughing *devas*.[259] According to Wijesekera,[260] Tālapuṭa seems to be the nickname of the village chief of *naṭa*s, who was known for his practice of keeping time by clapping while teaching his pupils the rudiments of rhythm, a method still practised by dance and music teachers. This perfectly fits the term *naṭagrāmaṇī*, used as a designation of Tālpuṭa. Keith[261] thinks that *naṭagrāmaṇī* is the 'troupe head of actors', the instructor of the other actors in their art (*naṭācārya*) and was also known as *sūtradhāra*. Bühler[262] had referred to *naṭagrāma*, a whole village inhabited by actors, which mentioned in a Jain story of the clever boy 'Bharata'. The name of the boy (Bharata) is also very significant. Most probably such villages had generations of such '*naṭa* preceptors' who were leaders of the *naṭa*s or heads of the village of the *naṭa*s (*naṭagrāmaṇī*).

The next interesting word, indicating identical sense in the above-mentioned reference of *Gāmaṇī Saṁyutta*, is *pubbakānām ācariyapacāriyanām naṭānām* . . .

258. *Mahābhārata*, Virāṭa-Parva, II.27.29.

259. *Saṁyutta Nikāya,* Gāmanī Saṁyutta, SIV, p. 306.

260. D.H.De.A. Wijesekera, *IHQ*, vol. XVII, no. 2, pp. 197-98.

261. A.B. Keith, *The Sanskrit Drama*, p. 360.

262. 'New Jain Inscription from Mathura', *EI*, vol. I, p. 381.

(traditional teachers who were actors) which Wijesekera[263] says 'refers to a genuine tradition regarding generations of such *naṭa* preceptors' of the past. Thus, the *naṭa* teachers mentioned in *Gāmaṇī Saṁyutta* were, in all probability, heads of the troupes or villages of the *naṭa*s. As the *naṭa*s known from Buddhist literature were mostly folk artistes, the style these teachers trained their pupils in must have been folk.

From *Jātaka* stories, we know that the family of *naṭa*s learnt and adopted their family art as their family profession. It is quite natural that the head of the family taught his art to his offsprings as means of livelihood. The art, thus, prospered as a family tradition, and the father or the head of the family acted as *naṭācārya*. Probably others too who were interested in the art joined the class. As the fame of the teacher spreaded, *naṭa*s from other places too, gathered around him, seeking his guidance, as generally happened with renowned teachers in ancient India, and thus, in due course, a settlement of *naṭa*s (*naṭagrāma*) may have been founded, headed by such *naṭa*s teachers (*naṭagrāmaṇī*).

Such *naṭācārya*s represented folk tradition, but there might have been scholars, with sophisticated taste and scientific approach, who might have studied dramatic art thoroughly and then drawn a code for *naṭa*s, e.g., *Naṭasūtra*. *Naṭasūtra*, an aphorism on the science of acting by Śilālin and Kṛśāśva, is mentioned by Pāṇini,[264] as we have already noticed. It had same importance in studies as an *āmnāya* or *chanda* had. This shows that Śilālin and Kṛśāśva were not ordinary *naṭa* teachers, maintaining the age old folk tradition by training novices; rather they were such *ācārya*s who tried to give drama a well-organised form and thus, probably, for the first time, the unsystematised and scattered folk tradition was systematised. This was the first step towards classicalisation of the art. Hence the contribution of Śilālin and Kṛśāśva, the *ācārya*s, to dramatic art is of great consequence, though, unfortunately, their work seems to have been lost. The *Naṭasūtra,* of these two *ācārya*s, must have been followed by the artistes and might have produced *naṭācārya*s, the instructors of the artistes, who might have been actors themselves trained by the *ācārya*s well-versed in *naṭasūtra*.

*Naṭācārya*s were there during Kauṭilya's time too. The Gaṇikādhyakṣa Prakaraṇa[265] of *Arthaśāstra* says that the king should arrange for the livelihood of

263. Wijesekera, *op. cit.*, p. 198.

264. *Aṣṭādhyāyī*, IV.3.129.

265. *KA*., Gaṇikādhyakṣa Prakaraṇa, 43.27.

a teacher who imparted the knowledge of singing, playing lute, flute and drum and similar other arts, to the girls earning their livelihood from stage appearance, prostitution and working as maid-servants. This not only proves the existence of *naṭācāryas* in Kauṭilya's time, but shows the wide field covered by their art. Their welfare was deemed to be the state's responsibility.

From the first act of Bhāsa's *Cārudattam,* we know that Vasantasenā was trained by her teacher in the art of voice-modulation, stage appearance and dance. This supports Kauṭilya who enjoins that teachers should be appointed to train prostitutes in theatrical arts.

Patañjali[266] describes the method of *naṭācāryas* of imparting training in dramatics. He says that they took their pupils directly to the stage,[267] made them observe the senior actors (or may be the instructor himself) performing thereon, and asked them to act accordingly. This is what the present-day actor-teachers do.

We do not know, for sure, if Śilālin and Kr̥śāśva were such *prayoktās* or instructors but Bharata, who flourished a century or two later than Patañjali, was both a theoretician and a practitioner. The date and identification of Bharata are two of the most controvertial problems of Indian history. As regards his date, generally, a period from second century BC to second century AD is tentatively assumed. But, identification of Bharata, the author of *Nāṭyaśāstra*, remains as puzzling as ever. The reference to Bharata and Ādi-Bharata, and quotations from these two, by Rāghavabhaṭṭa in his commentary on *Abhijñānaśākuntalam*,[268] make the problem all the more difficult. Not only this, there are passages in *Nāṭyaśāstra* where the word *bharata* is used not merely in the sense of a proper name or family name or in the sense of the family members (which naturally came to mean 'actor'), but in a still wider significance when the term *bharata* is used in the sense of back-stage worker.

Whether Bharata, the traditional author of *Nāṭyśāstra*, was known after these *bharatas* who were actors, sponsors and managers of dramatic representations or the latter were called so after Bharata, the author of *Nāṭyaśāstra*, cannot be said. Much has been said and written regarding the problem, but the fact still remains

---

266. *Mahābhāṣya*, I.4.29.

267. V.S. Agrawala, *Paṇini kālīna Bhāratavaraṣa*, p. 326.

268. M. Ghosh, 'Problems of Nāṭyaśāstra', *IHQ*, vol. VI, no. 1-2, pp. 75-76.

that we do not have sufficient and conclusive evidence to identify Bharata. In which case, we take him as an *ācārya* having an insight into dramatic art, whether folk or classical, with deep knowledge of the texts and theories of earlier dramaturgists, who composed a text himself with a purpose of giving drama the status of the discipline. There is no doubt about it that the text in its present condition has several later interpolations, as has happened with other ancient Indian texts also.

Bharata was an *ācārya*, both a teacher and a *prayoktā* (producer) as is evident from his work. That is why, his text is a real *śāstra* for theatre artistes and *ācārya*s both. He gives a long list of the qualifications of the *ācārya*s, in whom he vested the responsibility of maintaining the correct form of the art, recognised by people of higher and lower classes of the society alike. According to him, an *ācārya* should have memory, intelligence, sharpness, imagination,[269] creative faculty and capacity to shape the taught.[270] In fact, according to Bharata, *nāṭyācārya* was the overall incharge of the whole show. He was the architect of the theatre, chief actor, instructor of the other actors, performer of the preliminary rituals[271] and it was he who selected the play to be staged, assigned roles to actors and actresses[272] according to their appearance and temperaments, and introduced the play.

He seems to be a very important and competent person. While performing these duties *naṭācārya* was known as *sūtradhāra*.[273] Bharata has enumerated his natural and acquired qualities in his work. Anyone who had a knack of acting and organising could not become a *nāṭyācārya*, unless he was bestowed with some inherent natural qualities.[274] A person having natural qualities of intelligence, good memory, generosity, tolerance, self-control, etc., after going through a rigorous training in various arts and crafts related to drama and stage and getting well-versed in various fields of knowledge, including *Arthaśāstra*, *Kāmasūtra*, *Veśopacāra*, religion, philosophy, rituals, flora and fauna, and ways and habits of people belonging to different regions, could adorn the high position of *nāṭyācārya* or *sūtradhāra*.[275]

---

269. *NŚ*, XXXV.73.
270. *Ibid*., XXXV.71.
271. *Ibid*., II.50, 63; III.2-3, 17, 91-92, 101.
272. *Ibid*., XXXV.2-4.
273. *Ibid*., XXXV.71.
274. *Ibid*, XXXV.66-71.
275. *Ibid*, XXXV. 66-74.

It seems, thus, that to Bharata drama was not an ordinary art, inherited by *naṭa*s from their ancestors or a source of making money, but a noble art, almost a science and for coming into the field a *naṭa* as well as a *naṭācārya* had to go through a proper training. Bharata himself was a great *naṭācārya*, as is evident from his work which is an instruction for future actors and *nāṭyācārya*s in detail lest drama fall back into the vulgar art, as it had once become. His was the greatest attempt to synthesise folk and classical traditions. He added *Arthaśāstra*, *Kāmasūtra*, poetics and philosophy, the advanced and specialised studies of later times, to the humble folk art of *naṭa*s, raised it to a great height and contributed to the fulfilment of the symbiotic tradition of drama.

Bharata has mentioned the names of some *ācārayas* belonging to his tradition. It is difficult to say who among them flourished before Bharata and who later. Since some of them are mentioned by Bharata as *bhārataputra* (sons of Bharata), they may be taken as *ācārya*s who carried his tradition, but at the same time, on the same ground, they could be considered as belonging to a period prior to Bharata. One of them is Kohala, one of the hundred sons of Bharata.[276] In the concluding chapter, Bharata brings out that the rest will be discussed by Kohala.[277] He is considered to be the author of *Tālādhyāya*, and hence it seems that he was associated with dramaturgy, especially with music and dance. A work called *Dattila Kohalīya* is supposed to include the lectures delivered by Kohala to Dattila.[278] Abhinava refers to him as an actor. He often quotes Kohala in his commentary and cites differences between the views of Bharata and Kohala.[279] He had been quoted in *Bhāvaprakāśana*[280] and *Nāṭyadarpaṇa*,[281] in connection with the number of *rūpaka*s, etc. He is mentioned in *Rasārṇavasūtradhāra*[282] as an *ācārya*.

Bharata has mentioned *vātsya*, *śāṇḍilya* and *dhūrtila* in the concluding chapter.[283] Unfortunately, the works of these *ācārya*s, also, have not been found.

276. *NŚ*, I.26.

277. *Ibid.*, XXXVI.69.

278. K.H. Trivedi, *The Nāṭyadarpaṇa of Rāmacandra and Guṇacandra: A Critical Study*, p. 15, fn. 1.

279. Dr. Nagendra, *Hindi Abhinava Bhāratī*, pp. 9-10. 137, 416.

280. *Bhāvaprakāśana*, pp. 204, 210, 236, 245.

281. *Nāṭyadarpaṇa*, p. 23 (G.O.S.).

282. *Rasārṇavasūtradhāra*, I.51.

283. *NŚ*, XXVI.75.

They, too, are quoted by Abhinava.[284] Aśmakuṭṭa and Nakhakuṭṭa, these two *ācāryas*, are also mentioned in the first chapter of *Nāṭyaśāstra*,[285] though no mention is made regarding their work. The other texts mentioning these two *ācāryas* are *Nāṭakalakṣaṇa-ratnakośa*[286] and *Sāhityadarpaṇa*. The latter quotes two-and-a-half verses of Aśmakuṭṭa.

The next important *ācārya* is Dattila, quoted by Abhinavagupta in his commentary in connection with Dhruvā.[287] *Nāṭyaśāstra* refers to Bādarāyaṇa as one of the hundred sons of Bharata.[288] He had been twice referred to in *Nāṭakalakṣaṇa-ratnakośa*. Unfortunately the works of these *ācāryas*, who were probably predecessors of Bharata, have not been available. It seems that they were in the tradition of *naṭācāryas*, belonging to the class of Śilālin, Kṛśāśva and Bharata, who in their own way might have tried to make drama a dignified art, acceptable to both classes of audience — class and mass.

The tradition of *naṭācāryas* continued after Bharata too. A *naṭācārya* is mentioned in *Avadānaśataka*,[289] a second or third-century AD text, who came to Śobhāvatī from Dakṣiṇāpatha with his troupe to present *Buddha Nāṭaka* and himself played the part of Buddha. Thus, the term *naṭācārya* here denoted not merely 'dance master' but an instructor of the actors too, who had his own repertory which travelled from one place to another presenting plays, but such *naṭācāryas* were only *prayoktās* and not theoreticians. They are mentioned in the literature of succeeding periods of Indian history too.

In the Bhāṇa plays of the early Gupta period, *naṭācāryas* are mentioned. Bhāṇa *Padmaprābhṛtakam* says, 'The creeper that is a woman of the forest, which is *antaḥpura* (harem), is acting at the instruction of wind that is an *ācārya*.'[290] This shows that the girls of *antaḥpura* were trained by the *ācāryas*. Again, in the same

---

284. Dr. Nagendra, *op. cit.*, p. 10.
285. *NŚ*, I.33.
286. *Nāṭakalakṣaṇaratnakośa*, pp. 83, 427, 2766, 2775, 2904.
287. *Abhinavabhāratī*, vol. I, p. 203.
288. *NŚ*, I.32.
289. *Avadānaśataka*, VIII.75, p. 185.
290. *vātācāryopadeśādabhinayati latākānanāntaḥpura strī padmaprābhṛtakaṁ*
— *Caturbhāṇī*, p. 2

Bhāṇa[291] play, a disciple of *nāṭācārya* Gāndharvadatta, named Darduraka, who himself was a son of an actress (*nāṭeraka*) is mentioned. He had been to a *gaṇikā* Devasenā's place, to give the copy of the dialogues which she had to learn by heart to take part in the play, *Kumudavatī*. Though she was not well, she did not refuse, but out of her respect for the *ācārya*, accepted the same.[292] From the same play, we gather that *gaṇikā*s used to go to the house of their *ācārya* for obtaining training in dance.[293] Not only the prostitutes, but girls of noble birth too, during the Gupta period, were trained in the art under the guidance of *naṭācārya.* There used to be a special room for their classes as mentioned in Kālidāsa's *Mālavikāgnimitram.*[294]

Two *naṭācārya*s — Gaṇadāsa (who trained Mālavikā) and Haradatta (who trained queen Irāvatī) — are mentioned. Gaṇadāsa appreciates his disciple Mālavikā and remarks that it is seldom that one gets such a good disciple.[295] He also mentioned the clan of *guru*s. He says that he had been well-trained under the guidance of a *guru* and is a *prayoktā* instructor of the art himself.[296] This indicates the long tradition of teachers and their disciples who maintained their tradition of art and teachings. There were such teachers[297] who took their profession not as a means to make money but as a work in the service of the art — *nāṭya*. As Gaṇadāsa says boastfully that 'the teachers who impart training just for earning money are like traders and just as pure gold does not turn black even after being put into fire, no faults can be found in the performance if training is properly given'.[298] Kālidāsa has successfully portrayed the professional jealousies and pride of the *naṭācārya*s in the court.

Another work of Kālidāsa, *Raghuvaṁśa*, too mentions *naṭācārya*s. It says that bewitched by the charm of Agnivarṇa, when he played *mṛdaṅga*, female dancers

291. . . . *bhāvagandharvadattasya nāṭakācāryantevāsī-dardurakonāmanāṭerakaḥ*. . . . ,
— *Caturbhāṇī*, p. 50

292. *ācāryagauravāt pratigṛhītaṁ tatpatrakaṁtayā*. . . — *ibid*., p. 50

293. *ācāryagṛham nṛtyavāreṇa yasyati* — *ibid*., p. 58

294. *Mālavikāgnimitram*, Act I, *KG*, p. 187.

295. *Ibid*., pp. 187-88.

296. *Ibid*., p. 191.

297. *Ibid*., p. 194.

298. *Ibid*., p. 201.

forgot to dance and were ashamed of doing so, in the presence of their *ācāryas*.[299] Sometimes, the king (Agnivarṇa) himself played the part of *naṭācārya* and taught his female friends the art of dancing with gesture, sentiments and speech.[300]

The tradition of two types of *ācāryas*, known in the period under study, continued even during succeeding periods of Indian history. There were some *naṭācāryas* who were *prayoktās*, with a sound knowledge of the theoretical aspect of the art and others were merely *śāstrakāras*, i.e., dramaturgists, who laid rules, not only for the representation but also regarding the writing of the play, mostly on the lines of Bharata. To have an idea of the nature of their work and style, during later periods, a brief survey of the important literary and sculptural depictions of *naṭācāryas* is later taken up.

Kuṭṭanīmatam refers to a *naṭācārya* who migrated to Vārāṇasī from Kaśmīr after the death of King Anaṅga Harṣa.[301] Under his direction, the prostitutes of Vārāṇasī presented the first act of the play *Ratnāvalī* of Śrī Harṣa.[302] This *ācārya* was disappointed, as the prostitutes did not give drama priority and were more interested in their original profession, than rehearsing for the play[303] probably, these *ācāryas* were very hard task masters, who made their disciples tire out during the course of training. A mother, of a prospective *gaṇikā*, asks her female slave, to tell the *ācārya* that the tender body of my daughter will not stand the rigours of training.[304]

Rājaśekhara[305] mentions *naṭācāryas* as well-versed in the art of theatre. Sometimes, such *ācāryas* are depicted in sculpture as taking classes. For example, a frieze, showing a dance class, of Lakṣmaṇa temple, Khajurāho, depicts the *naṭācārya* as sitting on an *āsana,* holding an object in his right hand. A boy is dancing to his left, a woman, playing cymbals, is standing at the back left of the *ācārya*, a person is dancing, another is playing a drum, while some people are sitting on the

299. *Raghuvaṁśa*, XIX.14, *Ibid.*, p. 161.

300. *Ibid.*, XIX.36, *Ibid.*, p. 163.

301. *Kuṭṭanīmatam*, p. 799, ed. Narmadeshvar Chaturvedi.

302. *Ibid.*, p. 800.

303. *Kuṭṭanīmatam*, p. 796.

304. *Ibid.*, p. 3454.

305. *nāṭyācāryeṇa raṅgavidyādhareṇa* — *Bālabhārata*, Act I, p. 2.

floor and playing *tānapūrā* or *vīṇā*.[306]

Jayasenāpati, in his *Nṛttaratnāvalī*,[307] describes a perfect dancer of noble birth, with a sound knowledge of the science, who is a skilled teacher and has full control over his senses. This reminds one of the qualities of the *naṭācārya* described by Bharata, on the one hand and the tradition of such *ācārya*s, mentioned in classical Sanskrit literature, on the other.

Varadpande[308] had cited reference from south Indian inscriptions. From them, we infer that dance masters are attached to temples to train the *devadāsī*s. Some such teachers are individually mentioned, such as Achalan, who was well-versed in the technique of Bharata's *Nāṭyaśāstra*; his epithet, *naṭasevyo*, was given to him by other actors in respect.[309]

References to some of the theoretician *ācārya*s are found in Abhinavagupta's commentary — for example, Nandī[310] (Nandīkeśvara), Tumburu,[311] Sadāśiva,[312] Kātyāyana,[313] and Vārtikāra.[314] Some are mentioned by Śāradātanaya, such as Nandīkeśvara, Sadāśiva, and Subandhu,[315] while Dhanañjaya mentions Sadāśiva.[316] There were some like Bhaṭṭa Lollaṭa, Śrī Śaṅkuka and Bhaṭṭa Nāyaka, who wrote commentaries on Bharata's *Nāṭyaśāstra,* before Abhinavagupta and are mentioned and quoted by him, though except the commentary of Abhinavagupta, none of theirs is available. Later, dramaturgists like Dhanañjaya, Sāgaranandī, Rāmacandra, Guṇacandra, Śāradātanaya and Singbhūpāla, were mostly theoreticians, like Bhaṭṭa Lollaṭa, Śrī Śaṅkuka and Bhaṭṭa Nāyaka, but their contribution to drama is in no way less than that of the *prayoktā ācārya*s; both of them preserved and enhanced the classicalised tradition of drama.

---

306. R. Nath, *The Art of Khajuraho*, pl. LVII.
307. *Nṛttaratnāvalī*, VII.165-71.
308. M.L. Varadpande, *Religion and Theatre*, pp. 137-38.
309. *IA*, vol. X, p. 167.
310. *Abhinavabhāratī*, IV, p. 169.
311. *Ibid.*, p. 197.
312. *Ibid.*, p. 9.
313. *Ibid.*, XIV, pp. 245-46.
314. *Ibid.*, I, p. 170.
315. Dr. Nagendra, *op. cit.*, pp. 11, 13.
316. *Ibid.*, *op. cit.*, p. 11.

3

Actresses and Their Contributions to Theatre in Ancient India

Part I

atha rūpaguṇodāryasaubhāgyadhairya śīlasampannā ।
peśalamadhurasnigdhānunādikalācitrakaṇṭhā ca ।।
helābhāvaviśeṣajyāḥ sattvenābhinayena ca ।
mādhuryeṇa ca sampannā hyātodya kuśalāstathā ।।
svaratālayatijñyāśca tathācār yopasevikāḥ ।
caturā nāṭyakuśalāścopohavicakṣaṇāḥ ।।
rūpayauvanasampannā nāṭakīyāḥ prakīrtitāḥ ।

— *NŚ*, XXXIV.48-51

Women who have youthful age with physical beauty, good qualities, generosity, feminine charm, patience and sweetness of manners, and who possess a soft, sweet and charming voice, and varying notes in their throat, and who are experts in the representation of passion (*helā*) and feeling (*bhāva*), know well of representation of the temperament (*sāttva*), are skilled in playing musical instruments, have knowledge of notes, *tāla* and *yati*, and are associated with the master (of the) dramatic art, clever, skilled in acting, capable of using reasoning, positive and negative (*uhāpoha*), are known as actresses (*nāṭakīyā*).

THE above quote, from Bharata, proves not only women's participation in drama, but the highly advanced stage of their art too, which included music — vocal and instrumental, besides the main involvement with acting, which prospered under the guidance of *ācārya*s. Their accomplishments, during Bharata's time, indicate that it must have taken them a considerable time to attain excellence.

Literary and archaeological traditions speak of such female artistes who eventually grew into accomplished actresses — *naṭī* or *nāṭakīyā* of Bharata. In fact, the existence of female theatre artistes is as old as the history of the art itself.

It is evident from the still prevalent practices among aboriginals that in the primitive community, women took active part in ritualistic dance and in impersonation. It appears that women's participation in such performances would have started in the pre-historic period itself.

Dr. Ruben has mentioned the primitive drama of the Santals. In the case of Uraon, at the *Sarhul* festival, the marriage of the sun god with the mother earth is celebrated, wherein the roles of these gods are played by the priest and his wife.[1] Historically, too, the existence of female performing artistes in the form of ritualistic impersonator or entertainer may not be ruled out, even as early as the Indus Valley civilization. As mentioned in the previous chapter, the Indus Valley people had developed a taste for dance, music and perhaps impersonation too, as is indicated by the masks discovered from different levels,[2] the bronze figure[3] of the so-called danseuse from Mohenjo-Dāro and a male torso[4] in dancing pose from Harappā. Besides, a female figure with horns, hoofed legs, a long tail and a horned tiger is depicted on a fragment of a seal from Mohenjo-Dāro.[5] Kramrisch sees this figure as representing divinity, while Susan L. Huntington[6] thinks that the anthromorph is human because of the upright posture and the use of the forelimbs like arms rather than like the legs of a quadruped. It might be taken to be Eṅkiḍu of Sumerian Gilgamesh epic, attacking upon the zoomorph, but the breast-like form on the chest suggests that the figure is female and not Eṅkiḍu. She says that the meaning of the representation is still enigmatic. Could it suggest the ritual enactment of a myth? Moreover, it is interesting, as I have shown later, to observe a similarity between mother goddess depiction of the Indus Valley period and the later Śakti representation, both indicating association with the female generative power of

---

1. G.H. Tarlekar, *Studies in the Nāṭyaśāstra*, p. 13.
2. E.I.H. Mackay, *Further Excavations at Mohenjodaro*, p. 334.
3. See *figs*. I & II.
4. See *figs*. III & II.
5. Stella Kramrisch, *Indian Sculpture*, pl. II, fig. 9.
6. L. Susan Huntington, *The Art of India*, p. 22.

creation. The cult of Śakti had dance, music and drama as part of the esoteric Śākta ritual. If this similarity between mother goddess of the Indus Valley period and the later Śakti has any meaning one might speculate that the later ritual dancer perhaps had its origin in the Indus Valley period. Could we take the above-mentioned female figure as representing such a female ritual impersonator?

There are some references to the performance of maidens and courtesans in Vedic literature. At *Saman*, a Vedic festival, maidens' dancing skill was put to test and courtesans earned by singing and dancing.[7] *Taittirīya Saṁhitā*[8] and *Maitrāyaṇī Saṁhitā*[9] refer to women interested in dance and music. In *Mahāvrata*, another Vedic ritual mentioned in detail in *Śrauta-Sūtras*,[10] the wives of those engaged in sacrifice sang in order to obtain offspring and girls danced round the fire with water pitchers. In the Vedic tradition of marriage ceremony, mentioned in *Gṛhya-Sūtras*, at the bride's house, matrons whose husbands were alive danced to ensure that the marriage endured.[11] From *Atharvaveda,*[12] we know that women with loosened hair, beating their breasts and wailing, used to dance around the funeral pyre. These references show that the dance, an important part of dramatic art, was a social accomplishment for the girls of the period, which enabled them to partake in ceremonies and festivals.

Śatapatha Brāhmaṇa[13] mentions *sāmagāna* (recitation of *sāma*) as a duty specially delegated to women. This indicates three facts — either due to a naturally sweet voice women (priestesses) were considered most suitable to recite[14] or they used to recite *sāma* at domestic rituals or there was a professional class of female *sāma* reciters. But in the absence of any concrete evidence, we cannot say with

7. *Vedic Index*, vol. II, p. 429.
8. *Taittirīya Saṁhitā*, VI.16.5.
9. *Maitrāyaṇī Saṁhitā*, III.7.3.
10. A.B. Keith, *Śaṅkhyāyana Āraṇyaka*, 1907, p. vii, fn. 72.
11. *Śaṅkhyāyana Gṛhya-Sūtra* I.II.5.
12. *kṣipraṁ vai tasyadahanaṁ parinṛtyanti keśinirghnaḥ paninorsi kurvana papamailabam* — *Atharvaveda*, XII.5. 48.
13. *Śatapatha Brāhmaṇa*, XIV.3.11.35.
14. It is known that in Vedic period women were well educated, and they often performed sacrifices without taking help from the priest. — A.S. Altekar, *Education in Ancient India*, pp. 207-11.

certainty what the statement of *Śatapatha Brāhmaṇa* means. Though we are not certain about such female reciters being professional, we have some veiled references which indicate the existence of professional dancers in the *R̥gveda* itself.[15] There is reference to Uṣas in the text as revealing her beauty like *nr̥tu*, the female dancer, removing the garment in the form of darkness. This shows the existence and also, the style of dance performed by female dancers of the period. First, she puts her broidered garment on and then she reveals beauty (as a cow yields her udder so she bares her breasts, i.e., the dawn removes the darkness).[16] This may mean that as the dancer reveals her bossom while dancing, in the same manner, dawn reveals her beauty by removing the darkness.

Another reference is from *Atharvaveda,*[17] wherein a public dance of a woman, adorned with ornaments, in an assembly (*sabhā*) is mentioned. These references, from Vedic literature, show that there were female performing artistes during the Vedic period and probably, some of them were professionals. The passage which describes Uṣas, as a danseuse who bares her bosom to the audience, suggests that a class of danseuse of the period danced in minimum clothes. The reference reminds one of the obscene performances of *kuvalayā*, the actress, mentioned in *Avadānaśataka* and impudence of *naṭī*s mentioned in *Mahābhāṣya* (discussed later).

With the passage of time the dancer and probably, ritualistic impersonator of the Indus Valley period and dancer and musician of the Vedic period, grew into an actress who, like her male counterpart, was dancer, musician and actress, too. Their training in the art and acting style were similar, though in keeping with their different physical and temperamental qualities, slightly varied. As actresses were naturally gifted with greater grace and a sweeter voice than the actors, music and dance became their special field. They were known by the general term *naṭī* or *nāṭakīyā* but there were more than one class of *naṭī*s, based on the class of the society they belonged to. Hence, a study of the history and contributions of actresses to theatre in ancient India, on the basis of the broad division made for such a study, is proposed in this chapter.

---

15. *R̥gveda*, I.192.4. Griffith, tr., vol I, p. 155.
16. Griffith, *op. cit.*, p. 155.
17. *Atharvaveda*, II.36.1.

Professional Actress

Bharata mentions professional actress as *nāṭakīyā*. Another term for such actress is *naṭī*, the feminine form of *naṭa*, which occurs in Sanskrit plays, where she is generally the wife of *sūtradhāra* who aids her husband in introducing the play and is herself an actress. She is represented as devoted to him, fasting to secure reunion in another life,[18] fulfilling her domestic duties and playing her part in the play as well.[19] This type of professional actress was the most common one in ancient India. It was not considered wrong if the wife of a *naṭa* did the same job as her husband. In *Pādakuśalakamāṇavaka Jātaka*,[20] the wife of a *naṭa*, who was drowning, wished to learn at least one song which would enable her to earn her livelihood. This shows that she intended to carry on the profession of her husband. From Patañjali, we learn about the wives of actors serving as actresses.[21] Actors were reputed to live on the price of their wives honour (*jāyājīva*).[22] Rājaśekhara twice introduced the motive of a competition between actors to win the hand of an actress who had been offered by her father in marriage to the most adept of her suitors.

All these references show that the most common type of professional actresses were the wives of actors or in other words actresses chose their husbands from among the actors, so that they could continue their profession even after their marriage, as was suggested by Vātsyāyana.[23] One cannot say if they learnt the art as a family profession or underwent a proper training, but another professional, the *nāṭakīyā* of Bharata,[24] was a well-trained professional artiste. Bharata, while discussing three modes of representation, mentions *anurūpa prakṛti* in which roles are given to the persons of appropriate sex and age.[25] This means female roles were played by artistes of the same sex. Besides, his definition of *nāṭakīyā* also shows

---

18. *Cārudattam*, *BNC*, vol.II, pp. 4-5.
19. Kālidāsa, *Abhijñānaśākuntalam*, Act I, *KG*, pp. 4-5.
20. E.B. Cowell, *Jātaka Stories*, vol.III, p. 302.
21. *Mahābhāṣya*, VI.1.2.
22. The commentary on *Gītāya sūtaṁ nṛttāya śailūṣaṁ* — *Taittirīya Brāhmaṇa*, III.4.1.2.3, explains *anyasmai svabhāryā-pradānanimittakenannena jīvanaṁ* (as one who earns his livelihood by surrendering his wife to another); *Bṛhat-Saṁhitā*, V.74.
23. *Kāmasūtra*, VIII.1, 23-4.
24. *NŚ*, XXXIV. 48-50; XXXV.10.
25. *Ibid.*, XXXV.29.

that there were professional actresses who probably belonged to the class and troupes of *naṭa*s. From *Theragāthā,* we infer that there were five hundred actresses in the troupe of actors headed by Tālapuṭa.[26]

The magico-religious rituals often related to fertility cults of pre-Vedic period, containing ritualistic functions including dance and music performed by maidens as priestesses or oracles, influenced the later Vedic religion, as we know from the literature of the period. It is said in *Śatapatha Brāhmaṇa*[27] that a woman is broader at the hip and is contracted in the middle (or about the waist), and this should be the shape of the *vedī* which makes the altar pleasing to the gods. *Chāndogya Upaniṣad*[28] also states that 'Agni is male principle, while the altar containing it, is regarded as the female principle'. *Mahāvrata* ceremony, mentioned earlier, is another example of the influence of magico-religious rituals of pre-Vedic period on later Vedic religion. Such rituals continued to exist in popular folk cults.

One of the results of this amalgamation of Vedic and pre-Vedic beliefs was the rise of a class of women having the knowledge of dance, music and acting. In the beginning, the female entertainer may have performed this duty but gradually, at a later date, a class of female ritual artistes known as *devadāsī*s came into being, who underwent a special training for that purpose, and thus, their art took the form of a classical one. Others, trained by the *naṭācārya,* formed another and most important class of professionals, who either associated themselves with the existing theatrical troupes or formed their own troupes of exclusively female artistes,[29] specialising in different fields of theatre. There was a combination of folk and classical elements in their art. The '*desī*', included in classical dance and '*abhinaya*' (acting) in *Cilapdikāram,*[30] and '*Lokavṛtti*' often mentioned by Bharata, at a later date, are such folk elements that continued to exist in the classical art as its integral part throughout the history of dramatic art, giving rise to the symbiotic tradition of drama.

The existence of such professional actresses is indicated in the epics, too.

---

26. *Theragāthā*, 50.262.
27. *Śatapatha Brāhmaṇa*, I.2.5.16.
28. *Chāndogya Upaniṣad*, II.13.182.
29. See '*Strī-prekṣā*' section.
30. *Cilappadikāram*, canto III, p. 105, ed. V.R.R. Dikshitar.

According to Śānti-Parva,[31] descending on the stage (to perform dance or drama), making one's beauty a means of livelihood (*rūpopajīvanam*), selling meat and wine, as well as trading in iron and animal hides — all these acts are not considered good by the people. . . . Commentator Nīlakaṇṭha thinks that the term *rūpopajīvanam* here means living by performing shadow theatre. But, it seems more probable that the term is used to describe actresses and prostitutes because they earned their livelihood by their beauty — *rūpa*.[32]

The exclusive troupes of such professional actresses, which was different from those of *naṭa*s — with male and female artistes, is referred to in *Rāmāyaṇa* (Vadhūnāṭaka Saṁgha).[33] Such *saṁgha*s performed plays with female artistes only which were, probably, witnessed exclusively by women.

Pāli Buddhist texts, directly and indirectly, refer to female theatre artistes. *Cullavagga* refers to two monks, Assaji and Punabbasu of Kīṭagiri hills, who were very fond of theatrical shows: they used to spread their drapery and ask the danseuse to dance over it.[34] This shows that professional dancing girls visited such public fairs for earning money. Female dancers were specially called *lāsa*.[35] The Jain text *Aupapātika Sūtra*[36] also mentions that the city of Campā was frequently visited by female dancers performing *lāsya* dance. It is significant that the *lāsya* type of dance is attributed to Pārvatī.[37] In *Mūgapakkha Jātaka,*[38] Bodhisattva, born as the son of Kāśīrāja, wanted to escape from being a king and pretended to be crippled, deaf, dumb and morose. When he was sixteen, they wanted to test if he was normal, hence, it was decided to have dramas enacted before him. Some women full of graces and as beautiful as the daughters of the gods were summoned. They surrounded him and tried hard to delight him but in vain. It seems that these women were professional actresses who were invited to the palace to peform dance and music.

---

31. *Mahābhārata*, Śānti-Parva, 294.5-6.
32. M.L. Varadpande, *History of Indian Theatre*, p. 65.
33. *Rāmāyaṇa*, Bāla-kāṇḍa, 5.12.
34. *raṅgamajjhe pi saṁghātīm pattharitvā nacchakīm evam vadanti idha, bhaginī, nachasu iti — Cullavagga*, 1.3, pp. 19-20.
35. *Ibid*., 1.3, pp. 19-20.
36. *Anupapātika Sūtra*, 2, pp. 4-5 (*Jināgam Granthamālā*-13).
37. *Abhinayadarpaṇa*, 5, 6.
38. E.B. Cowell, *op. cit*., vol. IV, p. 7.

The professional performing female artistes are mentioned as *nāṭakitthiyo* in *Jātakaṭṭhakathā*,[39] who danced, sang and played musical instruments in front of Buddha. They were properly trained in dance and music. From other *Jātaka*s, like *Dasannaka*, we gather that often professional *naṭa*s were called to entertain the royalty; probably *naṭī*s, too, were invited for the same purpose. There were five hundred actresses in the troupe of Tālapuṭa, mentioned in *Theragāthā*,[40] who were all professionals, as already noticed.

Not only dancers but female entertainers, in the form of female acrobats, are also mentioned in Buddhist literature. *Dhammapada* mentions a female acrobat who was deeply loved by a youth, who later became an acrobat himself.[41] The reference reminds one of some depictions on railings at Bharhut and Bodh-Gayā, where a woman stands on the palm of a man (discussed later).

The Jain text, *Uttarādhyayana* commentary,[42] refers to professional female artistes. According to it, King Dummuha celebrated the festival *Indamaha* in Kampillapura. After raising the staff of Indra, danseuses danced on the occasion. They seem to have been professionals who were often invited to perform on public festivals, as we infer from Buddhist literature, too.

Kauṭilya mentions two types of such artistes, the first belonging to the troupes of the actors and the other comprising individual artistes. He suggests that female performing artistes should be engaged in espionage activity. He says that keepers of prostitutes (*bandhakīpoṣaka*), *plavaka*s, *naṭa*s, *nartaka*s, *śobhika*s, while performing plays, should make the chiefs of the ruling councils fall for beautiful young dancers of the troupe and make them quarrel among themselves, at the cost of their unity.[43]

In the first chapter of *Arthaśāstra*,[44] Kauṭilya mentions *kuśīlavā*, the feminine

39. . . . . *tāvadena nam sabbālaṅkārapatimaṇḍitā-nachagītādisu susikkhitā devakainyān viya rūpasobāggapatta itthiyo nānāturīyāni gahetvā samparivarayitvā abhirāmāpentiyo nachagīta vāditāni payojayiñsu. . . .* —*Nidānakathā, Jātakaṭṭhakathā*, p. 47

40. *Theragāthā* 50.262.

41. *Dhammapada commentary*, XXIV: 6, pp. 226-29.

42. J.C. Jain, *Life in Ancient India as depicted in Jain canons*, p. 216.

43. *KA*, XI.1, p. 672, ed. Garola.

44. *Ibid.*, 1.11, p. 34.

form of *kuśīlava*, among those female artistes who were employed for espionage work. She was perhaps a folk singer and earned her livelihood by singing. Such female artistes were employed by the state for episonage work because they were wandering artistes and got mixed with the crowd easily. The eleventh chapter of the text is full of references to women practising that art of music, dance, etc., and given to a life of easy virtue. In connection[45] with the method employed to creat splits among persons or to do away secretly with unwanted persons, the text speaks of some men and women engaged in artistic and other pursuits and moving closely with those in power. In the Mysore edition, such woman are mentioned as *kauśika striyonartakīgāyanā*. . . . But, T. Ganapati Sastri reads the text in his edition of the *Arthaśāstra* as *aditikauśikastriyaḥ* and, on the basis of the *Jayamaṅgalā* commentary on this portion of the text, interprets the word *aditi* as picture showing beggar. From *Mudrārākṣasa* we know that the spies of Kauṭilya worked in the guise of *maṅkha*;[46] probably there were women also practising the art of *maṅkha* to earn their livelihood. A late Jain text, *Triṣaṣṭiśalākā-puruṣa-carita,* also vaguely refers to a woman, Paṇḍitā, who utilised the art of *maṅkha* to help her mistress.[47] As for *kauśikastriyaḥ*, V. Raghwan[48] thinks that they were women of a class or community devoted to the arts of music, dance, toilette, etc., employed in court and engaged frequently in aiding love affairs.

It seems that during Kauṭilya's time, *kuśīlavā, nartakī* and *gāyanā* — the singing and dancing women, *aditi* — practising the art of *maṅkha* and *kauśika* (if we do not take the term with *aditi* as a compound word), having the knowledge of music, dance and acting and employed in the courts, belonged to the class of professional actresses. Such female artistes, engaged in episonage work, seem to have been in the king's employment and were, probably, spies trained in dramatic arts. There may not have been any relationship between them and *nartakī*, *gāyanā*, *kuśīlavā* or *aditikauśikastrī*, whose professions were aimed at pure entertainment, as Varadpande[49] says, but the reference indirectly shows the existence of such female professional artistes during Kauṭilya's time whose art the court employees learnt

---

45. *KA*, XI.1, p. 380.
46. *Mudrārākṣasa*, Act I.
47. *Triṣaṣṭiśalākā-puruṣa-carita*, I.650, *Jain Jātaka*, p. 69.
48. V. Raghvan, 'On the meaning of the word kauśika', *JOR*, Madras, vol. XV, p. 116.
49. M.L. Varadpande, *Traditions of Indian Theatre*, p. 31.

to serve their own purpose. The reference to *naṭī*, *nartakī*, *gāyanā*, *kuśīlavā* and *aditikauśikastrī* shows that female artistes had already secured an important place in different branches of dramatic art in the last few centuries before Christ and were in no way inferior than their male counterparts.

Some terracotta female figures of the Mauryan period found from *Bulandībāgh* seem to depict female dancers. According to V.S. Agrawala,[50] Sankalia and Dhavalikar,[51] these female figures, their costumes and poses suggest that they are dancing girls. The uplifted edges of their skirts (*ghāgharā*s) show the swinging motion of their body. These dancers are wearing earstuds, necklaces and girdles. The headdress of one of them[52] is extremely complicated and consists of a number of discs. Her long skirt (*ghāgharā*) is similar to present-day Maṇipurī dance costume. Sankalia and Dhavalikar find great affinity between the pose of the danseuse and present-day Maṇipurī and Nāgā dance poses and say that the figure proves that these dances are as old as the Mauryan period. It shows the great antiquity of Indian dance forms, whether Bharata mentions them or not. Another dancing figure[53] has a *ghāgharā* of different style but that too is uplifted indicating her whirling movement.

These terracotta figures of dancing girls are quite large in size and are characterised by smooth and sensitive modelling. They breathe the air of urban sophistication with their dynamic dancing movements, elaborate headdress and probably starched skirt (*ghāgharā*). According to Devangana Desai,[54] they reflect the tastes and interests of the royal family and the *śreṣṭhin* class and were probably produced by *rājakumbhakāra*s or royal potters. Their sophistication suggests that they represent professional dancers of a tradition which had already been classicalised and was popular among the higher class of the society.

Dancing, singing and recital of musical instruments by charming girls are depicted as part of worship on the railings of Bharhut, Sāñcī and Bodh-Gayā. The dance of celestial nymphs Alambuṣā, Miśrakeśī, Padmāvatī and Subhadrā depicted

50. V.S. Agrawala, *Bhāratīya Kalā*, p. 323.

51. Sankalia & Dhavalikar, 'The Terracotta art of India', *Mārg*, vol. XXIII, no. 1, p. 40.

52. *Ibid.*, p. 41, fig. 10.

53. *Ibid.*, p. 41, fig. 9.

54. Devangana Desai, 'Social Background of Ancient Indian Terracotta', *History and Society: Essays in honour of Professor N.R. Ray*, Calcutta, 1976, p. 149.

on the Presenjīt pillar at Bharhut[55] and a dance performed by female dancers on occasion of the division of relics of the Buddha, in accompaniment to music played by female artistes on a coping piece, are depicted at Bharhut.[56] At Sāñcī, too, a dance of a nymph on occasion of *Cuḍāmaha*[57] is depicted. It is obvious that in depicting such scenes sculptors would have been inspired by the dance of contemporary female artistes as there is not much difference in the style of the two dancers.

Such female artistes did exist in second century BC, to which date these depictions generally belong, because Patañjali[58] too mentions the wives of actors who served as actresses with an unsavoury reputation. Being asked by the audience, while on the stage, 'to whom they belong', the wives of actors responded 'to the audience'. The word *raṅgam gatā* clearly indicates that the wives of *naṭa*s performed on the stage and thus, it seems possible that in the second century BC, a date generally assigned to Patañjali, the wives of actors were professional actresses and they accompanied their husbands wherever their troupes went. Such travelling troupes of actors were in existence since the time of Kauṭilya, as we have already noticed.

In almost the same period, a female dancer is depicted at Rānīgumphā cave (Udaigiri, Orissa)[59] also, indicating that such dances and drama, performed by girls, were recognised in Jainism as they propagated the faith. There are nine sculptured friezes extending over the facade of the lower main wing and its immediate turn in the eastern end. Among these carvings is an interesting relief depicting a girl dancing gracefully under a pillared pavilion and four seated companions forming the orchestra. What interests us most is the dance posture which indicates a distinct element of nobility. The right hand of the danseuse seems to be in *patākā hasta*, a well-known hand gesture mentioned by Bharata[60] and still practised in Bharata Nāṭayam and Oḍissī styles of dance. In order to suggest a vigorous movement, the ribbon end of her headdress flows in lively manner behind her ear. Her hair is

---

55. See *Pl.* I.
56. C. Sivarammurti, *The Masterpieces of Indian Sculpture in National Museum*, pl. I.
57. See *Pl.* V.
58. *tadyathā naṭānām striyo raṅgam gatā yo yaḥ pr̥cchati kasyayuyamiti tam tam tvetyāhuḥ* . . . . — *Mahābhāṣya*, VI.1.13.
59. See *Pl.* XI.
60. *NŚ*, IX.18.

arranged in double plaits.[61] The depiction shows that the classicalisation of folk art (dance) had already begun.

A scene, depicting a similar dance performance by a young danseuse with five members of the orchestra, belonging to the second century BC[62] is found on a fragment of a running freize recovered from Kaṅkālī Ṭīlā, Mathurā, and it is housed at the Lucknow Museum (no. J. 354). The dance posture of the danseuse is very graceful. She, too, has her left hand turned towards her face in *patākā hasta* gesture, and her body shows her rhythmic movement. It is generally believed that the scene depicts the dance by Nīlāñjanā, the heavenly dancer, in front of Ṛṣabhadeva, the first *tīrthaṅkara*, but the dance style of *apsaras*es was that of professional dancers of the period, as shall be discussed later.

Another piece of art in terracotta recovered from Mathurā and belonging to second century BC, depicts a professional female dancer, performing to entertain a couple.[63] Since they are sitting under a tree, it seems that the scene represents an *udyāna goṣṭhī* (garden party), common during the period, which included dance performance by professionals. The left hand of the danseuse is about to rest on her hip and the right hand is raised in a style which suggests that she is about to revolve on her toes or has just revolved.

This was a common style, as a female artiste dancing in a similar style is depicted on a bracket figure, Totowa Gumpha no.2, Khaṇḍagiri, Orissa, also.[64] The beautiful danseuse is performing a dance to the tune of a stringed musical instrument played by a man, under a tree. The hands of the girl are almost in the same position as in the Mathurā example. The scarf of the danseuse, flowing in an attractive manner, indicates her swinging motion. This scene also represents a professional female artiste peforming in a garden.

Another dance performance by female professional artistes of the second century BC, is represented on the left wall of cave no. 10 of Ajantā.[65] There are fifteen female

---

61. Charles Fabri, *History of Art in Orissa*, p. 21; R.P. Mahapatra, *Jain Monuments of Orissa*, pp. 162-63, see *Pl.* XI.
62. See *Pl.* XII.
63. V.S. Agrawala, *Bhārtīya Kalā*, fig. 178.
64. R.C. Mahapatra, *op. cit.*, fig. 30.
65. G. Yazadani, *Ajanta*, part III, pl. no. 1.

artistes, of whom three are dancers and the rest musicians. Yazdani[66] has described the scene in detail.

> Two of the musicians have long trumpets, which may be either of horn or of metal. The others are clapping their hands to mark the time, or to produce the high pitch effect in music. Among the dancers, one has raised and curved her arms in a style which suggests that she is about to revolve on her toes. The other two have inclined their bodies on one side by bending one leg, and have curved their right arms gracefully upwards and placed the tips of their thumbs on their heads, while the left hand is placed on the hip on the same side, the object being primarily to keep the balance of the body while dancing in short wavy steps and also, to produce an effective pose by making two beautiful loops (or curves), one with the right arm and the other with the left.

The dance is being performed near the *bodhi*-tree. Yazdani[67] thinks that these women belong to the orchestra attached to the monastery, in the garden of which the *bodhi*-tree is shown, but it is more probable that they are professional female artistes invited to perform in the garden of the monastery on occasion of some religious festival. This shows the changed attitude of Buddhism towards dramatic arts.[68]

The dance scenes depicted at Bharhut, Sāñcī, Rānīgumphā, Totowa Gumphā, Mathurā and Ajantā provide vital information regarding the contemporary dramatic performance by female artistes or actresses who were gradually developing into artistes with sound knowledge of *nṛtta, gīta* and *vāditra* (dance, song and instrumental music) and also acting, exactly like their male counterpart, *naṭa*. We observe the following in the depicted scenes :

1. The dance was performed either in a pavilion, generally supported by pillars

---

66 G. Yazdani, *The History of the Deccan*, vol. VII-XI, p. 779.

67. *Ibid.*, p. 779.

68. Buddha in *Brahmajāla Sutta*, objected to monks attending such festivals or gatherings where theatrical arts were performed, chiefly because such performances stimulated erotic feelings of a person (*Dīghanikāya*, *Brahmajāla Sutta*, *sīla mattakam*, *cūdasīlam*, 10). For the same reason Aśoka, too, was against such gatherings where theatrical arts were performed with a touch of vulgarity. (Irāvatī, '*Aśoka ke Abhilekhon Men ullikhit samāja: Ek Samīkaraṇa*', *The Indian Journal of Buddhist Studies*, vol. 2, no. 2)

as is seen in Rānīgumphā and Mathurā examples, or in an open courtyard facing a building with open pillared balcony as is seen in Cūḍāmaho scene at Bharhut and Sāñci both,[69] or in a garden under a tree as is seen in the Ajantā example and in the second example from Mathurā.

2. The dance was accompanied by an orchestra consisting of the players of drums, harps, trumpets, a gong-like instrument with a small stick and hand clappers and vocalists.

3. Female dancers performed adorned with heavy ornaments, as the dancers in above-mentioned scenes are wearing girdles, bangles, necklaces and ear ornaments and less clothes. That reminds one of the reference to Uṣas in *R̥gveda*, mentioned earlier in this chapter, where she is described as baring her bosoms like a *nr̥tu* (female dancer).

4. From Bharata we gather that for graceful (*kaiśikī*) style Brahmā had provided Bharata with *apsaras*es and for that style women and women alone were supposed to be best suited. The above-mentioned examples from second or first century BC tell us that perhaps the dance part of a drama which needs such graceful movements of the body was performed by female artistes during this period, probably because they had physical beauty and grace.

5. It seems that the vocalists of the troupe were generally women, whether it was a troupe with mixed cast or exclusively of female artistes. The Cūḍāmaho scene from Bharhut[70] has four musician gods but the vocalists are three heavenly maidens. Similarly, the same scene from Sāñcī[71] also has four musician gods sitting in the foreground facing the holy Cūḍā, but at least three female figures in front of the dancer represent the vocalists. This became a common practice. In Bhāsa's *Pratijñāyaugandharāyaṇa,*[72] *naṭī* is asked by *sūtradhāra* to sing a suitable song. It has been already noticed how gradually the *naṭī* took the place of *kuśīlava*, the musician of the troupe.

---

69. At Rānīgumphā cave, there is an open courtyard facing a double-storyed building with pillared balcony. It is generally believed that the place was used as an open-air theatre.

70. See *Pl.* II.

71. See *Pl.* V.

72. *Pratijñāyaugandharāyaṇa*, Act I, *BNC*, vol. II, p. 3.

In Bhāsa's *Cārudattam*[73] also while going through a lane, the hero Cārudatta and Vidūṣaka hear enthralling music coming from a house. When Cārudatta appreciates it, Vidūṣaka says that he does not like singing men and reading (reciting) women. The man who sings appears like a priest and a woman who reads (recites) seems to be a cow without a nose. Later, Bharata[74] too voices the opinion that singing is a quality with which women are naturally endowed and if a man has a suitable voice it is his additional quality. Perhaps, Bharata too followed the traditional rules based on practical experience.

The female dancers in these sculptures seem to be professionals, either attached to some religious establishments who gradually gave rise to the *devadāsī* system, or were professional artistes invited or engaged to perform on festive occasions or at the time of worship as there was a custom in ancient India to appoint professional artistes to perform such duties.[75] Perhaps, this was the case in the Deccan too. The dance scene depicting two female dancers and one male dancer, carved in four episodes at Kondane, referred to in the previous chapter,[76] may be taken as its example. All these four episodes, probably, represent four important episodes of a popular folk play with some religious bearing. It is apparent that this dance style included *abhinaya* (acting) too.

On the facade of the *caitya* at Kārle, which belongs to nearly the same age as that of Kondane, are carved the figures of dancers in pairs of male and female. Yazdani[77] thinks that they are aborigines as is shown by their costume and ornaments. They probably represent folk artistes and show that the folk tradition of dramatic art flourished in the period along with the classical. Probably, such female artistes together with their male partners were invited to perform in religious

---

73. *Cārudattam*, Act III, *BNC*, vol. III p. 65.

74. *NŚ*, XXXII.503, 504.

75. In *Mahāvrata* ceremony, a harlot was called to perform a mock fight and to exchange abuses with a *brahmacārī* as part of the ritual. Kālidāsa in *Meghadūtam* mentions that *Līlāvadhu* (courtesan) was invited to the temple of Mahākāla to do the part-time job of a *devadāsī*. Bhāna's play *Ubhayābhisārikā* tells that *gaṇikā* Madanasenā was invited to the temple of Bhagavān Nārāyaṇa to present a *saṅgītaka* — musical opera (*Caturbhāṇī*, pp. 122-23).

76. See *supra*, pp. 40-41.

77. G. Yazdani, *op. cit.*, pp. 778-79.

establishments in the Deccan too. So would have been the case at Bharhut, Mathurā and Orissa as well. And sculptors, charmed by the art of the performers, depicted them in their art.

Bharhut sculptures depict entertainment consisting of gymnastic feats besides music and dance, such as a woman standing on the palm of one's hand[78] and remaining balanced upon an unsteady support.[79] A similar scene depicting a woman standing on the palm of a man (*yakṣa*) is found at Bodh-Gayā too.[80] From the Buddhist text, *Dhammapada*'s commentary we know that there were female acrobats.[81] Hence, it seems that such scenes may have been inspired by performances of female folk artistes who displayed acrobatic steps and postures.

Bhūtapūjā, which had acrobatic dance as its feature, was one of the many festivals known in the rituals of magico-religious cults. A number of folk theatres like *yakṣagāna* have taken their basic patterns from the *bhūta* dance.[82] Bharata, too, mentions that the performance of *mahācārī*, a ferocious dance, appeases hosts of *bhūtas*.[83] *Nṛtyaratnāvalī,* composed by Jaisenāpati, refers to *Bhūtamātṛmahotsava* and acrobatic dances performed on the occasion. Varadpande says,

> Probably the sophisticated classical dance style like Bharatanāṭayam, Kuchipuḍī and Oḍissī are evolved out of ritualistic dances in honour of the folk deities; they retain the forceful and acrobatic aspects inherent in the tradition.[84]

These dance traditions have folk elements improvised into a discipline, a classical form. In their original folk form, they probably had more acrobatic and less graceful postures. The female acrobats mentioned in Buddhist literature probably belonged to that nascent stage of the art. As mentioned in the previous chapter, *stūpa* worship

---

78. B.M. Barua, *op. cit.*, III, p. 67, fig. 72.
79. *Ibid.*, fig. 61, 65, 68, 73, 74.
80. B.P. Sinha, *Bhāratīya kalā ko Bihār Kī Dena*, fig. 43, 52.
81. *Dhammapada com.*, XXIV, 6, pp. 226-27.
82. H.K., Ranganath, 'Karnatak Theatre', quoted by M.L. Varadpande, *Religion and Theatre*, pp. 37-38.
83. *NŚ*, V.28.
84. M.L. Varadpande, *op. cit.*, p. 39.

contained dance and music. *Laṅghananaṭa*s (male acrobats) are depicted at Bharhut,[85] showing that acrobatic shows too were included in the ritualistic worship of *stūpa* or in the fairs held at the time of special worship. Could it be that the above-mentioned scenes depicting female figures in acrobatic postures represent the female counterparts of *laṅghnanaṭas*? From *Jātaka*s we know that such artistes visited fairs (*samajjā*) to earn money; in all probability female acrobats too might have done the same and while depicting *vṛkṣikā*s or *yakṣī*s, sculptors copied their postures. Such figures, i.e., *nāyikā*s standing on *guhyaka*s or *yakṣa*s[86] are found in Mathurā art of the Kuṣāṇa period also. There is one such depiction of an acrobatic dancer or *naṭī* on the front face of an upright pillar of the railing found from Sanghol, belonging to Mathurā art. The *naṭī* is represented as balancing a pot filled to the brim with water on the elbow of her raised arm. The danseuse is continuing her whirling movement without slowing down the tempo. The neat footwork is shown by placing the feet parallel to each other.[87]

On half a dozen pillars at Mathurā, a maiden is depicted as undoing her girdle or lower garment.[88] V.S. Agrawala thinks that they are sculptural depictions of dances prevalent in the period wherein the female dancer barred her body while dancing. This type of dance was most probably in tradition — the one vaguely referred to in *Ṛgveda* in Uṣas Sūkta, cited earlier. Such scenes are depicted at Bharhut too. *Avadānaśataka*, composed in the early centuries of the Christian era, describes a troupe of actors from south visiting Rājagṛha where the beautiful actress, Kuvalayā, the daughter of the *naṭācārya* of the troupe, seduced many pious monks by her histrionic talents and uncommon physical attraction. Kuvalayā's dance was obscene as she did exactly what is being done by the female figures on the pillars at Mathurā. The description shows that she too barred her body while dancing.[89]

Bharata[90] has enjoined that certain scenes should not be shown on the stage, one of them is undoing of the *nīvī* (knot of the lower garment). This instruction of

85. See *Pl*. III.
86. V.S. Agrawala, *op. cit*., p. 235.
87. See *Pl*. XXV.
88. V.S. Agrawala, *op. cit*., p. 250, fig. 343.
89. *upasaṁkramya bhagavataḥ purastātsthitvā nṛtyati gāyati vādayate strīliṅgāni stracinhāni strīnimittāni copadarśayati* — *Avadānaśataka*, VIII.175, p. 185.
90. *NŚ*, XXIV.296-97.

Bharata suggests the existence of such performances which were not acceptable to Bharata who wanted theatre to be a decent art. It seems that there was an unbroken tradition of this dance style, similar to the striptease dance of modern period. This obscenity had given a bad reputation to the *naṭīs*, mostly the wives of the actors who themselves did not mind it — hence were known as Jāyājīva.[91]

On the right half of a round pillar from Mathurā, a scene is carved, depicting a lady dancing with her right foot bent and left hand raised in a dancing posture. To the left, a male figure is playing a tabor and some other instruments corresponding to modern *ḍholak*, a cylindrical form of drum placed horizontally for playing. Some female members of the orchestra are also seen. One of them is playing a gong-like instrument, holding it in her left hand and has a small stick in the right. Two other female members are, perhaps, the vocalists.[92] This dance scene has the same features as the earlier scene from Mathurā, belonging to second century BC, mentioned earlier in this chapter.[93] The dance posture itself is almost identical. The performance is being held in a pillared pavilion which is slightly raised. The stairs are seen on the left, and the orchestra is sitting on the same level and facing the back of the danseuse who is wearing a thin transparent lower garment and heavy ornaments. The art of the danseuse shows that she belonged to the professional class that performed in public.

Individual female musicians, too, are depicted in Mathurā art — for example, a lady leaning on a tree is seen as playing a *vīṇā*.[94] A female figure on a pillar has been discovered from Sanghol recently.[95] It depicts a lady piping rapturous melodies from her musical instrument, which resembles a harmonica. She is standing on a seated lion. Her posture, the expression on the lion's face and also the rapt attention of the couple in the balcony indicate the sweetness of the notes rising from her harmonica. A sculpture, depicting a musician playing lute, was discovered from Swāt, Gāndhāra, and is now housed at Peshawar Museum. Though Marshall[96] has not mentioned it specifically, the drapery of the figure, which consists of two

---

91. *Bṛhat-Saṁhitā*, V.74.
92. Mathura Museum J., 268. *Mārg,* XV, no. 2 (Illus). no. 19, p. 36.
93. See *Pl.* XII.
94. V.S. Agrawala, *op. cit*., p. 235, fig. 352.
95. *Kushan Sculptures from Sanghol*, vol. I, ed. S.P. Gupta, fig. no. 216.
96. J. Marshall, *The Buddhist art of Gandhara*, fig. 65.

garments, the lower one of floor length, shows that the figure is that of a female musician.

There is another example of a female individual artist playing flute from Gāndhāra (see *Pl.* XXIV). It is interesting to note the standing posture of the artist. Her *tribhaṅga* posture reminds one of God Kṛṣṇa. Did the Gāndhāra sculptor view it as a common standing posture for playing flute or a comfortable one for playing flute among flutists? Or was it that he had seen some sculptural depiction of God Kṛṣṇa playing the flute and had taken it as a proper pose for playing that instrument while standing? It can be an interesting quest from the iconographic point of view, too. There is another example of a flute recital by a male artist from a sculptural depiction in Gāndhāra. The flutist in this sculpture is standing in the same pose (Ingholt Harald, *Gandhara Art in Pakistan*, pl. X 1).

Existence of a musician couple, like *naṭa* and *naṭī*, is known from the sculptures of the period. For example, a musician couple playing lute and cymbals has been discovered from Mathurā (see *Pl.* XXVII). A vaulted bracket from Gāndhāra depicts a musician couple standing on a lotus pedastal.[97] The bearded male plays a string instrument, while his female companion holds a clapper-type percussion instrument. It seems that they are professional musicians like *naṭa* and *naṭī*; their profession was music and dance. Such performing couples are often depicted in Indian art — for example, two dancing couples from Nāgārjunakoṇḍa.[98]

The tradition of inviting or engaging professional actresses to perform on religious festivals continued in the early centuries of the Christian era, too, which is indicated by another Gāndhāra sculpture,[99] depicting a sacrifice being performed by a Nāga king. On this occasion, two danseuses are seen as performing dance accompanied by a six-member-orchestra depicted on the right of the king and the queen. The instruments being played are drums, tambourine and flute. The dance posture of the dancers are also traditional: one hand raised and the other hanging, the feet in whirling motion.

Some ivory plaques, with beautiful carvings, have been discovered from Kapish. One of them depicts a dance performance by a young lady to the accompaniment of

97. S.J. Czuma, *The Kushan Sculpture: Images From Early India*, fig. 94.

98. R.J. Mehta, *Masterpieces of Female Form in Indian Art*, pl. 14.

99. Ingholt Herald, *Gandhara Art in Pakistan*, p. 399.

a drum, played by a female musician. Another scene represents a female flute player deeply engrossed in her art.[100] Such scenes indicate the existence and popularity of such performances of female artistes in the north-western part of India during the early centuries of the Christian era.

Some second-century-AD sculptures from Amarāvatī too depict such performances.[101] The scene depicting the division of the relics of Buddha among the eight claimants shows a dance performance by four female dancers. The dance gives an impression that it is a well-rehearsed programme. The figure in the centre in the background has turned both her hands, showing the *patākā hasta* gesture, towards her face. She is flanked by two dancers in identical dancing pose facing opposite directions; the figure in the centre in the foreground has just sat down while dancing in an attractive posture to let the spectators see the girl behind her, thus making a beautiful composition. On the left of the danseuses are seen the musicians. The two female lute players are clearly seen, a seated female figure in the background is probably playing a *ḍholak*-like drum and next to her is a female figure, probably the vocalist. Thus, the whole composition clearly shows that it is not a spontaneous dance performed by overwhelmed ladies, but a properly composed dance performance with regulated steps and postures. This indicates the advanced stage of the art of female professional artistes. A similar group dance performed by three female dancers is depicted in a Nāgārjunakoṇḍa relief.[102] The hand gestures and static postures of the dancers clearly represent Bharata Nāṭayam style.

In Bharata's *Nāṭyaśāstra,* we find detailed instructions for actresses, which indicates that by the time of Bharata, dramatic activities of female artistes must have taken a definite shape, and hence Bharata thought it proper to include directions for actresses too. *Nāṭyaśāstra* shows that actresses enjoyed equal importance in the field with actors, at times more than them, as some of the roles and duties were performed exclusively by them. The preliminary rituals in *Pūrvaraṅga* concerning dance were performed by actresses.[103] It seems that Bharata had realised that an actress was capable enough to do justice to male roles too, and

---

100. V.S. Agrawala, *op. cit.*, fig. 444 and 445, p. 281.
101. Bachopher, *Early Indian Sculpture*, pl. 125.
102. Amita Ray, *Life and Art of Early Āndhradeśa*, fig. 206.
103. *NŚ*, IV.281, 282.

hence, he enjoins that she may be given a delicate man's role.[104] In temples, palaces and houses of army officers, etc., dramatic performances were mostly staged by women in men's role.[105] Bharata's *nāṭakīyā* (actress) was a professional artiste who received proper training under the guidance of an *ācārya*.[106] Bharata's rule regarding *anurūpā prakṛti*[107] also tells that there were such professional actresses who did not hesitate to take part in a play with mixed cast, probably because most of them were wives of the actors and belonged to their dramatic troupe.[108] The picture of an actress that emerges from *Nāṭyaśāstra* is that of a perfect artiste with natural and acquired qualities of a professional theatre artiste, whose art prospered later in the Gupta period under favourable conditions.

The period between the fourth and the sixth century AD was a time of tremendous growth in the field of dance, drama and music as is reflected in the literature and the art of the period. It seems that these three arts which had already taken a definite form during Bharata's time reached their zenith during this period. Besides, during this period the amalgamation of folk and classical arts was completed and a perfect symbiotic tradition was formed in which the best of these two traditions were combined and at the same time their identity was retained. *Naṭa* and *naṭī*, the product of the folk tradition, had gone through centuries of proper training. They had their guilds with properly trained male and female artistes. This was the period when the art had become an embellishment for girls of noble birth too, as shall be discussed later in this chapter. This shows that the efforts of the *ācārya*s to establish the folk art of drama, which though strong was not recognised by the upper class of the society as respectable, as a classical art were now accomplished. *Ācārya*s on the one hand and *naṭa*s on the other, were trying to win the recognition of the people of both the classes, upper and lower, to establish drama as a respectable art. By the common efforts of these two, theatre eventually reached a stage where it got religious sanction — Brahmā was supposed to be the author of *Nāṭyaśāstra* and God Śiva contributed dance to drama — and social recognition, as people of all classes recognised it as respectable.

---

104. *NŚ*, XXXV.38.
105. *Ibid.*, XXXV.37.
106. *Ibid.*, XXXV.40.
107. *Ibid.*, XXXV.29.
108. *Ibid.*, XXXV.101.

This was the period when Kālidāsa wrote his plays. The *sūtradhāra* of his plays tells that they were witnessed not only by the common folk but by the learned class also, though they were presented by the *naṭa*s and their troupes whose origin was in folk tradition. Sculptures of the period too reflect a new turn in theatrical arts. A fragmentary sculpture from Nachanā Kuṭharā depicts *mahānaṭa* Śiva which is the earliest representation of the *tāṇḍava* motif so far known in Indian art and belongs to Gupta period.[109] Kālidāsa in all three of his plays dedicates his *maṅgalācaraṇa* to Śiva, showing that Śiva as the patron deity of theatrical arts was worshipped during the Gupta period. This indirectly shows the artistic leaning of the people during the Gupta period. This new awareness towards dramatic arts is noticed in the case of female artistes, too. The literature of the period refers to the professional female artistes of different types.

The Purāṇas refer to the dedication of maidens, skilled in theatrical arts, to the temples as a pious deed, which gave rise to the *devadāsī* system, the *devadāsī* being a kind of professional artiste. The *naṭī* of Kālidāsa's *Abhijñānaśākuntalam* is the wife of the *sūtradhāra* and she also seems to be sharing his responsibilities regarding getting the characters (actors) of the play duly prepared for the final show. Besides, she is well-versed in the art of singing: her haunting and melodious voice leaves the audience spell-bound.[110] The *naṭī* of the Gupta period, thus, belonged to that professional class of actresses which was known since at least the times of Patañjali and Bhāsa, i.e., she was the wife of the actor and was herself an actress belonging to the troupe.

The popularity of female professional artistes is reflected in the philosophical texts of the period. In *Sāṁkhya Kārikā* of Īśvarakṛṣṇa,[111] primal nature (*prakṛti*) is compared with a *nartakī* (female dancer): 'as dancer (*nartakī*) desists from dancing, having exhibited herself to the audience so does primal nature desist having exhibited herself to the Spirit'.[112] What interests us in this verse is the reference to *nartakī* as a professional artiste who performs in public. The reference shows not only the existence of such a professional dancer but also her popularity which made the author give this instance which was commonly known to people — they were familiar

109. V.S. Agrawala, *Gupta Art*, p. 34.

110. *Abhijñānaśākuntalam*, Prastāvanā, *KG*, pp. 3-5.

111. Generally ascribed to a period between first and fifth century AD.

112. *Sāṁkhya Kārikā*, 59, ed. S.S. Suryanarayana Sastri, p. 94.

with the danseuse who exhibited herself to the audience and left the stage. Such dancers performed in the *goṣṭhī* (assembly) also, arranged by the well-to-do people or people of artistic tastes. Such *goṣṭhīs* are mentioned in *Vasudevahiṇḍī*, written in about sixth century AD[113] and *Kāmasūtra*[114] where female professional artistes danced and competitions were held.

Some of the female figures depicted on the door-jambs or walls of the temples of Gupta period in dancing poses indicate a definite growth and refinement in the postures, hand gestures and steps of the dance. Some of the depictions are quite close to the postures described by Bharata. The dance is often depicted in accompaniment to a full-fledged orchestra. By this time devotional Vaiṣṇavism had already become one of the most popular religions, and it had dance, music and drama as an essential part of its ritual. We have seen how professional performing artistes were often invited to perform in religious establishments much earlier to the Gupta period. The depiction of female dancers in graceful postures on the door-jambs of Gupta temples suggests that this tradition was in vogue during the Gupta period too. On the right jamb of the door frame at Udayagiri cave no. 19, a female dancer is seen dancing in the aforesaid manner in the accompaniment of a guitar-like instrument played by her male partner, most probably a *naṭa*.[115] Her dance posture speaks of her proper training.

The paintings at Bāgh cave[116] also show some interesting scenes. There is a panel showing flying figures probably, casting flowers of blessings on the female group below. The rippling bodies of the girls, the subtle, slow, swaying movements of their torsos, suggest that the group is involved in dance. Their dance style seems to be *lāsya* and here, it seems to be a form of prayer.

Next to this is the large panel of the dance and music scenes, showing two male dancers surrounded by female orchestra in two different groups.[117] Both the scenes are full of strange rhythmic vitality. In the first scene, the animated group of dark brown women is engaged in playing accompanying musical instruments (drum,

113. *Vasudevahiṇḍī*, Dhammila Hiṇḍī, p. 28, Jain Granth Mālā-80.

114. *Kāmasūtra*, 41.1.15.

115. See *Pl.* XXXI.

116. *Mārg*, vol. XXV, no. 3, p. 15.

117. *Ibid.*, p. 11.

cymbals and beating sticks) to the vigorous male dancer. One of the seven musicians, a lithe young girl with a drum strapped to her body on the left of the dancer, is involved in active play, as is indicated by the three fingers of her right hand in the movement of striking the drum. The girl standing on the right of the dancer with upraised hands is obviously marking the time for the song which her open mouth seems to be uttering. Here, again, we see a female vocalist. Of the other female figures, the second on the right is shown with beating sticks, similar to modern Gujarātī *ḍāṇḍiā*.

The dance scene on the right has six female musicians, playing same instruments as in the first group. Describing it, Mulk Raj Anand says, 'Vibrant with joy, its sensuous appeal is redolent of the spirit of the period, when the ordinary folk loved the pleasure of life.'[118] The figures appear to be of tribal origin. As Bāgh hill was and is mainly a jungle land and the dominant population aboriginal Bhīls, who were not assimilated by Brāhmaṇism, it seems that Buddhist monks saw opportunities for their missionary work and Buddhist temples were excavated here at Bāgh.[119] We have seen that since the time of Bharhut and Sāñcī sculptures, dance and music formed part of Buddhist ritualistic worship. The above-mentioned paintings of Bāgh cave show that perhaps the instinctive love of Bhīl devotees manifesting itself in song and dance which these people of the forests loved was involved in the Buddhist ceremonies, which may have fully absorbed dance, music and drama as part of its ritual due to Hinduised Mahāyāna thoughts. In Brāhmaṇic religions such ritualistic dances were performed by professional artistes. Probably, this would have been the case with Buddhists, too.

V.S. Agrawala[120] thinks that the two dance groups, from Bāgh Cave, illustrate the performance of the Hallīsaka dance, one of the Uparūpakas, a musical drama acted by a troupe of women led by a man, representing folk style. This type of dance is referred to by Bhāsa in his plays.[121] In *Cilappadikāram*, the dance of the girls belonging to the cowherd community, similar to *rāsa*, is mentioned wherein two of

---

118. Mulk Raj Anand, *Album of Indian Paintings*, p. 52.
119. Mulk Raj Anand, 'Rhythm of Dance and Music in the Bagh Caves', *Mārg*, vol XXV, no. 3, p. 3.
120. V.S. Agrawala, *Gupta Art*, pp. 95-96.
121. *Bālacarita* Act, III, *BNC*, vol. I, pp. 55, 59.

them acted as Māyavan and Balarāma, i.e., male characters.[122] In Bhāgavata cult, *rāsa* performed by the cowherd God Vāsudeva and cowherdesses has similar features. If we study the paintings of Bāgh cave which depict a group of female musicians with a male dancer in the centre and themselves, showing the rythmic movements of their bodies, in the background, it would seem possible that they are performing some sort of folk dance-drama, most probably, Hallīsaka. This type of performance in a cave of Gupta period, probably by the aboriginals of the nearby forests representing folk style, is significant. The instruments (drums, cymbals, beating sticks) common to both the styles (classical and folk) of dance, indicate the amalgamation of folk and classical elements in the dramatic art of the period, representing the great symbiotic tradition of art.

The professional actress in the form of *naṭī*, the wife of *sūtradhāra*, was known in successive periods, too. In *Ratnāvalī* of Śrī Harṣa, she is addressed not merely as *ārye* but also as 'My dear' (*priye*) and all that by the *sūtradhāra*.[123] He tells his wife (*gṛhiṇī*) that his younger brother has dressed himself up for the role of Yaugandharāyaṇa. Thus, it seems that there were troupes of hereditary professional communities of actors in the seventh century AD, as there were much before then, since the times of Bhāsa and Patañjali, and their whole family, including wife of the director too, had drama as their family profession.

Dancing female figures in beautiful poses are found on some architectural fragments from Cittaurgarh at Bhīlwārā, Rajasthan, belonging to the late seventh century AD (now housed at Chittor Government Museum).[124] The dance postures are similar to that of Bharata Nāṭayam. As the rudimentary form of this dance style was already fixed during Bharata's time, it may be possible that the female dancers depicted on the above-mentioned fragments represent *naṭīs*, well-versed in the classical style of theatrical arts.

Since the present study confines itself only up to the seventh century AD, it takes only a cursory glance at the tradition of the female theatre artistes (professionals) which continued even in the later periods. In early medieval period, during Rājpūt rule, the spacious assembly halls of temples suggest that dance

122. *Cilappadikāram*, pp. 265-67.

123. *Ratnāvalī*, Prastāvanā.

124. Chittor, Government Museum no. 389, CIH 311; Chittorgarh, State Museum, No. 821 and 87, CIH, 401. See *Pls*. XXXIX, XL.

performances by the professionals in the form of ritual continued. There are many sculptures in Khajurāho temples depicting the *nāyikā* or *surasundarīs* expressing their inner feelings in graceful poses with a rare dramatic flare. It seems that in dramatising the entire psychological background of such sculptures the beautiful actresses and dancers performing in the temple on festive occasions would have been the source of inspiration for the skilled sculptors and may have provided a wide range of subject. There are many comic scenes also: for instance, in one of them the beard of a clown is being pulled by a woman,[125] which reminds us of the *vidūṣaka-ceṭī* combination.

In Orissa, at Sun Temple, Koṇārka, several female musicians are depicted in attractive postures.[126] South Indian temples belonging to the twelfth century AD such as Mārkaṇḍ Temple, Andhra Pradesh and temples at Belūr depict female musicians playing drums, flutes or some string instruments in beautiful poses. Some of them exhibit refined dance postures.[127] They all suggest the existence of professional dancers whose postures were copied by the sculptors in stone. Perhaps, the songs and music of female artistes from Kaliṅga were quite famous in early medieval period, as Bilhari inscription[128] states that Kalacuri king Yuvarājadeva was fond of the charming songs of the women of Kaliṅga.

Professional Actress from Royal Harem (Antaḥpura)

Besides the above-mentioned professional types of actresses, there is one very important type mentioned in our ancient literature and depicted in sculptures and paintings. This type of professional actress was associated with *antaḥpura* of the royal palace.

Bharata has specifically mentioned this type as a separate class, referring to her as *nāṭakīyā* and *nartakī*.[129] The description of *nāṭakīyā* he gives is that of a perfect actress who is bestowed with natural qualities of physical beauty, sweet nature and charming voice and who has proper training in music and acting. Similarly, the qualities of *nartakīs*, too, are described

---

125. Vidya Prakash, *Khajurāho*, p. 80.
126. R.J. Mehta, *op. cit.*, pl. 84, 86.
127. *Ibid.*, pls, 71, 73, 79.
128. H.C. Ray, *Dynastic History of Northern India*, vol. II, p. 760.
129. *NŚ*, XXXIV.48-50; XXXIV.32.

> women who excel by their beauty, are conversant with the sixty-four arts and crafts, courteous in behaviour, inured to hard work, skilled in dancing and songs, etc., are *nartakīs*.[130]

In his thirty-fourth chapter, Bharata again describes *nāṭakīyā*[131] differently as

> women in the royal harem who attend all the movements of the king, should be employed, when they are proficient in performing all classes of dance, in the theatre under the authority of the harem.

Ghosh[132] says that it is not clear why the *nāṭakīyā* has been described again by Bharata. Babulal Shukla Shastri[133] says that perhaps, for adding additional duties to the actress, she has been described again. To us, it seems, in the background of Kauṭilya's *Arthaśāstra*, that besides *nāṭakīyā*, the entertainer of the palace, some female spies were appointed by the state who had to go training in dramatic arts so that they could perform their duties, in the guise of *nāṭakīyā,* properly and effortlessly. That is why, perhaps, she had to attend to all the movements of the king for his safety and is mentioned separately by Bharata.

However, from *Nāṭyaśāstra,* this seems certain that it was a custom of the palace to appoint actresses in *antaḥpura* who served some political purpose too besides entertaining in addition to *nāṭakīyā,* the actress. Bharata[134] tells that it was Urvaśī who had introduced *nāṭya* in the *antaḥpura* of Purūravā, the ancestor of Nahuṣa. This reference shows that the custom was quite an old one.

Dramatic activities of the royal harem is mentioned in the *Rāmāyaṇa*. We are told that when peace and order prevailed, maidens used to go about in the evenings to gardens for recreation or to witness plays performed by women.[135] The ladies of Rāvaṇa's harem are mentioned as being well-versed in the art of singing, dancing

---

130. *NŚ*, XXXIV.51-3.
131. *Ibid.*, XXXIV.78, 79.
132. Tr. of *NŚ*, p. 210.
133. *NŚ* (Chaukhamba Sans. S. Sams.), vol. IV, p. 467.
134. *NŚ*, XXXVI.60.
135. *Rāmāyaṇa*, Bāla-kāṇḍa, 22, 12-13.

and playing musical instruments.[136] Arjuna as Bṛhannalā, in *Mahābhārata*,[137] requested King Virāṭa to appoint him in his *antaḥpura* to entertain its members and to train the womenfolk of the city of Virāṭa.

From *Jātaka* literature, also, it appears that kings did have dancing girls employed in their harems. According to *Gāndhāra Jātaka*,[138] kings of Gāndhāra and Videha were great friends. When the former renounced his kingdom and took to religious life, the latter too, gave up his large kingdom with 'sixteen thousand villages with storehouse filled and sixteen thousand dancing girls'.

Similarly, in *Kummāsapiṇḍa Jātaka,*[139] a *bodhisattva* born in a poor family gave his breakfast of four portion of sour gruel to four *pacceka buddha*s and in consequence, was born in the royal family of Vārāṇasī. There in his court he was attended by many people including troupes of dancing girls. In *Mahājanaka Jātaka*[140] also, in the palace, where people of his kingdom gathered in order to present offering to Mahājanaka, there were ministers, brāhmaṇas, wealthy merchants and beautiful dancing girls. Again, when he decided to lead an ascetic's life, it is said that he stopped to behold the dancers. In *Campeya Jātaka*[141] too, Sumanā, the wife of serpent king Campeya, offered 'sixteen thousand women gay with jewel and with ring' among many other things to the king of Kāśī, begging her husband's release. When Ugrasena, the king of Kāśī, visited Campeya's palace 'celestial harps made melody and fair serpent maidens danced'.

Some Jain texts, too, indicate that it was a custom to employ female theatre artistes in the *antaḥpura* of the palace. According to the story of *Kṣatriya Jamāli*, music was played in the uppermost storey of his palace and beautiful damsels presented thirty-two types of drama.[142]

We have seen that Kauṭilya too has mentioned such women artistes who were appointed to perform espionage work, besides entertaining. In connection with such

136. *Rāmāyaṇa*, Sundara-kāṇḍa, 10.32.37 to 45.
137. *Mahābhārata*, Virāṭa-Parva, 2.27-29.
138. E.B. Cowell, *op. cit.*, vol. III, p. 222.
139. *Ibid.*, p. 246.
140. *Ibid.*, vol. VI, pp. 28-29.
141. *Ibid.*, pp. 285-88.
142. *Dhammakahāṇuyoga*, Skandh V, Ninhava Kathānaka, Sūtra 2, p. 3.

women he mentions *Aditikauśikastriyaḥ*. Though the term *kauśika,* like the term *aditi,* is very controvertial, according to V. Raghavan,[143] they were a class of women devoted to dramatic art, employed in courts and engaged in aiding love affairs, as seen earlier in this chapter. He cites the example of *paṇḍitā kauśikī* mentioned in *Mālavikāgnimitram* who was well-versed in the art of dance, acting and toilette[144] and was there in the royal household of Agnimitra. Similarly, *paṇḍitā* of *Triṣaṣṭiśalākā-puruṣa-carita*[145] was the nurse of lady *Śrīmatī*. In the background of *aditikauśikastriyaḥ* of *Arthaśāstra* and *paṇḍitā kauśikī* of *Mālavikāgnimitram*, the term (or the name) *paṇḍitā* of *Triṣaṣṭiśalākā-puruṣa-carita* seems significant. Was it a common name instead of being a proper one and does it indicate that picture showing women (*aditi* of *Arthaśāstra* and *paṇḍitā* of *Triṣaṣṭiśalākā-puruṣa*) were well-versed in the arts of music and acting too? This is because we know that *maṅkhas* used to describe the pictures drawn on their scroll with the help of song and music in a very attractive manner. Do the terms *aditikauśikastriyaḥ*, *paṇḍitā kauśikī* together with *paṇḍitā* suggest that picture showing women had sound knowledge of theatrical arts and were appointed in the courts as a companion to the members of the harem and to do espionage work too if necessary?

From Bhāsa's play *Pratimānāṭakam,* we get comparatively more detailed information regarding such professional actresses. In the first act of the play, *pratihārī* asks a *cheṭī sārasikā* to go to the *saṅgītaśālā* and ask the actors to be ready for presenting a suitable play on occasion of Rāma's coronation.[146] This shows that in *antaḥpura* there used to be a *saṅgītaśālā* where dramas were performed. Moreover, this *saṅgītaśālā* had a rich *nepathya* (property storehouse?) in charge of a woman Āryā Rewā whose designation was *nepathyapālinī* and whose duty it was to keep the property in good condition. This *nepathya* had stage property and costumes stored in it as we know from the same play. *Avadātikā*, the *antaḥpura* attendant, brings a *valkal* and on Sītā's inquiry she explains that as Āryā Rewā, the incharge of *nepathya*, did not give a leaf of Aśoka tree, which was no longer required on the stage, she took this *valkal* instead.[147] This clearly shows the nature of the

143. V. Raghavan, 'On the meaning of the word *Kauśika*', *J.O.R.* Madras, vol. XV, p. 116.

144. *KG*, pp. 113-14.

145. *Triṣaṣṭiśalākā-puruṣa-carita* I.650, *Jain Jātaka*, Lahaura, 1925, p. 69.

146. *Pratimānāṭakam*, Act I, *BNC*, vol. II, p. 15.

147. *Ibid.*, pp. 18-19.

duties of professional actresses in *antaḥpura*. The term *āryā* used for Rewā, the in-charge of *nepathya*, indicates her respectable status and knowledge of the art too.

From Bhāsa's *Pratijñāyaugandharāyaṇa,* we infer that in such *saṅgītaśālās* of royal harems female musicians having mastery over the art were appointed. Vāsavadattā used to learn the art of playing *vīṇā* from a *vaitālikā*.[148] *Vaitālikā* is a feminine form of *vaitālika*, the well-known male musician and reciter. This reference confirms that female artistes excelled in this field of the art too.[149]

Aśvaghoṣa, in *Buddhacarita,* mentions *antaḥpura* artistes. When Siddhārtha's father, reflecting that the prince 'must see nothing untoward that might agitate his mind', assigned him a dwelling in the upper storeys of the palace, he was entertained there by female musicians and dancers, their art rivalling those of the beautiful *apsaras*es.[150] Such scenes are depicted in contemporary art of Gāndhāra. A relief represents Prince Siddhārtha being entertained by female artistes of *antaḥpura*. He is shown as reclining on a couch, and listening to female musicians playing the harp, the flute and the drum.[151] Aśvaghoṣa while describing the *mahābhiniṣkramaṇa* (renunciation) of Buddha gives a vivid description of *antaḥpura* attendants and female musicians who slowly fell into deep slumber. He says,

> One, as she lay there, supported her cheek on an unsteady hand, as if angry, abandoned the flute in her lap, dear though it was to her,[152] another lying with her bamboo pipe in her hand and her white robe slipping off her breasts, resembled a river with lotuses.[153]

This shows the existence of female artistes in the form of musicians in *antaḥpura*.

This description of Aśvaghoṣa, too, probably had inspired the Gāndhāra sculptors. In a relief, the top section shows Siddhārtha as reclining on a couch being entertained by female attendants with music and dance. The lady seated on the edge of the

---

148. *Pratijñāyaugandharāyaṇa*, Act II; *Ibid*., vol. II, p. 52.

149. The existence of *naṭī*, *gāyanā*, *kuśīlavā*, *aditi* (*maṅkha*) and *kauśika-strī* had already been noticed.

150. *Buddhacharita*, II.30; V.45, ed. Johnston.

151. See *Pl*. XXIX.

152. *Buddhacarita*, V.48.

153. *Ibid*., V.49.

couch is undoubtedly Yaśodharā, Buddha's wife. The lower section represents the great *mahābhiniṣkramaṇa*. In this scene female musicians of *antaḥpura* are depicted as sleeping in almost similar manner as described by Aśvaghoṣa, and Siddhārtha is ready to leave the palace. A female musician is depicted as reclining over her drum, resembling modern *ḍholak*, another is dozing and is resting her head on a *ḍholak* in her lap. These figures represent *antaḥpura* artistes.[154]

A similar relief has been found from Jamālgarhī. The upper part of the fragment shows Yaśodharā as sleeping on a couch, guarded by a Yavanī, behind whom four female musicians are crowded. The flutist and the harpist seem to be playing, but the drummer is fast asleep.[155]

The scene represents an old tradition of India, according to which the court or *antaḥpura* musicians sang and played musical instruments when the royalty went to bed and also, to wake them up in the morning.

A panel from Gāndhāra, housed at Chandigarh, Government Museum and Art Gallery, depicts *antaḥpura* musicians outside the bed chamber of Siddhārtha and Yaśodharā, providing such music for them (see *Pl.* XXVI).

Another scene of the same nature is depicted on a relief found in Kafirkot. It shows a Nāga king sitting on his throne and being entertained by *nāgī* musicians playing flute and lute. They also represent the *antaḥpura* artistes.[156]

Some palace scenes showing such female musicians are depicted in Veṅgī sculptures. On a fragment of a lintel, Prince Siddhārtha is shown sitting on a seat, flanked by two ladies and below them, on the floor, some women are playing lute and flute.[157] In a panel, belonging to third century AD, sleeping female musicians holding lute and harp are depicted. They seem to be the attendants of the royal harem.[158]

The custom of appointing *nāṭakīyā* in *antaḥpura* was quite common during successive periods of Indian history too. The rich tradition of dance, music and

---

154. See *Pl.* XXVIII, XXX; J. Marshall, *Buddhist Art of Gandhara*, fig. 92.
155. Ingholt Harald, *op. cit.*, pl. 41.
156. J. Marshall, *op. cit.*, pl. 56. fig. 82.
157. P.R. Ramchandra Rao, *Andhra Sculptures*, pl. CXIV, fig. 345.
158. R.J. Mehta, *op. cit.*, pl. 11, 12.

drama flowering in the palace, during the period between fourth and sixth century AD, is known from the contemporary literature. Dramatic activities of the royal harem, described by the great poet Kālidāsa, reflect the art of *antaḥpura* artistes of the Gupta period. The harem of Agnivarṇa, the pleasure loving king of Raghu dynasty, was full of capable female dancers with whom he himself played *mṛdaṅga*[159] and whom he taught three-fold acting (*āṅgika*, *vācika* and *sāttvika*).[160] Such dancers were not common folk artistes but were professionals trained under the guidance of *naṭācārya*s.[161] This shows that professional actresses and dancers who were appointed in the palace were well-trained artistes, as Bharata had described. Besides, their training or rather practising continued even after being appointed in the harem.

There were *naṭācārya*s appointed in royal herems to train the girls of the harem, as is known from Kālidāsa's *Mālavikāgnimitram*. Gaṇadāsa and Haradatta were two such *naṭācārya*s who were in charge of Mālavikā and Irāvatī respectively.[162] *Antaḥpura* had a *saṅgītaśālā* where dance competitions were held.[163]

The existence of *naṭācārya*s to train the female artistes of the harem is further confirmed by *Padmaprābhṛtakam*,[164] the Bhāna play of the Gupta period. It is said in this play that the creeper, who is the woman of *antaḥpura*, is acting on the direction of wind, who is an *ācārya*. Kālidāsa's *Vikramorvaśīya* also indicates the existence of *nāṭakīyā* as the *vidūṣaka* asks *nipuṇikā*, the *antaḥpura* attendant, 'where are you going leaving your musical recital aside'.[165] First part of *Vasudevahiṇḍī*[166] informs that the dancer at the court was known as *nadajjā* (Skt. *nāṭakīyā*) and sometimes sang and enacted popular stories through dance. Vasudeva was entertained in his house by palace dancers with the story of a caravan.

The *antaḥpura* entertainment of the Gupta period is depicted in sculptures and paintings of the age. A relief, housed at the Archaeological Museum, Gwalior,[167]

159. *Raghuvaṁśa*, XIX.13, 14, *KG*, p. 16.
160. *Ibid.*, XIX.36. *Ibid.*, p. 163.
161. *Raghuvaṁśa*, XIX.14. *Ibid.*, p. 161.
162. *Mālavikāgnimitram*, Act I, *Ibid.*, pp. 186-88.
163. *Ibid.*, *KG*, pp. 196, 198-99.
164. *Caturbhāṇī*, p. 2.
165. *Vikramorvaśīya*, Act, II, *KG*, p. 117.
166. *Vasudevahiṇḍī*, p. 282. A.P., Jamkhedkar, *Vasudeva-Hiṇḍī: A Cultural Study*, p. 108.
167. V.S. Agrawal, *Gupta Art*, pl. I, fig. 1.

depicts such dance performed by a female dancer, who is almost in a trance. Such dance performances by female artistes depicted in sculptures belonging to the earlier period had already been noticed, but the difference between this and the earlier examples lies in the style of dance, which had now clearly taken a classical form. The dancer is clad in an almost Bharata Nāṭyam style of *sārī* and a scarf is properly tied to her left shoulder which very decently covers her breasts too. Most likely, the dance is in the Bharata Nāṭyam style which demands measured, harmonious movements. According to Goetz,[168] this style of dancing which is still preserved in south Indian temples was already fully developed in its basic approach and movements in the Gupta age. One more advancement, in the performance, noticed in the panel is the provision of stuffed round cushions for the members of the orchestra who are all women. This shows that the scene represents a musical dance performance (*saṅgītaka*) by a skilled *nāṭakīyā* appointed in the *antaḥpura* who is entertaining the lady of honour, the woman depicted on the extreme left holding a lotus flower (*līlākamala*).[169]

Dancing in the same classical style is shown in an episode of the *Mahājanaka Jātaka*, painted on the left wall of cave 1, Ajantā, belonging to the Gupta period.[170] The dancer is wearing a skirt-like dress and a full-sleeved jacket of some embroidered stuff. Her ornaments include rich jewels and a crown. A pillared pavilion is seen in the background, indicating a dance performance of professional dancers, mentioned earlier in this chapter. The dancer is accompanied by a female orchestra having *tablās* (tympanum drum), *mṛdaṅgam*, a guitar-like instrument and two flutes. The pose of the dancer is very graceful: the curves of arms, wrists and hands suggest an emotional intensity, evidently in accord with the movement of the other parts of the body. This shows that the dance is being performed by a professional dancer representing classical style. The background of the scene indicates that the performance is being held in a palace.

In the same cave, there is another dance scene depicted on the left wall of the front gallery. The performance is shown as taking place in a royal pavilion in which a *nāga* king and queen are seated on a cushion in a mood of dalliance. The step of the dancer near the royal couple is not clear because she has moved behind the

168. H. Goetz, *Five Thousand Years of Indian Art*, p. 99.

169. V.S. Agrawala, *op. cit.* p. 103, pl. I, fig.

170. G. Yazdani, *op. cit.*, p. 780, pl. LX (a).

cushion but her raised arms, and the hand in which she holds a short stick, indicate that she is still dancing. The principal dancer may be seen near the feet of the *nāga* queen. The lower part of the dancer's body is damaged in the original painting, but the right hand placed on the hip and the right leg bent at the knee raised up to the knee of the left can easily be made out, and suggest that 'the dancer had poised herself on the feet, in readiness for a sinuous undulating movement'.[171] The two dancers of this painting, too, represent classical tradition of professional court artistes.

It seems that girls having a natural talent for dramatic art were brought up in the *antaḥpura* of the palace, and special training was provided for them. The royal family was always eager to witness their masterly performance. This tradition is known from Kālidāsa's *Mālavikāgnimitram.*[172] From Bāṇa's *Kādambarī*[173] also we know that at the palace of Ujjayanī there was such an arrangement. From the same source, we infer that the uppermost storey (*saudha*) of the palace, also known as *prāsāda kukṣī*, was the place where the king, with a few selected friends, used to witness *antaḥpura saṅgītaka* (dance and music performance of *antaḥpura* artistes), with the orchestra consisting of lute, flute, *mr̥daṅga*, etc.[174] We have already noticed that this practice is referred to in Jain literature also;[175] hence, it seems that this was an old tradition continued through the ages in the country.

It appears that there existed a full-fledged theatre in the harem of the palace during Harṣa's time because in his *Priyadarśikā* we get a rather conventional description where it is related that it was a lovely place with garden, columns adorned with hundreds of jewels, etc., and the *antaḥpura* professionals performed not only dance and music but a proper drama *Udayanacarita*, there on the stage.[176] This indicates that they were trained to take part in dramas too. Kālidāsa had also mentioned a few centuries ago that Mālavikā learnt *pañcāṅgābhinaya* under the

171. G. Yazdani, *op. cit.*, p. 780-1.
172. *Mālavikāgnimitram*, Act, I, *KG*, p. 188.
173. V.S. Agrawala, *Kādambarī ek sānskr̥tika adhyayana*, p. 104.
174. *vīṇāveṇumurajamanoharamantaḥpurasaṅgītakaṁ dadarśa* — V.S. Agrawala, *op. cit.*, p. 65.
175. *Dhammakahānayog*, Skandh 5, Ninhava Kathanak, Sūtra 2, p. 3.
176. *Priyadarśikā*, Act III, p. 52-68, tr. C.K. Nariman.

guidance of her *ācārya*[177] and in seventh century AD, we find a proper drama being performed by *antaḥpura* professionals. Thus, it seems that their training was that of a perfect actress.

The *antaḥpura* artistes performed on special occasions also — for example, birth of the royal heir. When Candrāpīḍa was born,[178] the belles of the harem danced and the whole atmosphere reverberated with the tinkling sound of their *ghuṅgharū* bells. The same happened when Harṣa was born.[179]

The professional actresses appointed at the harem were not merely performing artistes, but some of them excelled in their art and held the post of directors too. Bāṇa tells that Mukulikā was the *sūtradhārī* of Queen Rājaśrī's plays.[180] Since the plays in *antaḥpura* were performed by female artistes, it is quite natural that they were directed by a female director.

The tradition of *antaḥpura* artistes was, in fact, never out of vogue in India. This age-old tradition continued even after the period under consideration. Second part of *Vasudevahiṇḍī* (generally considered as written in eighth century AD) informs that music, dance, drama, Bhāṇa, telling stories, etc., were among the pastimes of *antaḥpura*.[181] Rājaśekhara in his *Viddhaśālabhañjikā*[182] refers to Kalakaṇṭhī, the actress appointed in the *antaḥpura* in the service of the queen.

The custom of keeping dancing girls in the royal court was so deep-rooted in the mind of the people of the eleventh and the twelfth century AD that even a great scholar and religious preceptor like Hemacandra writes that his royal disciple Kumārapāla used to be surrounded by a few good dancing girls in his court.[183]

Courtesan Actress

Among the female contributors to dramatic art, the name of *gaṇikā* or courtesan comes next to the professional actress. Her profession demanded skill in music —

177. *Mālavikāgnimitram*, Act I, *KG*, p. 188.
178. V.S. Agrawala, *op. cit.*, p. 82.
179. *Harṣacarita*, pp. 222-27, ed. Jagannath Pathak.
180. *nikaṭe nāṭaka sūtradhārī — Harṣacarita*, p. 248, text p. 247.
181. Jamkhedkar, *op. cit.*, p. 110.
182. *Viddhaśālabhañjikā*, Act III, p. 103.
183. *Commentary of Dvayāśraya Kāvya of Hemachandra*, IV.38.

vocal and instrumental, dance and acting besides other fine arts and her mastery over these arts raised her demand in the field of drama. *Gaṇikā* was included in the 'panel of the judges', i.e., the experts from different fields, in whom the responsibility of judging or evaluating the artistic qualities, merits and demerits of a performance was vested by Bharata.[184] This shows the prestigious position held by *gaṇikā* in the field of drama. Besides, Bharata had mentioned her together with other people associated with dramatic arts; this also shows her importance in the sphere of drama. According to Bharata,

> a woman who is always engaged in attending the teacher (*ācārya*) in connection with application of various arts and crafts, is endowed with amorous movements, emotions (*hāva*), feeling (*bhāva*), temperament (*sāttva*), sweetness of manner and is conversant with the sixty-four arts and crafts, is free from female diseases, is clear in her speech, clever and undaunted by fatigue is called a *gaṇikā* (courtesan).[185]

This leaves no doubt that a courtesan was an accomplished artiste, especially in the field of dramatic arts.

Existence and contributions of courtesans to dramatic arts is known since the time of *Ṛgveda*. *Saman,* the delightful, popular festival of the Vedic period, was marked by dance, music, archery, recitation, etc., and courtesans visited this festival to make profit on the occasion, obviously by exhibiting their art.[186] Besides, in a Vedic ritual *Mahāvrata*, a *brahmacārī* and a harlot exchanged abuses which were in a dialogue form.[187] This ritual probably had its origin in the fertility cult. Representing sexuality, the harlots radiate luck and prosperity. This was the reason why they were so often present at festivals, fertility ceremonies, religious holy days, etc., since the Vedic times. Besides their own profession which demanded a sound knowledge of dance, music and acting, their demand in such dramatic rituals and festivals also associated them with theatrical arts. Thus, the association of courtesan with theatrical arts goes back to the Vedic period as these two references indicate.

---

184. *NŚ*, XXVII.63.
185. *Ibid.*, XXXV.81-3.
186. *Ṛgveda*, IV.58.8; VI.75, 4; X.168.2.
187. A.B. Keith, *Śaṅkhyāyana Āraṇyaka*, p. 72.

In epic literature, courtesans are mentioned as beautifully dressed women in whom the responsibility of entertaining guests and soldiers was vested. In Udyoga-Parva,[188] courtesans are described as coming out to welcome Kṛṣṇa when he came on a mission of peace to the Kaurava court. Here, they are called *kalyāṇyaḥ* (those who are auspicious). In the same Parva, when the Pāṇḍava armies were about to start for battle, it is said that carts, markets and courtesans also accompanied them.[189]

From *Rāmāyaṇa* it seems that courtesans entertained the honoured guests during great sacrifices, because Vasiṣṭha called *naṭa*, *nartaka* and courtesans together with other artistes and ordered them to be ready for the performance of *aśvamedha* sacrifice by King Daśaratha.[190] Their duty on the occasion must have been entertainment, it seems. Again, while giving instructions to Lakṣmaṇa for the preparation of *aśvamedha*, Rāma asks him to send beautiful young maidens (courtesans), well in advance on the site of the sacrifice.[191] At the time of Rāma's coronation also, *tālāvacāra*s (dancers) and *gaṇikā*s bedecked in beautiful attire were present. Their presence on such occasions was necessary because they were considered as 'object of luck' and also because they made the occasion delightful by their performance. Their association with dance and music is known from the story of sage Ṛṣyaśṛṅga who was charmed by the beauty and art of singing of the courtesans.[192] Because courtesans were the custodians of art, kings felt proud in having them in their capital: this we gather from Lakṣmaṇa's statement who nostalgically remembering his beautiful home Ayodhyā, proudly says that it is adorned with beautiful courtesans.[193]

Courtesans as the custodians of art were known during sixth century BC also. Among Licchavis it was a custom to appoint the most beautiful girl of their race as *gaṇikā* who was known as *nagaraśobhanī* or *janapada kalyāṇī* and was regarded highly respectable.[194] One of the most famous *gaṇikā* was Ambapālī, whose invitation

188. *Mahābhārata*, Udyoga-Parva, 86, 15.
189. *Ibid.*, 151, 58.
190. *Rāmāyaṇya*, Bāla-kāṇḍa, 13, 7-8.
191. *Ibid.*, Uttara-kāṇḍa, 91.22.
192. *Ibid.*, Ayodhya-kāṇḍa, III.17.
193. *Ibid.*, Ayodhya-kāṇḍa, 51.21.
194. A.L. Basham, *The Wonder that was India*, p. 184.

Lord Buddha accepted without hesitation. Besides being extremely beautiful Ambapālī was known for her knowledge of dance and music, too. On festivals like *Chaṇa* and *Sabbarattivro,*[195] Ambapālī together with her few selected admirers and retinue joined the festival procession, singing and playing musical instruments.[196]

Some other courtesans are mentioned in Jain literature who had nice palatial residence indicating their prosperity. In *Rājapraśneyī Sūtra,*[197] the story of *ayohāraka* (one who carries iron) is narrated, wherein it is said that the friends of *ayohāraka* sold their pieces of diamonds and became wealthy. When they came back to their own city they spent their time comfortably witnessing thirty-two types of drama embellished with dance and music, performed by the beautiful damsels (*varataruṇī*s) at the upper storey of the beautiful palace.[198] These *varataruṇī*s seem to be the courtesans and not professional actresses because they are not mentioned as performing on the stage in public; instead people themselves visited their luxurious houses to witness their performance, as it happens in the case of courtesans generally. Their dwelling place indicates their comfortable life and thirty-two types of plays performed by them indicate their knowledge of drama, hence it seems that they belonged to the *gaṇikā* class of courtesans.

It appears that there was great demand for the dramas performed by *gaṇikā*s, and they were specially invited to perform the same on festive occasions. Śreṇika, to celebrate the birth of his son, asked eighteen *śreṇī*s to arrange the performance of plays with *gaṇikā*s as main characters.[199] Similarly, King Mahābala also ordered dance dramas by the best courtesans to be staged on the birth of his son.[200] Some highly accomplished *gaṇikā*s are mentioned by name, for example, Devadattā,[201]

---

195. *Dhammapadaṭṭhakathā* (PTS), vol. III, pp. 466, 279, 280.; B.C. Law, 'The Licchavis in ancient India', *Journal and Proceedings, Asiatic Society of Bengal*, New Series, vol. XVII, 1921, p. 266.
196. Divakar, *Bihar through the Ages*, p. 173.
197. *Rājapraśneyī Sūtra*, 267, p. 195.
198. We have seen that dance and drama was performed at the uppermost storey of the royal palace, too, called *prāsādakukṣī* during Bāṇa's time.
199. *Dhammakahāṇuyoga*, Skandh II, Meghakumāra Samaṇe, Sūtra 321, p. 159.
200. *Ibid.*, Skandha VI, Prakīrṇakakathānaka, Sūtra 250, p. 116.
201. *Dhammakahāṇuyoga*, Sūtra 108, p. 52.

the *gaṇikā* residing in the city of Campā. She had mastery over sixty-four arts, had all the sixty-four merits or qualities of a *gaṇikā*, was well-versed in eighteen languages and so on. The king himself had provided her with *chatra* (umbrella), *cāmara* (flywhisk) and *vijana* (fan). This, perhaps, indicates the custom, which is indicated by Buddhist literature, too, according to which an accomplished courtesan was appointed as *gaṇikā* by the state itself.

During Kauṭilya's time also *gaṇikā*s were appointed by the state, the chief criterion of the selection being proficiency in dance and music — vocal and instrumental, besides youth and beauty. In *Gaṇikādhyakṣa Prakaraṇa,*[202] he says that the superintendent of prostitutes should employ a woman noted for her beauty, youth and accomplishments, on a salary of one thousand *paṇa*s per annum to work as *gaṇikā*. Half of their salary should be given to their family. She could leave the service of the king only after giving twenty-four thousand *paṇa*s to him. Kauṭilya enjoins[203] that the king should provide the means of livelihood to persons who teach various arts including singing, playing musical instruments, dancing, acting and prostitution, etc., to *gaṇikā*s, *dāsī*s and actresses. This shows that dance, music and acting were included in the training of *gaṇikā*s who, like professional actresses, mastered these arts under the guidance of *ācārya*s. Thus, there was not much difference between a *naṭī* and a *gaṇikā,* profession wise. Dancing and acting style of *gaṇikā*s during Kauṭilya's time represented classical tradition. Kauṭilya[204] further says that the son of *gaṇikā* should be made the chief of the actors (*raṅgopajīvī*) and actors expert in *tāla* (*talavacāra*s). This also indicates the close association of *gaṇikā* with drama. Her son was considered the most suitable person to be appointed to that post because he had a suitable theatrical background provided by his talented mother.

It seems that *gaṇikā*s were trained by skilled *naṭācārya*s during Bhāsa's time too, following the tradition known from Kauṭilya. Courtesan Vasantasenā, the heroine of Bhāsa's play *Cārudattam,* was trained in stage-craft under the guidance of *naṭācārya*s. This seems certain when we read the play. While chasing Vasantasenā,

---

202. *KA*, *Gaṇikādhyakṣa Prakaraṇa*, 43.27.

203. *KA*, *Gaṇikādhyakṣa Prakaraṇa*, II.43.27.

204. *gaṇikāputrān raṅgopajīvinaśca mukhyam niṣpādayeyuḥ sarvatālāvacārāṇām* ।
— *Ibid.*, II.43.27

in the first act, Viṭa says[205] that she is changing her gait every now and then as she is an expert in the art of dance. In the same act, Viṭa warns Śakāra against leaving her hand, taking her as someone else, because she has been trained in changing her voice and is expert in the art of stage appearance.[206] Lastly, Śakāra specifically describes Vasantasenā as *nāṭakastrī* and *gaṇikādārikā*, i.e., an actress who is the daughter of a *gaṇikā*, in the same act.[207] All these references show that *gaṇikā*s during Bhāsa's period were great custodians of dramatic art. They received proper training under the guidance of *ācārayas* in various aspects of drama, such as dance, voice modulation and stage appearance.

Gradually, courtesan, a well-known figure in the field of drama, became the symbol of female sophistication and ideal qualities. This made the author of *Lalitavistara*[208] say that Siddhārtha wanted his wife to be as knowledgeable and accomplished in arts as a *gaṇikā*.

An inscription from Mathurā, belonging to first century AD,[209] records the construction of a residence of *śramaṇa*s, a small *arhat* temple, seats for *ācārya*s and a slab of stone by a *gaṇikā* named Nādā, who describes herself as the daughter of the *gaṇikā*, Dandā, the *leṇaśobhikā*. Here the terms *gaṇikā* and *leṇaśobhikā* are important for our study. The word *śobhika*, we have already noticed in the previous chapter, stands for theatre artiste, most probably an 'actor' in the well-known passage of *Mahābhāṣya*. Hence the word *śobhikā*, the feminine form of *śobhika*, would mean an actress and *leṇa* means cave; thus the word *leṇaśobhikā* would mean a cave actress. Here, in this inscription, this cave actress is a *gaṇikā* (a courtesan). There seems a tradition of cave theatre in our country in ancient times. Besides so-called Sītābeṅgā cave theatre, we have several literary references too regarding theatrical

---

205. *Chārudattam*, Act I.9, *BNC*, vol. II, p. 16.

206. *eṣā raṅgapraveśena kalānāṁ caiva sikṣayā* ।
svarāntareṇa dakṣā hi vyāhartuṁ tannamuchayatāṁ ।।
—*Ibid.*, p. 33

207. . . . *nāṭakastrī vasantasenā nāma gaṇikādārikā* . . .
—*Ibid.*, p. 36

208. . . . *śāstre vidhijñān kuśalā gaṇikā yathaiva* . . . .
—*Lalitavistara*, *Śilpasandarśaparivarta*, 350

209. *IA*, vol. XXXIII, p. 152.

activities in caves. Thus, it seems correct as Lüders[210] thinks that *leṇaśobhikā* was the special designation of courtesans who performed mimic representation in caves, such as one described by Bloch.[211] Thus, this inscription further confirms the association of *gaṇikā*s or courtesans with theatre during the first century AD.

While discussing Kuṣāṇa art of Mathurā, V.S. Agrawala[212] says that among Madraka Yavanas it was a custom to arrange Bacchanalian parties full of dance and music associated with the cult of Bacchus, mostly at the dwelling place of rich citizens or hetaera type of courtesans. The popular Kubera worship adopted this form of ritual. Bacchanalian scenes from Mathurā depict such *goṣṭhī*s (parties) at *veśavāsa* (courtesan's house). One such slab depicting Bacchanalian scene, belonging to the second century AD, has been found from the village Maholi.[213] On one side of the slab, a drunken woman is seen in half kneeling posture with a child holding a drinking cup and is supported by a man by the arm to prevent her from drooping. Standing beside the damsel, according to Sivaramamurti, is 'the old *kuṭṭanī*, who certainly had once all the charms and wiles associated with girls of the *veśavāsa*'.[214] The scene depicted on the other side also confirms that the sculpture represents a Bacchanalian party held at a courtesan's house. It shows a wealthy damsel moving away from a couple of youths following her. Her opulence is suggested by an umbrella held by a girl, her attendant. The scene is taken as representing the events depicted in the first act of Śūdraka's *Mṛcchakaṭikam* by Śivarāmamūrti,[215] where 'the courtesan Vasantasenā hurries home at dusk hotly pursued by Śakāra and his friend Viṭa'. The latter says that the jingling of her anklets and fragrance of her flowers betray her even in the darkness. The position of the anklets of the damsel in the sculpture and her attempt to cover her braid clearly show that she is courtesan Vasantasenā. The same event, more or less in similar style and language, has been described in Bhāsa's *Cārudattam* also.[216] Could it be possible that at the Bacchanalian parties in the house of the courtesans, which was marked by dance

---

210. *IA*, vol. XXXIV, 1905, p. 199.
211. *ASI*, *Annual Report — 1903-04*, pp. 123-27.
212. V.S. Agrawala, *Bhāratīya Kalā*, p. 257.
213. See *Pls*. XXI, XXII.
214. C. Sivarammurti, *Indian Sculpture*, p. 37.
215. *Ibid*., pp. 37-38; See *Pl*. XXI.
216. *Cārudattam*, Act I. 18, *BNC*, vol. II, p. 26.

and music, dramas, too, were performed? This sculpture probably depicts both, such gathering and performance, the former on the front and the latter on the back of the slab. What could be a more favourite drama for courtesans than the story of a courtesan's love affair, i.e., Bhāsa's *Cārudattam*.

It seems that courtesans were associated with theatre throughout the country during this period because *gaṇikās*, well-trained in dramatic arts, were the most suitable female artistes for playing female parts in the plays. Besides the wives of the actors, they were the only easily available actresses who could perform any role without hesitation. Their training in the field by the proficient *ācāryas*, at least since the times of Kauṭilya and Bhāsa, polished and modified their art which was necessary for their original profession also and thus, they gradually became the representatives of the classical tradition of dance, music and drama.

From *Cilappadikāram* we gather that in south too the courtesans excelled in theatrical arts which were highly advanced during this period, as is apparent from the details provided in the text concerning the arts. Mātavī, the charming courtesan of the city of Pumpukār, underwent training for seven years in dance, song and grace of form, succeeding in all the three; and at the age of twelve she was in a position to display her talents before the king. She was trained by a skilled teacher having a thorough knowledge of the art including the characteristics of the two schools of the dance: *deśī* (secular) and *mārga* (orthodox).[217] She had a separate teacher for music, an authority in the art of dramaturgy. She had knowledge of the two branches, *Vettiyal* (the branch relating to *akam* in the dramatic composition) and *Potuviyal* (the branch relating to *puram* in dramatic works), and exhibited it in her composition.[218] While performing, she was accompanied by an orchestra — consisting of *mṛdaṅgam*, flute, lute, pot and the vocalist. Her dance was perfect and scientifically correct.[219] This description shows that in south too, the courtesan actresses represented classical style of dance and drama, though having a knowledge of folk (*deśī*) style as well. In the tradition of Kauṭilya, they were trained by the *ācāryas* and they performed in the court on festive occasions accompanied by an orchestra. Here, also the courtesan seems to be a full-fledged actress having a sound knowledge of dramatic arts. The courtesans were probably invited to perform on

217. *Cilappadikāram*, Canto III, pp. 104-5.

218. *Ibid.*, pp. 106-7.

219. *Ibid.*, pp. 112-13.

religious festivals as Mātavī was on the occasion of *Talaikkol*,[220] a festival held in honour of Jayanta, the son of Indra.

This might have been the case in the Deccan too, it seems. At Nāgārjunakoṇḍa, a unique structure belonging to second or third century AD has been discovered by archaeologists.[221] On the basis of its architectural features, it is known as 'Nāgārjunakoṇḍa amphitheatre'. On entering the arena, to the right, there were some stone benches, one of them having an inscription on it, reading *kāmasara* or 'arrow of love'.[222] H.V. Sharma[223] thinks that it sounds like a Buddhist name of a person of either sex, while Varadpande[224] says that it might have been the name of the dancer or a leader of the dancing troupe attached to the theatre. To us, it seems the name of a courtesan-dancer, as the meaning of the name itself suggests, who probably used to perform in the theatre. Since the engraving of the inscription is not professional,[225] it seems that it was inscribed by one of the admirers of *kāmasara* and thus indicates her popularity. But it is only a conjecture, because nothing can be said on the basis of only such a short inscription like *kāmasara*.

In the period between fourth and sixth century AD, the age of cultural awareness, we have ample evidence, literary and sculptural, of the contributions of courtesans to theatrical arts. During this period, dance, music and drama were considered as the parts of *vaiśika śikṣā* (training of the courtesans). Vātsyāyana in his *Kāmasūtra* says that a courtesan must learn the sixty-four arts which include music — vocal and instrumental, dance, knowledge of drama and stories.[226] He further says that a courtesan endowed with character, beauty and virtues attains an honoured place in the society and acquires the rank of *gaṇikā*, if she is an expert at these sixty-four arts. This indicates that the *gaṇikā* enjoyed an honourable place in society for her deep knowledge of the sixty-four arts including drama. Vātsyāyana[227] clearly

---

220. *Cilappadikāram*, pp. 111-12.
221. *IA, 1954-55 — A review*, p. 22 Nāgarjunakoṇḍa.
222. *Ibid.*, p. 22.
223. H.V. Sharma, *The Theatre of the Buddhists*, p. 54.
224. M.L. Varadpande, *Traditions of Indian Theatre*, p. 63.
225. H.V. Sharma, *op. cit.*, p. 54.
226. *Kāmasūtra*, (tr S.C. Upadhyaya), III.12-20, pp. 73-78.
227. *Ibid.*, VI.VI.54-5, p. 221.

mentions *naṭī* as one of the types of courtesan. It seems that during the Gupta period courtesans were trained in various niceties of acting prescribed by Bharata, because in *Ubhayābhisārikā* of Vararūci, belonging to the Gupta period, Viṭa describes the accomplishments of *gaṇikā,* Priyaṅgusenā in the field of drama which gives an idea about the syllabus of their training in dramatic arts. She had command over four types of *abhinaya* (expressions of acting), thirty-two types of hand gestures, eighteen types of glances (expression with the eyes), six types of static postures, three types of gaits, eight *rasas* (sentiments) and three types of music — vocal and instrumental and dance.[228]

Another Bhāna play, *Padmaprābhr̥takam* of the same period, describes a *gaṇikā*, Magadhasundarī as humming a *caupadī*, song with four *padas*, named Vallabhā in a most melodious voice which was based on *ṣaḍaja grāma* (a kind of scale or *rāga*),[229] i.e., on classical *rāga*. These references indicate that in the Gupta period, too, the courtesans represented the classical tradition of theatre.

Bhāṇa *Padmaprābhr̥takam*[230] shows that *gaṇikās* were trained under the guidance of the *ācāryas*, who trained them not only in dance or music but also in drama, as was the case during Bhāsa's time. The script was sent to them beforehand by the *ācāryas* to learn it by heart. The *ācārya* was an object of great respect for the courtesans, because though Devasenā, the courtesan, was not well, she accepted the copy of the dialogue because of respect for the *ācārya*.[231]

As was the tradition in ancient India, such courtesan actresses were invited to perform dance or drama on special occasions. Varāhamihira,[232] while describing *Indradhvajotsava*, states that the roads were decorated and flanked by beautifully attired courtesans and squares were filled with actors, dancers and musicians, obviously to celebrate the occasion. When a son was born to King Dilīpa, courtesans, according to Kālidāsa's *Raghuvaṁśa*, danced to celebrate the occasion. They were

228. Vararūci, *Ubhayābhisārikā*, *Caturbhāṇī*, pp. 142-43. Some of these niceties of acting are mentioned in Bharata's *NŚ* — four types of *abhinaya* — *NŚ*, VI.23; thirty-two hand gestures — *NŚ*, IX.11-16; eighteen glances — *NŚ*, VIII.46-95 though *NŚ* has thirty-six static postures — *NŚ*, X.51; three gaits — *NŚ*, XII.XVI.

229. Śūdraka, *Padmaprābhr̥takaṁ*, *Caturbhāṇī*, p. 48.

230. *Ibid*., p. 50.

231. *Ibid*.

232. *Br̥hat-Saṁhitā*, 43.25, 26.

honoured as recognised artistes in the field of dramatic arts and were invited to perform at the royal palace for which they were paid in advance.[233]

Priyaṅgusenā, in *Ubhayābhisārikā*, was invited to the palace of Pāṭaliputra to perform *saṅgītaka purandaravijaya*.[234] The duty of welcoming honourable guests was given to the courtesans. When Kṛṣṇa reached Mathurā, courtesans together with King Ugrasena and citizens of the city came forward to welcome him and other Yādavas, as described in *Harivaṁśa*.[235] In the same text, *asura* King Vajranābha arranged *Kālotsava* (festival dedicated to *kāla*), on this occasion. Yādavas, disguised as the *naṭa*s belonging to the troupe of one Bhadranaṭa, performed a play called *Rambhābhisārā*. A beautiful *gaṇikā* from Dvārakā named Manovatī played the role of Rambhā, the heroine.[236] Earlier than this, the courtesans who had come from Dvārakā with Yādavas as *naṭī*s (actresses)[237] sang *chalikya gandharva* named *Devagandhāra*.[238] From the first part of *Vasudevahiṇḍī*, we infer that the *gaṇikā*s entertained the king or the priest performing sacrifices in the forest with dance recitals.[239]

Besides performing in the presence of the king or in the palace, courtesans were invited to do so at the residence of the royal officers too, it seems, because at a *prekṣā* held at the palace of *veśyādhyakṣa pratihāra droṇilak*, courtesan Mayurasenā performed a dance.[240] Besides such functions, courtesans were invited to perform in the temples too, as we know from *Ubhayābhisārikā*. *Gaṇikā* Madanasenā participated in a *saṅgītaka* called *Madanārādhanā* which was performed in the temple of Nārāyaṇa.[241] Such performances in temples by courtesans are suggested by the sculptures of the period also.

---

233. *Ubhayābhisārikā*, *Caturbhāṇī*, pp. 141-42.
234. *Ibid.*
235. *Harivaṁśa*, Viṣṇu-Parva, 55.12-13.
236. *Ibid.*, 92.28.
237. *Ibid.*, 92.60.
238. *Ibid.*, 93.23.
239. *Vasudevahiṇḍī* (T), pp. 101, 193.
240. Śyāmilaka, *Pādatāditakaṁ*, *Caturbhāṇī*, pp. 225-26.
241. *Ubhayābhisārikā*, *Caturvāṇī*, pp. 122-23.

Three stone panels[242] showing female dancing groups, obtained from the projections of the plinth of Devagarh temple belonging to a period between fifth and seventh century AD, are significant. As there was a tradition of inviting courtesans to the temple for performing *saṅgītaka*, these depictions may be taken as representing the same. In all the three groups, the central female figure is that of a dancer who is wearing a *svasthāna*[243] or a Scythian costume and is flanked by four female musicians holding various percussion instruments. Pratapaditya Pal is of the opinion that the dancer in the centre, in the context of the age, very likely represents a foreigner.[244] There are many references to foreign dancing girls and courtesans in the literature of the period. Bhāṇa play, *Pādatāditakam,* refers to a foreign courtesan Yavanī Karpūraturiṣṭhā, 'who used to speak in an unknown language which she uttered like a female monkey,[245] trying to explain its meaning by gesticulation'. Hence, either there was a fashion of wearing foreign dresses among dancing girls whose figures these panels depict or the central figure in these panels represent a Yavanī *gaṇikā* well-trained in the art of dance and music under the guidance of an *ācārya* who used to perform in the temples together with her companions.

The graceful dancing pose in all the three groups represents classical tradition of the art. The triangle of the dancer's legs in two of these panels[246] and hand gestures in all of them are similar to those of Bharata Nāṭyam.[247] Dancing pose of the danseuses and musical instruments played by the female figures in these panels are similar to those represented in other dance scenes depicted in sculptures and paintings of the period, referred to earlier,[248] i.e., drums, cymbals and two sticks, probably to mark the time — as it is done in Bharata Nāṭyam style of dance with the help of *taṭṭapalaḥ* and *taṭṭakaḷī* even today. Such dance scenes on the wall of the temple were probably meant as permanent dance offerings to the deity, as we

---

242. See *Pls*. XXXII, XXXIII, XXXIV.
243. V.S. Agrawala, *Gupta Art*, p. 104.
244. Pratapaditya Pal, *The Ideal Image*, p. 91.
245. *Pādatāditakaṁ*, *Caturbhāṇī*, p. 238.
246. See *Pl*. XXXII, XXXIV.
247. See *Pl*. XXII, XXXIII, XXXIV.
248. See *supra*, pp. 85, 86.

know from the literature of the period that offering dance and drama to the deity was considered a meritorious deed.

In *Saṅgītaka*, offered to the deity, first of all the instruments were played, then *devatā-maṅgala* (song in praise of god) was sung and finally the main dance started to the accompaniment of a song. It was not merely a dance performance but a sort of dance drama because it contained acting or *bhāva* part, too, as is known from *Ubhayābhisārikā*, where it is said that Priyaṅgusenā, the courtesan, was invited to perform *Purandaravijai saṅgītaka* imbibed with different *rasas*.[249] Courtesans were often invited to dance on the occasion of a sacrifice, being performed in hermitage. First part of *Vasudevahiṇḍī* says that on one of such occasions courtesans Cittasenā, Kaliṅgasenā, Anaṅgasenā and Kāmapadagā gave their performance in the spirit of Competition.[250]

It seems that not only in Brāhmaṇical but in Buddhist religious establishments of the period, too, such dances were performed representing classical tradition. At Auraṅgābād in Cave No. 7, belonging to sixth century AD on the left wall of the shrine, is an exquisitely carved panel,[251] representing a girl dancing in accompaniment of musical instruments being played by six other girls, three on each side, all deeply, engrossed in the rhythm of the dance and music. 'The big hipped moon breasted body of the dancer with slender arms and delicate fingers, is involved in dance in so ecstatic a manner that the triangle of the legs, with the phrasing of the lifted right foot, touch off rhythm itself. The coherence of the various limbs is fused into the total plastic expression of the *Bharata-Nāṭyam* pose.'[252]

The dance thus represents the classical tradition.

Amita Ray[253] is of the opinion that doctrinal and mythological change in Buddhism during this period, which had its impact at Auraṅgābād, was reflected by the philosophy of the *yogācāra* from about the fourth and fifth century AD. One of the important, though Indirect, hypothesis of *yogācāra* was that the human body

249. *Ubhayabhisārikā*, *Caturbhāṇī*, pp. 141-42.

250. *Vāsudevahiṇḍī*, 281.23; 183-25, tr. J.C. Jain.

251. See Pl. XXXVII.

252. *Marg*, vol. XVI, no. 3, Portfolio.

253. Amita Ray, 'Sculpture in Aurangabad', *Marg.*, *op. cit.*, p. 38.

was the receptacle of all intellectual, religious and spiritual experience, that all experience were but human. Such an ideology naturally tended towards bringing about some important changes in the viewing of the world. When to this was, added the doctrine of the *śakti* or the feminine energy as being integral to the *bodhisattva*, it came gradually to imply a new attitude towards women. This is reflected in the sculptures carved on the walls of Buddhist establishments, such as the one at Auraṅgābād Cave No. 7.

This new development in Buddhism, which may have changed its attitude towards theatre, was already being slowly effected by the impact of the Mahāyāna doctrine. This may be the reason why such dance scene are depicted in Buddhist caves. These depictions suggest that such dances, performed by professional artistes like courtesans invited to the temples, which was the custom of the period, had probably become part of Buddhist temple rituals.

Courtesans performed dance as part of the folk ritual too, because *Vasudevahiṇḍī* mentions a dance performance, in honour of a lake, by a Mātaṅgī girl, who looked like a mass of cloud dense just at the time of showers.[254]

Besides performing in the palace, residence of royal officers, temples — Brāhmaṇical and Buddhist, and hermitages, courtesans continued to perform in the caves during the Gupta period too, it seems, because Kālidāsa in *Meghadūta* refers to sport and frolics in a cave near Vidiśā. The *yakṣa* addresses a cloud:

> When you desire to rest, stay a while on Rāmagiri near Vidiśā . . . the caves of the mountain send out the seductive perfumes of courtesans and thus, bear witness to the youthful ardour of the citizens.[255]

Since, courtesans are referred to in literature as closely associated with theatrical arts and since caves were being used for such activities, the association of courtesans with caves is discernible. Again, in *Kumārasambhava,*[256] Kālidāsa speaks of *darīgṛha* (cave dwellings). *Vanecara* (men of the forest) would used these cave-dwellings for musical soirees with their women friends. In the fourteenth verse of the same *sarga* of *Kumārasambhava*, he says,

254. *Vasudevahiṇḍī*, tr. J.C. Jain, pp. 155-56.
255. *Meghadūtam*, *Pūrvamegha*, 27, *KG*, p. 292.
256. *Kumārsaṁbhava*, I.10, *KG*, p. 167.

> Youths and girls would frolic in these mountain caves. When, in the course of the romping, the girls, clothes were taken off, they would feel ashamed, a cloud would then suddenly stretch itself across the entrance to the cave, serving thereby as a curtain.

It seems that the description of the great poet, though containing many embellishments of imagery, are based on facts. We have already mentioned the reference to courtesan Leṇaśobhikā in a Mathurā inscription belonging to first century AD. Thus, it seems that the courtesans at the *śilāveśma* and women at *darīgṛha* mentioned by Kālidāsa probably belonged to that class of courtesans who performed in cave theatres.

There was one more important work that the courtesans did during this period, i.e., performing the duty of a *devadāsī*, probably because they were experts in the sixty-four arts. *Meghadūta*[257] of Kālidāsa refers to them at the temple of Mahākāla as *Līlāvadhu*, the bells of whose girdles jingled when they danced. It is stated that their hands ached by holding *cāmara*, as they were fanning the idol, and who would soothe their 'nail marks' with the first rain. Thus, it seems that courtesans were given the job of the part-time *devadāsī* also, though the term *devadāsī* has not been used by the poet.

Though courtesans continued to perform in public, as *gaṇikā* Rāgamañjarī had done, where she made amorous gestures to Prince Upahāravarmā in *Daśakumāracarita* of Daṇḍī,[258] in the post-Gupta period. They maintained their association with temples also, not as part-time *devadāsī*s but simply as artistes, even after the period under study. In *Kuṭṭanīmatam,*[259] we find an elaborate description of local *gaṇikā*s presenting the first act of the *Ratnāvalī* of Śrī Harṣa in honour of Samarabhaṭṭa (a prince of Devarāṣṭra) in the temple of Viśveśvara at Vārāṇasī.

Though the courtesans were still being trained under the guidance of *ācārya*s and the syllabus of their training contained *śāstra* of Bharata and Viśākhila, instrumental music (*ātodya*), dance and song,[260] they started losing that dedication

---

257. *Meghadūtam*, *Pūrvamegha*, 39, *KG*, p. 294.
258. *Daśakumāracarita*, VII, p. 87.
259. *Kuṭṭanīmatam*, verse no. 800.
260. *Ibid.*, verse 124.

and devotion towards theatrical arts which they had during the period under study, as we know from *Kuṭṭanīmatam*. The *naṭācārya*, in *Kuṭṭanīmatam*,[261] was not satisfied with his courtesan pupils for whom their other business was more important than the dramatic art.

But we have references to such *gaṇikā*s also who were embodiment of the different *śāstra*s and were talented poetesses. Rājaśekhara in his *Kāvyamīmāṁsā* says that the insight for poetry may be seen in women too, hence a *gaṇikā*, *naṭī* or a princess may be a poetess of great fame.[262] Again in the same text,[263] he gives a place, next to the poets of Bhūtabhāṣā, to *gaṇikā*s with other theatre people in the honourable *kavi samāja*.

Merutuṅga,[264] at a later date, had also referred to a hetaera of Gujarat, who pleased the Paramāra king, Bhoja. *Mānsollāsa*[265] shows that courtesans continued to be invited to the assembly of poets and scholars convened by the kings. But there is no doubt that the devotion, dedication and sobriety of earlier *gaṇikā*s in the field of art had become out of tune with the luxurious medieval aristocratic society. *Prabandhacintāmaṇi*[266] refers to a dance by a naked low woman witnessed by Parmardin of Kuntala. Thus, it seems that though the courtesans were still known for their knowledge of theatrical arts and the old custom of seeking a courtesan's presence, at the time of raising the flag staff of Indra, continued up to twelfth century AD, as is known from *Rājadharmakāṇḍa*[267] of Lakṣmīdhara, their art after the period under consideration was essentially dominated by eroticism.

Part II

Apsarases: The Celestial Dancers

Apsaras are mentioned in Indian literature right from the Vedas. In the Vedas, the

261. *Kuṭṭanīmatam*, verse 793-98.
262. *Kāvyamīmāṁsā* X, p. 132, tr. Kedarnath Sharma.
263. *Ibid.*, X, p. 55, ed. C.B. Dalas, 1924.
264. *Prabandhacintāmaṇi*, tr. Tawney, p. 186.
265. *Mānsollāsa*, II, p. 155.
266. *Prabandhacintāmaṇi*, tr. Tawney, p. 186.
267. B.P. Majumdar, *Socio-Economic History of Northern India*, p. 371.

term is used as *apsarasaḥ*, a constituent of two words — *apaḥ* and *sarasaḥ*; *apaḥ* is water and *sarasaḥ* is reservoir of water. They are referred to in *Ṛgveda* as aqueous nymphs.[268] *Ṛgveda* in general attaches the nomenclature of *asparasaḥ* to cloud. Thus, in this Veda, the relation of *apsaras*es to dance and music is not very clear. It seems that they are the deified form of water-vapour. A reference from *Śatapatha Brāhmaṇa*[269] suggests that *apsaras*es had power to change their form at will and they often appeared as acquatic birds. Warriors, who die in battle, are taken by the *apsaras*es in brilliantly coloured chariots of heaven.

In *Atharvaveda*,[270] the old belief of *apsaras*es being a water deity was preserved but some new aspects of their character were introduced. They are referred to as the wives of *gandharvas*[271] and a mystic touch is given to them in this context. The *gandharva* is referred to as the supreme soul[272] and *apsaras*es as their wives or Śaktis.[273] They have a mind-bewildering or fascinating power.[274] So, it appears that insanity was due to them.[275] *Apsaras*es were appeased and prayed for securing success in gambling.[276] In the fourth *maṇḍala* of *Atharvaveda,* the *gandharvas*, the husbands of *apsaras*es, are compared with dancing peacocks,[277] and the *apsaras*es are described as fond of dancing.[278] In connection with the charms uttered by women which created passionate yearning in the hearts of men for them, it is said that this yearning comes from *apsaras*es.[279] Thus, it seems that the vagueness in the concept of *apsaras*es which was there in the *Ṛgveda* was gradually yielding to the concept of

---

268. 'Apyā Yoṣa', *Ṛgveda*, X.10.
269. *Śatapatha Brāhmaṇa*, XI.5.1, 4.
270. *Atharvaveda*, II.2.5; IV.37.7.
271. *gandharvapatnibhyo-apsarābhyo* — *Ibid.*, II.2.5.
272. *bhuvanasyayaspatireka eva namasyovikṣvidyā* — *Ibid.*, II.2.1.
273. *Ibid.*, II.2.5.
274. *manomuhaḥ* — *Ibid.*, II.2.5.
275. *Ibid.*
276. *Ibid.*, IV. 38.1.
277. *anṛtyataḥ śikhaṇḍino gandharvasyapsarāpateḥ* — *Ibid.*, IV.37.7.
278. *Ibid.*, IV.38.13.
279. *Ibid.*, VI.130.7.

*apsaras*es as celestial dancers and wives of *gandharva*s, the celestial musicians, with their power to drive people mad by their beauty and art.

There were several religious ceremonies of the period which had ritual dance and song as an important part. For example, the *Mahāvrata* ceremony referred to earlier in which women, especially courtesans, took active part. For such rituals a class of female ritual dancer was coming into being. It seems that as ancient Indians had female artistes either as ritual dancers or entertainers they provided celestial ones to their gods. This is how the concept of *apsaras*es, the celestial dancers, who often act as the attendants of gods especially Indra, originated.

Bharata states that he applied four modes of expression, one of them was *kaiśikī vṛtti* (graceful expression) for which female artistes were needed. Brahmā then created *apsaras*es,[280] who proved themselves to be the most proficient theatre artistes[281] and maintained the tradition of drama in heaven. According to Bharata, *apsaras*es introduced the art on earth, too, as Nahuṣa says in *Nāṭyaśāstra* that it was Urvaśī who introduced drama in the *antaḥpura* of his grandfather Purūravas (*NŚ*, 36.60). Bharata gives a list of the names of the *apsaras*es. The description of *apsaras*es there also suggests that the author of *Nāṭyaśāstra* had professional female theatre artistes in mind while writing about *apsaras*es and the names of *apsaras*es given in *Nāṭyaśāstra* might have been the names of contemporary famous female theatre artistes.

Role and Functions of Apsarases and Courtesans

The role and functions of *apsaras*es in heaven were not very different from that of courtesans on earth. *Apsaras*es are described as celestial dancers who entertained gods. The entertainment of different deities in their respective assembly halls by *apsaras*es and *gandharva*s performing dance, music — vocal and instrumental, *nāṭaka* (drama), *kāvya* (poetry), *kathā* (story) and *hāsya* (comedies) is described in the *Mahābhārata*.[282] Similarly, *gaṇikā*s were appointed by the state on a fixed salary,[283] obviously for entertainment. According to Jain texts, *varataruṇī*s

280. *NŚ*, I.46, 47.
281. *Ibid.*, I.46, 47.
282. Sabhā-Parva, II.8.38; II.9.26; II.10.9-13; II.10.26; II.22.28; II.11.36.
283. *KA*, *Gaṇikādhyakṣa Prakaraṇa*, 27.1.

(courtesans) entertained people on the upper storey of their house.[284] *Kāmasūtra*[285] refers to such *goṣṭhīs* or conclave of citizens of a similar age and wealth, learning, intelligence and character who met either in the house of courtesans or at another suitable place and discussed poetry, drama and other arts as an entertainment. *Vasudevahiṇḍī*[286] also refers to such *goṣṭhīs*. *Harṣacarita* refers to *vārivilāsinīs* in the court of Harṣa.[287] The principal duty of *vārivilāsinīs* was to perform dance in royal courts and palaces. The king represented Indra, his court Indra's court and the *vārivilāsinī* women, the *apsarases*.[288]

Besides entertaining deities in their *sabhās*, *apsarases* are described as entertaining them individually too. Urvaśī accepted Purūravas as her husband for a certain period and while going away from Purūravas she says, With women there can be no lasting friendship, the heart of hyenas are the hearts of women.[289] *Apsaras* Rambhā is depicted as going to entertain Nalakūbara[290] and she tells Rāvaṇa who stopped her that she is, on principle, Nalakūbara's wife for that period. In *Cilappadikāram*,[291] Mātavī, the beautiful courtesan of Pumpukār, entertained Kovalan and considered him as her husband. Later, Sanskrit literature — *Kāmasūtra*, first part of *Vasudevahiṇḍī* and *Caturbhāṇī* — is full of such references where courtesans are described as entertaining people individually.

On the basis of the above-mentioned reference from *Rāmāyaṇa*, Projesh Banerjee says that since Rambhā told Rāvaṇa that it was her strict principle that the person whom she had decided to meet first would be her husband for that very day and none else,[292] it is quite clear that *apsarases* were not women of easy virtue as people think.[293] But to us, it is another instance of *apsarases* acting like courtesans for,

---

284. *Rājapraśneyī Sūtra*, 267.195.
285. *Kāmasūtra*, I.IV.35-6.
286. *Vasudevahiṇḍī*, Dhamila Hiṇḍī, 28.
287. *Harṣacarita*, II Ucchvāsa, 74-5.
288. V.S. Agrawala, *Gupta Art*, pp. 64-66, 91.
289. *Ṛgveda*, X.95.15.
290. *tasyāsmi kṛtasaṅketālokapālasutasya vai, temuddiṣyam ca me sarvaṁ vibhūṣanamidaṁ kṛtaṁ* — *Rāmāyaṇa*, Uttara-kāṇḍa, 26, 26.
291. *Cilppadikāram*, III.114.
292. *yathā tasya hi nānasya bhavo me pratitisthali* — *Rāmāyaṇa*, Uttarakāṇḍa, 26, 27.
293. P. Banerjee, *Apsarases in Indian Dance* p. 51.

like courtesans, Rambhā is described as having different husbands for different days. It was on principle that Rambhā would be the wife of the son of Rāvaṇa for that day.[294] Her 'principle' and sense of *dharma* (business ethics) was exactly like that of a courtesan who entertains that person first who books her first and for that day or period he is her husband or master.

The next important function of *apsaras*es, similar to that of courtesans, was to perform on occasion of sacrifice performed by pious kings. For example, they danced on occasion of the *aśvamedha* sacrifice performed by Yudhiṣṭhira[295] and King Marutta.[296] Courtesans also did the same. In *Rāmāyaṇa*, courtesans are depicted as entertaining the honoured guests during the *aśvamedha* sacrifice. Vasiṣṭha called *naṭa*, *nartaka* and *gaṇikā*s together with other artistes and ordered them to be ready for the performance of the great sacrifice by King Daśaratha. Rāma asks Lakṣmaṇa to send beautiful young maidens (courtesans) well in advance to the site of the *aśvamedha* sacrifice.[297]

Naṭa, *nartaka* and *gandharva* are often classed together, for example *naṭa*, *nartaka* and *gandharva* entertained the learned guests when King Paurava performed *aśvamedha*.[298] This also indicates that *naṭa*, *nartaka*, *gandharva* and *apsaras*es belonged to the same class and category of entertainers. It is said that the king felt proud to have *apsaras*es as well as courtesans in their capital.[299]

*Apsaras*es as well as courtesans are represented as taking part in celebrations held on such special occasions as child-birth, marriage and coronation. *Apsaras*es danced to celebrate the birth of the four sons of Daśaratha.[300]

In Uttara-kāṇḍa of *Rāmāyaṇa*, *apsaras*es danced to celebrate Rāma's coronation. There are references to the dance and drama performed by courtesans in literature on similar occasions, for example, Śreṇika, to celebrate the birth of his son, asks for

---

294. *dharmataste sutasyaham bhāryā rākṣaspuṅgava* — *Rāmāyaṇa*, Uttara-kāṇḍa, 26.23.
295. *Mahābhārata*, Aśvamedhika-Parva, Anugītā-Parva, 80.36.
296. *Ibid.*, Aśvamedhika-Parva, 1027.
297. *naryaśca bahavo nityaṁ yauvanśālinaḥ* — *Rāmāyaṇa*, Uttara-kāṇḍa, 91.22.
298. *Mahābhārata*, Droṇa-Parva, 57.4.
299. *Ibid.*, Droṇa-Parva, 61.6; *Rāmāyaṇa*, Ayodhyā-kāṇḍa, 51.21.
300. *nanr̥taścapsarogaṇaḥ* — *Rāmāyaṇa*, Bāla-kāṇḍa, 18.16.

arrangement of dramatic performances, with *gaṇikā*s as their chief characters.[301] Bāṇabhaṭṭa also refers to courtesans as dancing to celebrate the birth of Harṣa.[302]

There is a second-century BC sculptural depiction from Bharhut of four female figures with the figure of a child performing in accompaniment of an all-female orchestra.[303] They are generally taken as *apsarase*s as the names of the dancing figures are engraved on the panel — Alambuṣā, Miśrakeśī, Padmāvatī and Subhadrā. According to Lüders[304] this scene represents festivities on the occasion of Buddha's nativity.

*Apsarase*s performed on occasion of marriage of great men — for example, they danced to celebrate Rāma's marriage.[305] It was customary to invite theatre artistes on occasion of *svayaṁvara* and marriages.[306] Kālidāsa refers to the masterly representation of a play by *apsarase*s on occasion of Śiva's marriage with Pārvatī.[307]

*Apsarase*s danced to show heavenly pleasure on pious deeds of human beings, beneficial to both humanity and divinity. For example, *apsarase*s together with *gandharva*s danced and sang when Ahalyā was redeemed from her curse by Rāma,[308] as also when Indrajīt was killed by Lakṣmaṇa.[309]

There are some sculptural depictions of the performance of the *apsarase*s representing heavenly pleasure. At Bharhut,[310] four *apsarase*s, Alambuṣā, Miśrakeśī, Padmāvatī and Subhadrā, are depicted as dancing in the background of a three-storeyed building, *Vijayato prāsāde*, to celebrate *Cūḍāmaha*, a festival held in heaven to celebrate the reception of Buddha's hair there at the time of his *mahābhiniṣkramaṇa*. At Sāñcī, only one *apsaras* is seen as dancing on the occasion

---

301. *Dhammakahāṇuyoga*, Skandha II, Meghakumāra Samane, Sūtra 321, 159; Skandha VI, Prakīrṇaka Kathānaka, Sūtra 250.1186; *Bhāgavata Purāṇa*, 10, 3, 6; 4.11.
302. *Harṣacarita*, 186, 189.
303. See *Pl.* I.
304. H. Lüders, *Corpus Incriptionum Indicarem*, vol. II, Part II, *Bharhut Inscription*, p. 102.
305. *Rāmāyaṇa*, Bāla-kāṇḍa, 73, 38.
306. *Mahābhārata*, Ādi-Parva, 12.184; 16.28.
307. *Kumārasambhava*, VII.91. *KG.*
308. *Rāmāyaṇa*, Bāla-kāṇḍa, 49.20.
309. *Ibid.*, Yuddha-kāṇḍa, 9.90.66.
310. B.M. Barua, *Bharhut*, III, pl. X, II.

of this festival.[311] This continued to be a favourite subject in art and literature during later centuries, too. It is mentioned in Aśvaghoṣa's *Buddhacarita*[312] and is depicted on a relief from Gāndhāra.[313]

*Gaṇikā*s performed also on special festivals or festive occasions. In Udyoga-Parva of *Mahābhārata*[314] courtesans are described as coming out to welcome Kṛṣṇa when he came on a mission of peace to the Kaurava court. In Buddhist literature, *gaṇikā*s (*janapada kalyāṇī*) are mentioned taking active part in festivals as we have already seen in the 'courtesan' section. *Gaṇikā*s were invited to dance on such special occasions as appearance of *Vaijayanta Cakraratna* in the armoury of King Bharata as it is known from Jain texts.[315]

There was yet another role of *apsaras*es and courtesans in common as known from literature and sculpture, i.e., distracting the penance of sages, as a test to their self-control. This responsibility was often vested in *apsaras*es by Indra. The chief victims or lovers of *apsaras*es were Bharadvāja,[316] Vyāsa[317] and Viśvāmitra.[318] In Buddhist tradition, the abortive destruction of the penance of Buddha and other ascetics by the daughters of Māra (*apsaras*) is narrated. While doing so they are said to have performed dance and drama, as is known from *Aśokāvadāna*[319] where they are mentioned as performing dance and drama to attract Upagupta when people collected to listen to him. In a sculpture depicted in cave no. 36 at Ajantā, daughters of Māra are represented as dancing and tempting Buddha.[320] Exactly the same was the function of courtesans described in the story of sage Ṛṣyaśṛṅga who was charmed by their beauty and here, too, the courtesans charmed the sage as a duty given to them by the king himself.[321]

---

311. See *Pl*. V.
312. *Buddhacarita*, IV.57-58.
313. See *Pl*. XXIII.
314. *Mahābhārata,* Udyoga-Parva, 5.15.
315. *Dhammakahāṇuyoga*, Bharata Chakravarti Charitra, sūtra, 500.195.
316. *Mahābhārata*, Sabhā-Parva, 5103.
317. *Ibid*., 121.88.
318. *Rāmāyaṇa*, Bāla-kāṇḍa, 64.10.
319. *divyāścapsaras nāṭayituṁ pravṛttaḥ — Aśokāvadāna,* Pāṅśupradānāvadāna, 16.
320. Sel *Pl*. no. XXXVIII.
321. *Rāmāyaṇa*, Ayodhyā-kāṇḍa, III.17.

Thus, the similarity between the functions of the *apsaras*es and those of the courtesans clearly suggests that the concept of *apsaras*es came into being on the basis of the contemporary female theatre artistes, particularly courtesans. Gradually, these two terms, *apsaras* and *gaṇikā* became almost synonymous. In *Ṛgveda*,[322] Vasiṣṭha calls himself the son of an *apsaras*. In *Mahābhārata,* he is depicted as born of a *gaṇikā*[323] while the legend in Veda recounts that he was the son of Urvaśī. Thus, the terms *apsaras* and *gaṇikā* became interchangeable. This is the reason why *apsaras*es are clearly called *vārāṅganāḥ* (courtesans) in Udyoga-Parva[324] and *veśyā* in *Amarakośa*.[325] In *Harivaṁśa*, *apsaras*es are mentioned as entering into the body of the *gaṇikā*s at Piṇḍāraka Tīrtha by the order of Śrī Kṛṣṇa himself.[326] They presented plays based on the life of Kṛṣṇa and Balarāma.[327] This also indicates that *apsaras*es were the idealised concept of everything best in a *gaṇikā*. *Apsaras*es entering into the bodies of *gaṇikā*s refers to *gaṇikā*s excelling themselves in art and grace.

Traditionally, *apsaras*es have been classified into two categories — *laukika* (worldly) and *daivika* (divine).[328] This division indicates that possibly some courtesans known for the excellence of their art and beauty were raised to the status of *apsaras*es and were called *laukika apsaras*es.

Art of Female Theatre Artistes as Reflected in the Depiction of the Art of Apsarases

The representation of the performance of *apsaras*es in literature and sculpture provides some very important information regarding the art of contemporary female artistes.

(1) It is described in the Bāla-kāṇḍa of *Rāmāyaṇa* that *apsaras*es formed troupes exclusively of their own with female musicians.[329] This is an evidence of the

322. *Ṛgveda*, VII.33.
323. G.R. Bhandarkar, 'Foreign Elements in the Hindu Population', *IA*, vol. XI, p. 7.
324. *Mahābhārata*, Udyoga-Parva, 9.12.
325. *Amarakośa*, 52.17.
326. *Harivaṁśa*, Viṣṇu-Parva, 80, 41.
327. *Ibid.*, 80, 91.
328. R.P. Sharma, *Paurāṇika Kośa*, p. 25.
329. *nanṛtuścapsaraḥ saṁghaḥ* — *Rāmāyaṇa*, Bāla-kāṇḍa, 73, 38.

existence of *strī-prekṣā* — theatrical troupes of exclusively female artistes. The same *kāṇḍa* of *Rāmāyaṇa*[330] refers to *vadhūnāṭakasaṁghaśca,* female theatrical troupe. Thus, it seems that contemporary female artistes had their own troupes. It is further evident by some second-century BC sculptural depictions of theatrical troupes of *apsaras*es[331] where musical instruments of the orchestra, too, are being played by *apsaras*es only. But *apsaras*es are commonly referred to as dancing in accompaniment of music provided by *gandharva*s and together they formed their theatrical repertory.[332]

Vedic and post-Vedic references to *gandharva*s as the husbands of *apsaras*es who accompanied them in their dance performance as musicians, reminds one of the professional *naṭī* who was an active member of her *sūtradhāra* — husband's troupe, and also of that *naṭī* who danced in accompaniment of the music provided by her male partner.[333]

(2) The representation of *apsaras*es, in literature and sculptures, suggest that their art belonged to classical style. The earliest of them were trained by the great master, Bharata, himself.[334] The theatrical art that was imparted to them was in the form of a discipline and therefore, it belonged to the classical tradition. Bharata says that they were experts in *nāṭya* and its embellishments.[335] Wherever they are represented, either in literature or in sculpture, their mastery over the art is always emphasised and this mastery comes through proper training. They are depicted as perfect theatre artistes.

Though dance is described as their special field, they are said to have equal proficiency in singing and histrionic art. In Bāla-kāṇḍa of *Rāmāyaṇa,* it is said that Rambhā came first to tempt sage Viśvāmitra and sang beautifully

330. *Rāmāyaṇa*, Bāla-kāṇḍa, V.12.

331. See *Pl.* I.

332. *Mahābhārata*, Aśvamedika-Parva, Anugītā-Parva, 88.36; *Rāmāyaṇa*, Bāla-kāṇḍa, 49.20;73. 38;18. 16; Uttara-kāṇḍa, 131.39; Yuddha-kāṇḍa, 9.90.66.

333. See *Pl.* XXXI; also G. Yazdani, *Ajantā*, Part III, 777-8, pl. IV-V; J. Stanislow Czuma, *Kushan Sculpture: Images from Early India*, fig. 94; R.J. Mehta, *Masterpieces of Female Form from Indian Art*, pl. 14.

334. *NŚ*, I.46-53.

335. *nāṭyālaṅkāracaturaḥ*, — I.47.

in her captivating voice.[336] In some of the sculptures, depicting dance of the *apsaras*es, a few members of their all-female orchestra seem to be vocalists, as, though they are grouped with the members of the orchestra, they are not playing any instrument and appear merely as clapping to mark time, as often musicians do even today — for example, the figure in the background in the panel from Bharhut representing dance of the *apsaras*es.[337]

Similarly, in the *Cūḍāmaho* scene from Sāñcī, there are two female figures in the background besides those of the danseuse and the drum player; they, too, may be taken as vocalists.[338] The female figure, represented on the far left among the group of performing artistes on the relief from Gāndhāra, depicting the same scene, seems to be a vocalist too, who is not playing any instrument, but appears to be clapping to mark time while singing (see *Pl.* no. XXIII).

In Udayagiri panel, depicting the descent of Gaṅgā and Yamunā, too, there is a central dancing figure surrounded by five female figures. Three of them are playing different musical instruments; one of the two, on the left of the dancer, seems to be playing a small drum, the other, seems to be the vocalist,[339] since she does not seem to be playing any instrument. In Māravijaya scene from Ajantā too, the female figure standing behind the drummer, on the left of the dancer, seems to be the vocalist.[340]

As far as their proficiency in *abhinaya* is concerned, it is stated in *Nāṭyaśāstra* that *apsaras*es were good actresses. It is said that Brahmā created *apsaras*es for giving vent to *kaiśikī vṛtti*[341] and they take part in *nāṭya*.[342] *Aśokāvadāna* also refers to the *nāṭya* performance of *apsaras*es.[343] In *Vikramorvaśīyam,*[344]

---

336. *Rāmāyaṇa*, Bāla-kāṇḍa, 64, 16.
337. See *Pl.* I.
338. See *Pl.* V.
339. See *Pl.* XXXV.
340. See *Pl.* XXXVIII.
341. *NŚ*, I.45-6.
342. *Ibid.*, XXXVI, 60.
343. *apsaraso nāṭayituṁ pravṛttaḥ* — *Aśokāvadāna*, Pāṅśupradānāvadāna, 16.
344. *Vikramorvaśīyaṁ* III, Miśraviṣkambhaka.

Kālidāsa refers to a play 'Lakṣmī Svayaṁvara' performed by *apsaras*es and directed by Bharata. In Kālidāsa's *Kumārasambhava,* a drama was performed by *apsaras*es in which various dramatic forms were expressed in articulation and the musical modes corresponded to the varying moods and sentiments.[345] In *Harivaṁśa,* a play performed by *apsaras*es is mentioned, in which *apsaras* Citralekhā did the role of Pārvatī.[346]

On the basis of the above description of *apsaras,* it seems that the contemporary professional female theatre artiste was dancer, actress and musician all combined, and a professional, whether she was a *naṭī* or a courtesan, had to have a thorough knowledge of the art of *nāṭya.*

The contemporary classical style of dance that was adopted by the *naṭī*s is also reflected in the dance of *apsaras*es depicted in literature and sculpture. The dance posture clearly indicates that the art was turning into a discipline. In Bharhut examples,[347] the hands of the dancing *apsaras*es show *patākā hasta* gesture. Sivaramamurti also thinks that it illustrates the commencement of dance *Alārippu* still in vogue in Bharata Nāṭyam. In *Cūḍāmaho* scene,[348] from Sāñcī, the beautiful posture and curvacious and graceful hand gesture of the dancing *apsaras*es indicate classical style. The dance posture of a female figure identified as *apsaras* Nīlāñjanā, performing in honour of Ṛṣabhadeva,[349] represented on a frieze from Mathurā, also shows classical style with graceful static posture. The dance posture of the *apsaras* performing on occasion of *Cūḍāmaho*, represented on the relief from Gāndhāra, too, suggests classical style. The *patākā hasta* gesture of the artiste is noticed here as well (see *Pl*. no. XXIII).

The Udayagiri panel[350] is another example of the classical style, as suggested by the posture. The dance of an *apsaras* is depicted on a relief from Pahārpur, north Bengal, belonging to the seventh century AD. She is seen at a moment

345. *Kumārasambhava*, VII.91, *KG*, p.
346. *Harivaṁśa,* Viṣṇu-Parva, 117, 6-7.
347. See *Pls*. I, II.
348. See *Pl*. no. V.
349. See *Pl*. no. XII.
350. See *Pl*. XXXV.

of whirling and just before rising again. The forcefully bent knees, the weight on the left foot, the right arm thrown across the body, the left shoulder and left arm raised and the head bent and turned towards the right, clearly indicate classical style.[351] Another example, belonging to the seventh century AD, is from Ajantā, cave no. 26.[352] In this scene, representing *Māravijaya* of Buddha, the central figure is that of a danseuse with the right hand representing what seems to be *kapittha* hand gesture.

The refinement of the dance postures of *apsaras*es indicate the refinement that had come about in the art of the contemporary artistes. The delicacy of the art is reflected in the paintings also. For example, the paintings of Ajantā, cave no. 17 belonging to fifth century AD represent flying heavenly bodies.[353] In first scene, the back of a female figure (*apsaras*) is seen, depicted as playing a long flute. In the same cave, there is another flying figure of an *apsaras* depicted as playing cymbals. The *apsaras*, bejewelled and decorated with heavy necklace and tiara on her head, a scarf fluttering on her neck, delicate hands with long finger nails in gesture of playing the cymbals, shows the refinement, perfection and delicacy that had come in the art and the personality of the contemporary female artistes.

The dance posture of the two *apsaras*es depicted in the painting on the pillars of the facade of the Sittannavasal cave temple, generally taken as belonging to the seventh century AD, represents classical tradition of the art. The left arm of the first figure is stretched in *latā hasta* and the right arm bent in front represents *patākā hasta* gesture. The artist probably had no. 18 *karaṇa*, viz., *alāta* or no. 25 *karaṇa*, viz., *ūrdhvajānu* or no. 44 *karaṇa*, *latāvṛścika* in mind while painting this figure. Another figure, painted on the south pillar, has right arm showing *patākā hasta* and the left stretched out in *latā-hasta* pose, which is in accordance with the *vivartika karaṇa* of Bharata.[354] These figures show that the rules laid by Bharata were followed by the artistes belonging to the classical style.

---

351. S. Kramrisch, *Indian Sculpture*, pl. XXXII, fig. 80.

352. See *Pl.* XXXVIII.

353. Mulkaraj Anand, *Album of Indian Paintings*, pl. 30.

354. T.N. Ramachandran, 'Cave Temples and Paintings', *Lalita Kalā*, no. 9, April, 1961, pl. C and D.

(3) The description of the dance of *apsarases* in literature and art shows that they always performed in accompaniment of an orchestra provided either by *gandharvas* or by the *apsarases* themselves. In literature, *dundubhī* (drum),[355] *bherī* and *paṇva*[356] are the musical instruments mentioned as used by *apsarases* and *gandharvas*. In scuplture, in addition to these, *avanaddha* type of instruments (percussion instruments), some *tat* (string instrument) like *vīṇā*, *ghana* (metal instrument) like cymbals and *suśira* (wind instruments) like *veṇu*, too, are noticed. In some of the sculptures,[357] a percussion instrument with a stick is noticed. It is either a *ghaṇṭā* or something like *taṭṭakaḷī* used in Bharata Nāṭyam dance by teachers to teach their pupils the rudiments of rhythm. On the basis of these depictions, it seems that the contemporary female theatre artistes performed in accompaniment of a full-fledged orchestra. Vertical and horizontal, both types of drum were used. *Vīṇā*, too, was of two types — *vipañcī vīṇā* and *kacchapī*.

(4) In respect of costume, the description of *apsarases* giving performance indicates that they danced fully attired and adorned with ornaments. Rambhā did so while going to Nalakūbara.[358] It is supported by some of the sculptural depictions of *apsrases*.[359] They are seen as wearing anklets, girdle of several strings, necklaces and bangles. The style of the *sārī,* worn by the *apsarases*, is similar to that of the Bharata Nāṭyam dancers, with pleats in the centre. Heavy headdress is seen in all the examples. This might have been the costume of the contemporary professional danseuses.

(5) The representation of the dance of the *apsarases* give important information about the stage on which contemporary professional danseuses performed. In Aśvamedhika-Parva of *Mahābhārata,* Indra gave instructions to gods to erect a pavilion for *apsarases* to dance on the occasion of a sacrifice performed by *mahārāja* Marutta, specifying that it should have pillars and a staircase too.[360] This shows that contemporary danseuses danced on a raised stage,

355. *Rāmāyaṇa*, Bāla-kāṇḍa, 49, 20.

356. *Mahābhārata*, Anuśāsana-Parva, 107, 64.

357. See *Pl.* XII.

358. *sarvavibhūṣanaṁ kṛtaṁ* — *Rāmāyaṇa*, Uttara-kāṇḍa, 26.26.

359. See *Pls.* I, II, XII, XXXVIII.

360. *klṛptāḥ sthūṇāḥ kuratārohaṇāni* — *Mahābhārata*, Aśvamedhika-Parva, 10, 27.

temporarily constructed for the show in the form of a pavilion, around which the spectators sat. This is supported by sculptural depictions. The fragment of the frieze, from Mathurā, represents a pavilion type of theatre.[361] It is long hut-type, open to all sides. Its roof was supported by four pillars, three of which are visible. In Bharhut scene depicting four *apsaras*es and a child,[362] one pillar on each side of the performers suggest a pavilion in which the dance was being performed. That the professional female artistes of the period danced under such pavilions, is noticed in some other sculptures too, for example, dance scene from Rānīgumphā,[363] belonging to second century BC, and from Mathurā, belonging to second or third century AD, carved on the right half of a round pillar.[364]

Another favourite place for dance performance of *apsaras*es and therefore that of contemporary female artistes, was an open courtyard facing a building with open pillared balcony where spectators used to sit as is seen in *Cūḍāmaho* scene from Bharhut and Sāñcī.[365]

Female Performing Artistes in the form of Devadāsīs

The *devadāsī*, 'the female servant of gods', was a girl dedicated to serve the presiding deity of the temple in various ways, including the performance of dance and drama. In discharging her last-mentioned duty, the *devadāsī* contributed to theatrical art a great deal. She was properly trained to perform ritual dance, drama and music, hence, she may be considered as a form of female performing artiste. Though the *devadāsī* system, as an institution, came into vogue after 700 AD, its origin may be traced to girls associated with rituals performing dance and music in literature, epigraphs and sculptures of earlier period.

Origin of Devadāsī System

Association of theatrical arts with ritual is a very old Indian tradition. In Vedic *Mahāvrata* ceremony, there were songs sung by married women, dance performed

---

361. See *Pl*. XII.
362. See *Pl*. I.
363. See *Pl*. XI.
364. *Marg*, XV, no. 2, fig. 19, 36.
365. See *Pls*. II, V.

by maidens, dramatic dialogue between a harlot and a *brahmacārī* and ritual copulation, having magico-religious bearings. The last-mentioned rite indicates the influence of pre-Āryan fertility cults on Vedic rituals. Varadapande[366] rightly says that later *devadāsī*s performed many of the functions performed by women in *Mahāvrata* ceremony including dancing, singing, playing musical instruments and even, ritual copulation in temple under *tāntrika* influence.

The association of women with mystic ritual is known from the Buddhist text *Brahmajālasutta*[367] which refers to a girl possessed by the spirit *Kumārikāpañhaṁ* and also obtaining answer from God, *Devapañhaṁ,* called one of the lower arts by the Buddha. Rhys Davids thinks that here *kumārī* stands for the *devadāsī* or temple prostitute.[368]

The Pāśupata sect of Śaivism includes singing and dancing, together with *śṛṅgāraṇa*, i.e., showing oneself to be in love by means of amorous gestures, as if, seeing a beautiful young women was part of the *vidhi* or process to achieve *duḥkhānta* or final deliverance.[369] The relation of Pāśupata *ācārya*s with courtesans was known during later centuries, e.g., *Kuṭṭanīmatam*, an eighth-century text, refers to the intimate relations between a Pāśupata *ācārya,* Bhavaśuddhi and a dancing girl, Anaṅgādevī.[370] Varadpande says that probably these *ācārya*s needed dancers for their ritualistic Śiva worship.[371] This may have been the reason why later in medieval period ascetics are depicted on the temple walls in the company of women which reminds one of *Mahāvrata* ceremony which had dailogue between a *brahmacārī* and a harlot and ritual copulation as part of the ritual. This ascetic-courtesan or ascetic-dancer combination may have grown into a *devadāsī*-ascetic or a *devadāsī*-chief priest combination. Thus, the recongnition of theatrical arts as ritual, and woman as its performer gave rise to the belief that the best way to please gods was presenting dance, music and drama, especially performed by women.

---

366. M.L. Varadapande, *Religion and Theatre*, p. 48.
367. *Dīghanikāya*, *Brahmajālasūtta*, *Mahāśīla*, 26.
368. Rhys Davids, *Dialogue of Buddha*, I, Sacred Book of Buddhists, p. 24.
369. R.G. Bhandarkar, *Vaiṣṇavism, Śaivism and Minor Religious Systems*, pp. 122-33.
370. *Kuṭṭanīmatam*, 538.
371. M.L. Varadapande, *op. cit*., p. 48.

This belief is traceable quite early in India. Kṛṣṇa says in *Bhāgavata Purāṇa*[372] that he is immensely pleased by the enactment of his *līlā* (divine acts). It is said in *Harivaṁśa*[373] that the performer of *chalikya* dance is dear to Lord Nārāyaṇa. It is enjoined in *Agni Purāṇa*[374] that devotees should arrange *yātrā* in honour of deities, full of dancing, singing and sounding of musical instruments. Thus, inclusion of theatre and women in religious rituals gradually gave rise to the *devadāsī* system, with some influence of secular *śṛṅgāra*, too, as suggested by Devangana Desai.[375]

There is yet another reason for the rise of the *devadāsī* system in India. When sacrifice ceased to be the norm of worship and was replaced by temple worship, a different type of ritual was required. In Vedic sacrifice, ritualistic dance and impersonation was required only during the sacrifice. Female artistes, whether in the form of professional entertainers hired for the ritual or as ritual dancers, were free after the sacrifice was over. But a temple was a permanent religious establishment with regular rituals, therefore, a permanent attendant to the presiding deity was required. Hence, the *devadāsī* was introduced. The tradition of having temple girls was in vogue in the Greek and west Asian civilizations. Since India came into contact with them, directly and indirectly, an impact of their cultures might be considered as one of the factors responsible for the rise of the *devadāsī* system as an institution.

History and Contributions of Devadāsī to Theatrical Art

The first reference to *devadāsī* is in Kauṭilya's *Arthaśāstra*,[376] who says that a *devadāsī* retired from temple service may be employed in spinning work. Since Kauṭilya does not refer to the nature of her duty in temple, it is not clear if the term *devadāsī* is used here in the same sense in which it was used later in the country. She may be taken as an ordinary female attendant of the temple establishment. There is an inscription in Aśokan Brāhmī referring to *devadāsī* Sutanukā in Jogimārā

---

372. *Bhāgavata Purāṇa*, XI.11.13; XI.27, 44; XI.27.35.

373. *Harivaṁśa*, Viṣṇu-Parva, 89, 73-86.

374. *Agni Purāṇa*, 68.3, 12, 14.

375. Devangana Desai, *Erotic Sculpture of India*, p. 162.

376. *ūrṇāvalkakārpāsatūlaśaṇa kṣaumāṇi ca vidhavāny-aṅgākanyā pravrajitādaṇḍa-pratikāriṇībhī rūpājivāmātṛkābhirvṛddharājadāsibhirvyuparatopasthānadevadāsi-bhiśca kartayeta* — *Arthaśāstra*, II.23.2.

cave.[377] Adjacent to this is another cave — Sītābeṅgā, the so-called cave-theatre.[378] According to Bloch's translation, the inscription of the Jogimārā cave refers to one Sutanukā, the *devadāsī,* who was loved by the excellent among men — Devadinna, the skilled sculptor. But, Hara Prasad Sastri disagrees with the above renderings and translates the inscription as follows:

> I salute the beautifully formed one who shows us the gods. I salute the beautiful form that leads us to the gods. He is much in quest at Vārāṇasī. I salute the god given one for seeing his beautiful form.[379]

It seems that the reading of the inscription is controversial. Even if we take the reading as *devadāsī,* we cannot say if this *devadāsī*, Sutanukā, performed all those duties which were performed by the later *devadāsīs*. But the paintings in the Jogimārā cave depicting girls and musicians,[380] a theatre-like cave in the vicinity with an inscription which refers to 'poets and festivals when frolics and music abound' and Sutanukā's association with Devadinna, himself the artist, may suggest some association of *devadāsī* Sutanukā with theatrical art, though, one cannot say that this association was through temple ritual, as both the inscriptions are silent in this regard.

Writing about mother goddess and her association with the fertility cult in the light of James Frazer's theory, Devangna Desai cites a disc from Rūpar[381] belonging to 'Maurya-Śuṅga' period depicting a male figure, probably representing the priest or the male partner of the goddess with whom she, or her human surrogate — the *devadāsī* — mates annually, a small leaf structure or a 'shrine' on the right of the mother goddess and another male figure offering a round object to a fully clad female. Desai wonders if the female figure represents the human surrogate of the mother goddess, i.e., the *devadāsī* or a proto-type of the *devadāsī*.

Desai cites a steatite plaque (245-105 BC) also which was found from Rājgīr. It has three compartments. A female figure in the typical standing pose of mother

---

377. T. Bloch, *Archaeological Survey of India Report,* 1903-4, p.128.
378. *Ibid.*, pp. 126-27.
379. Hara Prasad Sastri, *JASB Proceedings 1902*, pp. 90-91.
380 T. Bloch, *op. cit.*, p. 130.
381. Devangana Desai, *op. cit.*, p. 11, pl. 1.

goddess is represented with her male partner, also nude on the first panel. In the middle panel, the male partner tries to please the female by offering her a cup. In the upper panel, the female is in dancing pose while the male partner plays a musical instrument.[282] Both these examples show the mother goddess and a male figure closely associated with that goddess. The second example shows most significantly a female figure in dancing pose. This suggests that there used to be a female associated with the cult of mother goddess in the third or the second century BC, who danced either as human surrogate possessed by the goddess or as her attendant who was later more popularly known as a *devadāsī*.

That music and dance had become a form of ritualistic worship during the second century BC is known from Patañjali, too, who states that the temples of Rāma, Keśava and Kubera vibrated with the sound of *mr̥daṅga*, *śaṅkha* and *paṇava*.[383] Since we know from *Arthaśāstra*[384] that the art of dance was taking a definite form and *naṭācārya*s were given the responsibility of training the courtesans,[385] it is posible that the ritual dancer, too, underwent a proper training in the art, as a discipline, with some such static postures and gestures that were suitable for temple ritual.

The enactment of *līlā* of different gods being a most common and favourtie subject of the *abhinaya* part of dance and devotion (*bhakti*) being its basis even now, noticeable in modern dance styles as Bharata Nāṭyam, Oḍissī, Maṇipurī, Kathaka, etc., suggest that temple ritual must have contributed to the origin of such dances. But, unfortunately, we have only one sculptural depiction of the performance of ritual dancer (Rājgīr plaque) and that, too, is quite poor in workmanship. Therefore, it is difficult to form an idea about the style and standard of their art but the closed eyes and rhythmic movement of the dancer of the Rājgīr plaque indicate her mystic ecstacy, dedication and absorption in the ritual she is performing. It might be possible that the girl in service of the goddess was a courtesan who was hired for the ritual. This is firstly, because it was customary to hire courtesans for such Vedic rituals as *Mahāvrata* ceremony, referred to earlier, in which dramatic dialogue between a harlot and a *brahmacārī*, and ritual copulation, were part of the magico-religious

382. Devangana Desai, *op. cit.*, p. 12, pl. 2.

383. *mr̥daṅgaśaṅkhapaṇavaḥ pritaṅgaḥ nadanti saṅsadi prāsādedhanapatirāmakeśavānām* — *Mahābhāṣya*, 2.2.34.

384. *Arthaśāstra* II.27.128.

385. *Ibid.*

ritual and secondly, because it was a fashion to hire courtesans to do the job of a part-time *devadāsī* during later periods of Indian history, too, though the term *devadāsī* was not attached to them.[386]

A Greek farce with Kannaḍa passages, belonging to the second century AD, had been discovered during the excavation undertaken by the Biblical Archaeological Association in Egypt. It refers to a beautiful girl, Charition, who was dedicated to the temple of 'moon goddess' in India and who was later rescued by her brother.[387] Varadpande[388] thinks that she may have been one of those dancing girls who were deported to India as attested by the 'Periplus of Erythrean Sea' (p. 42). Some of them were sold in the Veśa, but probably, a few were dedicated to the temple as temple-girls (*devadāsī*). This Charition may have been one such *devadāsī* dedicated to the temple of the moon goddess.

This Greek farce raises some questions. Charition was a Greek girl who was dedicated to the temple of moon goddess as an attendant. That she was devoted to the goddess is evident by the fact of her not being ready to take the ornaments of the goddess from the temple at the time of her escape with her brother. This might have been due to her background. Permanent appointment of temple girls as an institution was known not only to ancient Greece but to western Asia and Egypt, too. In Sumeria, it was considered honourable to dedicate beautiful girls to temples. A festival was organised on the day of the dedication to celebrate the occasion.[389] This system was known to Babylonians, too. In large temples of Babylon, Sippar and Ur, there were several unmarried girls dedicated to the presiding deity. They received the same amount of money from their father as they would have received at marriage, had they been given in marriage.[390] In Greece, too, girls were dedicated to temples, especially to that of Aphrodite.[391] In Egypt, the temples of Isis and

386. *Meghadūta*, I, 39, Chaturvedi, *KG*, pp. 122-23.

387. R. Shama Shastri, *Mysore Archaeological Report for 1926*, pp. 11-15; B.A. Saletore, '*Ancient Karnataka*', vol. 1 (History of Tuluva), pp. 592-7.

388. M.L. Varadapande, *op. cit.*, pp. 61-62.

389. C. Leonard Woolly, *The Sumerians*, p. 106 also, S. Goel, *Viśva kī Prācīn Sabhyatāyen*, p. 56.

390. S. Goel, *op. cit.*, p. 118.

391. C. Leonard Wooly, *op. cit.*, p. 108; P. Thomas, *Indian Women Through the Ages*, p. 236; Richard, Lewinsohn, *A History of Sexual Customs*, p. 26.

Osiris were well-known for their orgies and dancing of professional courtesans which formed the main attraction of the great feast and festival of these shrines.[392]

During their westward migration and settlement in Bactria, the Kuṣāṇas, who had their own tradition, came into contact with Greek and west Asian cultures. They might have introduced the tradition of temple girls, permanently appointed in the temples, the result of a composite culture, as an institution to Indians. Is this the reason why we get the first clear-cut reference to a girl dedicated to the temple on permanent basis as an attendant in *circa* second century AD ? And the temple to which she was dedicated was that of a moon goddess — a deity represented on Kuṣāṇa coins — Manaobago?[393] Could we think that Indian tradition of ritual dance performed by women, particularly courtesans, with some mystic influence was strengthened by these influences which came into India from western Asia? Is it for this reason that girls dedicated to temples on a permanent basis were called *devadāsī*? Because Kuṣāṇas, during whose rule Charition was dedicated to the temple, called themselves *devaputra* and the temple where they got their statues installed was called *devakula*.[394]

Though the term *devadāsī* was known to ancient Indians, as we know from *Arthaśāstra* and Jogimārā cave inscription, we cannot say if it was used in the same sense in which it was used later in India. Most probably, it denoted a simple female attendant, doing jobs other than ritual dance, for which courtesans were hired. We have references to courtesans hired for performing *saṅgītaka* in the temple.[395] Not only this, they did such other duties also which were performed by later *devadāsī*s, as we know from Kālidāsa.[396]

The Scythian dress of the dancing figures, accompanied by an all female orchestra from Devagarh[397] belonging to fifth or early sixth century AD, is also very significnat. We have already discussed, in the 'courtesan' section, that either there was a fashion

392. P. Thomos, *op. cit.*, p. 236; C. Leonard Woolly, *op. cit.*, p. 42, Richard Lewinsohn, *op. cit.*, p. 27.

393. B. Chattopadhyay, *The Age of Kushanas — A Numismatic Study*, pp. 59, 75, 76, 78.

394. Gritlivon M. Mitterwallner, *Kuṣāṇa Coins and Kuṣāṇa Sculpture from Mathurā*, pp. 54, 59.

395. *Ubhayābhisārikā*, *Caturbhāṇī*, pp. 122-23.

396. *Meghadūta*, I, 39, *KG*, pp. 122-23.

397. See *Pl.* XXXII; XXXIII. XXXIV.

of wearing scythian dress among dancers or they were Yavanī *gaṇikās*. Possibly, such *gaṇikās* did the job of part-time *devadāsī* in temples, during fifth or sixth century AD, because they were fully acquainted with this type of worship. But, gradually, the custom of dedicating beautiful maidens to temple was making its way in Indian society, probably because of foreign influence. According to *Padma Purāṇa,* one who offers beautiful maidens to God, attains heaven for one full *kalpa*.[398] Later *Bhaviṣya Purāṇa,*[399] states that one who consecrates a bevy of women, in honour of Sun God, goes to the highest region where shines the Sun. Since we do find reference to dancing girls in the temple of this God, probably, the instruction given in the Purāṇas were followed. In seventh century AD, Hieun-Tsang[400] mentions dancing girls at the sun temple of Multān.

As far as, the style of performance of *devadāsīs* is concerned, one can say that it must have been more ceremonial, and elaborate then the ordinary performance. In *Rauravāgam*[401] which relates to the construction, conservation and rituals of the temples, a list of protocols of *Śuddhanṛtta* is given in a separate chapter. It states that *gaṇikā* dancer (of the temple) should be personally clean and ritualistically purified by *ācamanīya*. She should be well-versed in the art of music and dance. *Suprabhedāgama* states that she should be physically fit and mentally tranquil. She should dance at fixed time in the *maṇḍapa*, a circular area marked by the priest, after invoking the presence of Naṭeśvara there. All these references show that the art of *devadāsī* had become classical. There may have been as hard and fast rule for the art also, which she presented to the deity as ritual, as it was for the rituals and cleanliness.

They were not only maintaining and enriching the classical style of theatrical art but were giving it a respectable position also, because their art was associated with religion. There association with religion was taken as any other religious ritual. This may have popularised the art of dance and music. This may have been the reason, why the art of dance became more popular in south than in north because *devadāsī* system was more popular there in south. The contribution of the dance of

398. *Padma Purāṇa*, Sṛṣṭikhaṇḍa, 52.99-100.

399. *Bhaviṣya Purāṇa*, 53.67.

400. A.S. Altekar, *Position of Women in Hindu Civilization*, p. 183.

401. P. Subrahmanyam, 'The Temple as the Focal Centre of Dance Art', *Kusumāñjali* New interpretation of Indian Art & Culture, *Sri C. Sivaramamurti Commemorative,* vol. I, p. 140.

devadāsī's to theatrical art is evident by the *bhakti* element, still being the pivot of many of the modern dance styles. Some of the dance styles, are derived from that of the *devadāsīs*, for example, Oḍissī style which is derived from the dance for *māharīs* (*devadāsīs*) of Orissa. They may have been a source of inspiration and subject for the temple sculpture.

Part III

Female Performing Artistes of Noble Birth

A passage from *Ṛgveda*[402] says that the daughter was first married to Soma, next o *gandharva* and Agni, and then to a man. This shows that girls were first taught to prepare *soma* juice, next they were instructed in *gandharva-vidyā*, i.e., dance and music, after that they were trained in the procedure of sacrifical ceremonies. Only after all these stages of instruction they were given in marriage to men. From the same source it seems that it was customary for girls to sing, while engaged in the preparation of *soma* juice. The girls were so well-versed in music that they would pray for a husband who was familiar with and appreciated the musical arts.[403]

Śatapatha Brāhmaṇa states that it is to him who dances and sings that women most readily take a fancy.[404] *Kauṣītakī Brāhmaṇa*[405] states that Sarasvatī would dance to the far-vibrating rhythmic beat of the contrasting, accented and unaccented, tones of the chanting Vedic priests and that it was out of this that Prajāpati Brahmā discovered the metrical scheme. The *Mahāvrata* ceremony also shows that during Vedic period unmarried girls and married women, both were conversant with dance and music.[406]

Existence of female artistes from noble families is known from *Mahābhārata* also.[407] Arjuna as Bṛhannalā was appointed in the *antaḥpura* of king Virāṭa to teach theatrical arts to the girls of *antaḥpura* and of the city. He taught such arts to

---

402. *Ṛgveda*, X.85.40.

403. *Kṛṣṇa Yajurveda*, VI.1.6.

404. . . . *anuyoṣāstasmādya evanṛttyati yo gāyati tasminnevaitā nimiślatamā-a-iva* ।
— *Śatapatha Brāhmaṇa*, III.2.4.6.

405. *sāmavedādimagitaṁ sañjagrāhpitāmaḥ*. . . — *Kauṣītakī Brāhmaṇa* 29, 5.

406. A.B. Keith, *Śāṅkhyāyana Āraṇyaka*, p. 72.

407. *Mahābhārata*, Virāṭa-Parva, II, 27-9.

princess Uttarā. There are some sculptural depictions of dance and music, belonging to second century BC, which indicate that girls of good families learnt and performed the art as part of worship. On the north pillar of western gateway, upper panel at Sāñcī there is a depiction of Nāgarāja Mucilinḍa and his family in the background of holy tree. On his left, some *nāga* girls are engaged in dance performance, accompanied by an orchestra, played by other girls.[408]

Vāsavadattā of Bhāsa's *Pratijñāyaugandharāyaṇa,* is an example of girls learning the art of music for sheer personal interest and excelling in it. Vāsavadattā was trained in the art of playing *vīṇā,* first, by a *vaitālikā* and later, by king Udayana himself, a renowned musician.[409]

A dancer, queen Candraprabhā of king Rudrāyaṇa, is mentioned in *Divyāvadāna.*[410] Queens usually had proficiency in classical music, too. King Duṣyanta and Vidūṣaka listen to a song being sung at *antaḥpura* in *Abhi-jñānaśākuntalam* and the Vidūṣaka says that probably queen Haṁsapadikā is singing in her sweet voice adorned with proper *laya* and *tāla.*[411]

It seems that during Kālidāsa's time the art of dancing was popularly cultivated. Members of royal household took interest in it. Irāvatī, the second queen of Agnimitra learnt dance under the guidance of an *ācārya* Haradatta.[412] Kālidāsa has given vivid picture of the dance master who took special classes of dance and trained such pupils, whom their royal patrons, desired to be so.

Probably, it was customary during this period to give shelter to girls belonging to a royal or a good family and to impart proper training through the *ācārya*s in *antaḥpura*, such as Mālavikā, the sister of Prince Mādhavasena, who was sent to the *antaḥpura* of King Agnimitra, saying that she will learn the art of singing, playing musical instruments and dancing.[413] She was trained by an *ācārya*

---

408. See *Pl.* VI.

409. *Pratijñāyaugandharāyaṇa*, II *BNC*, II.52.

410. *rudrānyaṇo rājā vinayaṁ kr̥tāvīcandraprabhādevī nr̥tye* ।
yāvad apareṇa samayena rudrāyaṇorājā vīṇāṁ vādayati candraprabhā devī nr̥tyati ॥
— *Divyāvadāna*, XXXVII.37.553

411. *Abhijñānśākuntalam*, V, *KG*, p. 36.

412. *Mālavikāgnimitram*, I, *KG*, p. 187.

413. *Ibid.*, p. 188.

Gaṇadāsa.[414] Similarly, a sister of Sumatī, the prime minister of Mādhavasena,[415] was appointed in the *antaḥpura* of Agnimitra, disguised as *paṇḍitā kauśikī* having a sound knolwedge of dance, music and drama and was made the judge in the competition held between Mālavikā and Irāvatī.[416]

Performance of dance, in honour of the presiding deity of the temple, was considered as an act of high merit.

> A queen took a vow that she would give a performance of dancing before the deity in a public temple, if a son was born to her. She kept her vow.[417]

Another example of female artistes from royal family is the heroine of Harṣa's play *Nāgānanda* who was first seen by the hero when she was playing *vīṇā*.[418] According to *Harṣacarita,*[419] Princess Rājyaśrī became proficient day after day in all the fine arts, dance and music. In Harṣa's *Priyadarśikā,*[420] Princess Priyadarśanā took part in the play *Udayanacarita* staged at the royal harem.

Theatrical arts continued to be a social necessity during the last phase of the seventh century. Girls of noble families took part in such rituals and festivals which had dance and music. A special type of dance called the 'festival of the ball' (*kanduka utsava*) was often observed by them. Daṇḍin[421] gives a detailed account of this dance, performed by a girl to acquire a virtuous husband. Princess Kandukavatī performed this dance in a masterly manner. This might have been in the tradition of ritualistic dance performed by maidens since Vedic period. Such royal female artistes belonged to the classical tradition of the art, since they were trained by the *ācārya*s, the representatives of classical tradition. They performed, mostly within the precincts of the royal palace and not in public because they practised their art exclusively for

---

414. *Mālavikāgnimitram*, p. 187.
415. *Ibid.*, p. 247.
416. *Ibid.*, pp. 196-98.
417. V.S. Agrawala, *Gupta Art*, p. 121.
418. *tataḥ praviśati bhumāviṣṭhā vīṇāvādayanti malayavaticeṭī ca . . .*
—*Nāgānanda*, I.25-30
419. *rājyaśrīrapi nṛttagitādiṣu vidagdhāsu akhīṣu sakalāsu kalāsu ca pratidivasamupacīyamānaparicayā . . .* —*Harṣacarita*, p. 140
420. *Priyadarśikā*, Act III.
421. *Daśakumāracarita*, pp. 149-53.

their aesthetic satisfaction. In their own way they contributed to the development of the art.

Dance, drama and music were cultivated and widely practised among the ladies of royal families during successive periods of Indian history, too. The love of a princess for drama is evident by the marriage of Avantisundarī, the Cāhmāna princess, with poet dramatist Rājaśekhara. Not only this, she herself presented *Karpūramañjarī*, a Sattaka type of drama.[422] This seems to have been something new for female artistes of noble family in the field of drama, since, rarely did this class associate itself with public theatre.

In south, too, this class of artistes are seen as performing in public during successive periods. There are several examples of queens being expert in dramatic arts and performing in public, from early medieval south. In subordinate court of the Hoyasala, Padmāladevī, Cāvalīdevī and Boppādevī, the three wives of Ballāl I, were highly accomplished in singing and dancing. Santalādevī, the wife of another Hoyasala king, Viṣṇuvardhana was known to be properly trained in dance and music.[423] Sāvaladevī, the queen of Kalacūrya — Sovideva, was skilled in these arts, and used to perform in public.[424] Lakṣmīdevī, the queen of Tribhuvanmalla Mallideva Coḷa *mahārāja*, was proficient in *kāvya*, music and dance.[425] There may be some exaggeration in what the inscriptions state but this seems evident enough that theatrical arts continued to be an important part of female education in this part of the country in early medieval period.

Part IV

Strī-Prekṣā

One of the most important features of female contribution to Indian theatre is *strī-prekṣā* — a dramatic performance presented entirely by female artistes. It seems that the terms used to denote such theatre or presentation were *Vadhūnāṭaka saṁgha* and *Strī-prekṣā*. The existence of such performances and theatrical troupes

422. *cauhānakulamaulimāliā reseharakaindyehini* ।
bhattuno kiri bhavantisundarī sa paunjaiyumedanicchadi ।।
— *Karpūramañjarī*, I/II, ed Durga Prasad, 1927

423. *Dynasties of Kanarese Districts* p. 485, n. I, *Epigraphia Karnatica*, II.132 (50).

424. *JBBRAS*, XVIII, p. 275.

425. *South Indian Inscriptions*, IX. (i), 273, II, pp. 36-56.

was indicated by Bharata, too.

One of the types of *lāsya*, the minor form of drama, was *puṣpagaṇḍikā* 'which has songs and various dances accompanied by various movements of men which were actually performed by women'.[426] Besides, 'the plays staged in a temple, palace or at the residence of a commander-in-chief or merchants, were enacted entirely by women'.[427] This was not a temporary arrangement; the actresses were especially trained to play male roles in certain types of plays. Bharata says,

> As natural amorousness is observed in women, their naturally graceful limbs are easily accessible to *sauṣṭhava*, and their sportful nature will be their additional quality or embellishment when they assume a male role.[428]

Not only this, Bharata enjoins:

> Delicate type of plays such as nāṭaka, *prakaraṇa*, *bhāṇa*, *vīthi* and *aṅka*, including erotic sentiment, should be produced by women,[429] and also that which includes ordinary (not exalted) incidents and requires an observance of proper tempo, *tāla*, *kalā* and regulated utterance of syllables.[430]

Following Bharata, later dramaturgists like Sāgaranandī and Nandīkeśvara, too, have recognised this type of theatre. Sāgaranandī, explaining *ceṣṭālaṅkāra* of *nāyikā*, defines *līlā* as one of the natural moods of women and 'imitation, in the presence of her friends, to divert her own mind from her beloved who has not come, of his dress, gait, speech, etc.'.[431] Nandīkeśvara says that *lāsya* form of dance was taught to Ūṣā, the daughter of Bāṇāsura, by Pārvatī who taught the *gopī*s of Dvārakā — from where the tradition was carried forward to women of Saurāṣṭra and later spread to other regions.[432] Thus, it seems that the tradition of dramatic performance by female artistes exclusively was popular and recognised by *ācārya*s, the representatives of classical tradition of theatre in ancient India.

---

426. *NŚ*, XX.141.
427. *Ibid.*, XXXV.37.
428. *Ibid.*, XXXV.41-2.
429. *Ibid.*, XXXV.48.
430. *Ibid.*, XXXV.51, 52.
431. *Nāṭakalakṣaṇa Ratnakośa*, 18.2606.
432. *Abhinayadarpaṇa*, 5, 6, p. 192, ed. V. Garola.

This type of theatre is mentioned for the first time in *Rāmāyaṇa*, as existing in Ayodhyā — *vadhūnāṭakasaṁghaiśca saṁyuktā sarvataḥ purīṁ.*[433] The term *vadhūnāṭaka saṁgha* may denote a theatrical troupe of exlusively female artistes. The story of sage Ṛṣyaśṛṅga who was enmeshed by the talented courtesans who sang and played flute and lute, also suggests the same.

Jain texts, too, mention the performance of *nāṭya* (dance/drama) by Śrīdevī in honour of Mahāvīra when he visited *caitya* Guṇaśīlaka during the reign of King Śreṇika.[434] Similarly, the performance of thirty-two types of drama by *varataruṇī*s, witnessed by Suṣeṇa Senāpati and play presented entirely by *gaṇikā*s, on the occasion of the birth of Śreṇika's son,[435] too, appear to be examples of *strī-prekṣā*. *Jātakaṭṭhakathā*,[436] a Buddhist text, also refers to the performance of *nāṭakitthiyo* (actresses) of divine beauty, in front of Buddha.

Kauṭilya mentions *strī-prekṣā* as different from *puruṣa-prekṣā*, because the amount of *paṇa*s imposed as fine on the women witnessing *puruṣa-prekṣā* without their husband's permission is prescribed by Kauṭilya as double than that imposed on witnessing *strī-prekṣā*.[437] This clearly indicates the existence of *stri-prekṣā* or all-female theatre during his time.

There are several sculptural instances of *strī-prekṣā* from the Śuṅga period — for example, a coping piece from Bharhut, depicting a dance performance entirely by female artistes accompanied by an all-female orchestra, on occasion of the division of Buddha's relics.[438] The next example is, again, from Bharhut, showing four divine damsels and a child performing dance, accompanied by eight female instrumentalists and three female vocalists.[439] Lüders thinks that the scene represents a dramatic performance on occasion of Buddha's birth.[440] The danseuse with turban, according to him, portrays Śuddhodana and the child, his newborn son. The famous *Cūḍāmaha* scene from Sāñcī is another example of female theatre, representing a divine

433. *Rāmāyaṇa*, Bāla-kāṇḍa, 5, 12.

434. *Dhammakahāṇuyoga*, Skandha III, Śramaṇika Kathānaka, sūtra, 234, p. 101.

435. *Dhammakahāṇuyoga*, Skandha II, Meghakumāra Samaṇe, sūtra 321, p. 159.

436. *Jātakatthakathā*, Nidāna Kathā, p. 47.

437. *KA*, III.3.

438. C. Sivaramamurti, *The Masterpieces of Indian Sculptures in the National Museum*, pl. 1.

439. See *Pl.* I.

440. H. Lüders, *Corpus Inscriptionum Indicarum*, II (ii) (Bharhut inscriptions) p. 102.

danseuse in the centre and a female orchestra with female vocalists on the left.[441] Similarly, the episode of Nāgarāja Mucilinḍa, depicted on the north pillar of western gateway[442] and heavenly scenes, depicted on the north pillar of eastern gateway[443] of the great *stūpa* at Sāñcī, represent female ballet troupes consisting of female dencers and members of orchestra. The musical instruments being played are tambourines, a harp and a flute in the first example and drums and harps in the second.

The dance scene from Rānīgumphā cave, Orissa, as already mentioned consisting of a danseuse and four female companions forming the orchestra, is a good example of 'female theatre'.[444] The instruments being played are *mṛdaṅga*, *dhakkā*, harp and flute.

A painting from Ajantā, cave no. 10, belonging to *circa* second century BC, depicts fifteen artistes, all female. Three of them are dancers and the rest musicians.[445] A sculpture from Vidiśā, belonging to first century BC,[446] is another example of female theatre. The scene depicts two dancing figures in the lower part of the panel (only partially seen), accompanied by a six-member orchestra. The instruments being played are flute, lutes, cymbals and *ḍholak*. The figure on the left of the *ḍholak* player seems to be the vocalist. In the centre, a *kalaśa* is visible. The scene may be taken as representing a religious festival performed by ladies in the inner apartment, having dance and music as its important part.

These sculptures and painting belonging to *circa* second century BC to *circa* first century BC and representing 'female theatre' imply that the tradition of *vadhūnāṭaka-saṁgha* of *Rāmāyaṇa* and *strī-prekṣā* of Kauṭilya continued during successive centuries of Indian history. The hand gestures and static postures of the dancers, with a lot of *abhinaya* part, too, suggest measured and harmonious movements. Thus, these artistes seem to represent classical tradition. The same is suggested by a fragmentary relief from Mathurā belonging to first century AD[447] depicting dance and music performance, exclusively by female artistes. On the left, three danseuses

441. See *Pl*. V.
442. See *Pl*. VI.
443. See *Pls*. VII, VIII, IX.
444. See *Pl*. XI.
445. G. Yazdani, *The Early History of the Deccan*, vol. VII-XI p. 779.
446. See *Pl*. X.
447. See *Pl*. XIII.

are seen; a hand visible on the extreme left shows that there were four of them. They are accompanied by a six-member orchestra.

Gradually, with the passage of time, more refinement came in the art of female artistes, representing 'female theatre'. This is noticed in the scene depicted on the fragment of a beam from Amarāvatī,[448] representing a group dance of female artistes in a most beautiful composition, accompanied by female musicians, already referred to. The *Kuraval* dance of cowherdesses, mentioned in *Cilappadikāram*, wherein the roles of Māyāvān (Kṛṣṇa) and Balarāma were played by girls, too, has the spirit of all-female theatre.

It seems that in a period between fourth and sixth century AD, the age of cultural renaissance, the tradition of *strī-prekṣā* flourished. Kālidāsa refers to a drama, *Lakṣmī Svayaṁvara*, written by Goddess Sarasvatī and performed by *apsaras*es like Urvaśī and Menakā in the court of Indra, in his *Vikramorvaśīyam*.[449] Similarly, the tradition of *antaḥpura saṅgītaka* performed by the *antaḥpura* artistes or *gaṇikā*s, too, shows the existence of all-female theatre. According to *Ubhayābhisārikā*, a Bhāṇa play of the Gupta period, *gaṇikā*s Priyaṅgusenā and Devasenā were invited to present a *saṅgītaka*, *Purandara Vijaya*,[450] in the palace of Pāṭaliputra. There used to be a *prekṣāgāra* or *nāṭyaśālā* for such presentations in the palace. The dramatic presentation of the episodes from the life of Kṛṣṇa by *apsaras*es to entertain Yādavas visiting Piṇḍāraka Tīrtha, referred to in *Harivaṁśa,* is another example of 'female theatre' or *strī-prekṣā*.[451]

Some sculptures belonging to the Gupta period represent female theatre, for example, the dance scene (housed at Archaeological Museum, Gwalior), depicting an elegant danseuse in the centre surrounded by female musicians;[452] the one carved on the wall, to the left of Varāha incarnation panel, Udayagiri, Vidiśā, depicting a divine danseuse, surrounded by a group of divine damsels playing different musical instruments;[453] and the three stone panels from Devagarh temple[454] consisting of a

448. Louis Frederic, *Indian Temple and Sculpture*; pl. 83.
449. *Vikramorvaśīyaṁ*, III, Miśraviṣkambhaka, *KG*, pp. 134-35.
450. *Caturbhāṇī*, pp. 141-42.
451. *Harivaṁśa*, Viṣṇu-Parva, 39.
452. V.S. Agrawala, *Gupta Art*, pl. 1. fig. 1.
453. See *Pl*. XXXV.
454. See *Pls*. XXXII, XXXIII, XXXIV.

dancing female figure in the centre, flanked by female accompanists, as described earlier in courtesan section. The dancing pose of the danseuses in these sculptures represent classical style. The last three examples, probably, represent *saṅgītaka* presented in the temple by female artistes like *gaṇikā*s which was customary during the Gupta period, as is known from the Bhāṇa plays of the period.[455]

The painting depicting the central figure of a danseuse, accompanied by a band of musicians, all women, in cave no. 1 at Ajantā, referred to earlier, is another example of female theatre.[456] The refined posture of the danseuse represents classical style.

The much-discussed dance scene from cave no. 7, Auraṅgābād, belonging to sixth century AD, represents a group of seven female artistes. The central figure is again that of a dancer representing classical style flanked by female instrumentalists, accompanying her in her performance.[457] This scene suggests that dance by female artistes had taken the form of ritual in Buddhist religious establishments also, as it was in Brāhmaṇical temples.

The dance scene representing Buddha's Māravijaya, belonging to seventh century AD, in cave no. 26, Ajantā,[458] referred to earlier in this chapter, is a beautiful example of 'female theatre'. This also depicts a female dancing figure in the centre, surrounded by female musicians, according to the tradition known since the Gupta period. The tradition of *antaḥpura saṅgītaka*, performed by the talented members of the harem, too, was known in the seventh century AD. *Saṅgītaka* was generally performed on the upper part of the palace. Women of *antaḥpura* performed when Harṣavardhana was born, as is mentioned in Bāṇa's *Harṣacarita*;[459] so did they, when Candrāpīḍa, the hero of Bāṇa's *Kādambarī*[460] was born. Śrī Harṣa also refers to a full-fledged drama, *Udayanacarita*, performed by female artistes of the harem in his *Priyadarśikā*.[461]

---

455. *Caturbhāṇī*, pp. 122-23.
456. G. Yazdani, *op. cit.*, LX.
457. See *Pl.* XXXVII.
458. See *Pl.* XXXVIII.
459. *Harṣacarita* pp. 222-27.
460. V.S. Agrawala, *Kādambarī eka Sānskṛtika Adhyayana*, p. 82.
461. *Priyadarśikā*, Act III, pp. 52-68, tr. C.K. Nariman.

The tradition of 'female theatre' continued during successive periods, too. Bhavabhūti, in his *Uttara-rāma-carita*, refers to a dramatic performance of selective episodes from Sītā's life by the *apsaras*es.[462] The popularity of all 'female theatre' may have induced Bhavabhūti to use it as a dramatic device.

In the eighth century AD, too, *gaṇikā*s continued staging plays in temples, as they did in the Gupta period. *Kuṭṭanīmatam*[463] refers to the performance of Śrī Harṣa's *Ratnāvalī* by *gaṇikā*s of Vārāṇasī in the temple of Viśveśvara, in which male parts too were adorned by them. Thus, the reference shows the existence of all-female theatre even after the period under study. The dramatic activities of temple girls mentioned in the Bayānā inscription of Citralekhā[464] and plays performed entirely by female artistes of *antaḥpura*, witnessed by king in the evening, mentioned in *Bṛhat-kathā-śloka Saṁgraha,*[465] also indicate the same.

The reason for the origin and popularity of female theatre in ancient India lay in the social prejudice. As people associated with theatre in ancient India were generally considered immoral and *śāstrakāra*s objected to women witnessing theatrical show,[466] female theatre of *strī-prekṣā* might have originated as a substitute. Possibly, in the beginning, it became popular in *antaḥpura,* where no outside male could enter. The *antaḥpura* professionals, having proper training, played male parts too. Later, it was adopted by courtesans and professional actresses too, performing outside the harem. It might be possible that *strī-prekṣā* was, in the beginning, a theatre of the women and for the women as is vaguely suggested by Kauṭilya, but gradually, it became open to all as is known from the sculptures depicting male members of spectators too, besides females, witnessing *strī-prekṣā*.[467]

---

462. *Uttara-rāma-carita*, Act VII, p. 162, ed. M.R. Kale, 1924.
463. *Kuṭṭanīmatam,* 800.
464. *EI*, vol. XXII, p. 124.
465. *dṛṣṭastrīpātranāṭakaḥ* — *Bṛhat-kathā-śloka Saṁgraha*, II.32.
466. *KA*, III.3; *Manu-smṛti*, IX.84.
467. See *Pl.* V.

4

Dramatic Troupes, Abhinaya, Stage and Auditorium

Part I — Dramatic Troupes

DRAMATIC troupes are often mentioned in ancient Indian literature as performing on special occasions. Bharata's *Nāṭyaśāstra* gives a detailed description of the troupes and their members. A dramatic troupe, in fact, is a natural outcome of a professional necessity. As there was a heavy demand for professional theatre artistes at the royal courts, at the houses of well-to-do persons and also, at different festivals, the bards, musicians and actors formed their troupes or *saṁgha* and as the art developed and became more complex and varied, it demanded the help of a larger number of artistes, from other fields of art as well. Artistes joined the professional cadre which gradually developed into distinctive professional troupes.

Members of the Troupe

As drama is a comprehensive art, embracing almost all fields of art, a dramatic troupe too, consisted of different types of artistes as its members. Our main source regarding the troupe and its members is Bharata's *Nāṭyaśāstra*. The actors and actresses, in a theatrical company or troupe, have been broadly classified as *sūtradhāra*, *pāripārśvika* or the assistant director, *vidūṣaka* or jester, *viṭa* or the flirt or parasite, *cheṭa* or the personal aids, *śakāra* or the inconsequential, *nāyaka* or the hero, *nāyikā* or the heroine, *gaṇikā* or the courtesan, *bharata*s or other actors and actresses and other personal attendants and messengers. Actors and actresses of the troupe were divided according to their qualifications into superior, mediocre and inferior actors. The above-mentioned ones were the chief actors and actresses of the troupe and it seems that they would have gradually come to be known by those names.

SŪTRADHĀRA

Sūtradhāra, the director, was one who gave regular practice to the actors and actresses in enacting the roles assigned to them. He chose them according to their natural characteristics, i.e., physical form, temperament, gait, calibre, speech and acting capacity and prepared them for the final presentation of the plays. His natural qualities, according to Bharata,[1] were intelligence, good memory, generosity, steadiness in speech, good health, sweetness (in his manners), tolerance, self-control, sweet-tongue, calmness, truthfulness and politeness. He should be impartial and free from greed for praise. This greed for praise, according to M. Ghosh, means:

> a hankering after uncritical praise which may come from the multitude and surely, stands in the way of a first rate artistic production. Besides these natural qualities, he should possess knowledge of characteristics (of everything concerning the theatre), refinement of speech, knowledge of rules of *tāla* and theory of notes and instruments. He should be conversant with practices of various religious sects, with polity and *Arthaśāstra*, with science of stars and planets and also, with working of human body, and should know about countries and people inhabiting them.[2]

All these qualities of *sūtradhāra* or director, enumerated by Bharata, seem a must for a director, even if we study them in the modern context. M. Ghosh rightly says:

> Hindus had very advanced ideas about the responsibilities of a director. He was required to be an expert, not only as regards acting but also in all those arts which together constitute a performance.[3]

He had an important role in the preliminaries (*pūrvaraṅga*) and often appeared in different roles in plays.

PĀRIPĀRŚVIKA

Sūtradhāra was assisted in his work by *pāripārśvika*, who was 'a person of the middling types' and had 'slightly lesser number of qualities than the director was to

1. *NŚ*, XXXV.72-74.
2. M. Ghosh, tr., *NŚ*, vol I, p. 222.
3. *Ibid.*, p. 222 fn.

possess'.[4] He seems to be the equivalent of modern assistant director. In Sanskrit plays, we find *pāripārśvika* giving information to *sūtradhāra* about the play and obeying his orders.[5]

BHARATA

The next important member of the troupe was *bharata,* whom we have already discussed.[6]

VIDŪṢAKA

Vidūṣaka was another important member of the troupe who was an actor *par excellence*, as he could imitate the manners of all people, was ready witted in disclosures made through pleasantry and shrewd. He must have been a popular character of the troupe who looked to people's entertainment.[7] His importance in the troupe is indicated by the allotment of a pivotal role to him in the dramatic preliminaries.[8] From Bhāsa and Aśvaghoṣa down to the latest dramatists, with a few exceptions, all have introduced the character with varying degree of success.

As far as his origin is concerned, he is a highly controversial character of Indian drama. Konow[9] thinks that *vidūṣaka* is an old figure of the popular stage which the classical drama had borrowed from the popular dramas of the wandering dancers and mimes, where the manners and the demeanour of the higher castes — especially of the brāhmaṇas — have been ridiculed exactly in the same manner as in the present time.[10] This seems possible, when we find a long tradition of folk drama dominated by *hāsya*.[11] Among the folk artistes of Vedic period, a comic actor was included, who was called on occasion of sacrifice, according to the *Puruṣa Sūkta* of *Vājasaneyī-Saṁhitā* of *Śukla Yajurveda*. In Buddhist *Jātaka*s also, such *naṭa*s are mentioned who made people laugh by their representations at the popular festival

4. *NŚ*, XXXV.74-75.
5. *Vikramorvaśīyam*, *KG*, p. 106. *Mālavikāgnimitram*, *KG*, p. 184.
6. See chapter 2.
7. *NŚ*, XXXV.92-93.
8. *Ibid*., I.62-63.
9. S. Konow, *The Indian Drama,* p. 23.
10. *Ibid*., p. 24.
11. M.L. Varadapande, *Traditions of Indian Theatre*, pp. 81-84.

Samāja. We have seen the reference of a *naṭa* who made half of his body dance while the other half remained stone still.[12] Tālapuṭa, in *Gāmaṇī Saṁyutta*,[13] refers to the actors who make people laugh 'To make people laugh' was one of the aims of folk drama. Hence, it is not altogether unlikely that *vidūṣaka* was the product of this folk tradition of drama.

In modern folk theatre also, *vidūṣaka* in the form of *songadyā* (Maharastra), *raṅgalo* (Gujarat), *mīrāsī* (Punjab), *konnagī* (Andhra Pradesh), *kaṭṭiyār* (Kerala), *munśījī* (*nauṭaṅkī* U.P.), etc., is always there. He is there, performing several roles on the stage — introduction of characters and linking the story of the play with present events, besides making intelligent remarks on contemporary political and social life, in the garb of humour.

In classical tradition, a character was needed who had to be a suitable person of certain status in whom the king could confine his love affairs, and who would gain access into the world of the heroine and her associates to help his royal friend in his amourous adventures, as the heroes of the classical plays were kings. Rangacharya[14] says that to fulfil this need, *vidūṣaka* of the Sanskrit plays was always a brāhmaṇa because a brāhmaṇa *vidūṣaka* could be a friend of status, sufficiently high for the king to confide in and as 'one must be deserving hero or harmless fool to seek the company and the confidence of the beauties of the harem' he is depicted as a fool,[15] but at the same time, he is a man of wide experience and observation who knows what to say, when and where.[16] He is a fatalist in a typically Hindu tradition.[17]

He amuses the audience and at the same time, he alone in the dramatic world comments and moralises on progress of events, not only in the play proper but in life itself in general,[18] and acts as a bridge between the audience and stage, speaking in Prākr̥t. This was what the *naṭa* of folk tradition used to do, in a crude form, with

---

12. See chapter 2.
13. *Saṁyutta Nikāya*, IV, p. 306.
14. Adya Rangacharya, *Drama in Sanskrit Literature*, p. 68.
15. *Ibid.*, p. 5.
16. *yathā nāma ahaṁ mūrkhaḥ tat kiṁ parihāsasya api deśakālam na jānāmi — Mr̥cchakaṭikaṁ*, III, p. 65.
17. Adya Rangacharya, *op. cit.*, p. 67.
18. Adya Rangacharya, p. 71.

some elements of eroticism and vulgarity to amuse the folk audience, which had prompted Kauṭilya to enjoin that actors should avoid commenting on socially sensitive things and making fun of country, castes, family (*gotra*) and certain schools of Vedic studies (*caraṇa*).[19] Thus, it seems possible that the popular comic actor of folk tradition was transformed into a *vidūṣaka* in classical tradition.

TAURIPA

A dramatic performance needs music — vocal and instrumental, to create a suitable atmosphere before and during the play. Hence, musicians and instrumentalists also became part and parcel of a dramatic troupe.

Bharata had included *tauripa* in his list of the members of theatrical troupe. He says, '*Tauripa* is skilled in playing *tūra*, has a liking for all the instruments and is an expert in playing them all, and possesses (all kinds of) musical instruments.'[20] Bharata has described, in detail, the instruments used by musicians, like *tauripa* in a dramatic performance, and their use. He divides the instruments into four varieties — *tat*, i.e., string instruments like *vīṇā*; *avanaddha*, i.e., percussion instruments like *mṛdaṅga*; *ghana*, i.e., metal instruments to mark the time like cymbals and *suśira*, i.e., wind instruments like flute.[21] He, further, says that there should be perfect harmony among music (vocal), instruments and drama.[22] In thirty-second chapter of *Nāṭyaśāstra,* he describes *dhruvā vidhāna* or the songs in detail which are sung in the course of the play. *Dhruvā* is so-called, because in it the word, *varṇa*, *alaṁkāra*, *yati*, *pāṇi*, *laya* are harmoniously fixed.

*Dhruvā*s are of five types: *prāveśikī* — sung when the character enters on the stage. *naiṣkrāmikī* — when he leaves the stage, *akṣevikī* — the song which indicates the change of mood, with the change of the medium or the slow tempo to quick tempo (or vice versa), *prāsādikī* — the song which calms the audience that are experiencing a different sentiment, due to *ākṣepa* and which burnishes the mood, already introduced, and *antarā* — the last one, the song sung when a gap or a mishap in the perfomance is to be covered up or when owing to the overpowering

---

19. *KA*, IV.76.1
20. *NŚ*, XXXV.94.
21. *Ibid.*, XXXV.2.
22. *Ibid.*, XXVIII.7.

feeling, there is a tense situation in the action, as when one is in deep grief, loss of memory, sleep or has fallen down.[23]

In the thirty-third chapter, Bharata describes *kutapa*, i.e., the correct seating place for the each member of the orchestra, on the stage.[24] The above description indicates the importance of *tauripa* in the troupe. Probably, he was equivalent of modern music director of the play, because he was expert in playing all kinds of musical instruments.

KUŚĪLAVA

Kuśīlava, the next member of the troupe, is described by Bharata as he who can apply the principles of instrumental music, is himself an expert in playing instruments, and is called *kuśīlava* because of his being *kuśala* (clever) and *avadāta* (refined) and free from agitation (*avyathita*).[25] From *Nāṭyaśāstra, kuśīlava* seems to be an expert musician of the troupe, but he is frequently mentioned in ancient Indian literature as an actor — as we have already seen.[26]

NAṬA

While enumerating the names of the members of the troupe, Bharata mentions *naṭa* twice. In verse no. 95 of the thirty-fifth chapter, he says that the meaning of the root *naṭ* is 'to act' and as he acts (*naṭayati*) again and again the stories of men with sentiments, states and temperament he is called a *naṭa*. In verse no. 100 of the same chapter, he says that the 'one who can apply the music of four kinds of instruments, and produce a play according to the meaning of the *śāstra*s, as well as his own reasoning, is called a *naṭa*'. It is not clear to us why Bharata has described *naṭa* twice and differently. In the first verse (no. 95), he lays stress on his quality of acting and in the second, on that of producing a play with the help of his knowledge of instrumental music.

One is tempted to think that the *naṭa* described in verse no. 95 is an actor, the chief actor of the troupe playing the role of hero, as he is different from *bharata* the

23. *NŚ*, XXXII.365-70.
24. *Ibid.*, vol. IV, p. 415 (Chow. Sans. Sansthan edn.).
25. *Ibid.*, XXXV.106.
26. See chapter 2.

actor, mentioned separately by the author of *Nāṭyaśāstra*, while the *naṭa* of verse no. 100 is a *prayoktā* (producer, director) who produces a play, applying the music of four types of instruments. Hence, it seems that this *naṭa* of verse no. 100 is that member of the troupe who helped the director either in the dance sequence of the play, for which knowledge of instrumental music is essential, or in musical representation like *lāsya* which has dance part also. Besides helping the director, *naṭa*, like *sūtradhāra*, was himself an actor with proper knowledge of music and dance, as the term *naṭa* means a dancer too. Later, dramaturgists have mentioned *uparūpaka*s, the minor forms of drama, full of dance and music. In such minor forms, *naṭa*s act as well as dance — for example, in *nāṭyarāsaka*, *rāsaka* and *hallīśa*.

As dance and music had always been popular entertainment, since pre-Vedic and Vedic times, it seems that such entertainments did exist in some form during Bharata's time too, though he does not mention them in his treatise. A few centuries later than Bharata, a painting in Bāgh cave depicts a dance performed by a *naṭa* surrounded by female musicians who themselves are, perhaps, dancing. The scene is identified with *hallīśa* type of representation by V.S. Agrawala,[27] as we have already seen. Bharata himself admits that there are many other forms of drama which are not mentioned by him.[28] Hence, it seems that there were such plays in existence during his time too in which dance performed or directed by *naṭa* had an important place, and Bharata describing a dramatic troupe in detail does not forget mentioning such *naṭa*s.

NĀṬAKĪYĀ

Next member of the troupe is *nāṭakīyā*, the professional actress. Bharata says that 'a woman who knows all about the playing of drums, *laya* (tempo) and *tāla* and is conversant with sentiments and is beautiful in all her limbs, should be made an actress'.[29] In the previous chapter, we have already mentioned the role of this professional actress, *nāṭakīyā* in the troupe.

PLAY-WRIGHT

The next important member of the troupe was the play-wright, one among the three

27. V.S. Agrawala, *Gupta Art*, pp. 95-96.
28. *NŚ*, XX.151.
29. *Ibid.*, XXXV.101.

most important members of the troupe — director, actor and play-wright. Bharata says that because he puts in (different) sentiments, states and temperaments, as taught in the *śāstras*, in different characters, a person is called a play-wright (*nāṭyakāra*).[30] Perhaps, his duty was to compose a play on any given theme, as each troupe had its own play-wrights.

He mentions that the *itivṛtta* or main story is the body of a *kāvya* or the play and that it has five divisions.[31] He then proceeds to explain the weaving of a story into a well-constructed plot. A play-wright must choose a good story and select a proper form for the play before he begins writing. The stories are of three varieties — *prakhyāta* or popular, *utpādya* (*kalpita*) or imaginary and *saṅkīrṇa* or mixed. Every story must profess an end. The character that achieves the purpose of a story by himself or with the assistance of his associates is styled *nāyaka* or hero, around whom centres the main plot, *ādhikārika* (*pradhāna*) *itivṛtta*. The associates that help the hero to achieve the purpose are called *upanāyakas* or minor heroes. If any incident in the life of any of the associates enhances the value of the main plot, it is also accepted by the author in the construction of a play as a *prāsaṅgika itivṛtta* or subplot.[32]

The effort of the hero is to be delineated in five stages (*kāryāvasthā*) namely, the beginning (*prārambha*), the striving (*prayatana*), the attainment slightly suggested by the means (*prāptisambhava*), the visualisation of the certainty of success (*niyata-phala-prāpti* or *niyatāpti*) and the attainment of the result (*phalayoga* or *phala-prāpati*).[33]

The means which are conducive to the attainment of the result are also five — the *bīja*, i.e., the seed or the germ; the *bindu*, i.e., the prominent point or the spread; the *patākā*, i.e., the subordinate incident; the *prakarī*, i.e., the main episode and *kārya*, i.e., all the effort for the purpose of the main plot or denouement.[34] In *patākā*, the characters get their purpose served even while helping the hero. The character in the *prakarī*, which is introduced for helping the hero, has no purpose of his own

30. *NŚ*, XXXV.99.
31. *Ibid.*, XXI.1.
32. *Ibid*, XXI.3.
33. *Ibid.*, XXI.7-12.
34. *Ibid.*, XXI.20-26.

and has no continuity. *Bīja*, *bindu* and *kārya* would be necessary in all plays while *patākā* and *prakarī* would be used when required.

The plot is developed through five *sandhi*s, i.e., junctures — *mukha* (opening in which the germ is created), the *pratimukha* (the expanding juncture), the *garbha* (sprouting of the germ), the *vimarśa* (pause over the germ that has sprouted) and the *nirvahaṇa* (bringing together the object of all the junctures).[35] The *nāṭaka* and *prakaraṇa* are to have five junctures. The number of junctures used is according to the nature of the play, i.e., *dim* and *samvakāra* would be without *garbha* and *vimarśa* while *prahasana*, *vīthī*, *aṅka* and *bhāṇa* would have only *mukha* and *nirvahaṇa*.[36] Each juncture has its *aṅga*s, i.e., the sub-parts which are sixty-four in all.[37] *Abhinava* has stated that the *mukha* has twelve sub-parts, *pratimukha* thirteen, *garbha* thirteen, *avamarśa* (*vimarśa*) has twelve and *nirvahaṇa* has fourteen. But, in his commentary, he has explained with illustrations, thirteen sub-parts of the *avamarśa* juncture. These sub-parts of the juncture are treated in the *Nāṭyaśāstra* to show how the plot should be well-knit from the angle of the language used in it. The sub-parts of the junctures are meant for the perfection of the play. What particular sub-parts are to be used in a particular juncture depends upon the play-wright. A good dramatist never makes a conscious effort to include or incorporate the sub-parts of the juncture.

Because Bharata prohibits certain difficult incidents like war, death, siege of a fortress, etc., and delicate incidents like sleeping, kissing, embracing, eating, etc., a play-wright had to employ more than one suggestive device. Since it is not feasible to present the complete life story of a hero in the course of a play, the minor incidents of his life, which are necessary for the progress of the play, are brought out by the play-wright through such devices. Such suggestive devices are called *arthopkṣepaka*s, such as *viṣkambhaka* and *praveśaka*, which are the introductory scenes, presenting medium and low characters, respectively. *Cūlikā* is an announcement from behind the scenes. *Aṅkāvatāra* are for continuity, the former for maintaining continuity between two acts and later, for general continuity.[38]

---

35. *NŚ*, XXI.35-41.
36. *Ibid.*, XXI.43-5.
37. *Ibid.*, XXI.51-62.
38. *Ibid.*, XXI.107-17.

If an entirely different meaning is derived in the rendering of a word or sentence, written to convey a particular meaning, it is called *patākā-sthānaka* or dramatic irony. They are of four kinds:

(i) The incidence of an uncontemplated novel, meaning of a word or sentence that promotes the intended objective, is the first kind of dramatic irony.

(ii) When a statement carrying double meaning, suitable to the occasion, is employed and expressed in a poetic language, it is called the second kind of dramatic irony.

(iii) The clarification of the meaning of a statement which is not clear by itself, in a subtle manner, in the form of a dialogue is called the third kind of dramatic irony.

(iv) When a statement with a twin meaning purports a different third meaning, suitable to the occasion, it is called the fourth kind of dramatic irony.[39]

Thus, when a play-wright chooses the life story of an ideal hero for writing a play, he first picks up attractive episodes, then the plot is developed through the junctures. The executive processes, suggestive devices, sub-parts and dramatic ironies appear in these junctures.

Unlike Greek tragedians, ancient Indian play-wrights did not have any restriction regarding time and place for the events and actions depicted in the play. The lapse of time between two acts (which was never more than a year) was indicated by introducing scene (*praveśaka*) and the only restriction regarding place or locality was for the human character — that they were always to be placed in Bhāratavarṣa.[40]

BACKSTAGE WORKERS

People associated with theatre know the importance and indispensability of the backstage workers, without whom a play cannot be a success. As Bharata was a *prayoktā* and had seen dramatic troupes intimately, he knew this fact and did not forget the backstage workers while enumerating the names of the troupe members.

---

39. *NŚ*, XXI.29-33; P.S.R. Appa Rao, and P. Ramasastry, *A Monograph on Bharata's Nāṭyaśāstra*, p. 51.

40. *NŚ*, XX.99. M. Ghosh, tr. Introduction, p. xxxii.

Mukuṭakāra

First of all, Bharata mentions *mukuṭakāra*, the crown maker, who makes masks and various special dresses together with headgears (*śīrṣaka*, *pratiśīrṣaka*) suited to various characters. This artist, thus, provided facilities for *āhāryābhinaya*. His work is described in detail in *Nāṭyaśāstra*.

Bharata says that crowns should be used for gods and kings. They are of three varieties: *pārśvagata*, *mastakin* and *kirīṭa*. The first was used in the case of gods, *gandharvas*, *yakṣas*, *pannagas* and *rākṣasas*; second, in the case of middling gods; and the third, in the case of suprerior gods. In the case of inferior gods, *pārśvagata* was used. The *mastakin* was employed in the case of kings. The *keśamukuṭa* (with the locks of hair tied) was used in the case of *vidyādharas*, *siddhas* and *cāraṇas*.[41]

Masks were employed in the case of *rākṣasas* and demons. Bharata says that they should have tawny hair and green beard. For the superior amongst the demons, *pārśvagata* should be used. Crowns were to be used when the head was shaven as in the case of sacrifice and when the hair is not long. He further says that the half crown should be used in the case of commanders, princes and *mahāmātras*; ministers, *kañcukīya*, leaders of the guilds of merchants and priests should have turbans.[42]

All these headdresses were made by *mukuṭakāra*. Bharata describes the masks made by him and also the method employed by the artist. Masks are to be used when characters with two or three heads, etc., are to be represented, or when the character covering his own face impersonates that of the other. The *ghāṭī* of the masks should be thirty-two *aṅgulas* in measure or of appropriate measure and should be prepared out of bilva paste and cloth or bark of trees, etc. The mask should be made with ashes or husk of paddy mixed with bilva paste. Then, it should be covered with strips of cloth smeared with bilva paste. After drying it, the holes are to be made for ear, nose, etc.[43] Probably, artificial hands and legs were made by *mukuṭakāra* according to the need.

Ābharaṇakṛta

The maker of the ornaments (*ābharaṇakṛta*) was another important member of the

---

41. *NŚ*, XXIII.135-38.
42. *Ibid.*, XXXV.138, 140.
43. *Ibid.*, XXIII.175-83.

troupe doing similar job regarding *āhāryābhinaya*. Bharata[44] says that he makes ornaments according to various roles. He used to make ornaments for men and women according to the fashion of the caste of the characters. The ornaments of the divine and royal males were *cūḍāmaṇi* (crest jewel), worn on the top of the head, *kuṇḍala* (earrings), *mocaka* (ear pendant) worn in the central part of the ear and *kīlā* at the top of the ear. Among the ornaments of neck were *muktāvalī* (pearl necklace), *harṣaka* (having the shape of a snake, etc.) and *sūtraka* (golden neck chain), etc. Ornaments of the finger were *vetikā* (golden ring) and *aṅguli-mudrā* (ring with various designs). *Hastali valaya*, *rūcaka*, *culikā*, etc., were hand ornaments and *talaka* (worn below the navel) and *sūtraka* (worn still lower) were those of the waist.

The ornaments for female characters are also described. *Śikhāpāśa*, *śikhāvyāla*, *piṇḍīpatra*, *cūḍāmaṇi*, *makarikā* and *muktājāla* are the head ornaments. *Kuṇḍala*, *karṇikā*, *karṇavalaya*, *patrakarṇikā*, *karṇamudrā*, *karṇotkīlaka* (ear top), *śikhipatra* (ear ornament studded with multi-coloured jewels, in the shape of peacock feather), etc., are ear ornaments. *Muktāvalī* (pearl necklace), *vyālapaṅkti*, *mañjarī*, *ratnamālikā*, *sūtraka* are of the neck. *Aṅgada* (arm band), *valaya* (arm ring), jewelled net for bosom are others along with *kaṭaka*, *kalāpi*, *śaṅkha*, *mudrāṅgulīyaka* for fingers, *talaka* (set with network of pearls), *mekhalā* (girdle), *raśanā* (another kind of girdle) for hips, *nūpura*, *kiṅkiṇī*, *ghaṇṭikā* for ankles, *pādapatra* for shanks and toe ring and *tilaka* for toes.[45]

This variety of ornaments, for the males and the females, indicates the fine work of *ābharaṇakṛta*. Bharata says that the ornaments should not be heavy, for this would cause fatigue to actors and actresses.[46] Hence, the golden ornaments should have only a thin covering of gold. The jewels should be studded in lac so that they would not cause exhaustion. This shows that the *ābharaṇakṛta* had to take extra care in making the ornaments, since they had to be light as well as realistic. Like actors, *mukuṭakāra* and *ābharaṇakṛta,* too, would have been properly trained by the artists in the respective fields, as technical knowledge was necessary for their work. Possibly, they belonged to that particular artisan class or caste that practised these arts as family profession, later, they joined the theatrical troupe

---

44. *NŚ*, XXXV.103.
45. *Ibid*, XXII.15-41, 196.
46. *Ibid.*, XXXV.46-48.

because of their personal interest in dramatic arts, and gradually, their hobby became their profession.

Mālyakṛta

Similar would have been the case with *mālyakṛta*, the next back-stage worker, who made five kinds of garlands.[47] Garland was considered as one of the ornaments.[48] They are of five types. The first, is *veṣṭim*, in which along with flowers, leaves and green grass are woven decoratively. The second type is *vitata*, in which many garlands are interwoven. The third is *saṁghātya* in which the thread is woven through the flowers, or many bunches of flowers are woven together. In *granthima*, the fourth one, the flowers are knitted together with knots and the fifth is *pralambita*, *a* long garland hanging down.[49]

Veṣakāra

The next back-stage artist is *veṣakāra*. In him was vested the responsibility of costume and make-up, it seems. Bharata described the female and male costumes in detail, according to the status and region the characters belonged to and also, according to the situations in the play. Hence, a *veṣakāra* was expected, it seems, to have a knowledge of dresses and costumes of different countries and had to be an imaginative artist who could give shape to the ideas of the director regarding the sentiments he wanted to portray through the costume and make-up of the character. This is because it is through make-up and costume that the audience is given a complete picture of the nature of the character, his nativity, period and state of mind. An actor or actress should look exactly like the character he or she is going to portray on the stage; only then would Bharata's *parakāya-praveśa*[50] be possible, i.e., the transmigration of the soul. Just as the soul of an individual enters the dead body of another individual, and behaves like him, an actor gets into the physical characteristics of the role, with the aid of the costume and make-up, and then, behaves likewise, yet not losing his inner identity and this miracle is performed by such back-stage artistes as *veṣakāra*.

---

47. *NŚ*, XXXV.104.
48. *Ibid.*, XXIII.10.
49. *Ibid.*, XXIII.10-11.
50. *Ibid.*, XXXV.24-7.

Bharata has described the costume of various females, for example — *vidyādharī*, *yakṣī*, *apsaras*, *nāgī*, *munikanyā*, *siddha* women, *gāndharvī*, *rākṣasī*, *devī* and *divya-nārī* in detail.[51] Women on earth should be dressed according to their countries — for example, Āvantī ladies should have curly hair, Gauḍī mostly curls having *śikhāpāśa* and braid of hair, etc.[52] Similarly, dress should match the situations and the characters, for example, the women whose lovers have gone abroad and those that are afflicted with calamity should have one braid of hair and the dress soiled.[53]

Male costume, according to Bharata, is of three types:[54] *śuddha* (white), *vicitra* (variegated) and *malina* (soiled). *Śuddha* dress should be used when a religious activity is to be performed — for example, while going to a temple. *Vicitra* dress should be used in the case of gods, demons, *yakṣa*s, *gandharva*s, *nāga*s and kings of amorous nature and *malina* for lunatics, intoxicated persons, travellers and those in calamity.[55] Sages and monks should have dress according to their rules.[56]

Citrakāra

It seems that *aṅgaracanā* or making up the face and the body with grease paints, etc., would have been one of the functions of *citrakāra*,[57] one of the back-stage artists who knew painting. It seems that besides painting things concerning *nepathya*, he did the above-mentioned job, too or at least helped the *veṣakāra* because the art of *aṅgaracanā* needs a sound knowledge of colour combination and command on brush.

Bharata says that there are four original colours — black, blue, yellow and red. The derivative colours are to be prepared by mixing them proportionately. In the mixture, the ratio of the strong colour to the weak should be one to two. Thus, knowing these rules of colour combination, the body should be painted.[58] Gods, *yakṣa* and divine nymphs are to be painted *gaura* (fair); Rudra, Arka, Druhiṇa and Skanda with golden colour; Soma, Vṛhaspati, Śukra, Varuṇa, stars, *samudra*,

51. *NŚ*, XXIII.51-62.
52. *Ibid.*, XXIII.63-7.
53. *Ibid.*, XXIII.71-72.
54. *Ibid.*, XXIII.118.
55. *Ibid.*, XXIII.119-24.
56. *Ibid.*, XXIII.125.
57. *Ibid.*, XXXV.105.
58. *Ibid.*, XXIII. 75-83.

Himavat, Gaṅgā and Balarāma — white; Mars red; Buddha, Hutāśana — yellow; Nārāyaṇa, Nara and Vāsukī — *śyāma* (dark); demons, goblins, mountains, Yama and sky — dark blue. The men in six *dvīpa*s have colour of burnished gold. All but those who live in Uttarakuru should have golden colour. The people of Bhadrāśva should have white and of Ketumāla, blue. *Gandharva*, *yakṣa*, *pannaga*, *vidyādhara* and *pitṛ*s should be of various colours.

In Bhāratavarṣa, the kings should have lotus colour, yellowish white or dark blue; happy men should be yellowish red. Wicked people and those possessed of evil spirit, diseased, people who work hard and those of inferior birth like *dhīvara*, *ḍom*, etc., should have the colour of *badara* (plum) and those engaged in penance should be black. The colour should be used according to the need of the situation, country and birth. Kirāta, Barbara, Āndhra, Draviḍa, Kāśī, Kośala, Pulinda and Dakṣiṇātya should be generally black. Śaka, Yavana, Pahlava, Bāhlika and those in the northern region should be generally *gaura*. Pāñcāla, Śaurasena, Mahiṣa, Oḍra, Magadha, Aṅga, Vaṅga and Kaliṅga should be dark blue. Brāhmaṇas and kṣatriyas should be *gaura*, vaiśya and śūdra, *śyāma*.[59]

The knowledge of painting was necessary for the make-up of female characters too, as the forehead *tilaka* mark was to be painted and designed with great care, especially having the semblance of flowers. On the cheeks *tilaka* and *patralekhā* were painted.

Rajaka

There was a dyer (*rajaka*)[60] too in the troupe who was so-called because of his knowledge of dying (*rañjana*). He probably helped *veṣakāra* in providing suitably dyed and washed clothes.

Kāruka

Kāruka,[61] the craftsman, fashioned different objects out of lac, stone, metal and wool,[62] for the construction of sets and model work (*pusta*), i.e., various objects or

---

59. *NŚ*, XXIII.92-109.
60. *Ibid*., XXXV.105.
61. *Ibid*., XXXV.105.
62. *Ibid*., XXXV.105.

pieces grouped together and modelled to represent mountains, vehicles, chariots of gods, palaces, forests, armours, shields, flagstaffs, etc., for creating the necessary illusion on the stage. Bharata says that this could be achieved in three ways. The first is *saṅdhima* (joined), i.e., preparation of the necessary shape and form of the objects for the stage requirements with the help of pulp, mats, bamboo, leather, cloth, etc. The second is *vyājima*, i.e., animation of the objects by means of mechanical device, and the third is *veṣṭima*, i.e., creation of an object with drapery — for example hill, carriages, celestial cars, shields, armours, banners, elephants or trees.[63]

Probably, one of the *kāruka*'s important function was the construction of the stage. In ancient literature,[64] this term, *kāru*, occurs frequently, meaning an artisan (*śilpakāra*). According to Manu,[65] the term means a carpenter, weaver, barber, washerman and cobbler. Thus, it seems that the function of the *kāruka* of the dramatic troupe was multilateral in the back-stage world.

The above account shows that each member of the dramatic troupe of Bharata's time had different important duties to perform, to make that aesthetic representation successful which is known as drama. Drama was, thus, not merely acting, dancing, singing or writing plays but construction of theatre, its decoration, painting, dyeing, washing, making garlands, costumes and ornaments, etc., also. Hence, each member of the troupe had collective as well as individual importance. Bharata's description of the troupe clearly reflects his practical experience regarding the art and confirms that he was himself a *prayoktā*. The general term for such *prayoktā*s in *Nāṭyaśāstra* is 'Bharata'; from *sūtradhāra* to *rajaka* are called 'Bharata'.

We do not find such comprehensive description of a dramatic troupe in any other text on dramaturgy, the reason being that Bharata was a *prayoktā* while the later *ācārya*s were mere *śāstrakāra*s. Though Dhanañjaya, Sāradātanaya, Sāgaranandī, Viśvanātha and Śiṅgabhūpāla, etc., have dealt with the traditional characters of drama, they did not discuss theatre artistes, whether performing or back-stage. Some of them have mentioned theatre people like *sūtradhāra*, *pāripārśvika*, *saṁsthāpaka* and *kuśīlava* but never those who work behind the curtain and whose importance only a *prayoktā* would understand.

---

63. *NŚ*, XXIII.6-9.

64. *Yājñavalkya-Smṛti*, II.249; *Viddhaśālabhañjikā*, I.13; *Naiṣadhīyacarita*, I.38.

65. *Manu-Smṛti*, V.129.

Sāgaranandī had mentioned *sūtradhāra*, *pāripārśvika*, *kāvyaprasthāpaka* (*saṁsthāpaka*), *nartaka*, *naṭa* (*śailūsa*), *bharata*, *sūta* (*strījīvī*), *raṅgācārya* (*mahānaṭa*) and their wives *lāsikā*, *nartakī* and *naṭī*.[66] Śiṅgabhūpāla[67] has mentioned *kāru* as the companion of the heroine, but to him *kāru* is *rajakī*, the washerwoman and *śilpakārī* is *vīṇāvādinī* (lute-player). Sāradātanaya gives a comparatively clearer view regarding *prayoktā*s (theatre people), for example, *sūtradhāra*, *naṭa*, *naṭī*, *pāripārśvika*, *kuśīlava*, *vidūṣaka*, *śailūṣa* and *bharata*, but none of them are back-stage artistes.[68] It seems that later dramaturgists were concerned with playwriting rather than producing. They were becoming more theoretical and less practical, while Bharata was a *prayoktā ācārya* whose rules and instructions were based on practical experience.

It seems that most of the members of the troupe were from the same family — for example, *naṭī* seems to be the wife of *sūtradhāra* who aids him in the opening scene, as is known from Sanskrit plays. In Bhāsa's play *Cārudattam,* she is his wife. She is often addressed as *ārye* and *priye*, a common way of adressing one's wife. In Kālidāsa's *Śākuntalam,* she addresses *sūtradhāra* as *āryaputra*, showing that he was her husband.[69] She was an expert in singing. In *Mṛcchakaṭikam*,[70] *Ratnāvalī*[71] and *Mudrārākṣasa*[72] also, she is *sūtradhāra*'s wife (*gṛhiṇī*). He addresses her as *priye* (my dear). Not only husband and wife, but other members of the family, too, were active members of the troupe.

From *Avadānaśataka,*[73] we know that a *naṭācārya* from Dakṣiṇāpatha (south) visited the city of Rājagṛha with his troupe. His beautiful daughter Kuvalayā was in his troupe, and people raved for her whenever she appeared on the stage. We have seen the reference to two generations of 'Śailālaka family' of Mathurā in previous chapters. The members of this 'Śailālaka family' may have formed a troupe

66. *Nāṭaka Lakṣaṇa Ratnakośa*, 2160-85.
67. *Rasārṇava Sudhākara*, I.89-93.
68. *Bhāvaprakāśa*, 10, p. 288.
69. *Abhijñānaśākuntalam*, Act I, Prastāvanā, *KG*, p. 3.
70. *Mṛcchakaṭikam*, p. 16, ed. M.R. Kale (rev. edn. 1972).
71. *Ratnāvalī*, Prastāvanā.
72. *Mudrārākṣasa*, Prastāvanā.
73. ... *yāvaddakṣiṇāpathannaṭācārya āgataḥ tasyaduhitā kuvalayā nām abhirūpa darśanīyā* ... *yadā raṅgamadhyamavatarati* ...

— *Avadānaśataka*, VIII.75, p. 185

of their own. In the *prastāvanā* of *Ratnāvalī*, *sūtradhāra* informs *naṭī* that his younger brother is appearing in the role of Yaugandharāyaṇa.[74] Similarly, the elder brother of *sūtradhāra,* in *Karpūramañjarī,* played the role of Devī.[75] Thus, it seems that *naṭa*s had adopted drama as their family profession. Probably, the father trained his children in the art and formed a family troupe, together with other artistes. The chief *naṭī*, *nāṭakīyā* or *nartakī,* mentioned by Bharata, may often have been the wife of the chief *naṭa*, *sūtradhāra* or *naṭācārya*, and performed one of the important roles, as she seems to have been an expert in music and acting. Thus it seems that gradually, a hereditary professional caste of actors was coming into being.

Inter-troupe Rivalry

Often there was rivalry between two troupes. This is indicated by Kauṭilya's *Arthaśāstra*.[76] He says that if artisans and actors, criticise each others' profession, they would have to pay certain *paṇa*s to the state as penalty. This criticism must have been generated by rivalry between two troupes. This rivalry is indicated by Bharata's *Nāṭyaśāstra* also. We know from the twenty-seventh chapter of the text[77] that competition between dramatic troupes were held and the winners were awarded. Naturally, one rival troupe tried to prove other as inferior and incompetent; for this they went even to the extent of hooting and demoralising the actors performing on the stage. Bharata has mentioned such disturbances under the category of *parasamutthābādhā*.[78] To prove a play useless, the rival party laughed or cried loudly at wrong places, went on whispering throughout the play or threw cowdung or ants on the stage[79] to disturb the artistes, especially the female characters.[80]

---

74. *nanu ayam mam kavīyāna bhrātā gr̥hītayaugandharāyaṇa-bhūmikaḥ prāptā eva.*
— *Ratnāvalī*, Prastāvanā

75. *Karpūramañjarī*, Prastāvanā. p. 11, ed. Durgaprasad, 1927.

76. *KA*, III.75.18.

77. *NŚ*, XXVII.75-78.

78. *Ibid.*, XXVII.19.

79. *athasitaruditavisphoṭitānyotkuṣṭanālikāpātaḥ* ।
gomayalośca pipilīkāvikṣepāśvārīsambhūtaḥ ॥
— *Ibid.*, XXVII.21

80. *sukumāra prakr̥teḥ strīpātra prāyasya trasnotpāditena siddhivighātāya paśoḥ veṣaṁ kr̥tvā sukumāra prayoktāraṁ bhīṣayati sāmājikam vā. . .*
— *Abhinavabhāratī*, vol 3, pp. 311-13

Probably, the rival troupes bribed people to cause such disturbance during the play.[81]

The rivalry between *naṭācāryas* is depicted in Kālidāsa' *Mālavikāgnimitram.*[82] Rivalry between troupes and actors continued to be a common feature in the field of theatrical art, even after the period under study. Rivalry between two schools of acting is mentioned in an inscription from Paṭṭadakal.[83] The inscription is signed, at the end, by 'Achalada' and refers to the growing popularity of a new work on dance following the precepts of Bharata which secured a decisive victory for the school of Bharata, against the votaries of the rival school or schools, referred to as *paranaṭa* and *kuṭilonnatanaṭa*, i.e., the hostile actor who is crookedly eminent. In *Anargharāghava*[84] of Murārī, the actor declares that he has come to exhibit a superior sort of drama to that played by a rival, and asserts that the dearest desire of a player is to satisfy the public and to win back the favour he has lost.

This rivalry might have had a good effect on the art, so far as it inspired the actors to refine their art and technique in a competitive spirit, but

> it would have been damaging for the history of the art if, as one may assume, every theatrical troupe zealously guarded use of the script of its successful plays, written by the poet or writer of that particular troupe, from its rivals. Under such circumstances, plays have little chance of outliving the time of their first production. As the popularity of a particular play decreased it came to be altogether lost.[85]

Could this be the reason as to why we do not find plays of poets like Kaviputra and Saumilla?

Travelling Troupes

Troupes of actors used to wander, far and wide, in search of favourable opportunities for presenting their shows. The performances were to adorn a festive occasion, such as religious festivals, the consecration of a king, a marriage, the taking possession of a town or a new estate, the return of a traveller, and the birth of a son. The

81. *NŚ*, XXVII.22.
82. *Mālavikāgnimitraṁ* Act, *IKG*, pp. 187-97.
83. *IA*, vol. X, p. 167.
84. *Anargharāghava*, I.3.
85. M. Ghosh, 'On the Origin of the Hindu Drama', *IHQ*, vol. XXXI, p. 213.

troupe travelled from one place to another to perform on such occasions because this would have been monetarily rewarding.

Travelling troupes of *naṭas* are mentioned in *Jātakas*. *Tittira-Jātaka* says:

> He has (as porter of the tradesman) wandered in Kaliṅga kingdom, he has engaged in trade, stick in hand, he walks over the country road. With Naṭas he had wandered.[86]

The reference to *naṭa* in *Kaṇavera Jātaka* shows the same. As *naṭas* and their troupes were known for wandering and presenting shows, Sāmā says to them:

> There is no place that you do not visit. You visit grāma (village), nigam (cities) and rājadhānī (capital) and present dramatic performances, sing and dance on the stage and allure people.[87]

Anupapātika Sūtra, the Jain text, while describing the city of Campā, says that it was frequently visited by theatrical troupes.[88]

Kauṭilya enjoins that the theatrical troupes from some other country, performing in the state should pay five *paṇas* as *prekṣā-vetana*.[89] He further says that actors must camp at one place during rainy season and stop moving.[90] This shows that during his time, too, actors wandered from place to place presenting their shows. This was one of the reasons why he utilised them and their art for spying.

The troupe of a *naṭācārya* in *Avadānaśataka,*[91] came to the city of Rājagṛha from south. *Mahāvastu* mentions a travelling troupe coming from Taxila to Vārāṇasī (*Mahāvastu*, vol. II, p. 169). From Chinese accounts, we infer that actors were invited in *vihāras* to stage the stories of renunciations, as those of Sāriputra and Maudgalyāyana.[92] Bharata[93] also took his dramatic troupe to Kailāsa, to present a play in honour of Lord Śiva.

---

86. V. Fousball, *The Jātaka*, vol. III, p. 541.
87. E.B. Cowell, *Jātaka Stories*, vol. III, p. 41.
88. *Aupapātika Sūtra*, II, pp. 4-5.
89. *KA*, II.43.
90. *Ibid.*, IV.76.
91. *Avadānaśataka*, VIII.75, p. 185.
92. Quoted by Kunjunni Rāja in his book *Kuṭiyāṭṭam*, *Chinese Literature*, Part III, p. 149.
93. *NŚ*, IV.6-7.

Kāmasūtra informs about such wandering troupes performing in the temple of Sarasvatī on occasion of a festival. Vātsyāyana, the author of *Kāmasūtra*, says that after performing once, the actors should repeat their performance if there is a strong demand or else return gracefully.[94] *Harivaṁśa*[95] tells that the troupe of Bhadranaṭa used to visit Bhadrāśva, Ketumāla and other places frequently. We have seen how Yādavas visited the city of Vajranābha, disguised as the members of a theatrical troupe. This shows that it must have been a common practice of the troupes to visit different cities.

Vasudevahiṇḍi also informs about such touring troupes: 'people entertained themselves at public dramatic performance[96] which were sometimes enacted by companies of actors who moved from place to place entertaining the people'.[97] An inscription from Canjeevaram informs about a troupe of actors who had enjoyed certain privileges, like those, that they had been enjoying in Śoḷamaṇḍalam, for staging certain plays (*kūttu*) at Kāñcīpuram and in all other villages of Toṇḍai Maṇḍalam.[98] The reference shows that they performed at several places, wandering from one to another.

History of Troupes

The history of dramatic troupes goes back to at least the age described in epics. In *Rāmāyaṇa,* such troupes are frequently mentioned. Describing the festivities at the time of Rāma's coronation, it is said that the troupes of *naṭa*s and *nartaka*s (dancers) delighted the citizens by their performances.[99] Not only this, the age of *Rāmāyaṇa* witnessed the performance of all-female theatrical troupes too, as already mentioned.[100] It seems that it was not a rare thing; Ayodhyā had such troupes all over the city.[101] *Rāmāyaṇa* and *Mahābhārata* often mention performing artistes as

---

94. *Kāmasūtra*, Part I. IV, Sūtra 22-33.
95. *Harivaṁśa*, Viṣṇu-Parva, 92, 48-50.
96. *Vasudevahiṇḍī*, p. 320.
97. *Ibid*., p. 292.
98. *A.R. Ep*., 1921, No. 42; also Pt. II, Para 68.
99. *Rāmāyaṇa*, Ayodhya-kāṇḍa, 6.14.
100. See chapter 3.
101. *vadhūnāṭakasaṅghaiśca saṁyuktaṁ sarvataḥ purīṁ* — *Rāmāyaṇa*, Bāla-kāṇḍa.5.12.

a group, *gāyaka-vādaka-nartaka* or *sūta-māgadha-vaitālika,* probably indicating the existence of their dramatic troupes.

Gāmaṇi Saṁyutta,[102] a Buddhist text, mentions the troupe of Tālapuṭa, who was the chief of the village of *naṭa*s. Probably, the *naṭa*s of the village had formed a troupe. In *Kaṇṇavera Jātaka,*[103] also a troupe of *naṭa*s is referred to, whom *gaṇikā* Sāmā requested to go from one place to another, singing a song, in the festival *Samāja*, which conveyed her feelings towards her lost love.

In Jain literature, they are often mentioned in plural number[104] which indicates the existence of their troupes. Besides, there are some very clear references to theatrical troupes, in Jain texts. Bharata Chakravarti, at the time of his coronation, entered into the pavilion with *strī-ratna*, thirty-two thousand *ṛtu-kalyāṇī*s, thirty-two thousand *janapad-kalyāṇī*s and thirty-two thousand theatrical troupes, divided into thirty-two groups.[105]

The existence of theatrical troupes is indicated by Kauṭilya's *Arthaśāstra* too. Kauṭilya says that *bandhakīpoṣaka* (prostitute keepers), *plavaka*, *naṭa nartaka* and *śobhika*, while performing plays, should make the chief of the councils fall for beautiful young dancers of the troupes, and make them quarrel among themselves at the cost of their unity.[106] This reference shows the existence of theatrical troupes with female members.

Dance performance, in accompaniment to vocalists and an orchestra, depicted on the railings of Sāñcī and Bharhut *stūpa*s indicate that there must have been such troupes during second and first centuries BC, too. *Avadānaśataka,*[107] composed in first or second century AD, mention the troupe of a *naṭācārya* from south, as noticed earlier. *Mahāvastu* mentions a troupe of *naṭa*s coming from Taxila to

---

102. S. IV, p. 306.

103. V. Fousball, '*The Jātaka*', pp. 61-2.

104. *battīsaibaddhehiṁ nāḍaehiṁ varataruṇīsaṁpauttehiṁ. . . — Dhammakahāṇuyoga*, Bharata Chakravarti Kathānaka, Sūtra 524. pp. 211-12; *Ibid.*, IV. Śramaṇopāsaka Kathānaka, sūtra 72.

105. *Ibid.*, Bharata Chakravarti Carita, Sūtra 576, p. 240.

106. *KA*, XI.1.

107. *Avadānaśataka*, VIII.75, p. 185.

Vārāṇasī.[108] The Mathurā inscription,[109] referred to earlier in this chapter, mentions two generations of a *śailālaka* family who must have had their own troupe.

The reference to Yādavas, who visited the capital of *asura* King Vajranābha in the guise of a theatrical troupe of the famous *naṭa* Bhadra, with courtesans as actresses, in *Harivaṁsa,*[110] also shows the existence of such troupes which were invited to perform at various places.

Harṣa would have staged his plays with the help of such troupes.[111] According to the Chinese account, King Śilāditya composed the story of *bodhisattva* Jīmūtavāhana. It was set to music. He had it performed by a band of actors, accompanied by dancing and acting.

Some medieval south Indian inscriptions frequently mention such troupes. A troupe of actors is mentioned in Tanjavur inscription of Rājendra Coḷa (year sixth),[112] who had to perform drama entitled *Rājarājeśvara Nāṭaka* in the Rājarājeśvara temple.

Part II - Abhinaya or Histrionic Expression

The best and the earliest available text containing directions regarding the representation of a play or the method adopted in acting, covering each field of the art, by the theatre artistes in ancient India, is *Nāṭyaśāstra* of Bharata. Hence, a study of *abhinaya* or acting will be undertaken on the basis of this text.

Bharata says that broadly speaking there are two methods or aspects of presenting a play — the first is the presentation of the joys and sorrows of the world, as close to reality as possible and secondly, the assumption of various roles on the stage by the actors which is more conventional than real. The first aspect is known as *lokadharmī* or proximity to the ways of the world and the second aspect is known as *nāṭyadharmī* or theatrical presentation, depending entirely on *abhinaya* or histrionic expression.[113] *Dharmī* may also be interpreted as schools of acting —

108. *Mahāvastu*, vol. II, p. 169.
109. *EI*, vol. I, p. 381.
110. *Harivaṁśa*, Viṣṇu-Parva, 55.12-13.
111. *A Record of Buddhist Religion as Practised in India*, pp. 163-64.
112. *South Indian Inscriptions*, vol. II, pp. 306-7.
113. *NŚ*, XIV.69-73.

lokadharmī is realistic school and *nāṭyadharmī* is conventional school. *Naṭyaśāstra* incorporates both the schools in a proper proportion, so that the entire production becomes thoroughly enjoyable. These two schools are prevalant even today and show the relevance of Bharata's instructions.

In the twenty-second chapter of *Nāṭyaśāstra*, Bharata describes *vr̥tti*s or modes of expression. He has classified them into four for the sake of convenience. They are *bhāratī vr̥tti* or vocal expression (speech proper); *sāttvatī vr̥tti* or emotional expression; *kaiśikī vr̥tti* or delicate expression and *ārbhaṭī vr̥tti* or virile expression. According to *Nāṭyaśāstra*, Brahmā, the creator, derived these four modes of expression from the four forms of combat God Viṣṇu employed to conquer Madhu and Kaiṭabha, the two demons.[114]

Vr̥tti or modes of expression may be taken to be synonymous with what is commonly called acting. Acting with words proper is *bhāratī vr̥tti*; acting with the face and other parts of the body, in which the expression is the result of mental responses, is called *sāttvatī vr̥tti*; bodily action, generally demonstrative, is *ārbhaṭī vr̥tti*; *kaiśikī*, the fourth one, is a distinctive delicate form of bodily acting or speech and has been classified as a separate mode of expression. Hence, one can say that *kaiśikī vr̥tti* is a delicate form of all the three modes of expression motivated by the mind, the word and the body.

The importance of the modes of expression is determined by the *rasa* they are intended to produce. The delicate mode of expression (*kaiśikī*) will be present in creating the *rasa*s of *śr̥ṅgāra* and *hāsya*. The *sāttvatī vr̥tti*, motivated by thought, is employed to produce the *rasa*s, *vīra*, *adbhuta* and *śānta*. The *ārbhaṭī vr̥tti* is employed to produce the *rasa*s, *raudra* and *bhayānaka*, and *bhāratī vr̥tti* to produce *vībhatsa* and *karuṇa rasas*.[115] Action is the soul of drama. It is through action that plot develops. In the absence of action, the drama would come to a stand-still. This is the reason why *vr̥tti*s are called the mothers — the birthplace of drama.[116]

Not only costume but language or dialect, manner, custom and profession of the character speak of his regional identity. This is called *pravr̥tti*, i.e., the local usage. The regions are broadly divided by Bharata into four divisions, taking into

114. *NŚ*, XXII.2-14.

115. *Ibid.*, XXII.64-5.

116. *Nāṭyadarpaṇa*, III.103.

consideration the common characteristics possessed by them and overlooking the minor differences. They are 'Oḍramāgadhī', i.e., the eastern, 'Āvantī', i.e., the western, 'Dākṣiṇātya', i.e., the southern and 'Pāñcālī', i.e., the northern.[117] P.S.R. Apparao[118] says that it may be stated broadly that *dharmī* relates to *āṅgika abhinaya* or expression through movements and gestures, *vr̥tti* to *vācikābhinaya* and *sāttvikābhinaya* or expression through voice and speech and expression through responsive emotional reactions and *pravr̥tti* to *āhāryābhinaya* or expression through make-up and costume.

When *dharmī*, *vr̥tti* and *pravr̥tti* are decided, the next important thing is the art of acting. The Sanskrit word for acting is *abhinaya* which is derived from the root *nī* with *abhi* prefix and *acha*, suffix,[119] meaning 'to lead towards'. Thus, *abhinaya* is the art which conveys the poet's meaning or mood and the nature of the play in the fullest degree to the spectators. This *abhinaya* or histrionic representation covers all human activity which is divided into the physical, verbal and the mental. In performance, dress and make-up, etc., are helpful to produce the proper effect immediately. Hence, they are also included in *abhinaya*. The four fundamental types of expression are classified as *āṅgika abhinaya* or expression through movement and gestures, *vācikābhinaya* or expression through voice and speech, *sāttvikābhinaya* or expression through responsive emotional reactions and *āhārya abhinaya* or expression through costume and make-up.[120]

In addition to these four fundamental types of *abhinaya*, Bharata describes two more *abhinaya*s in two separate chapters — *sāmānyābhinaya* (chapter 24) and *citrābhinaya* (chapter 26) — which do not have a separate entity as such but comprise special features of the four types of *abhinaya* which have not been dealt in earlier chapters. *Sāmānyābhinaya* incroporates special features in respect of the three *abhinaya*s — *vācika*, *āṅgika* and *sāttvika*, and *citrābhinaya* deals, in greater detail, with *āṅgika abhinaya*, conveying ideas through symbolic representation.

Sāttvika Abhinaya

All the gesticulation of mental states is *sāttvika abhinaya* but prominence is given

117. *NŚ*, XIV.36.46.

118. P.S.R. Apparao, *A Monograph on Bharata's Nāṭyaśāstra,* p. 57.

119. *NŚ*, VIII.6.

120. *Ibid.*, VI.24.

to the gesticulation of the temperamental states (*sāttvika bhāva*) because of the peculiar mental effort which is necessary for their presentation.[121] *Sattva* is the capability of an actor to bring into being the pleasure and pains experienced by others, making them his own and presenting them on the stage, though he might not have been subject, in real life, to pleasure and pain of the type and form he is portraying on the stage. But he might have vicariously recorded in his mind the pleasure and pains actually experienced by others in the world. Besides, he receives instructions from his *ācārya*. As a result of constant practice and the innate *sattva* or emotional response, he is able to bring into play the respective emotions he has directly or indirectly exprienced. He presents the emotions on the stage, whenever called upon to do so, without losing himself in the emotion he portrays. The expressions depending on this *sattva* is called *sāttvika abhinaya*.

Bharata, in the seventh chapter of *Nāṭyaśāstra*, describes permanent states (*sthāyī bhāva*), transitory states (*śañcārī bhāva*) and temperamental states and their representation by the *anubhāva*, which is necessary for *sāttvika abhinaya*.

Among the permanent states, the first is *rati*; it is represented by smiling face, sweet words, contraction of eyebrows, sidelong glances and the like. *Hāsya* is represented by smile, laughter, etc. *Śoka* is represented by shedding tears, lamentation, change of colour, paralysis, insanity, etc. *Krodha* is represented by extended nostrils, upturned eyes, throbbing cheeks, etc. *Utsāha* is represented by steadiness, boldness of undertaking, etc. *Bhaya* by trembling hands and feet, dryness of the mouth, perspiration, etc.; *jugupsā* by contracting all the limbs, spitting, etc., and *vismaya* by wide opening of the eyes, looking without winking, etc.

Among transitory states or *sañcārī bhāva,*[122] the first is *nirveda* represented by weeping, deep breathing, etc. *Glāni* is represented by weak voice, lustreless eyes, pale face, etc. *Śaṅkā* is represented by constantly looking about and hesitating movement; *asūyā* by finding fault with others, casting glances in jealousy, knitting eyebrows, etc. *Mada* by sleeping in the case of superior persons, laughing and singing in the case of middling ones and crying and using coarse words in that of low ones. *Śrama* is represented by gentle rubbing of the body, contraction of mouth, very slow gait, etc.; *ālasya* by aversion to any kind of work, drowsiness, etc.; *cintā* by

---

121. *NŚ*, VII, vol. I, p. 377, Chow. San. Sansthan. edn.

122. *Ibid.*, VI, pp. 304-5, 391-492, VII, pp. 28-92 (Chow. San. Sansthan edn. 1978).

deep breathing, sighing, agony, etc.; *moha* by want of moment, excessive movement, falling down, etc.; *smṛti* by nodding of the head, raising up the eyebrows, etc.; *dhṛti* by enjoyment of objects attained, absence of regret for the unattained, etc.; *vrīḍā* by covered face, drawing lines on the ground, etc.; *capalatā* by harsh words, rebuke, etc.; *harṣa* by brightness of the face, embracing, etc.; *āvega* by looseness of limbs, falling down on the ground, sudden retreat, etc.; *jaḍatā* by not uttering any word, aversion to all work, etc.; *garva* by disrespect for others, etc.; *autsūkya* by sighs, drowsiness, etc.; *nidrā* by heaviness of face, relaxed body, etc.; *apasmāra* by throbbing, sighing, etc.; *supta* by deep breathing, dreaming, etc.; *vibodha* by yawning, etc.; *amarṣa* by shaking the head, etc.; *avahittha* by speaking otherwise, etc.; *ugratā* by killing, etc.; *mati* by instructing pupils, etc.; *vyādhi* by shivering, desire to roll on the ground, etc.; *unmāda* by laughing and weeping without any reason, etc.; *marana* by looseness of the body, closed eyes, etc.; *trāsa* by contraction of limbs, etc.; and *vitarka* by various discussions, etc.

Among the temperamental states (*sāttvika bhāva*),[123] the first is *sveda* represented by taking up the fan, etc. *Stambha*, the second, is represented by being inactive, smileless, etc. *Kampa* is represented by quivering, etc.; *aśru* by wiping the eyes full of tears, etc.; *vaivernya* by alteration of the colour of the face with effort by putting pressure on the artery; *romāñca* by repeated thrills, etc.; *svarabheda* by broken and choked voice; and *pralaya* by motionlessness, falling on the ground, etc.

Āṅgika Abhinaya

The movements of various parts of body, portraying emotions to express the ideas, is called *āṅgika abhinaya*. The parts of the body that are involved in movements and gestures have been divided into three categories — *aṅga*s, *upāṅga*s and *pratyaṅga*s or major, minor and subsidiary limbs, respectively. Head, hands, waist, chest, sides and feet are known as *aṅga*s, or the major limbs. Eyes, eyebrows, nose, lower lip, cheeks and chin are known as *upāṅga*s or minor limbs. Bharata has mentioned the word *pratyaṅga*s or the subsidiary limbs but he does not name them. Nandikeśvara[124] names them clearly as shoulders, upper arms, back, stomach, thighs and shanks. He also says that, according to some authors, wrists, knees, elbows and

123. *NŚ*, VII.94-100.

124. *Abhinayadarpaṇa*, 43.

neck are also minor limbs.[125] Bharata, however, has described the nature and use of most of the above subsidiary limbs. The gestures of limbs are divided into three types; *mukhaja* — those of the face; *śārīra* — those belonging to the body; and *ceṣṭākṛta* — those resulting from movement (of entire body).[126]

MUKHAJA ABHINAYA

In *mukhaja abhinaya*,[127] the movements of the head, the major limb, together with the minor limbs are given in detail. Thirteen movements of the head are treated, such as *ākampita* or slow vertical vibration of head used in giving hints, recognition, etc.; *kampita* or fast vertical vibration used in anger, arguments, etc.; *dhūta* or slow sideways vibration of the head used in unwillingness, dejection, etc.; *vidhūta* or fast sideways vibration used in attack of cold, terror, etc.; *parivāhita* or horizontal vibration used in wonder, joy, etc.; *adhūta* or lifting upwards, used in showing arrogant will, etc.; *avadhūta* or lowering down used in communicating a message, calling, etc.; *añcita* or bending to one side applicable in sickness, swooning, etc.; *nihañcita* or bending to a side to meet a raised shoulder, to be used by women in pride, affected indifference, etc.; *parāvṛtta* or turning away, used in turning away the face, looking back and the like; *utkṣipta* or bending backward, used in lofty objects and divine things; *adhogata* or bending down, used in shame and sorrow; and *lalita* or gyratory movement used in fainting and sickness, etc.

After this major limb, head, Bharata deals with the movement of minor limbs — for example *dṛṣṭi*[128] or glances (expression with the eyes) which is thirty-six in all and are, broadly divided into three main categories, eight *rasa* glances, eight static emotional glances and twenty transitory emotional glances.

The first among *rasa-dṛṣṭi* or *rasa* glances is *kāntā* or the pleasant, next comes *bhayānaka* or the terrified, then *hāsya* or the humorous, *karuṇa* or the pathetic, *adbhuta* or the wondrous, *raudrī* or the furious, *vīra* or the valorous and *vībhatsa* or the repugnant. There is, yet, a ninth glance, the *śānta dṛṣṭi* or the blissful glance.

The *sthāyī bhāva dṛṣṭi* or static emotional glances are *snigdhā* or the lovely,

---

125. *Abhinayadarpaṇa*, 44.
126. *NŚ*, VIII.9-13.
127. *Ibid.*, VIII.17-26.
128. *Ibid.*, VIII.38-93.

hṛṣṭā or the joyful, *dīnā* or the pitiful, *krodhā* or the angry, *dṛptā* or the bold, *bhayānvitā* or the terrified, *jugupsitā* or the disgustful and *vismitā* or the surprising.

The *sañcarī bhāva dṛṣṭi* or transitory emotional glances are *śūnyā* or the blank, *malinā* or the shrouded, *śrāntā* or the tired, *lajjānvitā* or the bashful, *glānā* or the depressed, *śaṅkitā* or the doubtful, *viṣādinī* or the despairing, *mukulā* or the partially closed, *kuñcitā* or contracted, *abhītaptā* or the distressed, *jihmā* or the jealous, *lalitā* or the delicate, *vitarkitā* or the reasoning, *ardhamukulā* or the half-closed, *vibhrāntā* or the confused, *viplutā* or the disturbed, *ākekarā* or the oblique, *vikośa* or the full-blown, *trastā* or the frightful and *madirā* or the intoxicated.

The disposition of *tārakas*[129] or the pupils in expression is of nine varieties — *bhramaṇa* or the turning round; *valana* or moving the eyeballs obliquely; *pātana* or relaxing; *chalan* or trembling; *sampraveśana* or drawing in; *vivartana* or turning sideways in sidelong glances; *samadvṛtta* or raising up; *niṣkrāma* or going out and *prākṛta* or natural.

The disposition of the pupils in *darśana,*[130] or additional glances, in looking at objects is of eight varieties — *sama darśana* or balanced look; *sacīkṛta* or half-closed side look; *anuvṛtta* or observing look; *ālokita* or startled look; *vilokita* or searching look; *pralokita* or side look; *ullokita* or upward look and *avalokita* or downward look.

Expression with *putas*,[131] or the eyelids, that generally follow the movements of the pupils is of nine varieties. They are *unimeśa* or separated; *nimeśa* or closed; *parasṛta* or fully separated; *kuñcita* or contracted; *sama* or normal; *sphurita* or throbbing; *pihita* or eyelids closed with efforts and *vitāḍita* or upper eyelid suddenly striking the lower one.

Expression with *bhrū* or eyebrow[132] is of seven varieties, which generally follow the movement of the pupils and eyelids. They are *utkṣepa* or raised; *pātana* or lowered; *bhṛkuṭi* or knitted; *catura* or pleased; *kuñcita* or bent; *recita* or raised and *sahaja* or natural.

---

129. *NŚ*, VIII.95-9.

130. *Ibid.*, VIII.104-8.

131. *Ibid.*, VIII.109-16.

132. *Ibid.*, VIII.117-27.

Expression with *nāsikā* or the nose[133] (nostrils) is of six varieties. They are *naṭā* or repeated depressed; *mandā* or balanced; *vikṛṣṭā* or expanded; *socchvāsā* or inhaling; *vikūṇitā* or contracted and *svābhāvikā* or natural.

Expression with *gaṇḍas* or the cheeks[134] is of six varieties — *kṣamā* or sunken; *phulla* or booming; *ghūrṇa* or expanded; *kampita* or throbbing; *kuñcita* or contracted and *sama* or normal.

Expression with *adhara* or the lower lip[135] is of six varieties — *vivartana* or awry; *kampana* or throbbing; *visarga* or protruding; *vinigūhan* or drawn-in; *sandaṣṭaka* or biting the lower lip and *samudgaka* or pouted.

Expression with *cibuka* or the chin[136] is dependent upon the movement of the tongue, teeth and lips and is of seven varieties: *kuṭṭana* or grinding the teeth; *khaṇḍana* or lips coming together repeatedly; *chinna* or closing the lips tightly; *cukṣita* or parting the lips; *lehita* or licking the lips; *sama* or normal and *daṣṭa* or biting the lower lip. The movements of lips and teeth are in reality the movement of the chin because they contribute to the expression with the chin.

Expression with *āsya* or the mouth[137] is of six varieties: *vinivṛtta* or awry; *vidhūta* or obliquely widened; *nirbhugna* or corner of the mouth lowered; *bhugna* or widened; *vivṛtta* or opened and *udvāhita* or corners of the mouth raised.

In *mukhaja abhinaya* should be included *mukharāgas*[138] or the colours of the face which depend upon the emotion expressed and the *rasa* created. The colour of the face is *svābhāvika* or natural, unnatural and indifferent mood, *prasanna* or pleasant, in wonder, laughter and love, *rakta* or red, in intoxication and in the heroics, the terrible and the pathetic and *śyāma* or dark, in the terrible and the odious.

There are nine movements of the *grīvā* or neck: *sama* or natural used in meditation etc.; *natā* resulting when the face is bent down, used when wearing

133. *NŚ*, VIII.128-33.

134. *Ibid.*, VIII.134-38.

135. *Ibid.*, VIII.139-44.

136. *Ibid.*, VIII.145-50.

137. *Ibid.*, VIII.151-58.

138. *Ibid.*, VIII.159-67.

ornaments, etc.; *unnatā*, taking place when the face is upturned, used in looking up; *trayasrā*, resulting when the face is turned sideways, used in carrying burden, etc.; *recita*, moving round, used in churning, dance, etc.; *kuñcita*, taking place when the head is bent, used in pressure of weight, etc.; *añcita*, taking place when the head is turned back, used in hanging to death, etc.; *valitā*, resulting when the face is turned sideways, used in looking with bent neck; and *vivr̥tta*, taking place when the face is towards the front, used in going towards one's own place.

ŚĀRĪRA ABHINAYA

The second division of physical gesticulation is *śārīra* or expression with the body,[139] which is the co-ordinated expression of the various limbs in response to an expression through a particular main limb. In this division, Bharata treats the movements of hand, breast, sides, waist and legs with their parts, i.e., shanks, thighs and feet.

Here, the *hand gestures* are very important. The hand is very eloquent in physical gesticulation. The number of hand poses is sixty-four in all, which is subdivided as the hand poses to be used in dramatic representation and those in dance. The *asaṁyukta* or single-hand poses are twenty-four and *saṁyukta* or those with both the hands are thirteen. The remaining twenty-seven hand poses are to be used mainly in dance, i.e., in the *karaṇa*s, etc.

Some of the *asaṁyukta hasta*s or single-hand gestures include *patākā* or the flag, the finger extended and closed and the thumb bent, used to represent blows struck by others, excessive heat, urging, great joy, in saying 'I too', 'Me too', etc. The same hand with the other hand in *patākā* with fingers moving was used in representing fire, rain, shower, etc., and *tripatākā* or the flag indicated by the third finger of the *patākā* hand bent, used in calling descent, bidding goodbye, raising up, salutation, the wearing of turban, etc. *Kartarīmukha* or the scissors, the forefinger of the *tripatākā* hand is bent at the back of the middle finger in this gesture. It is used in showing way, decorating the feet or dyeing them, etc. *Ardhacandra* or the half moon, where all the fingers together with the thumb are bent like a bow, is used in indicating a young tree, the digit of the moon, conch, jar, the thinness or fatness of the waist, etc. Similarly each single-hand gesture conveys some ideas. The remaining single-hand gestures are *arāla*, *śukatuṇḍa*, *muṣṭi*, *śikhara*, *kapittha*, *kaṭakāmukha*, *sucīmukha*, *padmakośa*, *sarpaśiras*, *mr̥gasīrṣa*, *kāṅgula*, *alapallava*,

139. *NŚ*, IX.4-204.

bhramara, *haṁsasya*, *haṁsapakṣa*, *saṁdaṁśa*, *mukula*, *ūrṇanābha* and *tāmracūḍa*.[140]

Similarly, combined or *saṁyukta* hand gestures are also very expressive. One of the *saṁyukta* hand gestures is *añjali* or the joint palms. It is used in representing great gods when held on head, respectable elders when near one's face, and friends when on breast. In *kapota* or the pigeon hands, both the *añjali* hands, meet at their side. It is used in indicating an approach with modesty, salutation and talk with venerable persons; it is held on the breast. Women represent cold and fear with this hand placed on the bosom and shaking. Similarly, remaining *saṁyukta* hand gestures also convey different *bhāvas*. They are as follows — *karkaṭa*, *svastika*, *khaṭakāvardhamānaka*, *utsaṅga*, *niṣādha*, *ḍolā*, *puṣpapuṭa*, *makara*, *gajadanta*, *avahittha* and *vardhamāna*.[141]

Even though the twenty-four single-hand gestures use only one hand normally, the second hand is also used in expression in an uncombined state. In all the thirteen coupled hand gestures, both the hands combine to produce the desired effect. *Nṛttahasta*s or the ornate hand gestures are, also, coupled hand gestures. They are used mainly in dance and have limited use in drama.[142]

All the hand gestures should be accompanied by expressive eyes, eyebrows and facial colour, etc., in a performance.[143] The experts should use the hand gestures in conformity with the popular usage, taking into consideration the *karaṇa* (movements), *karma* (object), *sthāna* (sphere), *pracārayukti* (appropriateness) and *kriyā* (mode). In dramatic representation, there is no idea that cannot be conveyed through hand gestures. The general position of the hands, in histrionic expression, are of three varieties — *uttāna* or upwards, *pārśvagata* or sidewards and *adhomukha* or downwards.

The use of the hand gestures and movements is prohibited in certain situations by Bharata, such as sadness, fainting, shyness, disgust, grief, weakness, dream, inactivity, disease, fever, fear, chillness, intoxication, panic, madness, thought, meditation, snowfall, pain, bondage, drowning, talking in sleep, excitement and

---

140. *NŚ*, Vol. II. pp. 47-63 (Chow. Sans. Santhan edn.).

141. *Ibid.*, IX.132-52.

142. *Ibid.*, IX.178-210.

143. *Ibid.*, IX.211.

cutting nails. Proper acting, in such situations, should be achieved through responsive emotional reactions and voice and speech.

After hands, the next is expression with *vakṣa* or the chest[144] which is of five varieties. *Ābhaṅga*, i.e., the breast is slightly bent, back high, shoulders slightly bent and at times loose. It is used in expressing hurry, dejection, fainting, sorrow, fear, disease, broken heart, the touch of cold objects, rain and shame; *nirbhaṅga* or the straight indicates paralysis, accepting with respect, look of surprise, speaking truth, etc.; *prakampita* or heaving which is used in laughter, weeping, fear, asthma, etc.; *udvāhita* or raised which indicates breathing, looking at lofty objects, etc., and *sama* or normal, used in normal position.

Expression with *jaṭhara* or the belly[145] is of three varieties: *kṣāma* or sunken used in laughter, weeping, inhalation and yawning; *khalva* or depressed used in sickness, penance, hunger, etc., and *pūrṇa* or full used in exhalation, fatness, disease and gluttony. According to some dramaturgists, there is another variety, viz., *sama* or normal.

Expression with *kaṭi* or the waist[146] is, again, of five varieties: *chinnā* or twisted indicating exercise, hurry and looking round; *nivṛttā* or twisted one turned square, used in turning round; *recita* or turned round, used in moving round on all sides; *prakampita* or quick lateral movement, used in the gaits of hunchback persons, dwarfs and persons of low type; and *udvāhita* or raised, used in the movements of fat persons and the graceful gait of women.

Next are the movements of *uru*, *jaṅgha* or thighs,[147] five in number: *kampana* or vibrating, used in the gaits of low type characters and in fear; *valana* or drawing the knees inwards, used in the easy gait of women; *stambhana* or stationary, used in nervousness and dejection; *udvartan* or drawing the knees inward and moving them and *vivartana* or drawing the heels inwards, used in moving about in confusion.

Expression with *jaghana*s or the shanks[148] is, also, of five varieties: *avarita* or repeated cross-wise movement of the shanks, used in the moving about of *vidūṣaka*;

144. *NŚ*, X.1-9.
145. *Ibid.*, X.18-19.
146. *Ibid.*, X.21-26.
147. *Ibid.*, X.27-32.
148. *Ibid.*, X.33-39.

nata or bent, used in sitting and standing position; *kṣipta* or thrown out, used in excercise and dance; *udvāhita* or raised, used in movements like going quickly and *parivṛtta* or twisted, used in classical dance and the like.

Next come the movements of the feet[149] which are, again, five in number: *sama* or normal used in natural poses; *agratala sañcāra* or moving on the toes, with the heels raised, used in urging, pounding, standing posture, pressing, striking the ground, etc.; *añcita* or reverse movements of the *agratala sañcāra*, used in movements when the forepart of the foot is injured, turning round, striking by foot and in various *bhrāmarī* movements; *kuñcita* or feet with an arched sole and bent toes, used in noble gait, turning round to the right and vice-versa, the *atikrānta* steps; and *udghaṭita* or raising on the toes and hitting the ground with the heels, used in *udghaṭita karaṇa*, once or more in the high or medium speed.

The leg movements are constituted of the movement of thighs, shanks and feet. The thigh should follow the movements of the feet.

After treating the gestures of the individual limbs separately, the movements of the body are dealt with. *Kārī* is the movement of the limbs below the hip. In *kārī* the movement of the feet is prominent, which is accompanied naturally by the movements of shank, thigh and also, waist. *Kārī*s are to be used in *nṛtta*, i.e., classical dance; in the *ceṣṭita*, i.e., the gaits of various persons and in fight.

CEṢṬĀKṚTA

The third division of physical gesticulation is *ceṣṭākṛta,* in which the body has to move. *Ceṣṭākṛta abhinaya* is of two types — the one pertaining to *gatipracāra*[150] or the expressive movement and the other, *nṛtta* or the rhythmic movement of the body as in dance. *Gatipracāra* prescribes the modes in which a character has to walk, stand, sit and lie down, in order to give proper expression as the situation or the emotion demands. This has great importance in drama. *Nṛtta* or the rhythmic movement of the body in a play does not establish any particular aspect but embellishes the play when accompanied by instrumental music.

Bharata has vividly described the movement or *gati* of a character at the time of

149. *NŚ*, X.40-56.

150. *Ibid.*, XIII.1-189.

his entry on the stage,[151] and gait according to the characters,[152] situations,[153] and *rasas*.[154] He describes the following stage movements which should be more indicative than real movement, in darkness,[155] disposition of a charioteer,[156] climbing and descending high building, tree, mountain,[157] etc., getting into water and coming out of it,[158] boating,[159] riding,[160] flying,[161] etc. In drama, such actions cannot be realistic but can only be established by such histrionic expression — for example, in drama a character dies but the actor who has taken that role does not. Hence, he has to enact death through expressions.

Bharata then describes the movements of a *viṭa*,[162] a *kañcukīya*,[163] a *vidūṣaka*,[164] a *cheṭa*,[165] a *śakāra*,[166] the sickly,[167] the stout,[168] the intoxicated,[169] the mad,[170] the disabled like lame and crippled, the dwarf,[171] the animal and the birds.[172] Next, he describes the three main *sthāna*s or postures of women, used in action and in

151. *NŚ*, XIII.4-11.
152. *Ibid.*, XIII.21-28.
153. *Ibid.*, XIII.30-40.
154. *Ibid.*, XIII.48-75.
155. *Ibid.*, XIII.87.
156. *Ibid.*, XIII.88-90.
157. *Ibid.*, XIII.96-100.
158. *Ibid.*, XIII.101-4.
159. *Ibid.*, XIII.105-7.
160. *Ibid.*, XIII.108.
161. *Ibid.*, XIII.93-95.
162. *Ibid.*, XIII.110-11.
163. *Ibid.*, XIII.112-13.
164. *Ibid.*, XIII.137-39.
165. *Ibid.*, XIII.146-47.
166. *Ibid.*, XIII.148-50.
167. *Ibid.*, XIII.115-17.
168. *Ibid.*, XII.119-20.
169. *Ibid.*, XIII.121-22.
170. *Ibid.*, XIII.123-30.
171. *Ibid.*, XIII.131-34.
172. *Ibid.*, XIII.152-57.

talking to others.[173] He then describes the movement of young women,[174] the old, the child, hand-maids, half-women, tribes women, children and eunuchs.[175]

Bharata, also, describes the posture of men and women in sitting[176] and reclining.[177] In this connection, he has also described the different types of seats provided in palaces and other houses.[178]

The *sāmānyābhinaya*[179] or general histrionic expression pertaining to *śārīrābhinaya* or the expression with the body has been classified into six categories. *Vākyābhinaya* or vocal expression, is used in conveying through speech the various meanings of a sentence, in consonance with the respective *bhāva*s and *rasa*s. *Sūcābhinaya* or indicative expression with speech is used to indicate the meaning of a sentence through other branches of expression, before the actual sentence is spoken. *Aṅkurābhinaya* or indicative expression bereft of speech is used to express the meaning of a sentence through the limbs improvised by the actor or actress. *Śākhābhinaya* or expression through arms and legs is used in expressing an emotion in consonance with the movement of the head, face, thighs, shanks and feet. *Nāṭyāyita* or interdramatic expression, in which the same characters in a play are employed as actors and audience for expressing a new theme that conveys a new idea or enhances the values of the main theme. *Nivṛtyāṅkura* or vicarious expression is used in places where the meaning of a sentence spoken by a character is interpreted by another character, through indicative expression, as though the meaning relates to himself.[180]

Vācika Abhinaya

Speech has been described as the main component of drama, since it allows the character to express all emotions, provides the basis for the instrumental and vocal

---

173. *NŚ*, XIII.160-68.
174. *Ibid.*, XIII.172-76.
175. *Ibid.*, XIII.180-88.
176. *Ibid.*, XIII.196-205.
177. *Ibid.*, XIII.221-27.
178. *Ibid.*, XIII.206-20.
179. *Ibid.*, XXIV.41.
180. *Ibid.*, XIV.41-48.

music that accompany histrionic expression, and by itself is an independent branch of histrionic expression. The play and its production on the stage enjoy an equal importance in a dramatic presentation. So, *vācikābhinaya*[181] or voice and speech has been dealt from both the author's and actor's viewpoint but our present study would consider its relevance to the actor.

Though *vyākaraṇa* or grammar is mainly concerned with playwriting, an actor should also have the knowledge of the same to understand the beauty of the word, and to clearly express its meaning in its pure form, particularly in the case of drama, where *pāṭhya* or speech (text proper) occupies an important place. The languages used in drama are mostly Sanskrit and Prākr̥t.

SANSKRIT PĀṬHYA OR SPEECH IN SANSKRIT

Sounds may be classified into consonants and vowels, which are commonly called letters. These sounds, both articulate and inarticulate, originate from eight points in the body: chest, throat, head, root of the tongue, teeth, nose, lips and the palate.

The combination of letters results in the creation of words, and knowledge of the identity and value of words is essential. In this connection, it is necessary to know about the following words or parts of speech — *nāma* or noun; *ākhyāta* or verb; *nipāta* or adverb; *upasarga* or preposition; *pratyaya* or terminal syllable, especially in Indian languages; *taddhita* or nominal affix; *vibhakti* or case; *liṅga* or gender; *saṅdhi* or conjunction of words and *samāsa* or grouping of words (compound words).[182]

PRĀKR̥T PĀṬHYA[183] OR SPEECH IN PRĀKR̥T

When the language is different from Sanskrit but akin to it and is in its unrefined form, it is called Prākr̥t. Prākr̥t exists in several forms, differentiated by regional variations. There are three forms of speech in Prākr̥t, evidenced by usage in drama — *samāna* or equivalent to Sanskrit, *vibhraṣṭa* or deformed and *deśīgata* or colloquial.

Grammar is as vast as an ocean and it is not possible for an actor to know all

181. *NŚ*, XV.2.
182. *Ibid.*, XV.23-24.
183. *Ibid.*, XVIII.2-3.

about it. Hence, Bharata indicated that it is enough if an actor had as much fundamental knowledge of grammar as was essential for a proper delivery of speech in drama.

Even though the language of the play may be perfect, without its impressive utterance, it would fail to make its impact. Not only this, but the difference in utterance would cause a change in meaning, which could be out of place in a given situation. It is possible to have contrary feelings like respect and contempt to be produced by the help of modulation of voice. Hence, it is absolutely necessary to render the text of the play on the stage with *kākusvara* or modulation in voice. In this connection, *pāṭhya* or recitation is described to possess six qualities essential for effective performance. They are *svara*s (notes), *sthāna*s (voice registers), four *varṇa*s (the manner of uttering notes), *kāku* (variations in inflexion), six *alaṅkāra*s (modes of enunciation) and six *aṅga*s (modes of rendering).

The *svara*s or notes are seven, i.e., *ṣaḍaja*, *r̥ṣabha*, *gāndhāra*, *madhyama*, *pañcama*, *dhaivata*, and *niṣāda*. These notes are to be used in different sentiments as follows — *madhyama* and *pañcama* in the erotic and the comic; *ṣaḍaja* and *r̥ṣabha* in the heroic, the furious and the marvellous; *gāndhāra* and *niṣāda* in the pathetic and *dhaivata* in the odious and the terrible.[184] *Abhinava*[185] makes clear the use of the seven notes in the recitation. These notes are musical, when they are possessed of *rakti* (produced by the specific musical intervals between these notes). The specific distances are not expected in the recitation. Only the change of voice to suit the experession is essential.

The voice, with the modulation, is produced from the chest, throat, and head which is *mandra* (low), *madhya* (medium) and *tāra* (high), respectively. When conversing with a distant person, the voice would be loud; when not far away, the medium, and when near, low.[186] In the delivery of speech, it is good to start with *mandra svara*, generating from the chest, brighten it with *tāra svara,* generating from the head and end it with *madhya svara,* generating from the throat. This achieves a good rendering of the text.[187]

---

184. *NŚ*, XIX.38-40.

185. *Abhinavabhāratī*, vol. II, pp. 385-86.

186. *NŚ*, XIX.41-42.

187. *Ibid.*, XIX.42-43.

Varṇa or the four fundamental variations in intonating speech are *udātta* or the bold; *anudātta* or the normal; *svarita* or the circumflex and *kampita* or the vibrating. In *hāsya* and *sṛṅgāra rasa*, *svarita* and *udātta*; in *vīra*, *raudra* and *adbhuta rasas*, *udātta* and *kampit*; in *vībhatsa* and *bhayānaka rasas*, *anudātta*, *svarita* and *kampita* modes or intonation predominate in rendering the text.[188]

Kāku or the variations in inflexion is of two kinds, *nirākāṅkṣā* (without expectancy) as the sentence is completely expressed and *sākāṅkṣā* (with expectancy) as the sense of the sentence is not completely expressed. The latter has notes from the throat and the breast, and begins with a high pitch and ends in a low pitch, and its *varṇa* and *alaṅkāra* are not complete; the former has notes from the head, beginning with a low pitch and ending in high pitch and its *varṇa* and *alaṅkāra* are complete.[189]

The six *alaṅkāra*s or the modes of enunciation are *ucca* or the high; *dīpa* or the bright; *mandra* or the base; *nīca* or the low; *druta* or the fast and *vilambita* or the dilated. Bharata has described in great detail the uses of these six kinds of enunciation.[190]

*Aṅga*s or the six processes in which speech is rendered are *viccheda* or the punctuated; *arpaṇa*, the recitation which fills the auditorium with graceful modulation of voice; *visarga* or disinterested, used in finishing a sentence; *anubandha* or the continuous which is the absence of separation between words or not taking breath while uttering them; *dīpana* or the brilliant is gradual augmentation of notes; and *praśamana* or the flowing is the lowering of the notes of high pitch, without making them discordant.

Bharata instructs about pause, *virāma*, in the delivery of speech which is very important for an actor to know. The pause should be after completion of meaning and not according to the metre, as the meaning depends on the pause. It is found in practice that there occurs pause even after one, two, three or four syllables. In a play, words occur containing a small number of syllables, in cases of *sūca* and *aṅkura*. That is why care should be taken about pause. When the two hands are busy, the recitation should be with proper eye movements and with pause expressive of

188. *NŚ*, XIX.43.
189. *Ibid.*, XIX.44.
190. *Ibid.*, XIX.45.

meaning. Pauses should be used when the word meaning is completed or breath is exhausted, or when there is a long compound, quick utterance or confusion or many meanings. Pause should be observed at the end of the foot of a verse or according to breath. One should not pause where it is not prescribed and should not have excited utterance when sorrow is to be expressed.[191]

SĀMĀNYĀBHINAYA[192] OR GENERAL EXPRESSION PERTAINING TO VOICE AND SPEECH

Speech should form the force behind the six varities of general expression with body. In consonance with the emotion and *rasa*, the general modes of speech are twelve: *ālāpa* or address; *pralāpa* or prattle; *vilāpa* or lamentation; *anulāpa* or repetition; *saṁlāpa* or dialogue; *apalāpa* or alteration of words; *saṁdeśa* or messages; *atideśa* or agreement; *nirdeśa* or indication; *vyapadeśa* or pretext; *upadeśa* or instruction and *apadeśa* or quotation.

There is, yet, another style of general expression in speech which is divided into seven categories: *pratyakṣa* or in the presence; *parokṣa* or in the absence of a character or characters; *bhūtakālika* or the past; *vartamānakālika* or the present; *bhāvikālika* or the future; *ātmastha* or pertaining to self and *parastha* or pertaining to others.

CITRĀBHINAYA[193] OR PARTICULAR EXPRESSION PERTAINING TO VOICE AND SPEECH

In particular expression, *ākāśa vacana* or speech directed to a character not on the stage; *ātmagata* or the soliloquy; *apavārita* or exclusive speech; *janāntika* or the aside; *karṇokta* or the whisper; *punarukti* or redundant speech; *svapnāyita* or talking in one's sleep; and *maraṇa* or death; etc., are discussed by Bharata as *citrābhinaya*.

Thus, the success of the representation depends, mostly, upon the actors. Actors are not supposed to repeat the dialogue of a drama in a parrot-like cold way, but have to reproduce with appropriate gesture of hands and feet, modulation of voice (in accordance with the emotion to be conveyed) and appropriate expressions on the

---

191. *NŚ*, XIX.60-67.
192. *Ibid.*, XXIV.49-57.
193. *Ibid.*, XXVI.85-104.

face, without which the drama will fail to make the emotional appeal to the spectators or to give them aesthetic delight (*rasa*).

Āhāryābhinaya or expression through make-up and costume

Āhāryābhinaya or expression through make-up and costume is the fourth type of *abhinaya*. Essentially, in drama, figure and form provide the spectacle and are called *rūpa*. Because *rūpa* is assumed in a drama, it is called a *rūpaka*; this shows the importance of make-up and costume in a dramatic representation. Abhinava[194] says that it is like a wall for the painting in the form of the performance with all the representation. Even if all the other histrionic representations are absent, the particular character is determined by the special dress and make-up. The other three forms of gesticulation are connected with the actor's physique but the *āhārya* is something that is externally added. The actors and actresses should create the physical characteristics of the roles they play by applying appropriate paint and wearing appropriate headgear or hairstyle and costume, in order to conceal their natural characteristics and to appear like the characters themselves.[195]

Āhāryābhinaya is four-fold — *pusta* (the model work), *alaṅkāra* (decoration); *aṅgaracanā* (painting of body); and *sajīva* (living creatures), details on which we have already studied in connection with dramatic troupe.[196]

BHARATA AS A PRAYOKTĀ: A REVIEW OF THE ACTING STYLE KNOWN FROM NĀṬYAŚĀSTRA

Bharata's instructions regarding modes and forms of expression are quite comprehensive, and relevant even today. Though, at a first glance, they appear to be a confusing list of terms, leading one even to doubt, if during Bharata's time the actors understood these terms, remembered them while on the stage and comprehended their significance. But, a re-reading puts anyone beyond doubt that Bharata's minute details were meant not only for his time but he wrote for posterity. The motivating force behind this monumental work was not merely instructive, but to preserve the great art for the future time. Like the *ācārayas* of the rich Indian

---

194. *Abhinavabhārati*, vol. III, pp. 112-13, (G.O.S. Baroda).
195. *NŚ*, XXIII.10, 15-41, 51-62, 75-83, 92-109, 118-24, 137-38, 175-83.
196. See chapter 3.

tradition,[197] he conceals nothing of his encylopaedic knowledge, pours forth his wisdom in the great treatise, welcoming pupils thirsty for knowledge to have their fill. To give drama a dignified status, maintain the great tradition as an art form and impart all this to a *supātra* was the aim of Bharata.

Bharata's *Nāṭyaśāstra* serves a two-fold purpose, as basic or fundamental to beginners and as a storehouse of veritable knowledge for experts to polish their art. There is nothing artificial in his instructions regarding the forms of expression. He merely speaks of the innate human qualities. Even if we put *Nāṭyaśāstra* aside, we would do exactly the same, as Bharata instructed, while on stage. Who will not classify the modes of expression in the way he did, though one may not name them as he did.

In many ways, Bharata was not an innovator but more of a codifier who rendered and explained everything in the light of human behaviour. Many of the static postures, hand gestures or other forms of gesticulation have merely been explained by him in keeping with the ways of the world. For example, when someone is necked out, the hand assumes the shape of the half-moon. That is why, that particular hand gesture is named as *ardhacandra hasta* or half-moon hand gesture. Two half-moon hands are used when ladies arrange their hair or put it in order. Similarly, the half-moon hand gesture is used on various other occasions. Bharata has given names to the hand gestures depending on the shapes the hand assumes, defined them and indicated their uses in his text for those to whom he could not demonstrate, personally. The expressive hand gestures are only chosen from nature, hence natural and there is no artificiality about them; the actors of his time did not have to memorise them. Bharata never imposes his ideas over the director or the actor. At the end of almost each chapter, he asks director or producer to get the idea of those expressions which have not been dealt with by him, from the ways of the world. Thus, the individual creative faculty which gives a distinct touch to every artiste is retained, and Sylvain Levi's[198] comment on Indian dramaturgy, that 'the artistic genius, that creative faculty which gives to rare individuals a fascinating originality has no name in Sanskrit', seems baseless.

---

197. *Milinda-Pañho* 1, p. 142; *ācāryo-apyanācāryo bhavati śrutpariharmājaḥ*
— *Āpastamba Dharmasūtra* XI.8.28

198. Sylvain Levi, *The Theatre of India*, vol I, p. 20.

The expression through other limbs is, also, very realistic. For example, the expression through the movement of chest and belly are exactly same as an actor of today would do. Whose belly would not contract while yawning, laughing and crying?[199] Similarly, the gaits of men, women and eunuchs are, also, very natural. If a person has seen a eunuch closely, he will appreciate Bharata's observations,[200] and an actor would walk exactly in the same manner as described by Bharata while playing a eunuch.

One must not forget that the names given to these expressions are in Sanskrit which was not far from the language known to the actors and directors of Bharata's time. These terms were actually demonstrations given by an *ācārya* for his pupil actors. We do find difficulty in memorising them but the pupil actors of Bharata's time did not. They were not 'terms' for them, but were part of instructions or direction, which an actor receives from his *ācārya* and reproduces it on the stage. It is as simple as we direct our pupil actor in Hindi — *haṅsatī huī āṅkheṅ rakkho* or in English — 'keep your eyes smiling'. The actor of present time knows what the director means by that because it is in his own language and not a term to learn by heart. Bharata explains this expression as *hāsya-dr̥ṣti* in Sanskrit, the language of his time.

Besides, Bharata had an added difficulty: he had to instruct those pupil actors also who were not present in his class and were not going to receive instructions from him, personally. Hence, Bharata had to describe these expressions of eyes (and those of other major and minor limbs) in such a vivid manner that his pupil of the future would get his ideas in their real sense. Hence, his instructions are not 'formulas and recipes presenting an amazing analogy with chemistry' as Sylvain Levi[201] comments. Perhaps, his western mind could not comprehend the many gems of purest ray serene, the unfathomable depth of *Nāṭyaśāstra*. Hence, his limitations have led him to consider *Nāṭyaśāstra* merely as a handbook containing 'a long list of technical terms distributed into categories by innumerable divisions and subdivisions'[202] and not the account of a practical adventurer, the wisdom of an active *naṭācārya*.

199. *NŚ*, X.18.

200. *Ibid.*, XIII.184.

201. Sylvain Levi, *op. cit.*, p. 20.

202. *Ibid.*

The movements of actors and actresses on the stage and their facial expressions in various situations described by Bharata under *sāmānyābhinaya* are, also, very natural. For example, Bharata says that a *nāyikā* who is waiting for her lover to come should ask the time, should go to the door the next moment, and lean on the door-jamb, return back with tears in her eyes and drop herself loosely on the seat, should think about all sorts of disasterous happenings that might have happened to him.[203] This is what an actress would do in this situation on the stage, not only in India but all over the world. This sort of acting or movements and expressions beautifully depict the psychological condition of the *nāyikā*. There are many other similar instances of realistic direction of Bharata. He often describes the psychology of women to enable the actress to live that character properly.[204] Hence, the statement of Sylvain Levi that 'the Indian genius which excels in ontological speculations has no special interest in psychological analysis' seems incorrect.

While describing *vācikābhinaya*, Bharata says that the knowledge of grammar is a must for an actor. This shows Bharata's practical experience as a director; his instructions are based on experience. People associated with drama know how an actor spoils a play with his mispronunciation and poor language. Similarly, Bharata knew the importance of pause in dialogue delivery.

Bharata's practical experience is seen in his instructions regarding *āhāryābhinaya* also, showing that ancient Indian style of acting was realistic up to a great extent, and was based on practical experience of directors and actors. For example, Bharata says, heavy ornament or armours made of iron or wood are not suitable for stage as they hinder free movement and are, thus, inconvenient.[205] They also make the artiste sweat; the artistes may faint on the stage and the play could be spoiled.[206]

The art of acting, it appears, must have taken the form of an advanced art during Bharata's time, to which he himself contributed. The modes of expression and representation of a play by the actors of his time must have been, it seems, a real aesthetic experience for the audience.

---

203. *NŚ*, XXIV.245-50.
204. *Ibid.*, XXIV.265-73.
205. *Ibid.*, XXIII.47-48.
206. *Ibid.*, XXIII.206-8.

Generally actors, trained by skilled *ācāryas*, applied the rules of *śāstras* while acting. That would have been the classical style of acting. But, from *Nāṭyaśāstra* itself, it appears that there were such actors also who had not been trained by *ācāryas* and acted spontaneously, imitating people.[207] But, they too were bound by the instructions given by the director. These two types of acting were known *ābhyāntara* and *vāhya,* respectively.[208] M. Ghosh is of the opinion that often trained actors performed freely, leaving the rules aside. To us, it seems that this might have been due to folk effect on the actors, who themselves belonged to the common folk, later trained by the *ācāryas*; and these two styles were adopted by the great master Bharata, probably to give due importance and recognition to those artistes also who, though having a natural talent for histrionic art, were not trained by the *ācāryas*. This was one of his attempts to provide recognition to the art of drama, whether folk or classical, which finally gave rise to the great symbiotic tradition of Indian theatre.

Part III - Stage and Auditorium

Though we find a specific reference to a theatre building, for the first time, in Bharata's *Nāṭyaśāstra*, a 'theatre structure' is known to have existed and used by the theatre artistes much before the time of Bharata in ancient India. It seems that there had been a long period of experiments in the field. Eventually theatre architecture reached its perfection during the age of Bharata, as is evident by the complex architecture of theatre halls referred to in Bharata's *Nāṭyaśāstra*, which duly fulfils the necessities for a dramatic representation.

Open Air Theatre

In the beginning, theatrical shows were performed in open air, as is indicated by *Ṛgveda*, which refers to the thickening cloud of dust that arose from dancer's feet.[209] The story of the origin of drama narrated in *Nāṭyaśāstra,* also, suggests that originally plays were presented in open air and theatre was a later development — being constructed as a protective measure against undesirable elements.[210]

---

207. *NŚ*, XXIV.79.
208. *Ibid.*, XXIV.77, 79.
209. *Ṛgveda,* X.72.6.
210. *NŚ*, I.78-81.

Raṅga is the most common word to denote a stage. *Gāmanī Saṁyutta*[211] mentions *raṅga* in the sense of a stage. *Cullavagga*[212] also uses *raṅga* in the same sense while referring to a festival *Samāja*. In such gatherings, probably, a temporary open air structure was erected for the artistes to perform and for spectators to gather around them. This temporary construction was in vogue during the period depicted in *Jātaka*s, too. The word *raṅga* or *mañca* was used for a stage even during that period. The *Ayoghar Jātaka* refers to jugglers who perform on the stage.[213] *Guttila Jātaka,* also, refers to *raṅga* — 'at the palace door a pavilion was set up and throne was set apart for the king in the gay pavilion' to witness the competition held between the master lute player Guttila and his pupil Musila. 'In the courtyard they were fixing the seats circle on circle, tier above tier'.[214] *Mahāpanāda Jātaka* also refers to a similar auditorium in which 'seats were erected in circles on circles and tiers above tiers', in the city of Bhaddiya to let the citizens witness the magnificence of rich Bhaddaji.[215] *Vidhurapaṇḍita Jātaka,* also, mentions the performance of theatre artistes, crowds of men and women gathered to witness the show and 'their seats, tiers beyond tiers'.[216] The description shows that a temporary circular open air auditorium was erected for the audience and a circular space, in the centre, was left out for the artistes to perform. Such structures were known as *raṅgamaṇḍala*. Most probably, planks of wood were used to erect such amphitheatres.

A *prekṣāgāra*, mentioned in *Harivaṁśa,* seems to be the culmination of this type of theatre. It was a permanent structure, instead of being temporary, and was more elaborate in comparison to the *raṅgamaṇḍala,* mentioned in the *Jātaka*s. This *prekṣāgāra* of Kaṁsa, where wrestling match between Kṛṣṇa and Balarāma on the one hand and Cānūra and Muṣṭika on the other was held, was in the vicinity of his palace and not inside it, because it is said in the text that Kaṁsa came out of his palace and inspected the arrangements at the *prekṣāgāra*.[217] It seems that it

211. *raṅgamajjhe . . .* — *Gāmanī Saṁyutta*, IV, *Saṁyutta Nikāya*, p. 306.

212. *Cullavagga*, I.3, pp. 19-20.

213. *raṅgamajjhe . . .* — *Ayoghar Jātaka*, E.B. Cowell, *Jātaka Stories*, vol. IV, p. 308.

214. *Ibid.*, vol. II, p. 175.

215. *Ibid.*, p. 229.

216. *samajjā ca ettha vattanti ākiññā naranāribhiḥ mañcatī mañceti mañcānam uparibaddhamañce. . .* — V. Fousboll, *The Jātaka*, vol. IV, p. 277.

217. *Harivaṁśa*, Viṣṇu-Parva, 28.5.

was a two-storeyed structure as a broad staircase[218] led to the *mañcas* (seats or chairs). It appears that one side of the enclosure was left unenclosed for entrance where an intoxicated elephant stood, waiting to trample Balarāma and Kṛṣṇa.[219] The building was divided into a number of compartments with passages running inside.[220] Each was provided with *mañcas* which were arranged in raised tiers one behind the other.[221] It seems that the circular space in the centre was left out for the spectacular performances which were arranged by Kaṁsa for the entertainment of his subjects. Most probably, it was an enclosed open area and not a stage inside the palace, as is indicated by the reference to cowdung powder sprinkled in abundance on the floor of the performing area or the *prekṣāgāra*.[222] Thus, the performing area and seating arrangement of this permanent *prekṣāgāra* was in the traditional style, known since the time of *Jātaka*s.

Cave Theatre

During the Mauryan period we come across a permanent theatre, i.e., the cave theatre, which was not alien to ancient Indians, as some Western scholars have believed, though it was not very common. Two caves, Jogimārā and Sītābeṅgā, have been discovered at Rāmgarh hill in old Surguja state. The Sītābeṅgā cave gives the impression of a cave theatre. T. Bloch[223] thought that 'we may look upon it as an Indian theatre of the third century BC'. A.C. Bidyabhushan[224] has described the cave as follows:

> The cave is 6' high inside or even less in some places. At the far end of the cave, is a high platform. The entrance to the cave is 17' wide and the cave is 44' long. At the centre it is about 12' 10" wide and about 6' high. On three sides there are two tiers of seats, the inner set being two inches higher than the outer one. The side with the double bench facing the entrance is 8' 6"

---

218. *Harivaṁśa*, Viṣṇu-Parva, 28.8.
219. *Ibid.*, 29.17.
220. *Ibid.*, 28.9.
221. *Ibid.*, 28.8,9; 29.2,3.
222. *Ibid.*, 28.12.
223. *ASI*, *Annual Report 1903-04*, p. 126.
224. A.C. Bidyabhushan, 'The Dance Theatre at Rāmgarḥ', Wilson, Raghvan & Pisharoti, *Theatre of the Hindus*, p. 219.

wide. The seats behind the entrance are set rather lower than the rest. There are small stone seats by the walls.

The row of rock-cut benches arranged in terraces in the shape of a crescent, in front of the entrance, was called 'steps' by Begler but to Bloch,[225] it does not seem correct as there is no means of entering the cave from the south, where the stairs are cut. 'They would be very suitable as benches to seat an audience watching some play or similar performance acted in front of them'. He further says that 'there is sufficient space in front of the small rock-cut amphitheatre for the erection of stage'. 'The two holes cut into the floor at the entrance were made to hold wooden posts, to which the curtain was fastened to shut out the cold air of the winter nights, when the audience retired to the interior'. Konow[226] thinks that perhaps the holes were meant for the support of the beams of the curtain serving as screen for performing shadow play, which does not seem probable, because we do not find any reference to theatre construction of any type, especially for shadow play, in ancient literature of the country. Besides, the existence of shadow play itself during the period is doubtful.

Bloch thinks that the inscription of this cave referring to 'poets venerable by nature and swing festival (*dule* = *ḍolā* = swing; Vasaṁtīyā = the vernal full moon in Phālgun = *Vasantotsava*), when frolics and music abound and people tie (around their neck's garlands) thick with jasmine flowers', also suggests that the cave was a theatre.[227] Bloch translates the inscription of the adjoining cave Jogimārā as 'Sutanukā by name, a *devadāsī* made this resting place for girls. Devadinna by name skilled in painting'. He says that this cave was a place for *devadāsī* Sutanukā and girls of her class to lie down. These girls must have been actresses, employed in the theatre (Sītābeṅgā) close to the place where they retired for rest.[228] But, his translation is not accepted by all.[229] Besides, Burgess did not agree with the opinion of Bloch, saying that Sītabeṅgā is the solitary example of its kind and no trace of such caves has been found elsewhere, and hence, this cave cannot be taken as a theatre, though he accepts that in ancient India cave were probably used, at times,

---

225. T. Bloch, *op. cit.*, p. 126.
226. Sten Konow, *The Indian Drama*, pp. 5-6.
227. T. Bloch, *op. cit.*, pp. 125-26.
228. *Ibid.*, *op. cit.*, pp. 129-30.
229. A.C. Vidyabhusan, *op. cit.*, p. 224.

for entertainment of various forms.[230] Lüders has supported Bloch, citing references from ancient Indian literature and inscription.[231]

Bloch thinks that the cave theatre at Sītābeṅgā bears a certain resemblance to the plan of a Greek theatre, as this too has rock-cut seats rising in terraces above each other. But, this does not seem correct because this type of seating arrangement for audience was known, since the time of *Jātaka*s, as we have already noticed. Ancient Indian literature, also, suggests the existence of such cave theatres or pleasure resorts, in the light of which Sītābeṅgā does not seem a solitary example of cave theatre. In Ādi-Parva of *Mahābhārata,*[232] Kṛṣṇa and Arjuna are mentioned as visiting the mountain Raivataka to witness the performance of *naṭa*s and *nartaka*s. Again, in Aśvamedhika-Parva of *Mahābhārata*, it is said that Kṛṣṇa heard the songs sung by men and women, and the sound of musical instruments being played by them, coming from Raivataka mountain while returning to *Dvārakā* from Hastināpura.[233] The caves of the mountain were brightly lit as if it was day-time.[234] This shows that the hilltop was a favourite place for holding festivals, having theatrical shows, and also that, caves were utilised as a place suitable for presenting such shows.

Jain texts, also, refer to Raivataka mountain as a favourite place of *apsarase*s and *vidyādhara*s, where festivals were held frequently.[235] There is a list of festivals given in *Rājapraśneyī sūtra,*[236] the Jain text, including *Girimaha* and *Darīmaha*, the festivals associated with mountain and cave respectively. These two must have been festivals performed on the hilltop. Buddhist text *Cullavagga*[237] refers to *Girigga*

---

230. A.C. Vaidyabhusan, *op. cit.*, p. 221.

231. *IA*, vol. XXXIV, Sept. 1905, pp. 199-200.

232. *Mahābhārata*, Ādi-Parva, 61.3,4,8,9,12.

233. *Ibid.*, Aśvamedhika-Parva, 69.3,4.8,912.

234. *Ibid.*, 69.7.

235. . . . *revaye nāmaṁ pavvaye hotthā. . . accharāganmadeva saṅgha-vijjāharamihuṇa sañichiṇṇe nicchachaṇaye. . .*
— *Dhammakahāṇuyoga*, Skandha II, Niṣadha in Ariṣṭanemitīrtha, Sūtra 78, pp. 32-33.

236. *Rājapraśneyī Sūtra*, 215.

237. *Cullavagga*, VI.1, p. 243.

Samajjā where dancers performed, and musicians sang and played musical instruments. Thus, it seems that organising festivals and holding theatrical shows on hilltops, was a common practice. From *Jātaka*s, we know that in such gatherings a temporary auditorium was erected by fixing the seats circle on circle, tier above tier. The necessity of an auditorium of this sort may have been felt during the folk festivals like *Girigga Samajjā*, *Girimaha* or *Darīmaha,* always popular in ancient India. Excavation of Sītābeṅgā cave may have been generated by this necessity, though not a very common one. The use of caves for such entertainments is vaguely indicated by a reference in Bhāsa's *Avimāraka*.[238] In the fourth act of the play, Meghanāda, a *vidyādhara*, coming across the sky with his wife, says that they had spent the morning in north Kuru, had bath in Mānasarovara and had a blissful time in the cave of Mandarācala.

Bharata[239] also took his troupe to Kailāsa, the abode of Lord Śiva, to present a play in his honour. Though it is not mentioned in *Nāṭyaśāstra* whether the play was performed in a cave of the Kailāsa mountain or elsewhere, Bharata's preference for cave-like construction of theatre is known.[240] He favoured this type of construction for better acoustic effects, which is proved by the remarks of Abhinavagupta[241] in his commentary, which clearly stresses the advantage of *anuraṇan*, the resounding, which was helpful in diffusing the sound to the four corners of the hall.

Aśvaghoṣa refers to *Giriyagga Samāja* in his dramas.[242] The Mathurā inscription,[243] belonging to the first century AD and referring to a *gaṇikā* named Nādā, the daughter of *gaṇikā* Daṇḍā, the *leṇaśobhikā*, shows the existence of a class of courtesans who performed in caves, as mentioned in the earlier chapter. *Śobhikā*, the feminine form of *śobhika*, the actor, whould mean an actress and *leṇa* meaning cave shows that *leṇaśobhikā* was a cave actress;[244] this indicates the popularity of such theatres.

---

238. *bhūyo mañdarakandarāntareṣvāmoditaṁ yauvanaṁ.*
 —*Avimāraka*, Act IV.10, *BNC*, vol. II, pp. 97-98.
239. *NŚ*, IV.6-10.
240. *śailaguhākāro* . . . —*NŚ*, II.85.
241. *Abhinavabhāratī*, G.O.S., Ch. 54.
242. F.W. Thomas, 'Notes on the Edicts of Aśoka', *J.R.A.S.*, 1914, p. 752.
243. *IA*, vol. XXXIII, p. 152.
244. Lüders., *IA*, vol. XXXIV, Sept. 1905, p. 199.

In *Meghadūta*[245] of Kālidāsa, *yakṣa* tells Megha that when you desire to rest, stay a while on Rāmagiri near Vidiśā. The caves of that mountain (*śilāveśma*) send out the seductive perfumes of courtesans and thus, bear witness to the youthful ardour of citizens. In *Kumārasambhava*[246] Kālidāsa says that *vanecara* (men of forests or hunters) would use these cave-dwellings (*darīgṛha*) for musical soirees. Again, in the same text he says that 'youths and girls would frolic in these mountain caves. When, in the course of the romping, the girls' clothes were taken of, a cloud would suddenly stretch itself across the entrance to the cave, serving thereby as a curtain'.[247] This shows that Kālidāsa was acquainted with such caves, where dance and musical performance, presented by courtesans, were held. Besides these clear references, there are some vague ones also in Kālidāsa's writings to caves as pleasure resorts.

At the time of Indumatī's *svayaṁvara*, her *sakhī* (friend or attendant), while introducing a suitor to her, says that if she would marry him, she can witness the dance of peacocks, sitting on the rock-benches of the caves of Govardhana mountain, wet with rain show.[248] As caves were common pleasure resorts for kings to witness dance and music performances, they, often, luxuriously constructed artificial mountains in their harems. Kālidāsa, in *Raghuvaṁśa*, describes the life of the pleasure-seeking King Agnivarṇa of Raghu's line and says that he spent his time on the 'Kṛtrimādri' (artificial mountain) during rainy season.[249] One such *krīḍā parvata* (lit. toy mountain) is mentioned by Bāṇa in his *Kādambarī*. We are told that Candrāpīḍa came to the 'Krīḍā Parvata', followed by the maids of Kādambarī who were good at playing lute, flute, etc.[250] The musical talent of the maids suggests that theatrical shows were performed on *krīḍā parvata*.

Skanda Purāṇa, also, vaguely refers to the theatrical activities at Raivataka mountain during the age of Pratihāra king Mihirabhoja. The *Vastrāpatha Māhātmya* section of *Prabhāsa-khaṇḍa* of *Skanda Purāṇa*[251] refers to a doe-faced woman,

245. *Meghadūta*, I.27. *KG*, p. 292.
246. *Kumārasmbhava*, I.10. *Ibid*., p. 167.
247. *Ibid*., I.14. *Ibid*.
248. *Raghuvaṁśa*, VI.51. *KG*, p. 48.
249. *Ibid*., XIX.37. *Ibid*., p. 163.
250. *Kādambarī*, p. 296, ed. M.R. Kale, 1928.
251. H.C. Roychoudhury, *I.H.Q*., v, pp. 129-30; B.N. Puri, *The Gurjara Pratiharas*, p. 58.

accompanying a herd of deers, in the forest of Raivataka, her capture by the *balādhyakṣa* and her revelation at Kānyakubja referring to the sanctity of the water of Suvarṇalekhā, and holy spots of Saurāṣṭra. The interesting point in the incident is the doe-face of the woman. Could we take it as a mask? Is it possible that the mountain Raivataka had some sort of a dramatic tradition associated with festivals like *Girigga Samajjā* since the epic age which continued during Pratihāra reign, too? Rājaśekhara, while mentioning four types of poets, in his *Kāvyamīmāṁsā*,[252] refers to poets who compose poems, sitting in the quiet mountain caves or in an underground apartment. This reminds one of the inscription of Sītabeṅgā cave referring to poets.

It seems that since the hilltop was a quiet place where theatrical shows, associated with festivals or otherwise, could be held without any disturbance and it provided a suitable background, it became a favourite place for shows. Originally, natural caves served the purpose of the auditorium, with some modifications, for a small gathering, but gradually the fashion of excavating caves specially to serve this purpose came into being. Architectural features of Rānīgumphā cave at Orissa clearly shows that it was used as a theatre on festive occasions.[253] The open courtyard, in front of the cave, was probably used as open air theatre and the terrace of the cave as amphitheatre. On the terrace, there is a throne-like seat which was, probably, for the high priest to witness the performance held in the courtyard. 'The whole, forming a brilliant and moving pageant, amidst the dark encircling groves'.

The religious establishments, in the form of caves, had provision for dance and musical performance which had, gradually, become a part of ritual in Brāhmaṇism, Buddhism and Jainism, alike. Most probably, the Tīnathāla cave of Ellorā also served the purpose of theatre on religious festivals. A.C. Vidyabhushan[254] thinks that Buddhist cave at Auraṅgābād,[255] two caves at Nāsik, the Uparkoṭ cave at Junāgaḍh and caves of Kunda and Mahad had facilities for dancing and singing.

It seems that probably there was a tradition of using cave as theatre in ancient India. But such theatres were for a small private gathering as is indicated by the

252. *Kāvyamīmāṁsā*, p. 53, ed. C.D. Dalal, Baroda.

253. Percy Brown, *Indian Architecture*, pp. 29-30.

254. A.C. Vidyabhusan, *op. cit.*, p. 221.

255. *Archa. Surv. Western India*, vol. III, PL. LIV, fig. V.

size of the Sītābeṅgā cave and also by the literary references. Besides, theatrical performances in Buddhist or Brāhmaṇical caves were in the form of religious ritual, witnessed by the members of the establishment or the devotees. It does not seem possible that they were used as regular theatre halls, visited by a large number of theatre-goers, because such natural or excavated caves were generally in remote places.

The preference of Indians for hilly regions as a suitable place for holding theatrical shows must have inspired them to construct a theatre on a hill slope at Nāgārjunakoṇḍa.

According to the Archaeological report,[256] a quadrangle, 54' 6" × 44', belonging to second or third century AD was discovered at Nāgārjunakoṇḍa. It has seats on all the four sides, except for a passage in the middle of one of its sides, for entering into the quadrangle, and a regular flight of steps, on the opposite side, leading to linear rectangular space, at a height of twenty feet. On both sides of this rectangular opening, there are carved steps leading higher up into another rectangular space. Another pair of curved flight on steps lead to a third rectangular space, behind which there are two identical enclosures, the left one containing a broken idol of a Buddhist goddess Hārīti.[257]

This seems to be a temple of this goddess.[258] R. Subrahmaniam, under whom this architecture was excavated and reconstructed along a hill slope, surmised it to be a theatre on the basis of three of its features: (a) the quadrangular arena, (b) the multi-tiered seating, and most important of all (c) its excellent acoustic condition.[259] H.V. Sharma thinks that it is a Buddhist theatre, and says that all the Mahāyāna Buddhist conventions of the practice of performing arts, in a way of following certain tradition, called for either a square or rectangular area for the activity. The seats for the spectators all around the performing area, with proper entries and exits, should simply be natural for such an arenal activity.[260] Possibly plays, on Buddhist themes, were performed here in this theatre. Other Buddhist mouments on the

256. *Ind. Archa 1954-55, A Review*, Nāgārjunakoṇḍa. p. 22.

257. H.V. Sharma, *The Theatres of the Buddhist*, p. 48.

258. *Ind. Archa. 1954-55, A Review*, Nāgārjunakoṇḍa, p. 22.

259. H.V. Sharma, *op. cit.*, p. 47.

260. *Ibid.*, p. 50.

site, also, indicate the same. Sharma thinks that the quadrangle or the arena is almost square and wonders if it was made on the model of Bharata's *caturasra madhyama* type of theatre.

Though, south India had trade relations with Greeks and Romans in early centuries of the Christian era, the architecture of Nāgārjunakoṇḍa amphitheatre is not an example of Greek or Roman influence as H. Sarkar[261] and M.N. Deshpande[262] believe. It has only a very general type of similarity with Greeco-Roman amphitheatre. Greeco-Roman amphitheatres are oval or semi-circular with a raised platform, the Skene, being long and narrow. At the back of this stands a building with many pillars and entrances, while the Nāgārjunakoṇḍa theatre is quadrangular and unlike Greek theatre, one part of it lies on a hill slope and the other part at the foot of the hill. 'What was the orchestra in the Greek theatre, happens to be the actual performing area, in the case of the Nāgārjunakoṇḍa theatre'.[263] Seats for the spectators, in the form of steps, were known in India since the very early times. Such seating arrangement is mentioned in the *Jātaka*s and is found at Sītābeṅgā cave, as we have already seen. Bharata, too, prefers this type of arrangement (*sopānākṛti pīṭhakāni*).[264] Hence, the seating arrangement is, undoubtedly, indigenous. This quadrangular theatre of Nāgārjunakoṇḍa seems to be in the tradition of socio-religious hill-revelry, known since the time of *Mahābhārata,* as we have already noticed. Desire for convenient seating arrangement and acting area kept motivating people for experimenting in the field and this theatre is an example of the final phase of that search. Its Indianness is obvious and is beyond doubt, as it is clear that this is a construction of those who were accustomed to constructing a temporary theatre by keeping wooden planks, one above the other in circle, to provide seats to the spectators, leaving a place in the centre as the acting area. It is natural for a Mahāyāna centre like Nāgārjunakoṇḍa to have produced a theatre of this kind, because, as we have noticed in the earlier chapter, the Hinduised Mahāyāna sect of Buddhism had adopted theatre as a means to propagate the faith; what could have been a more suitable place for such construction than the hills. But

---

261. H. Sarkar & H.N. Misra, 'Nāgārjunakoṇḍa', *ASI*, p. 22.
262. M.N. Deshpande, Presidential Address, *Indian History Congress Proceeding of the Twenty-fifth session*, 1963, p. 31.
263. H.V. Sharma, *op. cit.*, p. 53.
264. *NŚ*, II.95.

as said earlier, this type of theatre was not very common. This expensive construction seems to be a product of the upper class of the society, and thus, belonging to the classicalised tradition of Buddhist drama, though the entry may not have been restricted; some seats might have been reserved for the royalty and a few selected people. The common folk continued to have their shows in the pavilion type of theatre known throughout the history of the country.

Pavilion or Maṇḍapa Type of Theatre

This was the most common type of theatre known to ancient Indians. Its existence is indicated since the age depicted in *Mahābhārata*. From *Mahābhārata,* we know that theatrical shows were performed on occasion of sacrifices, but no permanent structure for such shows are mentioned. Perhaps, a temporary pavilion was erected for the show, which, in due course, may have given rise to temple theatre. In Aśvamedhika-Parva of *Mahābhārata*,[265] Indra gave instructions to gods to erect a pavilion for *apsaras*es to dance on the occasion of a sacrifice performed by Mahārāja Marutta, specifying that it should have pillars and a staircase, too. Thus, it seems that it was a raised stage, temporarily constructed for the show in the form of a pavilion, around which the spectators sat.

The existence of pavilion type of theatre is known from *Bhadraghaṭa Jātaka* too, which refers to a rich merchant's son who had made a pavilion across the road and sat down with his friends to drink and witness the performance of dancers and other theatre artistes.[266] Most probably, the spectators sat around this pavilion either on the ground or on the seats, arranged in 'tiers above tiers'.

A pavilion type of temporary, but highly decorated, theatre is mentioned in the Jain text, *Rājapraśneyī Sūtra*.[267] It says that Sūryābhadeva, who came to worship Lord Mahāvīra when he was residing at Āmalakappā, constructed a *maṇḍapa* as *prekṣāgṛha* supported by hundreds of pillars. There was a stage and seats for spectators too inside that *maṇḍapa.* This shows that *prekṣāgṛha* or play house was in the form of a *maṇḍapa* or pavilion, constructed for the performance of *nāṭyavidhi*s, presented by Sūryābhadeva in honour of Lord Mahāvīra. We have some sculptures and paintings showing such stage or theatre.

---

265. *Mahābhārata*, Aśvamedhika-Parva, 10.27.
266. E.B. Cowell, *op. cit.*, vol. II, p. 294.
267. *Rājapraśneyī Sūtra*, 74, p. 47.

A fragment of a frieze belonging to second century BC and discovered from Kaṅkālī Ṭīlā at Mathurā[268] has a scene depicting a pavilion type of theatre. It is an oblong type, open on all sides. The roof is supported by four pillars, three of which are seen.[269] They have slender plain shafts and a small capital. 'The superstructure consists of a triangular frame fitted with joints and covered with L-shaped tiles'. The danseuse and accompanying five members of the orchestra, are accommodated on the stage with their musical instruments.[270] The spectators are outside the pavilion in the open air.

Another example belonging to the same period is from Rānīgumphā cave.[271] The bottom storey corridor of the cave depicts a danseuse, accompanied by an orchestra, performing in a pavilion, the roof of which is, again, supported by pillars, two of which are visible — having a plain shaft and a capital of inverted lotus. Here, the pavilion is rectangular.[272] Fabri[273] thinks that the pavilion is a *nepathyagṛha*. The design carved on the entablature of the pavilion, according to him, is the well-known *zikkurat* or stepped tower motif imported from Mesopotamia. But the pavilion, in this frieze, seems to be the proper dancing or acting area, as the dancer is seen performing inside the pavilion and not in its background. Here, the pavilion does not accommodate all the members of the orchestra; a few are seen outside it, probably because the sculptor wanted to depict the dancer prominently.

The next example of this pavilion type of theatre is from Mathurā, belonging to the Kuṣāṇa period, carved on the right half of a round pillar.[274] This scene depicts a danseuse performing under a pavilion accompanied by an orchestra. The orchestra and the danseuse are accommodated in the rectangular pavilion. Here, the stage is slightly raised; in comparison to the first example from Mathurā, one can see the stairs on the left. The superstructure is supported by, probably, six pillars, of which three are seen. They are exactly like those of the earlier example from Mathurā, i.e., with plain slender shaft and a small capital. The tiles of the superstructure are

---

268. See *Pl.* XII.

269. M.L. Varadpande, *Traditions of Indian Theatre*, pp. 56-57.

270. *Ibid.*, p. 56.

271. See *Pl.* XI.

272. M.L. Varadpande, *op. cit.*, p. 55.

273. Charles Fabri, *History of The Art of Orissa*, p. 20.

274. *Marg*, vol. XV, no. 2, fig. No. 19, p. 36.

square in shape instead of being L-shaped. Probably, such common pavilion type theatres were made of timber and were 'theatre of the people', belonging to the folk tradition of drama which, in due course, was adopted, modified and enlarged by the classical tradition.

*Raṅgaśālā*s or *nāṭyaśālā*s of the royal harem are known since the time of Bhāsa. In his *Pratimānāṭakam*,[275] he mentions a theatre with *nepathya* where costumes were kept. But nothing is known regarding its architecture. Kālidāsa, also, mentions a *prekṣāgāra* in his *Mālavikāgnimitram*,[276] where performances were held and which accommodated the artiste, orchestra and spectators as well. A *saṅgītaśālā* is mentioned in *Abhijñānaśākuntalam*.[277] Kālidāsa, like Bhāsa, does not describe its architecture, obviously because the scene does not demand it.

A theatre or *nāṭyaśālā* of royal harem is depicted in a painting of the fifth or sixth century AD from Ajantā, cave no. 1.[278] The painting is in a damaged condition but we do get an idea of the theatre. The scene depicts a dance performed by danseuses, two of whom are visible, in a royal pavilion. Here, the pavilion is much larger than the earlier examples of pavilion type of theatre. Here too, the superstructure is supported by pillars. Three of them are easily seen. Unlike the earlier examples, the round-shaped shafts of pillars are beautifully carved. Cushion capital of one of the pillars is clearly seen. The pavilion here accommodates not only the performing artistes but also the audience who are in the form of a Nāga king, his queen, a princely person and a large number of maid-servants and male guards. The dance is being performed in the centre between the two important spectators, the royal couple and the princely person.

The *prekṣāgāra* of harem described by Harṣa in his *Priyadarśikā*,[279] also, seems to belong to this type. He says that it was lovely with golden columns, the invariable part of pavilion type of theatre. It seems, thus, that 'pavilion' was the most common type of the theatre, known throughout the history of the country. It was a temporary timber construction in the case of the common folk and a permanent, lavishly decorated pavilion, when in royal palaces. Varadpande rightly says that

275. *Pratimānāṭakaṁ*, Act. I, *BNC*, vol. I, pp. 18-19.
276. *Mālavikāgnimitraṁ*, Act. II, *KG*, pp. 198-203.
277. *Abhijñānaśākuntalam*, Act V, *ibid*., p. 56.
278. G. Yazdani, *The Early History of the Deccan*, PL. LXb.
279. *Priyadarśikā*, p. 46. Columbia University, Indo-Iranian Series No. 10.

> Bharata developed this unit (or idealised it) into a full-fledged theatre hall. He added two *mattavāriṇīs* at both sides, green room (*nepathyagṛha*) at the back and extended the roof, above the heads of the audience, also. The basic four-pillared structure remained in his theatre under the name *raṅgapatha*.[280]

Bharata endeavoured to make drama a dignified art, and hence, combined the best of the folk and classical traditions of theatre. One of the efforts for achieving this end was forming a proper stage out of this common folk structure, because he must have felt that the open air performance witnesses disturbances and the attention of the audience is diverted in such theatres ruining the *siddhi*. He talks about this practical problem in a mythical language in his *Nāṭyaśāstra*. He says that as the open-air performance meets with disturbance from some dissatisfied members of the audience (*rākṣasas*), the closed theatre becomes a necessity.

He describes three types of theatre, *vikṛṣṭa* (rectangular), *caturasra* (square) and *trayasra* (triangular). They were of three sizes, *jyeṣṭha* — the large one, had measure of hundred and eight *hastas*,[281] *madhyama* — the medium, sixty-four *hastas*, and *avara*, the small, thirty-two *hastas*.[282] Out of these types, *jyeṣṭha* may be used in the case of gods, *madhyama*, in the case of kings and *avara* in the case of ordinary people. Abhinava explains that *jyeṣṭha* may be used in the case of dramas where gods were heroes as in Dim, etc., *madhyama*, where kings were heroes, as in *prakaraṇa*, etc., and *avara*, where ordinary persons are heroes as in *bhāṇa*, *prahasana*, etc. Out of all these types, *madhyama* is proper for mortals. It may be sixty-four cubits in length and thirty-two cubits in breadth. The theatre must not be bigger than this. Otherwise, it will lose its acoustic properties. If a *maṇḍapa* is very extensive, words uttered would become faint and indistinct, facial expressions can not be observed properly and the subtleties of music will go unnoticed by the spectators far away from the stage.[283] Bharata prescribes various rituals to be performed at the time of laying the foundation and building the edifice on an

---

280. M.L. Varadpande, *op. cit.*, p. 57.

281. One *hasta* = 1½ ft.

282. *NŚ*, II.7, 8.

283. *Ibid.*, II.21-24.

auspicious day. The *naṭācārya* had to observe fast for three days.[284] This was to give sanctity to the construction associated with dramatic art. This was one of the efforts of Bharata to promote the folk art of drama to the status of an art, recognised by the upper class including ritualistic priests.

The main parts of the theatre hall mentioned by Bharata are as follows:

(i) *Nāṭyaveśma, nāṭyamaṇḍapa* or *prekṣāgṛha* — The theatre building.

(ii) *Maṇḍapa* — edifice, pavilion or theatre building.

(iii) *Mattavāriṇī* — Two square boxes on both sides of *raṅgapīṭha*. Scholars are of different opinion regarding the place and form of this part.

(iv) *Raṅgapīṭha* — Base of the stage proper.

(v) *Raṅgaśīrṣa* — Surface or top of the stage.

(vi) *Nepathyagṛha* — Green room.

(vii) *Ṣaḍ-dāruka* — A wooden part six in number or a wooden six-piece unit.

(viii) *Prekṣakānāṁ niveśanaṁ* — Auditorium.

Regarding the stage proper with its above-mentioned main parts, the scholars are of different opinion, because the text of the *Nāṭyaśāstra* is very corrupt and commentary of Abhinavagupta is, also, very confusing.[285] From the text of *Nāṭyaśāstra,* it appears that whatever be the shape or the dimension of the theatre, one-half was turned into an auditorium (*raṅgamaṇḍapa*) in which seats were constructed, rising one *hasta* higher gradually, so that the spectators would be able to witness the performance comfortably,[286] and the other half was divided for the performance (*raṅgabhūmi*) as stage. The stage, i.e., acting area, was further subdivided into three equal parts, each part further away from the auditorium half.

---

284. *NŚ*, II.49.

285. P.K. Acharya, 'The Playhouse of the Hindu Period', *Dr. S. Krishnaswami Aiyangar Commemorationg Volume*, 15th April 1938, p. 363; D.R. Mankad, 'Hindu Theatre', *I.H.Q*, vol. VIII, no. 3, p. 485; M. Ghosh, 'The Hindu Theatre', *I.H.Q.*, vol. IX, no. 1-2, p. 593; D.R. Mankad, 'Hindu Theatre', *I.H.Q.*, vol. IX, no. 3-4, p. 973; V. Raghavan, 'Hindu Theatre', *I.H.Q.*, vol. IX, no. 3-4, p. 991.

286. *sopānākṛti . . . ,* — *NŚ*, II.95.

The one nearest to the auditorium was called *raṅgapīṭha* and the one nearest to the green room (*nepathyagṛha*) was called the *raṅgaśīrṣa* and was on a level higher than the *raṅgapīṭha*. The remaining third of the stage was called the *nepathyagṛha* or green room, which was in the back of the stage. Regarding *mattavāriṇī*, D.R. Mankad thinks that it was some special portion of *raṅgapīṭha*.[287] Subba Rao[288] understands *mattavāriṇī* to be on the front of the *raṅgapīṭha*. As it represents Airāvata, he takes it to mean 'a line of intoxicated elephants' on the front side of the stage, a sort of decoration. Rangacharya,[289] thinks that in Indian tradition elephant is a guarding deity (*diggaja*). The two sides of the stage had two elephants, on the back of whom were platforms on the level with the *raṅgaśīrṣa*, where God Indra or similar important personages were to be seated. *Mattavāriṇīs*, seem to be a breadth-wise extention of *raṅgapīṭha,* on both sides, having four pillars each and thus, forming square box of eight *hastas*. The purpose of *mattavāriṇī* was, perhaps, to leave some space on both sides of the stage proper which may be utilised as one of the *kakṣyas* during the play. Thus, it seems that during Bharata's time, a proper stage, with different sizes and shapes, had developed which might be taken as an enlargement of the popular pavilion type of theatre.

Cilappadikāram[290] also describes a pavilion or *maṇḍapa* type of stage for dance performances. It was eight *kols* in length, seven *kols* in breadth and one *kol* in height.[291] It had two appropriate doors, for entrance and exit of the dancer. The stage proper had pillars, also, because it is said that the lamp illumining the stage was so placed that the pillars did not cast shadows. The screen of some sort was used for the stage as the text says that the single screen and the screen between the two pillars, to the right of the stage, besides the over-hanging curtain, were well manipulated by ropes. The stage had a canopy painted with many beautiful pictures.

Stage or theatre halls are mentioned in books on architecture. V. Raghavan in

---

287. D.R. Mankad, 'Hindu Theatre', *I.H.Q.*, vol. VIII, no. 3, p. 485.

288. D. Subba Rao, 'A critical Survey of the ancient Indian theatre in accordance with Bharata's Nāṭyaśāstra and its commentators', *J.O.I.*, vol. II, no. 2, pp. 196-97.

289. Adya Rangacharya, *Drama in Sanskrit Literature*, p. 215.

290. *Cilappadikāram*, p. 110, ed. V.S. Diksitar.

291. The *kol*, which was a piece of bamboo, with the length of a span between every two of its joints, and with twenty-four thumb breadth, was a standard.

his article 'Theatre Architecture in Ancient India'[292] has mentioned the types of theatre known from literature and *Śilpaśāstra*. For example, *Viṣṇudharmottara* mentions only two types of theatre, rectangular and square. The theatre should not be too small or too big, for there would be congestion in a small one and the show would become indistinct in a big one. The *Saṅgīta Mārttaṇḍa* of Nārada supplies a literary account of an unspecified type of the stage and the auditorium.[293] In this description, the construction and details are wanting. The playhouse (*nāṭyaśālā*) is stated to be sixty-four cubits with four corners and twenty-four pillars and furnished with various paintings, walls of various shapes and decorations.[294] Chapter 10 of Śāradātanaya's *Bhāvaprakāśa* says that the palace of a king should have three kinds of theatre — circular, square and triangular.[295] In an account given in *Saṅgītaratnākara* of Niḥśaṅgadeva,[296] the reference to the architectural features is very casual and scanty; no specific reference is made to the shape, size or dimension of the stage or the auditorium.

These references show that there were such theatre halls, besides simple and temporary folk theatres, in ancient India, which were built with scientific knowledge of acoustics, light, ventilation, safety, security and were meant for regular theatrical shows. These architecturally — developed theatre halls were fundamentally inspired by Bharata. The *nāṭyamaṇḍapa*s of temples of a later date are also a developed form of the same style. Some later texts on architecture refer to the temple theatre. *Mānasāra*[297] refers to temple and palace theatres. Here, the theatres are stated to be built in continuation of the temple and the palace.[298] Again in the chapter on pavilion it is stated that

. . . . thus, should be the Śālā pavilion and the Kṛta pavilion; the wise,

---

292. V. Raghavan, 'Theatre Architecture in Ancient India', Wilson, Raghavn, Pishroti, *Theatre of Hindus*, pp. 160-61.
293. *Saṅgīta Mārttaṇḍa*, V.2-9.
294. P.K. Acharya, 'The Playhouse of the Hindu Period', *Dr. S. Krishnaswamy Aiyangar Commemorating Volume,* 15th April 1936, pp. 369-70.
295. V. Raghavan, *op. cit.*, p. 161.
296. *Saṅgītaratnākara* VII.1331-61.
297. *Mānasāra*, XLVII.1-3, 26-33.
298. P.K. Acharya, *op. cit.*, pp. 371-72.

(architect) should build the theatre underneath the pinnacle of a ten parts square.

The elevation, the thickness of the walls, the varandahs, and the sheds with yards and the shapes of pavilion: these five features are described in order.[299] Temple theatre accommodate audience and performers, both.

It seems that the temple theatre, too, grew out of the basic pavilion type of theatre. The *mahāmaṇḍapa* of a fully-developed Khajurāho temple has a raised square platform in the centre and its ceiling is supported by four pillars installed on four corners of the platform, which reminds one of the pavilion type of theatre. It is generally believed that music and dance performances were held in *mahāmaṇḍapa*s of Khajurāho temples. The *naṭamaṇḍapa*s of Orissa temples, too, seem to be built on the same pattern. Some of the present folk theatre still use a frame supported by four bamboos, as their acting area, as in *yakṣagāna* style of theatre. This folk type of simple theatre structure was borrowed by the classical tradition and became highly decorated *nāṭyamaṇḍapa* (stage and auditorium), larger than the original examples in its size, as is seen in Ajantā paintings. Gradually, it was enlarged by the *ācārya*s, like Bharata, with the help of *sūtradhāra*, the architect,[300] to provide due facilities to performing artistes, on the one hand and to spectators, on the other; thus, it became a permanent theatre house, representing symbiotic tradition of threatre.

---

299. *Mānasāra*, XXXIV.2467-7, 34 quoted by P.K. Acharya, *op. cit.*, p. 377.

300. Adya Rangacharya, *Drama in Sanskrit Literature*, pp. 36-37.

5

Social and Economic Status of Performing Artistes

SOCIAL status of performing artistes is, in fact, the story of origin, rise and fall of the art itself, as their position in the society reflects the attitude of people towards the art. Actually, it was a love and hate relation between actors and society. Performing artistes never enjoyed a respectable place in society, though their art always remained exceedingly attractive to people, even after being prohibited or almost banned by the authorities or religious preceptors.

It is interesting to study why the people, responsible for evolving the natural instinct of man — to imitate — into a great art, always belonged to the lower strata of the society, how they earned their livelihood and what was their way of life. In the absence of any written source, we are not sure whether such artistes in the form of priests and priestesses, or people having a talent for the art, who were given the duty of performing magico-religious rituals of a dramatic nature, adopted the art as their profession during the Indus Valley period. Similarly, little is known regarding their social status.

As for the Vedic period, it seems that there existed a class of minstrels who composed songs and sang them. In this class brāhmaṇa (other than priest) and kṣatriya (*vīṇāgāthin*s) were included.[1] We do not know if such individual brāhmaṇa and kṣatriya minstrels, enjoyed the status of a brāhmaṇa or kṣatriya respectively, or that of musicians, but we do know about *sūta* and *māgadha*, the well-known minstrels. Though *sūta* was included in eight *vīra*s and eleven *ratnin*s of the Vedic period,[2] he did not enjoy a respectable place in the society, as indicated by the fact that immediately after the jewel offering ceremony, which the king performed in

1. See chapter 2.
2. *Vedic Index*, Vol. II, p. 462.

the house of *ratnin*s, among whom *sūta*, too, was included, he had to perform certain rites for expiating the sin committed by putting these unworthy persons of low classes or castes in contact with the sacrifice.[3] Similarly, *māgadha,* the other minstrel, is associated with *vrātya* in *Atharvaveda,*[4] indicating his low position. sūta in epics, is the offspring of a kṣatriya father and a brāhmaṇa mother. *Māgadha* was that of a vaiśya father and a kṣatriya mother.[5] Thus, both, were *varṇasaṅkara*s, that indicates lower status of these two artistes of the Vedic period. Another theatre artiste of the Vedic period, *kāri*, who practised fun-making as an art to create laughter in others and thus earned his livelihood, too belonged to the common folk.[6] *Śailūṣa,* too, seems to have been an artiste of folk tradition, absorbed in the classical tradition at a later date. He, too, belonged to the lower class of the society as already noticed in the earlier chapter.

In epics, too, people associated with theatre often worked with śūdras. In Śānti-Parva, only śūdras are recommended to impersonate female character.[7] In Anuśāsana-Parva (Dānadharma-Parva), it is said that generally people belonging to low castes take to acting. Thus, it seems, that though theatre artistes were invited on auspicious occasions like sacrifice, birth of a child, marriage and coronation for entertainment, they enjoyed in no way a better status than the śūdras. The *Mahābhārata* says that *gāyaka* (vocalist), *vādaka* (instrumentalist) and *nartaka* (dancer) should not be invited to a *śrāddha* ceremony. They were among those from whom a brāhmaṇa is not to take food.[8]

*Śailūṣa*s (actors) belonged to the same lower class of the society who practised customs unfit for dignified people of Āryan society, as we know from *Rāmāyaṇa.* Sītā says that Rāma is behaving like a *śailūṣa,* in leaving her behind, in someone else's hand.[9] Theatre artistes had, most probably, formed a class by now, because they are, generally, mentioned in epics as a group — *gāyaka*, *vādaka*, *nartaka* or *sūtamāgadha vaitālika*, etc.

---

3. *ŚB*, V.3.2.2.
4. *Atharvaveda*, XV/2/1-4.
5. *Mahābhārata*, Anuśāsana-Parva, 48.2571-3.
6. R.C. Hazara, 'The Professional Jester of Vedic Age', *IHQ*, vol. XXXVIII, no. 2-3, p. 198.
7. *Mahābhārata*, Śānti-Parva, 295.4-5.
8. *Mahābhārata*, 37.31.
9. *Rāmāyaṇa*, Ayodhya-kāṇḍa, 30.

The picutre of the theatre artiste that emerges from Buddhist texts, is that of an entertainer, who was ill-famed and had lower status in society. This was the reason why Buddha debarred monks from attending their shows.[10] *Jātakas*, though often describing their profession as a popular art, indicate that they did not have a respectable place in the society. Female artistes appear as temptress.[11] They danced in public and mixed freely with people, flirting even with monks. A female dancer danced on the drapery of the monks Assaji and Punabbasu.[12].

Jain texts are full of references to theatre artistes who were invited on special occasions, as was customary in ancient India, but they seem to have belonged to the lower class and were folk artistes like *jallā, mallā, maṅkha, naṭa, nartaka, kahaga, plavaka*, etc. Most of them feature in Buddhist texts.

To Kauṭilya, singing and dancing were among the duties of the śūdra.[13] In *Kaṇṭaka Śodhana Prakaraṇa* he says that 'they (actors) are thieves, in effect, though not in name'; thus, he included them in the list of anti-social elements.[14] He says in *Puruṣavyasana Prakaraṇa*[15] that 'among many other bad effects of drinking, one is that the man develops intimacy with bad people like singers and develops "attachments" to skill in lute and songs'. Thus, it seems that during Kauṭilya's time, theatre artistes were common folks having no social respect at all. He enjoins that the king should protect his people against the deceit of the merchants, artisans and *kuśīlavas*.[16]

According to Baudhāyana,[17] as quoted in *Kṛtyakalpataru, kuśīlava* was an offspring of an *ambaṣṭha* from a *vaidehī*, i.e., not very respectable. Āpastamba[18] speaks of *śailūṣa*, another theatre artiste, as holding same status as *rajaka* and *vyādh*. This, also, shows that theatre artistes did not enjoy a respectable place in

---

10. *Cullavagga*, 5.1.6.
11. *Mūgapakkha Jātaka*, E.B. Cowell, *Jātaka Stories*, vol. VI, p. 7.
12. *Cullavagga*, 1.3.
13. *śūdrasya dvijātisuśruṣā vārtā kāru kuśīlava karma ca, KA*, I.3.
14. *Ibid.*, IV.76.1
15. *Ibid.*, VIII.129.3.
16. *Ibid.*, IV.76.1.
17. P.V. Kane, *History of Dharma*, vol. II, Part I, p. 78.
18. IX.32. *Ibid.*, pp. 96-97.

society. Their character was, also, abominable; their women particularly were famed to be immoral. Hence, the lexicographers consider the term *jāyājīva*, i.e., one who depends on his wife for subsistence, as a synonym for an actor. This might have been the reason why Baudhāyana[19] says that to live on the stage (*raṅgopajīvana*) was one of the minor sins (*upapātaka*).

Manu did not have a good opinion about theatre artistes, either. He says[20] that *naṭa* is the same as *khasa* — a kṣatriya caste, originally but reduced to the status of śūdras by the absence of *saṁskāra* and the absence of contact with brāhmaṇas. But *śāstrakāra*s, it appears, had been aware of the influence which the stage was exerting on the people, in spite of prohibitions and restrictions, hence, they were very vehement in denouncing the profession of actors. Manu,[21] along with Yājñavalkya,[22] says that a brāhmaṇa cannot accept any food from the stage artiste (*raṅgāvatārin*). The evidence of *kuśīlava*[23] or *raṅgāvatārī*[24] is not valid. Manu says that the judge would consider the *kuśīlava* as a śūdra and the king should drive him out from the town. He[25] warns brāhmaṇas against involving themselves with dramatic arts. Manu[26] states that a king who is involved in *kāmaja varga*, i.e., in vices, loses *dharma* and *artha*, and the one involved in *krodhaja varga* destroys himself. He explains *kāmaja varga* as *tauyatrika*, i.e., dancing, singing and playing on musical instruments. This means that too much indulgence of a king in dramatic arts destroys his kingdom and prosperity.[27]

The performing artistes were so abominable that it seems that those who came to be associated with theatre people lost their social prestige, even if they belonged

---

19. II.1; II.13.
20. *Manu-smṛti*, X.22.
21. *Ibid.*, IV.214-15.
22. *Yājñavalkya-smṛti*, I.161.
23. *Manu-smṛti*, VIII.65.
24. *Yājñavakya-smṛti*, I.70.
25. *Manu-smṛti*, IV.15.
26. *Ibid.*, VII.46; VII.47.
27. Abhinava had explained that this prohibition is only for the king and that, too, to remind him of his primary duty, towards his kingdom and people, and is neither for actors nor for poets, whose professions are acting and writing plays respectively, nor for the audience that itself never enacts. — *Hindī Abhinava Bhāratī*, Dr. Nagendra, pp. 39-42

to the upper class of the society, and were placed in the same social class as those of performing artistes. *sūta* seems to belong to this class. Originally, he held an important position in Vedic political circle, but gradually, in epics, he came to be known as herald. Probably, brāhmaṇa and kṣatriya lute players and composers of songs too, gradually, came to be associated with theatre people due to the commonness of the profession and were, eventually, included in the troupe. They may have been absorbed in the class of *sūta*s and *māgadha*s.

By the first and second century AD, the original position of *sūta*s was totally forgotten and they were classed with other theatre people. *Cilappadikāram*,[28] while describing the city of Pukār, informs that there were separate quarters where dwelt *sūta*s, *māgadha*s, religious dancers, astronomers, rock dancers, prostitutes, actresses, bagpipe musicians, drummers, baffoons and jesters. Here, *sūta* and *māgadha* are classed with other theatre artistes. Scholars like Rangacharya[29] believe that *sūta* or *sauti*, the bard of epics, was a person talented in acting other roles while reciting the epic. He is the one who has grown into the *sūtradhāra* of Sanskrit dramas. In Sanskrit dramas, *sūtradhāra* is often called a brāhmaṇa, though not enjoying the prestigious status of the same, as no Vedic brāhmaṇa accepts his food.[30]

It happened with Vedic brāhmaṇas, too. In canto XIII of *Cilappadikāram,* it is said that Kovalan and Kannakī reached a village inhabited by brāhmaṇas who wore the sacred thread but they were given to music and dancing, having fallen from the Vedic life.[31] Such brāhmaṇas were said to be *ambanavar* as they did not pursue their *svadharma*, society regarded them as socially inferior. In the same context, we are told that brāhmaṇa *kauśika* met Kovalan and delivered to him a love message given by his beloved courtesan Mātavī.[32] V. Raghavan says that he is so abruptly introduced that *kauśikan* does not seem his proper name.[33] A commentator of *Cilappadikāram*, Aḍiyārkkunallār interprets the *kauśika* as *bandīkauśika*, a minstrel. It seems that *kauśika* is a common name for persons devoted to music and arts, and also, acting as aides and messengers in love affairs. Thus, we see that if a

28. *Cilappadikāram*, Canto IV, p. 122.
29. Adya Rangacharya, *The Indian Theatre*, p. 18.
30. *Cārudattam*, Prastāvanā, *Mṛcchakaṭika*, Prastāvanā.
31. *Cilappadikāram*, Canto XIII, p. 217.
32. *Cilappadikāram*, p. 218.
33. V. Raghavan, 'On a Meaning of the Word Kauśika', *J.O.R.*, Madras, vol. XV, p. 115.

person belonging to the upper class of the society associated himself with theatrical arts or with people associated with those arts, he lost his original status and was classed with the lower rung of artistes.

An almost contemporary text *Mānasāra*,[34] on architecture, says while describing the construction of Nandyāvarta village of brāhmaṇas that 'to the west of the village, the houses of instrumentalists and theatre for courtesans should be made'. This reminds one of the village of those brāhmaṇas who had adopted singing and dancing as their profession in *Cilappadikāram*.

This 'change of status' probably happened with kṣatriyas, too. Discussing the meaning of the word *kauśika*, V. Raghavan[35] says that *kauśika-strī* mentioned in Kauṭilya's *Arthaśāstra* refers to a class of women who specialised in the arts of song, dance, toilette, love affairs, etc., and were in employment of kings and nobles. *Parivrājikā kauśikī* of Kālidāsa's *Mālavikāgnimitram*,[36] who was an expert in the arts of dance, music and acting, seems to belong to this class. Towards the end of the play, it is said that she belongs to kṣatriya *varṇa*, still she is called *kauśikī*. Thus, it seems that though people loved theatrical arts throughout the history of the country, the performers of the art were always considered as detestable and people associated with them and their art lost status.

Even when the art reached its zenith and became very popular during successive periods of Indian history, people associated with theatre continued to belong to the same lower class of the society. According to *Vāyu Purāṇa*,[37] the *sūta* was to preserve the pedigree of kings and greatmen and tradition about learning and books but he was not authorised to study the Vedas.

Naṭa, according to *Atri-smṛti*,[38] is one of the seven *antyajas*, i.e., *rajaka*, *carmakāra*, *naṭa*, *buruda*, *kaivarta*, *meda* and *bhilla*. *Vedavyāsa-smṛti* figures him among twelve *antyajas*. According to *Viṣṇu-smṛti*,[39] to step into the stage is one of the occupations of Ayogava, the son of a śūdra and a vaiśya woman. Like Manu,

34. *Mānasāra*, Grāmalakṣana, IX.231-2, ed. P.K. Acharya.
35. V. Raghavan, *op. cit.*, p. 114.
36. *KG*, pp. 113-14.
37. *Vāyu Purāṇa*, vol. I, I.33-38 and vol. II, 1.1.39.
38. *Atri-smṛti*, 199.
39. *Viṣṇu-smṛti*, 16.8.

later *smṛtikāra*s also warn brāhmaṇas against involving themselves with dramatic arts. Gautama[40] says that if a brāhmaṇa indulges himself in singing, dancing or even playing a musical instrument, he would be excommunicated from the sacrifice and other religious functions.

All these references indicate that people associated with theatre were low class people, having very little social prestige. They are often classed with *antyaja*s, i.e., untouchables. Even if they were generously allowed to study, that was only to praise the kings and the great men and preserve their heroic deeds, as *sūta*s and *māgadha*s did. Studying Vedas was out of question for them. It seems that there were different grades of performing artistes, socially. *sūta*s and *māgadha*s were slightly better than *naṭa*s. But, theatre artistes in general belonged to the common folk.

Reasons

The reason for the *śāstrakāra*s being so vehemently against the actors and for actors being so ill-famed, lies mostly in the actors' lifestyle. From the very beginning, it seems that there was some sort of vulgarity in their performance. In *Ṛgveda,* Uṣas had been compared with a dancer — 'as the dancer (female) bares her bosom to audience, Uṣas, too, reveals her beauty by removing the darkness'.[41] This shows that female dancers in Ṛgvedic period danced with at least half of their body bare.

Again, we find a harlot performing a religious rite in *mahāvrata*, a Vedic ritual, in which, in course of a dialogue, as part of the ritual, she exchanges sexual abuse with a *brahmacārī*,[42] as already referred to. Most probably, the sexual abuse in the form of dialogue was a substitute for the act itself. Similarly, *māgadha,* in course of time, was substituted for an ascetic brāhmaṇa or *brahmacārī*. This rite has been taken as one of the rudiments which evolved the great art, drama. But, what interests us, is the involvement of courtesan and *māgadha*, the two theatre artistes, in the rite whose close association with drama we have already seen. Besides showing their participation in this ritual, of a dramatic nature, it shows one thing more. These two artistes were given the duty of performing this rite because they were known for their easy virtue and did not hesitate in performing this rite which had most probably its origin in fertility cult.

---

40. *Gautama-smṛti*, 15.18.
41. *Ṛgveda*, I.92.4.
42. J. Gonda, 'Ascetics and Courtesan', *Adyar Library Bulletin*, vol. XXV, part I, 1961, p. 78.

In *Rāmāyaṇa* too, though kings proudly patronised *gaṇikās* (courtesans), *naṭas*, *nartakas*, *māgadhas*, *sūtas*, *vaitālikas*, etc., these people were still ill-famed because of their low morals, especially the wives of *śailūṣas*, who were virtually prostitutes, as we infer from Sītā's saying, in *Rāmāyaṇa*, already referred to. Besides, most of the female artistes were courtesans, as we gather from both the epics, who had little hesitation in working with male actors. Being a courtesan, their moral standard was low. They are often mentioned as temptresses, using their art for that purpose, as we know from the story of sage Ṛṣyaśṛṅga who was charmed by the voluptuous courtesans who danced and sang in front of him.[43] The reference to *apsarases* are actually that of female artistes, either courtesans or professional dancers who behaved like courtesans, in the guise of divine dancers. They, also, were temptresses, as we know from both the epics.[44]

Jātakas are full of references to *naṭas*, and there, too, their notorious aspect is obvious. A *naṭa* is described as a tricky person who wins property by relating ill tales.[45] He is a poor man earning sufficiently only in the fairs and festivals, but due to bad habits spends a large amount of his earnings on drinks and ends his life by drowning in a river, as in *Pādakuśalakamāṇavaka Jātaka.*[46] *Bhadraghaṭa Jātaka* narrates the story of the son of a rich merchant who spent his money on actors and dancers, and died as a pauper.[47] *Telapātta Jātaka*[48] mentions a beautiful and talented dancer *janapada kalyāṇī*. People were mad after her. Female dancers flirted with people, even with monks as we have already noticed. Thus, it seems that though people loved the art of actors and actresses, they were notorious in their eyes, because of their obscenity. Buddha prohibited monks from attending song, dance, and instrumental music and witness *pekkhā* which was nothing but a dramatic representation.

Kauṭilya[49] had laid certain rules for actors from which we gather that while

---

43. *Rāmāyaṇa*, Ayodhya-kāṇḍa, III.17.
44. Like *apsarases*, they, too, distracted the penance of sages, as we have seen in *apsarā* section.
45. *Lābhagaraha Jātaka*, E.B. Cowell, *op. cit.*, vol. II, p. 287.
46. *Pādakuśalakamāṇavaka Jātaka*, V. Fousball, *The Jātaka*, vol. III, p. 507.
47. *Bhadraghaṭa Jātaka*, E.B. Cowell, *op. cit.*, vol. II, p. 294.
48. *Telapātta Jātaka*, *ibid*, vol. I, p. 232.
49. *KA*, IV.76.

performing, these actors crossed the limits of decency. He warned them against passing comments on some socially sensitive things and hurting people's feelings. He enjoins that actor must avoid making fun of country, caste, family, a certain branch of Vedic studies and representing copulation of men with women. Such strong prohibitions, themselves, show that they indulged in presenting such scenes on stage. We have already noticed how Kauṭilya had equated them with theives. Aśoka, also, banned such festivals which contained obscene representations, which is evidenced in his rock edict I.

According to *Mahābhāṣya*,[50] on being asked by the members of the audience to whom they belonged, the wives of the actors (*naṭas*) used to say that they belonged to the audience. *Avadānaśataka* refers to an obscene dance of *kuvalayā*, the actress, who bared her body shamelessly, while dancing.[51] A Mathurā pillar, also, depicts a female figure undoing her lower garment.[52] Hence, it seems that the performance of female artistes had vulgarity which would have been difficult for a dignified audience to put up with. That is why, perhaps, Manu[53] had stated that wives of *caraṇas* lived by prostitution and that a man conversing with another man's wife, commits an offence, and is liable to a fine, but anyone can talk with an actor's wife and no offence is committed.[54] 'Actors and their wives were so immoral that the question of their moral sentiments being offended does not arise at all'. Vātsyāyana also, enumerates actresses or *kuśīlava-bhāryā* among the women easily available for making love.[55]

Bharata himself tries to explain this contemptible position of actors in the society. In India, historical facts are often presented in the garb of mythical stories. Following the same pattern, *Nāṭyaśāstra* states that once, sons of Bharata presented farcical or comical satire insulting Vedic sages, which had some elements of vulgarity, too.[56]

50. *Mahābhāṣya*, VI.1.13.
51. *upasaṅkramya bhagavataḥ purastatsthitvā nṛtyati gāyati vādayate strīliṅgāni strīcinhāni copadarśayati* — *Avadānaśataka*, VIII.75, p. 185.
52. V.S. Agrawala, *Bhāratīya Kalā*, 343.
53. *Manu-smṛti*, I.8.362.
54. *Ibid.*, VIII.362.
55. *Kāmasūtra*, V.1.54.
56. *NŚ*, XXXVI.33-5: Kauṭilya, also, had enjoined that actors should not make fun of Vedic studies or castes. Hence, it seems that it had been a habit of the actors to make fun of these.

The sages were enraged and cursed the misbehaving sons of Bharata, 'O! Brāhmaṇas! you are arrogant and ill mannered. You are hereby relegated to śūdra status, your progeny shall, also, be born as śūdra and will always breed actors and dancers'.[57] This reference shows that as Bharata's sons, i.e., actors, some of whom were brāhmaṇas (as the sages addressed them as brāhmaṇas), were vulgar in their representation, partly according to the taste of the common folk for whom they impersonated, which was undigestable for the upper class of the society, they were considered as śūdra. Thus, it seems that this obscenity and vulgarity was there in drama before Bharata, which he tried to eliminate. That is why he prohibited certain scenes being shown on the stage.

Describing the origin of drama, in his first chapter, Bharata has said that people all over the world have taken to vulgar ways.[58] Here, he includes the audience too. It seems to be a reference to the kind of theatre that must have existed before Bharata, a theatre catering to the undisciplined and uninhibited tastes of the audience whom Bharata characterises as śūdra, for whom the *Nāṭyaveda* was created.[59] He, thus, wanted to ameliorate not only the artistes but also the taste of the audience.

One is inclined to think that a few centuries before Bharata, the slackening of morality, resulting in obscenity or vulgarity in the popular theatre, must have prompted Kauṭilya to lay a certain code of conduct and restrictions, but since this failed to make any lasting impact, the same was reiterated by Bharata, who tried to give a classical touch and dignity to drama. It seems that folk artistes of pre-Bharata period, though carrying a strong theatrical tradition, remained somewhat vulgar; this was the reason why theatre artistes are always looked down upon by the *śāstrakāra*s. Bharata, being himself a *prayoktā*, had a keen eye for dramatic arts; he knew how to promote the art and secure a right place for it in the society. The popular folk tradition, most probably, to match the taste of the common folk, had developed some undesirable elements, as we have noticed earlier. Bharata had realised that to make drama an art, acceptable to both the classes upper and lower, it was necessary to eliminate such elements and aquire social and religious or Vedic sanction. Hence, he combined the best of the two traditions and giving, thus, a

57. *NŚ*, XXXVI.38-41.

58. *Ibid.*, I.9.

59. *Ibid.*

dignified form of a discipline to drama, he worte his great treatise on the art for the actors. Thus, drama took a definite shape and a respectable position as an art with this symbiotic tradition, which was formed by a combination of folk and classical traditions of theatre.[60]

This symbiotic tradition brought some important changes in the attitude of people towards actors and their art. We have seen that scriptures, whether Brāhmaṇical, Buddhist or Jain, were not much in favour of drama and *naṭa*s; the *naṭa*s are always classed, in the scriptures, along with those, whose company was not much sought after by the people of noble birth. Buddha especially was always against such entertainments. But in *Lalitavistara*, Buddha is described as well-versed in theatrical arts.[61] Moreover, he wishes to marry a girl who is well-versed in various *śāstra*s, as a *gaṇikā*.[62] Aśvaghoṣa adopted this media to propagate Buddhist teachings. Vaiṣṇava *bhakti* cult stressed the importance of theatrical arts as a means of salvation. Moreover, kings like Gautamīputra Sātakarṇī[63] and Samudragupta[64] took pride in their knowledge of theatrical arts. Not only *gaṇikā*s like Vasantasenā were trained in dramatic arts but princesses like Mālavikā and Queen Irāvatī[65] too, were trained by *naṭācārya*s. It seems that the position of *naṭa*s in the society improved a bit, as *naṭācārya*s are known to be patronised by the kings; Haradatta and Gaṇadāsa were appointed in the inner apartments of the palace in Kālidāsa's *Mālavikāgnimitram*. They were properly trained in the art.[66]

Harivaṁśa describes how *naṭa*s were felicitated by sages and kings. Bhadranaṭa was given a boon by the sages to look exactly like the character he was going to play

---

60. Such attempts were made by some *ācārya*s, before Bharata's time too, it seems, but as their works are not available, Bharata seems to be the only surviving evidence of such attempt. It is known that *Naṭasūtra* was composed by Śailālin and Kṛśāśva, mentioned by Pāṇini (*Aṣṭādhyāyī*, IV.3.110-11). Kāśika says that *Naṭasūtra* had same place in studies, as an Āmnāya or Chanda had. V.S. Agrawal, *Pāṇini Kālīna Bhāratavarṣa*, pp. 312-22.
61. *Lalitavistara*, Śilpasandarśanparivartaḥ, 14-20, ed. Lefmann.
62. *Ibid.*, p. 350, ed. Śāntibhikṣu Śāstrī.
63. Nasik Cave Inscription, Line 8th, R.B. Pandey, *Historical and Literary Inscription*, p. 53.
64. Allahabad Pillar Inscription, Line 27, *ibid*. p. 76.
65. *Mālavikāgnimitram*, *KG*, p. 187.
66. *Mālavikāgnimitram*, *KG*, p. 191.

on the stage.[67] Not only this, he received another boon from the sages at the time of *aśvamedha* sacrifice performed by Vasudeva which must have improved his social status. Being asked by the sages to ask for a boon, he said that he would like to be honoured for his art, in the form of a boon. The greatest boon or honour, he felt, was being treated as equal, in accepting and sharing meals (food) with *dvija*s (brāhmaṇas).[68] This shows that even during the Gupta period, *naṭa*s were treated as inferior, and brāhmaṇas did not accept their food, as was the case during Bhāsa's[69] time also, but a *naṭa* even daring to ask for such an honour as a boon shows the change in the attitude of the general public, including that of the ritualistic brāhmaṇas towards the art. Again, when the Yādavas visited the capital of *asura* king Vajranābha in the guise of *naṭa*s with courtesans, as actresses, they had been treated cordially and gifts were given to them.[70]

It seems that persons who misbehaved with *gaṇikā*s were punished.[71] This seems quite a pleasant change, when we recount the account of the actresses and their immodesty in *Mahābhāṣya* and *Avadānaśataka*. Special seating arrangements were made for *gaṇikā*s in *raṅgaśālā*s as we know from *Harivaṁśa*, in context of Kaṁsa's *raṅgaśālā*.[72] They were allowed to dance with *kulavadhū*s (noble ladies) on special occasions like childbirth.[73] From *Vasudevahiṇḍī,* it seems that in several cases, they married princes and, though remaining inferior than the princesses, were raised to a higher status.[74] Bharata was called *muni* which indicates the honour he received.

One very important member of the dramatic troupe *sūtradhāra*, who apart from contributing to the direction and management of the play, adorned a role too, is often mentioned as a brāhmaṇa. Some scholars like *Raṅgācārya*,[75] think that it was *sūta* or *sauti*, the bard, who was a person talented in acting other roles while reciting epics, who grew into the *sūtradhāra*. *sūta* did belong to the classical Vedic

---

67. *Harivaṁśa*, II.91.26-8.
68. *bhojyo dvijānām sarveṣāṁ bhaveyam munisattamaḥ — ibid.*, II.19.29.
69. *Cārudattam*, Prastāvanā.
70. *Harivaṁśa*, 93.11-13.
71. *Caturbhāṇī*, p. 80.
72. *Harivaṁśa*, II.31.9.
73. *Caturbhāṇī*, p. 80, *Harṣacarita*, pp. 186-89.
74. A.P. Jamkhedkar, *Vasudevahiṇḍī: A Cultural Study*, p. 68.
75. Adya Rangacharya, *The Indian Theatre*, p. 18.

tradition but there, too, he belonged to the lower class of the Āryan society,[76] and later belonged to that symbiotic tradition which gave rise to drama as a most delightful art. *Sūtradhāra* is always addressed as 'Ārya'.[77] The *sūtradhāra* of *Ratnāvalī* is respectfully called *sabahumāna*. This shows that the artiste was respected for his art.

After being properly trained in the art which had now become a science, the lifestyle and conduct of actors and actresses must have undergone a vast change, since they were now found in the company of respectable persons like kings and poets. According to a legend, Vasumitra, the son of Agnimitra, was slain amidst his actors by his enemy.[78] Agnivarṇa, in Kālidāsa's *Raghuvaṁśa,* was always surrounded by actresses and dancers.[79] Bāṇa enumerates, in the *Harṣacarita*, among his friends, an actor and an actress.[80] Bhartṛhari,[81] refers to the friendship of the actors with kings. Bhavabhūti, too, had actors for his friends.[82] Poets like Bāṇa and Bhavabhūti, could not have had those *naṭa*s for their friends who gave folk shows like the ones mentioned in earlier literature, and whose occupations account for the censures of the law books and *Arthaśāstra*. Poet Rājaśekhara's wife was the *prayoktā* (producer) of the Sattaka *Karpūramañjarī.*[83] Thus, she, a Cāhamāna princess and the poet, also, must have had close association with such *naṭa*s. The *naṭa*s who had close association with poets seem to have been educated and cultured actors who had learnt the art, according to the tenets laid down by Bharata. Thus, it seems that the attempt of Bharata to give the art and the artiste a respectable place in society was successful up to a certain extent for at least, they were recognised for their art. But, even after being honoured and felicitated for their marvellous art, getting royal patronage and respectable company, they never enjoyed a very high position. This was true with artists in other fields, too. The reason was that the classical tradition of drama represented by the Sanskrit plays followed the rules prescribed by Bharata

---

76. *ŚB*, V.3.5.
77. *KG*, pp. 3, 185.
78. *Harṣacarita*, p. 192, text p. 198.
79. *Raghuvaṁśa*, XIX.5,14,19,36. *KG*, pp. 160-63.
80. *Harṣacarita*. p. 75.
81. III.57.
82. *Mālatīmādhava*, Act I, *Sūtradhāra*, p. 10, ed. M.R. Kale.
83. *Karpūramañjarī*, Prastāvanā, p. 10, ed. Durgaprasada.

(rather, too, faithfully without reasoning and without realising, the hidden object of Bharata behind a rule and thus, lacking the spirit of *nāṭaka* as we find in Sanskrit plays, after Bhavabhūti), but folk tradition could not put that mask on for a very long period and gradually, adopted their original style up to a certain extent. That is why we still find some obscenity or undesirable elements in folk tradition of drama, but at the same time the reminiscence of classical tradition is also there because somewhere in the hoary past, *ācārya*s had tried to modify the popular tradition of their art and unconsciously, they still retain those elements.

With the passage of time, some artistes representing classical tradition lost their original respectable status, for example, *gaṇikā* took the form of ordinary prostitute and so did the *devadāsī*.

In *Kuṭṭanīmatam*, we have seen that *naṭācārya* was disappointed in his courtesan pupils because they gave more importance to their original profession, rather than drama. He says that the courtesan cannot give a good performance, as they lack *sattva-bala,* due to their fondness of meat, wine and men. The statement indicates that *gaṇikā*s had lost those qualities for which they were honoured, as artistes. Their cheap performance[84] and love for prostitution, which might have been financially more profitable, were among the reasons for the decline in their status.

As for *devadāsī*, it seems that since she was considered the consort of the deity of the temple, her social status, originally, was quite high: she was one of the honourable members of the temple functionaries, and her deep knowledge of dramatic arts earned respect from the connoisseurs of the field for her. As the *devadāsī*'s position in the temple degenerated, her status in society, also, degenerated and she was treated as a temple prostitute. She is often referred to by that term.[85] *Devadāsī*s became women available to all though dedicated to God. When Durlabhaka Pratāpaditya II fell in love with a merchant's wife, the merchant proposed to the king, of offering her to the temple, so that she would be available to the king as a temple dancer.[86] This reference shows the change in the social status of temple dancers. Thus, she was dragged down from her respectable elevated position to the level of a commoner — an ordinary courtesan.

---

84. *Prabandhacintāmaṇi*, tr. Tawney, p. 186.
85. Santosh Chatterji, *Devadāsī*, pp. 32-33.
86. *Rājataraṅgiṇī*, IV.36.

Several reasons contributed to this fall, chief amongst them being financial in nature. During the heyday of this system, *devadāsīs* were employed by the temple and received definite endowments for maintenance.[87] Rich endowments raised their financial status and some of them had their personal property, at least in the Western Deccan, as is known from the donations made to the temple of Queen Lokamahādevī by a dancing girl in the eighth century AD. But, gradually, as the popularity and sanctity of the system waned, generous endowments became rare. 'The proceeds from the offerings of the devotees, gradually, became meagre, with the result, that the food received by them, from the *bhog* of the deity, was so much reduced, that it was impossible for the numbers of the *devadāsīs* to be sustained'. Hence, she was forced to seek other means to substantiate her income, when not engaged in her legitimate duties. They acted in stage shows, danced and sang in social functions, held in well-to-do households, and the more accomplished were paid highly. Thus, gradually, they turned into temple prostitutes.

Thus, either due to financial problem, vulgarity in performance or loose morals, performing artistes, gradually, lost that respect which they had earned with great difficulty. But the artistes appointed in the royal court, or those who received royal patronage in some way or the other, still held respectable status and were honoured for their art. According to Rājadharmakāṇḍa section of the *Kr̥tyakalpataru*,[88] the king was required to give money to the ordinary actors, according to their ability. The director of the play was to be honoured with betelnut and flowers; but there was a decline in the status of performing artistes in general, in early medieval period, though their art, whether classical or folk, still had the same attraction which it formerly had since the very beginning. Thus, people throughout the history of India despised their way of life but loved their art.

Glimpses of the Everyday Life of Performing Artistes

Interestingly, certain instructions of Bharata laid for *naṭa*s and some stray references to performing artistes in ancient literature of India reveal some important facts regarding their everyday life and way of living.

87. Tanjore temple inscription of Rājarāja Coḷa, *South Ind Ins*, vol. II, part III, p. 259; Hebbal inscription, A.S. Altekar, *Raṣṭrakūṭas and their times*, p. 295. Bagali inscription, *South Ind. Ins.*, vol. IX (i) p. 80; Shirur inscription, *ibid.*, IX (i) p. 85, 1.17.

88. *Kr̥tyakalpataru*, pp. 180-81.

REGULAR EXERCISE

The actors and actresses had to prepare their body for the tedious training by performing regular exercise. Bharata enjoins that for keeping the body flexible and swift, for quick action and bringing about *sauṣṭhava,* in *āṅgika* expression, an actor should perform exercise. One who is in the field of drama would understand the necessity and importance of exercise.

The National School of Drama, New Delhi, had prescribed Yoga in its curriculam, for bringing flexibility in the body of the students. Bharata says in the context of practising *cārī*s that an actor should perform exercise, either on the floor or 'high up in the air', and should have body massaged with oil or with, barley gruel, before he begins exercises.[89]

GOOD DIET

Besides exercise, another important thing for an actor, according to Bharata, is good diet. He says[90] that 'for the strength of body, one should take proper nasal medicine and get oneself purged, take oily food, juice of sugarcane and sharbat'. As vitality is dependent on one's nourishment, and exercise is dependent on vitality, one should be careful about one's nourishment. When bowels are not purged and one is very tired, hungry, thirsty, has drunk too much (water), eaten too much, one should not take exercise. Since drama was the profession of performing artistes, they must have followed these rules seriously.

PHYSICAL CHARM

Physical charm was one of the basic qualities of a *naṭa* or *naṭī*. *Nāṭyaśāstra* includes beauty and grace in the list of those qualities which a female artiste should have, no matter how small the role she is going to play, as *rūpa* (beauty), *śrī* (grace) and *navayauvana* (youth) were included in the *abhinaya siddhi* (excellence in acting) of a dancer.[91] Even for male roles, physical charm was necessary. In Sanskrit plays,

---

89. *NŚ*, XI.96-8; The *Kathakali* dancers massage and thus, prepare their body for the difficult dance postures, even today.
90. *Ibid*., XI.97-9.
91. *Caturbhāṇī*, p. 44.

the hero and heroine always possess this quality. That is why Bharata has prescribed exercise for actors.

Thus, performing artistes had to keep themselves physically fit and attractive for the sake of their profession. It was such an important quality for an actor that they tried hard to hide their age and prolong their youth. One such old actor is mentioned in the *bhāṇa Padmaprābhṛtakam*.[92] In this *bhāṇa*, an old *viṭa*, *Mṛdaṅgavāsulaka* of the dramas, is sarcastically, described as hiding his age by a *kaupīna*, i.e., even after applying dye to his hair and different types of cosmetics to his face and body, he still looked his age. Explaining the word *purāṇanāṭakaviṭa*, Moti Chandra says that it implies that *Mṛdaṅgavāsulaka*, the above-mentioned *viṭa*, was an actor taking part in the plays of the *veṣa*, who began to play the part of *viṭa* only due to his age.

BHRŪKUṀŚA

From *Mahābhāṣya,*[93] it appears that the *naṭa*s kept long hair, a thick beard and a bushy moustache. This was, probably, to enable them to play roles like those of sages and also of female characters, if necessary. *Mahābhāṣya* itself provides evidence of men playing roles of women. It mentions the term *bhrūkuṁśa*, while commenting on a *vārttika* of Kātyāyana, which was used to denote a man who made up as a female. Bhaṭṭojī's commentary on that *vārttika* says that because he (*bhrūkuṁśa*) conversed through the movements of his eyebrows or because of the charm (*kuṁśa*) of his eyebrows a male dancer, in the garb of a woman, is called *bhrūkuṁśa*.[94] The term occurs in *Amarakośa*,[95] also, carrying same meaning — a male dancer in a female apparel.

In Sanskrit plays, also, we have such references where male actors played female roles. In *Mālatīmādhava* of Bhavabhūti, *sūtradhāra* played the role of Kāmaṅdakī

---

92. *suṣṭhu tāvadanena nīlīkarmasnānānulepanaparispandena jarākaupīnapracchā-danamanuṣṭhitaṁ*

— *Padmaprābhṛtakam*, *Caturbhāṇī*, pp. 25-26

93. *Mahābhāṣya*, II.4.77; II.i.69.

94. *Siddhānta Kaumudī*, Samāsaśrayaḥ Vidhi Prakaraṇa.

95. *strīveśadhārī puruṣa* — *Amarakośa*, p. 17. (Poona, Orient Book Agency, 1941)

and Pāripārśvīka, that of Kāmaṅdakī's disciple Avalokitā.[96] In *Karpūramañjarī*, the elder brother of *sūtradhāra* appears in the role of Devī.[97] Probably, it was a common practice of folk artistes, as it is even today. Such folk artistes may have inspired Viśākhadatta's Candragupta, to disguise himself, as Dhruvasvāminī, for killing the wicked Śaka king in *Devīcandraguptam;* and Daṇḍin's, Puṣpodbhava to disguise himself as Bālacandrīka's female companion to kill wicked Dāruvarmā.[98] Bharata[99] has mentioned this type of role as *rūpānusāriṇī,* when man plays the role of a woman. This is another example of Bharata's attempt to combine folk and classical traditions and shows that actors often played female parts, most probably in the absence of suitable female artistes. This method was, thus, adopted by the *ācārya*s too, but generally, plays were enacted by the mixed cast, i.e., men in men's roles and women in women's.

Close Relationship Among Performing Artistes

Actors had close associations with courtesans and musicians as they were fellow workers and often belonged to common dramatic troupes. Courtesans were actresses, and music was an integral part of drama. In the above-mentioned *bhāṇa* play of the Gupta period, i.e., *Padmaprābhr̥takam,* the actor (*viṭa*) is affectionately called *Bhāvajaradgava* (old bull) by courtesans. He is described as coming out of the house of Nāgadatta, the musician.[100]

HABIT OF DRINKING

Stricture against drunken actors on stage[101] clearly shows that some actors had taken to drinking and in their drunken state lost self-control, forgot their dialogues and behaved indecently. *Naṭa*s' habit of drinking is known from the *Jātaka*s, also.[102]

---

96. *naṭa-saugata jagataparivrājikayaḥ tu kāmaṅdakyāḥ prathamāṁ bhūmikāṁ bhāva evādhite tadantevāsinyāstu ahaṁ avalokitāyāḥ*
— *Mālatīmādhava*, p. 10, ed. M.R. Kale
97. *Karpūramañjarī*, p. 11, ed. Durgaprasad, 1927.
98. *Daśakumāracaritam* — Pūrvapīṭhikā, pp. 76-78, ed. Chaukhamba Sanskrit Series.
99. *NŚ*, XXXV.31.
100. *Caturbhāṇī*, pp. 25-26.
101. *NŚ*, VII.44.
102. *Pādakuśalakamāṇavaka Jātaka*, V. Fousball, *The Jātaka*, vol. III, p. 507.

REHEARSALS OF THE PLAYS

We have some stray and rare references to the nature of the rehearsals of the plays in ancient Indian literature, which had great importance in the life of the theatre artistes. It appears from the *Mahābhāṣya* of Patañjali that actors were trained on the stage itself. He refers to *naṭa* teachers of dance, initiating novices, not through recitation of dramatic texts, but by the direct method of taking them to the stage,[103] which is no doubt the best way of teaching drama or acting. Art is the blessing bestowed by the *guru*, hence, the novices reverentially took to cater to all the needs of the *ācārya*, even working for him as errand boys, during the course of their preparatory training, as Darduraka had to do in *bhāṇa Padmaprābhṛtakam.*[104]

It seems that scripts were sent to the actors and actresses beforehand so they could learn it by heart, as we infer from the above reference, from *Padmaprā-bhṛtakam*, to the script of 'Kumudvatī Prakaraṇa', which was sent by the *ācārya* to *gaṇikā* Devasenā through Darduraka, a disciple of the *ācārya.*[105] It was written on a *tālapatra* (palm leaf).[106]

Economic Status

We do not have any definite information regarding the economic status of the performing artistes during the Vedic period. It seems that in the Vedic period, some theatre artistes were appointed in the service of the kings. As we have already seen, *hasanam upamaṁtrinaḥ* were fun-makers associated with the king and were recognised as state officers.[107] Probably such artistes received a fixed salary in the manner known in that period. Those who were given the duty of performing rituals of a dramatic nature would have received remuneration of some sort but that would

---

103. *Mahābhāṣya*, I.4.29; V.S. Agrawala, *Pāṇini Kālīna Bhāratavarṣa*, p. 327, fn. 2.

104. *aham tu devasenāṁ draṣṭumācāryena preṣitosmi iti* ।
atha kena kāraṇena? kiṁ bravīṣi?
kumudvatībhūmikā prakaraṇamupanayeti iti ।।
— *Padmaprābhṛtakam / Caturbhāṇī,* p. 50

105. *Ibid.*, p. 50.

106. *priyavādinike, kimidaṁ tālapatre abhilikhitaṁ? kiṁ bravīṣi nāṭakabhūmikā iti.*
—*Ibid.*, p. 54

107. R.C. Hazara, 'The Professional Jesters of the Vedic Age', *I.H.Q.*,vol. XXXVIII, no. 2-3, p. 194.

not have been the only source of their livelihood. Some of them like *śailūṣa* and professional female dancer (*nṛtu*) used to entertain people, specially in the fairs and festivals like *saman* and thus, earned their living. *Kāri*, the funmaker, is mentioned in Vedic literature as distinct from *hasanam upamaṁtrinaḥ* which indicates that they were different from the court-jesters and must have made their livelihood by amusing the common rung of the people.[108] Such artistes, generally, depended on festivals and special occasions for earning and their financial status would not have been very sound and stable.

By the age described in the epics, they had probably formed a community as they are, generally, referred to as *sūtamāgdhavaitālikaḥ* or *naṭanartakagaṇikāḥ*. Some of them, like *sūta,* were employed by the court. Probably, some female dancers and dance teachers, too, were employed in the harem, as we gather from the reference to Arjuna as Bṛhannalā. Such performing artistes must have been financially better off than the common *naṭa*s. It cannot be said whether the earnings of common folk theatre artistes, from their performance, were sufficient enough, or they had to seek other sources of income.

From Buddhist and Jain texts, also, it appears that dancers were appointed in the service of the kings. *Gāndhāra*,[109] *Kummāspiṇḍa*,[110] *Mahājanaka*[111] and *Campeya*[112] *Jātaka*s describe such dancers in the court of the kings. They must have been a little higher in status in the artistes' community, and most probably, received a good salary, as would have been the case in the age described in the epics. Some of the female artistes who had been appointed as *janapada kalyāṇī* enjoyed a respectable position and rich life, as we have noticed in the case of Ambāpālī. It is said in *Mahāvagga*[113] that Ambāpālī, the famous *gaṇikā* of Vaiśālī, took fifty *kārṣāpaṇa*s for a single night.[114] Some courtesans were really rich, as we

---

108. R.C. Hazara, *op. cit.*, p. 198.
109. E.B. Cowell, *op. cit.*, vol. III, p. 222.
110. *Ibid.*, p. 246.
111. *Ibid.*, vol. VI, pp. 28-29.
112. *Ibid.*, vol. IV, pp. 285, 288.
113. *Mahāvagga*, p. 286.
114. G.S.P. Miśra, 'The Vinaya Evidence on the means of entertainment, in the age of Buddha', *Ind. Ant.*, vol. I, 1964, p. 190.

know from *Kaṇṇavera Jātaka*,[115] which is a story of a courtesan Sāmā, whose price was a thousand pieces of money and who had a suite of five hundred female slaves. It was so, perphas because she was a favourite of the king. The palatial dwelling place of the female dancers, described in Jain literature,[116] also indicates that some of the female dancers or courtesans were financially better off.

On account of the comparatively greater respectability and the high salary, which the court artistes enjoyed, the effort of most of the artistes was to somehow get into the king's service; as, however, this fell to the lot of only a very few, other tried to serve under rich private persons. *Bhadraghaṭa Jātaka*[117] describes the story of a rich merchant's son who was always surrounded by actors. Very often such artistes are referred to who were in service of young tradesmen, like the one in *Bhadraghaṭa Jātaka*, 'whom they helped, along with other parasites, to squander their paternal property'. Tumblers, runners, singers and dancers, etc., received, each one of them, one thousand from the squandering and pleasure seeking merchant's son and made him, in short time, a beggar.

In contrast to these parasite artistes, there were many who earned their bread with difficulty, by catering for the amusement of people at festivities. In *Pādakuśalakamāṇavaka Jātaka,*[118] a *naṭa* is mentioned who lived in a village, not far from Vārāṇasī and went with his wife into the town, where he got money through dancing and singing and playing his *viṇā*. They were so poor that the wife of the *naṭa*, instead of crying and trying to save her husband when he was drowning, with his *vīṇā* tied to his neck, due to excessive drinking on their way back, was anxious to learn, at least, one song which would enable her to earn her livelihood, after the death of her husband. Her worry for bread was greater than her loss.

*Naṭa*s were always eager to attend festivals, as this was an opportunity to earn money. Jain texts, also, inform about such artistes who depended on such festivals and auspicious occasions for earning money.[119] As however, such festivities, in spite of their frequency, formed only an occasional break in their daily life, the *naṭa*s led

115. E.B. Cowell, *op. cit.*, vol. III, p. 40.
116. *Rājapraśneyī Sūtra*, 267, p. 195.
117. E.B. Cowell, *op. cit.*, vol. II, p. 294.
118. V. Fousball, *op. cit.*, vol. III, p. 507.
119. *Dhammakahāṇuyoga*, Sūtra 576, p. 240; Sūtra 168, p.54; Sūtra 277, p. 108.

at other times a miserable life, as did the *naṭakula* (*naṭa* family) in *Ucchittha-Bhatta Jātaka*.[120] This family maintained itself by begging and even the *bodhisattva* had no other way of earning a livelihood, than through alms. It seems that *naṭa*s did not do any other job besides their original work, i.e., the art which they had adopted as their profession.

We do not know if these artistes had organised themselves as a caste, as such professions, in course of time, developed into castes and are mentioned as such in *Dharmaśāstra*s. Their art, no doubt, had taken the form of their family profession, as we come across words like *naṭakula* (dancer's family), 'conch blower family', a 'drummer family',[121] 'son of an elephant tamer', etc.[122] This tendency towards organisation as a community, based upon a common profession, was present during the Mauryan period too, as Kauṭilya always mentions them as a community or group,[123] formed on the basis of a common profession.

The coming of the Mauryas represents a definite landmark in Indian history because the Mauryan emperors unified the greater part of India under one sceptre; this brought great changes and new outlook in political, intellectual, psychological and social spheres. This is reflected in the sphere of dramatic arts, also. For the first time, a most comprehensive treatise on polity — *Arthaśāstra* — was composed. Its author, Kauṭilya, saw dramatic arts from a different angle. 'His attitude towards the art, is not that of a *rasika* or art lover, his approach was totally utilitarian'. He is concerned with the well-being of the king and state, hence, for the first time, in his treatise, we find the salaries of performing artistes mentioned and the tax they had to pay to the state for providing them facilities. This must have brought a change in the economic status of the performing artistes as a whole because the instructions and rules, laid by Kauṭilya, were for both types of theatre artistes — common folk artistes and those employed by the state.

During Kauṭilya's time, it seems that the state provided regular employment for some performing artistes, who were helpful to the state in some way or the

120. E.B. Cowell, vol. II, p. 117.

121. *Saṅkhadhamakakula*: V. Fousball, *op. cit.*, vol. I, p. 284; *Bherivādakakula*. *Ibid.*, vol. I, p. 283.

122. *Ibid.*, vol. II, p. 221.

123. *naṭanartakagāyakavādakavāgjīvankuśīlavaplavaka-śobhikacāraṇastrivyavahāriṇāṁ* . . . . . — *KA*, II.43.27; III.66.1; III.69.13, etc.

other, as for spying or those included in personal staff. In *Bhṛtyabharaṇīyam Prakaraṇa*,[124] while discussing the salary of state employees, Kauṭilya says that *kuśīlava*s, should be given two hundred and fifty *paṇa*s per year, the makers of musical instruments five hundred *paṇa*s and *paurāṇika*s and *māgadha*s one thousand *paṇa*s per year.

In *Gaṇikādhyakṣa Prakaraṇa*[125] he says that a young and beautiful women should be appointed by the state on a salary of *paṇa*s one thousand per annum to work as *gaṇikā*. If she wants to leave the king's service, she will have to pay twenty-four thousand *paṇa*s to him. Kauṭilya enjoins[126] that the king should provide the means of livelihood to persons who teach various arts, i.e., dancing, singing, acting, prostitution, etc., to *gaṇikā*s, *dāsī*s and actresses.

Besides artistes who were state employees, Kauṭilya had thought about the common folk artistes, too. He says that theatre artistes present their shows to earn money, hence people should give them proper remuneration. If artistes, i.e., *kuśīlava*, *vāgjīvan*, etc., perform without fixing remuneration, prior to their show, they may be given wages as decided by experts in the field.[127]

Probably their remuneration was paid from the money collected from the people of the village or the locality, where the show was going to be held, because the state had made it a sort of compulsion on the people to contribute money for organising shows or dramatic performances. Those who had not contributed were not allowed to witness the *prekṣā*.[128] At another place, Kauṭilya clearly says that the state should arrange for the livelihood of the theatre artistes, from the money or tax collected from the cities and villages.[129]

Since, the state provided financial facilities to performing artistes, in return, they were required to pay a tax to the king from their earnings called *durga*.[130]

---

124. *kuśīlavāstardhātṛtīyaśatāḥ* । *dviguṇavelāścaiṣaṁtūryakarāḥ* ।
— *KA*, V.91.3

125. *KA*, II.43.27.
126. *Ibid.*, II.43.27.
127. *Ibid.*, III.69.13.
128. *Ibid.*, III.66.10.
129. *Ibid.*, II.43.
130. *Ibid.*, II.22.6.

Kauṭilya says that, at hard times, half of the income of prostitutes and actors (*kuśīlavas*), should be taken away as a state tax, to fill the royal treasury.[131] Besides these artistes belonging to the king's own kingdom, those who visited his country, from other states, were required to pay *prekṣā vetana* of five *paṇa*s per show, a sort of entertainment tax.[132]

We do not know if the system prescribed by Kauṭilya continued during successive periods too. Performing arts had become very popular, not only among common folk but in upper class, too, as we infer from Bhāsa's plays. It seems that actors and female dancers were employed by the state in the king's service during this period also as the *Nepathyapālinī-Rewā*[133] of *Pratimānāṭakam* and *Vaitālika* of *Pratijñāyaugandharāyaṇa*[134] show. They must have been appointed on fixed salaries. Besides, drama and dance was gradually becoming part of temple worship, Brāhmaṇical, Buddhist and Jain alike, as the sculptures of the pariod indicate, as we have already noticed. Hence, some female artistes may have been employed by the state, for temple service too. We do not know about the system of wages given to them during the period, but it appears that this was done either by the temple authorities or by the patron king.

Gradually, some of the actor-families prospered. In an old inscription, from Mathurā,[135] already referred to, a list of presents to Jain religious establishment by a *gaṇikā* Nādā or Naṅdā is mentioned, who was the daughter of *gaṇikā* Daṇḍā, the *leṇaśobhikā*. She seems to have been Jain by faith and financially in good state. This shows that dramatic art was a flourishing business, adopted by the artistes as family profession during early centuries of Christian era. Another Jain inscription, from Mathurā[136] states that the dedicators of the stone, who consecrated either 'on the site sacred to' or 'in the temple of' the divine lord of Nāgas, Dadhikarṇa, were the sons of those *śailālaka*s who were famous as the 'Chandaka brothers'. Here the term *śailālaka*s, according to Bühler, stands for an actor, in accordance with the

131. *KA*, V.96.2; II.43.27.

132. *teṣāṁ turyamāgantukaṁ pañcapaṇaṁ prekṣāvetanaṁ dadyāt* —*Ibid*., II.43

133. *Pratimānāṭakam*, Act I, *BNC*, vol. II, pp. 18-19.

134. *Pratijñāyaugandharāyaṇa*, Act II, *Ibid*., vol. II, p. 52.

135. *IA*, vol. XXXIII, p. 152.

136. *EI*, vol. I. p. 380.

meaning inferred from the references to such artistes in earlier literature. Thus, in first or second century AD, at Mathurā, play acting was the business of particular families, as was the case with the families of *gaṇikā* Nādā and *śailālakas*. These two inscriptions indicate the prosperity of the actors which enabled them to donate lavishly.

There are some references in *Nāṭyaśāstra* which indicate vaguely that Bharata had considered the professional aspect of drama, too, for the financial benefit of those who had adopted the art as their profession. To learn and practice the art in the manner prescribed by Bharata, was a whole time job and a person who was dedicated to the art in the true sense of the word and wanted to promote it needed financial security, too. Hence, generally speaking, midnight, noon-time, twilight and meal times were prohibited by him[137] for presenting dramatic shows because if performed, during the above-mentioned times, drama will attract very limited audience, which means little money. Besides, the artistes and their troupes[138] mentioned in *Nāṭyaśāstra* show drama as a flourishing business which gave financial shelter, not only to actors, actresses and directors, but to writers, *mukuṭakāra*, who fashioned various types of crowns, *ābharaṇakṛta,* who prepared ornaments, *mālyakṛta,* who made garlands, *veṣakāra*, the dresser, *citrakāra*, the painter, *rajaka*, the dyer and *kāruka,* who fashioned objects by means of lac, stones, iron and wood. All these artistes belonged to the lower class of the society, as we infer from the law books.

Later, as peace and prosperity prevailed in the country, during the Gupta period, comforts and luxury in life increased and this must have affected the theatre business too, for the better. We have several scenes depicting performance of theatre artistes in sculptures and paintings of the period, already referred to in earlier chapters. The luxurious garments, heavy ornaments, voluptuous poses of female artistes and trance-like absorption of performing artistes of the period in their art, indicate that they were heavily paid. In Gupta period, too, the artistes employed by the court were financially in much comfortable state than the common folk artistes, but the popularity of performing arts in the period shows that folk artistes, too, were financially in better position than their ancestors mentioned in *Jātaka* stories.

Dramatic troupes were invited to perform on festivals. *Kāmasūtra* says 'every

137. *NŚ*, XXXVII.80-85.

138. *Ibid.*, XXXV.66-109.

fortnight or every month, an assembly of citizens must be convened in the temple of goddess Sarasvatī'. Actors, from near and far, should be invited, to perform on the first day; on the second day of the festival, the actors should be rewarded by the temple authorities. There were two types of actors: those whose fees was fixed earlier and those whose fees was not. The latter usually received gifts from the citizens spontaneously, during or after the show.[139] Thus, it seems that generally the system of payment was same as mentioned by Kauṭilya who says that the actors, who have not fixed the remuneration prior to their show, should be given wages as decided by the experts in the field, i.e., spontaneously. From *Kāmasūtra* it seems that actors who fixed their fees first and then performed were paid by the temple authorities. The text further says that it is the duty of the citizens to co-operate with the temple authorities in every way — in difficulties or in celebration. Monetary help from the audience or citizens may have been included in this 'co-operation' as was the system during Kauṭilya's time, when the whole village contributed for such shows.

During early medieval period, after the period under consideration, we have reference to rich theatre artistes in the form of courtesans. Some inscriptions mention such *gaṇikās* from south who had constructed temples or donated lavishly for temples. A dateless inscription of Vijayāditya's reign[140] (AD 696 to 733), from Mahākūṭa, mentions the king'ṣ favourite mistress Vīṇāpoligal, and records her performance of *Hiraṇyagarbhadāna* and her precious gifts to the deity. Similarly, Chelebbe who endowed three pillars in the Vijayeśvara temple and perhaps, also, Matibbadammā, who contributed to make two other pillars of the temple, were other women of the same class.[141] The amount of their donations indicates that economically they were well off. At a later date, courtesan Kumudikā, mentioned in *Kathā-sarit-sāgara*,[142] also seems to have belonged to the same economic status because she owned hundred elephants, twenty thousand horses and a house full of precious jewels. She had her own army.[143]

Besides getting remuneration for performance, girls who performed in temple

---

139. *Kāmasūtra*, I.IV.27-33, p. 82.
140. *IA*, vol. X, p. 103.
141. *Ibid.*, 170, CXII and CXIII.
142. *Kathā-sarit-sāgara*, X.2-21.
143. *Ibid.*, X.2-42.

on festival days, individual actors and troupes of actors too, in early medieval south, received gifts of lands, a daily allowance of paddy and sheep, etc., for their performance.[144]

This shows that, in spite of the prejudices, the actor received affection and favour of kings and people, both. Due to this popularity, for his skill, he received gifts besides his wages which must have helped him strengthen his financial status.

---

144. Pattamadai inscription; *Annual Report on South Indian Epigraphy; Annual Report on Indian Epigraphy*, 1916, no. B.557; Tiruvengavasal inscription, *ibid.*, no. 253; Big. Canjesvaram inscription, *ibid.*, 1921, no. 42; Tanjavur inscription of Coḷa Rājendradeva, year 6; *South Indian Inscriptions*, vol. II, pp. 306-7; Tiravadi inscription of Uttamacoḷadeva; *Annual Report on Indian Epigraphy*, 1921, no. 398.

Appendix I

Spectators

IN Indian tradition, drama is considered to be a narration of action and emotions, as observed in the world. Bharata uses two phrases in this connection, one is *karmabhāvānukīrtana* and the other is *karmabhāvānudarśana*. It is not mere *anukīrtana*s but representation, *anudarśana*, that distinguishes drama from the other forms of literature-drama, is, thus, a *dṛśya kāvya*. *Daśarūpaka*[1] also says, 'Drama is an imitation of various actions and it is called (*rūpaka*) because it is represented'. A drama is essentially a thing to be visualised, and its consummation lies in its being represented on the stage. Bharata was fully aware of this fact; he regarded the performance of a drama as far more important than the composition of the drama itself. The judgement of drama, thus, should properly rest with the people, called upon to witness it, i.e., the spectators.

Successful representation of a play depends not on one but three requisites, all of vital importance, namely excellent composition, masterly direction and 'connoisseurs' — spectators. Of these three, spectators are of prime importance. Drama being representational, the presence of spectators is a must for its survival. The origin and progress of drama reflects the gradual change and refinement that came in the taste of spectators. The comprehensive form of drama comprising, dance, song, music, histrionics, etc., was, it seems, to cater to the variegated interest and tastes of the spectators. Bharata[2] says that there is nothing that is not comprehended in *nāṭya*, either knowledge, erudition, action, art or craft.

The prologues of Sanskrit plays show that it was the cherished desire of the poets to get the approval of those learned spectators who were competent enough to form an opinion about, appreciate or criticise the representation. The prologues

---

1. *Daśarūpaka*, I.8.
2. *NŚ*, XIX.122.

while highlighting the theme, focussing on the special features of the proposed performance, tried to arouse the interest of the spectators, leading them to a receptive mood. Most important for a producer or a play-wright was the way his play was received by the spectators. Kālidāsa and Harṣa call them as *abhirūpa-bhūyiṣṭhāpariṣada* or *guṇagrāhiṇipariṣada.* Kālidāsa was apprehensive about the success of his play *Vikramorvaśīyam* and requests the learned spectators, 'Arouse your good will, let our subject and hero, elicit your respect. Listen with attention, to this work of Kālidāsa'.[3] In *Mālavikāgnimitram*, he upholds the connoisseurs, against the plays of renowned play-wrights like Bhāsa, Saumilla and Kaviputra,[4] and says, as if giving an explanation, 'old does not always mean good, and new does not always mean bad. Discerning people rely on their judgement, only fools go by what others say'. In his *Śākuntalam*, the dependence of producers and play-wright on the opinion of spectators, is spelled out, when the *sūtradhāra* says, with great modesty to the *naṭī* who seems to be sure of success, 'Will the experts be satisfied? This is for me, the real criterion for the merit of a play'. Even the best artist hesitates to trust his own judgement.[5] *Pādatāḍitakam*,[6] a *bhāṇa* play, of poet Śyāmīlaka of the Gupta period, says that labour and pains taken by the poet in writing a play are repaid by the tears and joy of the spectators.

For Śrī Harṣa, too, the spectator of refined taste was a must to judge the success of a play. His *sūtradhāra* says,

> Śrī Harṣa is a skillful poet, the spectators are men of refined taste, the adventures of our hero are interesting and we know our profession as actors. Each one of these factors would be sufficient to assure the success of the play. It is our good luck to have them all together.[7]

Thus, the prologues of Sanksrit plays clearly show the important role played by the spectators in a dramatic representation. People collected to witness a dramatic spectacle, had different expectations from it. It is by way of exemplifying the tastes of such persons, of different categories, that the *Nāṭyaśāstra* says,

---

3. *Vikramorvaśīyam*, Act I, *KG*, p. 106.
4. *Mālvikāgnimitram*, Prastāvanā, *ibid.*, p. 184.
5. *Abhijñānaśākuntalam*, Prastāvanā, *ibid.*, p. 4.
6. *Pādatāḍitakam*, *Caturbhāṇī*, p. 150.
7. *Ratnāvalī*, I.5, p. 9. ed. Krishnarao Joglekar, 1959.

> Young people, are pleased to see (the presentation of) love; the learned, a reference to some (religious or philosophical) doctrine; the seekers after money, to the topics of wealth and the passionless, the topics of liberation. Heroic persons are always pleased in the odious and the terrible sentiments, personal combats and battles; the old people in Purāṇic legends and tales of virtue; and common women, children and uncultured persons are always delighted with the comic sentiment and remarkable costumes and makeup.[8]

These divergent tastes of the spectators were taken into consideration by Bharata, when he formulated his theory of success or *siddhi* which is actually the reactions and response of the spectators regarding the play. *Siddhi* is one of the essential constituents of *nāṭya,* as enumerated in the sixth chapter[9] and is elaborated in the twenty-seventh chapter of *Nāṭyaśāstra*. What he means by the term is the success of the performance gauged by the satisfaction of the spectators and the gratification of the performing groupe what Abhinava in his commentary, the *Abhinavabhāratī*, puts, as the attainment of the purpose saught.[10]

This should be borne in mind before studying the *nāṭya siddhi* of Bharata that 'creation of art', 'enjoyment of art', and 'evaluation of art' are three different, physical and mental actions, and each has its own importance. Out of eleven subjects discussed in the first twenty-six chapters of *Nāṭyaśāstra,* ten are related to the 'creation of art' (of drama-*nāṭya*); but *siddhi*, discussed in the twenty-seventh chapter, is related to the 'enjoyment' and 'evaluation of art'. Generally speaking, these two mean nearly one and the same, because both being products of the interaction between drama and the spectator, thus, differ only in degree and not in kind. The subtle difference is based on the person and the piece of work, each resulting out of his own capacity for enjoying the aesthetic pleasure, resulting out of his social environment, *saṁskāra*, character, age, sex, culture, etc. In experiencing or enjoying art, these factors which form the personality of an individual have an important role to play. On the other hand, though the personality of a person who evaluates and judges the artistic qualities of the performance is also formed on the same basis, yet he is expected to have some special qualification — critical faculty and knowledge regarding the art

8. *NŚ*, XXV.59-61.
9. *Ibid.*, VI.10.
10. *siddhirnāma sādhyaprayojana sampattiḥ* — *Abhinavabhāratī*, vol. III, 'Popularity is an Index of Śuccess' — XXXV.124; XXVI.113.

he is about to judge. This quality distinguishes him from the persons who merely enjoy the art, and thus, gives him a separate class and importance in the *siddhi*. This might have been the reason why Bharata classified the people or spectators into three categories: (1) *darśaka*, (2) *prekṣaka*, (3) *praśnika*.

Darśaka

The ordinary spectators were called *darśaka,* who represented society as a whole; brāhmaṇa, kṣatriya, vaiśya, śūdra, deity, *dānava*, *gandharva*, men, women, children, youths, old men and women, father-in-law, mother-in-law, son and daughter-in-law were included in the class of *darśaka* or ordinary spectators.[11] There were no rules or restrictions for entry laid for ordinary spectators.

Prekṣaka

People with special qualifications who were invited to evaluate a play and who were competent enough to pass the final verdict were called *prekṣaka*. The word *prekṣaka* has been grammatically derived as *pra+ikṣ+aka* — (*vuṇ* or *ṇvul*); hence, it has got a derivational meaning of a person who looks at or is viewing or intending to view or judge a performance. A *prekṣaka* is, thus, not merely an onlooker but a person who is competent enough to form an opinion about and appreciate the performance. Bharata describes the qualities and responsibilities of a *prekṣaka* — an ideal *prekṣaka* is one who has full control over his senses, possesses a pure character and is skilful in weighing the merits and demerits of the play.[12] One of the most important qualities of the *prekṣaka* is *bhāvānukaraṇa*, i.e., there should be a sort of self-identification on the part of the *prekṣaka* with the person on the stage, with regard to the *bhāva* generated.[13] But all these qualities cannot be expected in every member of the audience, which consists of persons of three levels, the high, the low and the average. Hence, an individual to whom a particular dress, profession, speech and an act belong as his own, should be considered fit for appreciating the same.[14] If a play, following the rules of the art of drama laid in *Nāṭyaśāstra*, proved itself to be a success, it achieved the *siddhi* and this was decided by the *prekṣaka*.

---

11. *NŚ*, XXII.228; XXVII.59-61.
12. *Ibid.*, XXVII.53.
13. *Ibid.*, XXVII.61.
14. *Ibid.*, XXVII.55-58.

Thus, *siddhis* is directly related to the representation of play.[15] The success or *siddhi* of *prayoga* or representation of a play is of two kinds: (i) *daivikī* (divine), (ii) *mānuṣī* (human). They are based on different moods (*bhāva*) and sentiments (*rasa*) and are expressed in three forms — vocal, physical and mental, the first two pertaining to the human and the last to the divine.

DAIVIKĪ SIDDHI

The divine *siddhi* is two-fold. The first is related to the *prayoga* (representation of the play) and the second, to the entire auditorium and the spectators therein. One is the wholesome disposition of the spectators, fully imbued with the appropriate moods; the other is the fullness of the auditorium and prevalence, therein, of an atmosphere of undisturbed calm,[16] i.e., when the representation of rhetorical sentiments and emotions attains the highest level of art the entire auditorium packed with spectators drops into pindrop silence and there is such attention which is not disturbed by any kind of distraction, noise or accidents. When the spectators are so spellbound that they forget themselves and thus, there is no physical, vocal or any other type of response on their part, the success of the performance may be regarded as *daivikī*.[17]

MĀNUṢĪ SIDDHI

The greatest success of the play lies in *daivikī siddhi,* but in a dramatic representation, imbibed with different moods and sentiments, special class of spectators (*prekṣaka*) had their responsibilities and in discharging them, they contributed to *daivikī siddhi*. The physical, vocal and mental responses of the *prekṣaka*s, during the performance, were precisely studied. The vocal and physical responses are five each in number, thus, making a total of ten elements for the human type. They are *smita*, *ardhahāsa*, *atihāsa*, *sādhu*, *aho*, *kaṣṭam*, *pravṛddhanāda*, *avakṛṣṭa*, *pulakaromāñca* and *abhyutthānachela-dānāṅgulikṣepaḥ*.[18] The first eight constitute the *vāṅgamayī siddhi* (vocal responses) and the last two, the *śārīra siddhi* (physical responses). It is natural for spectators to response physically and vocally to the

15. *NŚ*, XXVII.1.
16. *Ibid.*, XXVII.1-17.
17. *Ibid.*, XXVII.17.
18. *Ibid.*, XXVII.4-15.

actions, moods and sentiments, represented by the actors on the stage. Bharata, who was eager to record everything he knew in a classified manner, for the actors of the future, classified the reactions of spectators, too.

Bharata was not controlling or regulating the responses of the spectators, as he is often accused of; these responses are mostly involuntary expressions, depending upon the intensity of the feelings produced in the minds of the spectators. A *sahṛdaya* spectator would respond, in the manner described above, even without being instructed by Bharata. Bharata named the responses, only, to provide a proper criterion for the assessment of the performance. The purpose of defining and explaining the ten elements of *mānuṣī siddhi* was to instruct the *prekṣaka*s regarding their primary duty, because the ten forms of reactions of the *prekṣaka*s aided the *praśnika*s or the judges in deciding the merits and demerits of the play and the *artha* and *patākā* (trophy) was awarded to the best dramatic troupe, actors and actresses, on the basis of this record. At the same time, it inculcated a sense of appreciation for good performance in the ordinary spectators (*darśaka*s).

Praśnika

The literal meaning of the term *praśnika* is 'the person related to *praśna* or question'. In the case of dispute, about the assessment, the services of experts to the point of dispute was sought.[19] These experts were called *praśnika*s and were a sort of 'panel' of the judges. Two important responsibilities were vested in them — to settle disputes, in every possible point, regarding the art of drama, and to judge or evaluate the artistic qualities, merits and demerits of the performance impartially.

Since the responsibility of the *praśnika*s was greater than that of *prekṣaka*s, only highly qualified and competent persons, with a sound knowledge of the art, of drama were appointed, as the members of the 'panel of the judges'. This was the reason why the qualifications of the *praśnika*s are described more elaborately than those of *prekṣaka*s.[20]

A close study of the qualifications of the judges enumerated in *Nāṭyaśāstra* shows that some of them pertain to the individual character and nature of the people chosen as *praśnika*s, such as pure or good character, high birth, quiet demeanour,

19. *NŚ*, XXVII.62.

20. *Ibid*., XXVII.65.

maturity, etc., and some to their knowledge of art of drama, such as proficiency in six *aṅga*s of *nāṭya*, four kinds of *abhinaya*, four kinds of musical instruments, acquaintance with arts and crafts, capacity to discern moods and sentiments, etc., while others were necessary for an impartial judgement, such as impartiality, devotion to virtue, etc. It seems that the art of drama had, already, become so mature and developed during the age of Bharata that it was beyond the capacity of an ordinary man to discern the merits and demerits of a dramatic performance. Since it is not possible for a person to possess all these qualifications, the dramaturgists had suggested to constitute a panel of judges, consisting of an expert of sacrifice, an actor, an expert on prosody, an expert on language and grammer, an expert on weapons, a painter, a courtesan, a musician and a royal officer.

Although Bharata considers *siddhi* as one of the principal factors in dramatic presentation, in fact, as the most important end being aimed at, subsequent writers on dramaturgy seem to have practically, ignored it. The reason seems to be the great emphasis that came to be placed on *rasa* as the central element in the drama to be delineated by the actors and enjoyed by the spectators, and everything else being considered as the means to achieve this end. The commentary of Abhinavagupta has served to highlight this aspect. *Siddhi* is the achievement of success and both human and divine factors contribute to it. The success is the satisfaction of the spectators and this satisfaction results from aesthetic pleasure, which is called *rasa*. Bharata has mentioned *rasa* in the sixth chapter of *Nāṭyaśāstra* in a succinct manner.[21] Ghosh thinks that the reason for emphasis on *rasa,* lies in the outlook of spectators of the superior order

> who did not stop at the popular appreciation of play. They took the matter quite seriously and as was the wont of the Indians of every times, made an attempt to find out the philosophy of it. It was not enough for them that the spectators enjoyed witnessing a successful dramatic performance. They were, also, curious to find out the process, through which, it provided enjoyment to them and discovered, what may be called, the psychological basis of this enjoyment — *Rasa*. (M. Ghosh, Tr. *NŚ*, Introduction p. XXXVI.)

Mass and Class

The classification of the audience into three catergories — *darśaka*, *prekṣaka* and

21. *NŚ*, VI, p. 228.

praśnika by Bharata, suggests that there always had been two basic types of the spectators, say mass and class. *Darśaka* type of spectators were in the first category and *prekṣaka* type in the second, while *praśnika*s were experts from different fields.

In the earliest phase of dramatic art, when it was in the form of primitive ritual dance and enactment, spectators were not different from the performers, since the whole community participated in the ceremony. Gradually, the people having a knack for dances and impersonation were given the responsibility of performing such ritual dance and enactments and thus, two important elements of dramatic art — performers and spectators — came into being. At this stage, the art had a form of socio-religious celebration and spectators were a mass of people, taking part in the celebration as well as entertaining themselves. With the passage of time, ritualistic dance and impersonation gave rise to the folk form of dramatic art, attracting the mass.

From Buddhist literature, we gather that folk form of dramatic art was commonly enjoyed by the people as a whole, mostly during folk festivals and celebrations, which were often attended by the 'class' type of spectators, too. In such cases, special seating arrangement was made for them. In *Guttila Jātaka,*[22] it is said that a pavilion was set-up at the palace door, for the lute recital, by Guttila and Musila and a throne was set apart for the king. He came down from the palace and took his seat, upon the *dīvān* in the gay pavilion. All around him were thousands of slaves, women beauteously apparelled, courtiers, brāhmaṇas, citizens. In some special cases, festivals with theatrical shows were organised in the palace-yard and the king witnessed the show from his palace window.[23]

After the intervention of *ācārya*s, this simple folk art was, gradually, turned into a classical one, as noticed earlier and some important changes came in the sphere of drama. Drama took the form of a regular, well-organised art. Actors had to go through a proper training and the learned spectators, known as *sahṛdaya* and *sumanasa*, i.e., *prekṣaka*, forming 'class' type of audience, were there to appreciate their skill, who were different from the 'mass', i.e., *darśaka*, gathered to witness a spectacle and being easily satisfied. Classical plays were often staged in the palace and audience of such plays, too, belonged to 'class' category of spectators, witnessing and encouraging classical tradition of drama.

---

22. E.B. Cowell, *Jātaka Stories*, vol. II, p. 175.
23. *Ibid.*, vol. III, p. 208.

Drama itself had grown into several forms. Some of them like *bhāṇa* type of *prahasana* were for the common masses, and they had every sign of popular origin and vogue, while *nāṭaka* and similar other types of drama were written primarily for the higher classes of the society, for the assembly of the learned critics, without whose approval a drama would stand nowhere. It is in such types as *prahasana* that the 'masses' would get their familiar figures, the rogue, the scoundrel, the vagabond, the courtesan and such things, as quarrels, fight and violence, all in their *prākṛt* speech and wrapped in fun.

The reason for the existence of the two traditions of drama — folk and classical — lies in the fact that there were two types of people (spectators) for whom it was presented, though entry of either class was not barred in dramatic representation belonging to both traditions, except those meant exclusively for royalty.

The *uparūpaka*s, which include the latest varieties of drama and are conspicuous by being overlooked by Bharata, who was one of those *ācārya*s who endeavoured to give drama the status of an art, recognised by both classes of the society — lower and upper, show that primitive kind of drama, abounding in songs and dances, pantomimic shows and exhibitions, kept the popular stage engaged and was a great source of delight to the common people, the 'mass' category of spectators. Rangacharya[24] thinks that the *uparūpaka*s represent the earliest known form of the Indian theatre. Most of these are dance dramas, a majority of them have 'low' characters and low humours; a few of them, are concerned with love stories, the language in most of them is dialect. They represent an earlier tradition of theatre, catering to the undisciplined and unhibited tastes of the audience, belonging to the 'mass' or folk class of spectators. In course of time, when the classical drama came into existence, it certainly contributed elements to its formation. *Ācārya*s, like Bharata, took the best of this tradition, too, besides that of classical tradition, to make drama a popular as well as a respectable art. This folk tradition continued throughout the history of our country. Even in our own days, we do find a theatre of this kind with common folk as spectators. In it, we get a simple continuation of the most ancient theatrical principle — often the performer and spectator are one, forming a unity through the circles, in which they sit around the improvised booth of the stage, while actors walk up to and from the dressing room through the clearing, which the spectators, obligingly afford, as and when, necessary.

---

24. Adya Rangacharya, *The Indian Theatre*, p. 3.

Seating Arrangement

Regarding the seating arrangement for the spectators, it appears that in the beginning, it might have been an open space, around the place left for the performance, in the centre, where spectators were seated. In folk festivals like *samāja* which had theatrical activities as its chief feature, ordinary people were seated on *mañcas*, made by themselves and the rich folk on *śībikās*, as we infer from *Mahābhārata*.[25] This means that there were separate seating arrangement for rich people. Special *mañcas* were made for princes and people of the capital at the *samāja* held at the *svayaṁvara* of Draupadī.[26]

From the *Jātakas*, it seems that common people were seated on the seats arranged in 'tiers above tiers', while special throne was set apart for honourable audience like kings.[27] The sculptural depictions of the Śuṅga period, also, show that spectators were, generally, seated on the floor. For example, the famous *cūḍāmaha* scene, depicted at Sāñcī,[28] shows a group of deities seated on the floor, watching the dance of a divine danseuse in the centre, while others are standing with folded hands. The second century BC frieze from Kaṅkālī Ṭīlā, Mathurā,[29] depicts a dance performance by a young danseuse, the spectators sitting in the open air. Some of them, in the front row, are seated on the floor, while those in the back row are standing.

The Rānīgumphā cave, Orissa which is, generally, taken as serving the purpose of an open theatre also, shows that the common spectators, who may have been monks and devotees, were seated on the floor of the terrace of the upper storey but a rock-cut stone seat on the terrace indicates that it was provided to the high priest of the establishment.[30]

It seems that in a theatre hall, spectators were not segregated on the basis of sex and men and women used to sit together. *Vidhurapaṇḍita Jātaka*[31] describes a

25. *Mahābhārata*, Ādi-Parva, 7.134.9-14.
26. *Ibid.*, 12.184.126.
27. *Guttila Jātaka*, E.B. Cowell, *op. cit.*, vol. II, p. 175.
28. See *Pl.* V.
29. See *Pl.* XII.
30. Percy Brown, *Indian Architecture*, pp. 29-30.
31. E.B. Cowell, *op. cit.*, vol. VI, p. 135.

crowd of men and women, gathered to witness theatrical performances, as seated together on the seats 'tiers beyond tiers' created in the miraculous jewel. Bharata[32] had enjoined that certain scenes should not be shown on the stage as a *nāṭaka* is witnessed by the father and the son, the mother-in-law and the daughter-in-law (all sitting together).

Kāmasūtra,[33] also advises a young man, wishing to seduce a girl, to sit next to her while watching a play and try to flirt with her. Again, it says at another place that in the first three days, immediately after marriage, a couple should abstain from love. Instead, they should have a bath, eat together and witness a dramatic performance or *prekṣā*.[34] From *Harivaṁśa,*[35] it seems that there used to be a special pavilion for courtesans and ladies of the harem in a royal *prekṣāgṛha* (theatre) where men were also seated.

The seating arrangement in a theatre is described in *Mānasāra,* which varies in accordance with the shape of the theatre and in consideration of its being attached to a temple or palace or built independently, for the use of the general public. In an open variety of theatre, build in the courtyard of the temple,

> all kinds of seats are assigned for ordinary, special and occasional uses to *cakravartin* and other classes of kings, queens, as well as for the gods to be seated, together, with their consorts, as also, for the accommodation of ordinary people.[36]

The seats of wood, stone and bricks for the ordinary public, according to *Mānasāra*, should be arranged in compartments, partitioned by dwarf walls.[37] In a closed variety of the palace theatre, the seating arrangement is more specifically shown in *Mānasāra*. The first row corresponded to stall and facing the stage, is occupied in the centre, by the court ladies (*varāṅganā*), having the learned courtiers, on their

32. *NŚ*, XXIV.299.
33. *Kāmasūtra*, III.4.10.
34. *Ibid.*, III.2.1.
35. *Harivaṁśa*, Viṣṇu-Parva, 29.9.
36. *Mānasāra*, XLVII.26-9.
37. P.K. Acharya, *An Encyclopaedia of Hindu Architecture*, *Mānasāra Series*, vol. VII, pp. 273-74; P.K. Acharya, 'The Playhouse of the Hindu Period', *Dr. S.K. Krishnamurti Aiyangar Commemorating Volume*, 15 April, 1936, p. 372.

right and the bards on their left. Immediately behind the court ladies is the royal seat, on the left of which seats are reserved for the harem (*antaḥpura*) and on the right, is the seat for the chief queen and others.[38]

The seating arrangement for the audience is clear to some extent in the *Saṅgītaratnākara* of Niḥśaṅgadeva.[39] Though the text was written after the period under study, it contains an elaborate detail regarding seating arrangement and helps in throwing inferential light to the arrangement in the later part of the seventh century AD, too.

> In the variegated music hall, decorated with flowered walls, various flags and jewelled pillars, the president (king) is seated in a beautiful lion throne (in the middle of the auditorium). To his left, should be seated the court ladies of the harem, but the chief ones (queens) should be to his right. Behind, there should be the seats for the chief treasurey officers, close there to, should be the learned expert in human study as, also, the humourous poets and the clever people, conversant with all customs. The honourable astronomers and astrologers and physicians should be seated among the learned. To the right (left side behind the court ladies), should be seated the Council of Ministers, and therein should, also, be the seats for the honourable military officers and others. Fashionable males and females should be seated, surrounding the court ladies. In front of the king, and behind them, should be the female guards, full of youth and beauty and holding beautiful chowries and tinkling bracelets. The forward (guards) should be in the left side, having in front the vocal singers, conversationalists, bards learned and talking pleasantly, expert in panegyric and clear in all tunes. Thereafter, should be the family members, in the surrounding places. The dexterous (guards), holding canes, should be kept sealed.[40]

This type of seating arrangement was made when special *saṅgīta-sabhā* was held for the king and the royal household. It seems that there must have been the utmost variation in the character of the audience, according to the place and circumstances of representation. At great festivals, when plays were performed in the temple,

---

38. P.K. Acharya, *An Encyclopaedia of Hindu Architecture*, p. 274.
39. *Saṅgītaratnākara*, VII.1351-61.
40. *Dr. S.K. Krishnaswamy Aiyangar Commemorating Volume*, 15th April, 1936, p. 371.

there must have been admission for as many as could be crowded in; in private exhibition the audience may well have been more select. The fact that the dramas must have been largely unintelligible to all, i.e., ordinary spectators or 'mass' type of spectators, save a select few of the audience, i.e., *sahṛdaya-prekṣaka* or 'class' type of spectators, would not matter much. A drama was essentially a spectacle and people from all walks of life and different likings were allowed to witness the show. The popularity of the play must have depended on spectators as a whole, though the artistic level was judged and appreciated by the 'class' type of spectators. This was the case with the classical tradition of drama; the folk play was thoroughly enjoyed and understood by them. As a rule, the entire populace of the village contributed their share of money for holding such performance, since the very early age, as we gather from Kauṭilya,[41] who says that one who does not give his share of money, for the show, should not be permitted to witness it and if, he does so, secretly, the double of his share should be levied from him, as a penalty. According to *Kāmasūtra,*[42] it is the duty of the citizens to co-operate with the temple authorities, who help citizens in organising *samāja* in temple of goddess Sarasvatī, in every way — in difficulties or in celebrations. Again, in case of emergency, the temple may require the help of the audience. This help may have been monetary, too, as said earlier.

Thus, it seems that spectators, for whom the plays were written and staged, directly and indirectly contributed to drama in many ways — in popularising it, in pointing out the shortcomings and thus improving the artistic level of the play, in giving a convenient shape and form to theatre hall, since, comfortable seats were necessary for enjoying a play and maintaining folk and classical tradition of drama, by demanding such shows.

---

41. *KA*, III.10.
42. *Kāmasūtra*, I.IV.27-33.

Appendix II

Story of the Origin of Drama Narrated in Nāṭyaśāstra

PEOPLE, at the beginning of *tretā-yuga,* were leading a mixed life of misery and happiness, subjecting themselves to the lamental passion of lust, greed, rancour, and miserliness. So, Indra and other gods approached the creator of the universe, Brahmā and requested him to create a fifth Veda, pleasing both the eye and the ear, instructive and enjoyable to all sections of people. Since some of them are denied the privilege of learning the four Vedas. Brahmā conceded and went into meditation, recollecting the four Vedas for creating a fifth Veda.[1]

Brahmā in his meditation decided to name the fifth Veda as *Nāṭya* which being instructive and enjoyable with stories from history and legends would led the people towards righteousness, delineate the proper order of living and finally, bring prestige to those that learned it. He took recitation (*pāṭhya*) from the *Ṛgveda*, the song from the *Sāmaveda*, histrionic expression (*abhinaya*) from the *Yajurveda* and sentiments (*rasa*) from the *Atharvaveda*.[2]

After the creation of the *Nāṭyaveda,* Brahmā asked Indra to produce this piece called *Itihāsa*, but the god pleaded his inability. Brahmā, then, vested the responsibility of its production in sage Bharata.[3] Bharata, in his turn, taught *Nāṭyaveda* and also, its proper application to his hundred sons.[4] He, also, taught them to play various *bhūmikās* or roles suitable to them. Among the four *vṛttis* or modes of expression, *bhāratī* or vocal expression (speech proper), *ārbhaṭī* or virile expression, and *sāttvatī* or emotional expression were employed by him in the

1. *NŚ*, I.7-13.
2. *Ibid.*, I.14-18.
3. *Ibid.*, I.19-23.
4. *Ibid.*, I.25.

production, but the result did not satisfy him. So, on the request of Bharata, Brahmā created *apsaras*es to present *kaiśikī vṛtti* or delicate expression[5] and entrusted instrumental music to sage Swāti and the vocal music to sage Nārada and other *gandharva*s or the celestial musicians.[6]

The origin of modes or styles of expression (*vṛtti*) is connected with the fight of Viṣṇu with the demons Madhu and Kaiṭabha. The demons challenged the lord for a battle. They fought with their fists and knees, using various harsh words of mutual conflicts, shaking the ocean as it were by words of censure. Lord Brahmā, listening to their wordy warfare, spoke, 'Is this *Bhārati vṛtti,* proceeding from speech alone, increasing stage by stage? Please kill them'. Then Lord Viṣṇu said, 'I have created this *Bhāratī vṛtti* for the purpose of my work. This will be the style of speakers abounding in words. I shall kill them today'. The two demons fought with perfect gestures and movements of the limbs, as they were experts in the method of battle. The earth felt an excessive burden, due to the steps of Viṣṇu planted on earth, in the course of the fight. The *Bhāratī style* was born there. This is another derivation of the word *bhāratī,* from the word *bhāra* (the burden) which was felt by the earth.

The jumping movements of the wielder of *sārṅga* bow, sharp, intensely brilliant and full of *sattva* (i.e., strength) and without any confusion, gave rise to *sāttvatī vṛtti*. The God moved, sportively, with various *aṅgahāra*s and tied up the tuft of his hair, gracefully. This gave rise to the *kaiśikī vṛtti*.

Ārbhaṭī was produced by various personal combats, which were full of energy and excitement and which arose out of many foot movements.[7]

Bharata with the help of Sage Swāti and Nārada, *gandharva*s, *apsaras*es and his sons produced a play called *asura parājaya* (the defeat of the demons), in the open air at the time of the festival of *Indradhvaja* or Indra's flag.[8]

The production of *asura parājaya* offended the demons since the play was pointing toward their destruction. They disappeared from the auidence under the leadership of Virūpākṣa and owing to it, the speech, movements and memory of the

5. *NŚ*, I.41-50.
6. *Ibid.*, I.50-51.
7. *Ibid.*, XX.2-14.
8. *Ibid.*, I.55-58.

actors and actresses were paralysed.[9] Indra angered at the discovery of the hand of the demons in disturbing the production, beat them with his *jarjar* or flag-staff.[10] The production started again and the remainder of the demons started to frighten the actors and actresses with their guiles. Then Brahmā ordered Viśvakarmā, the celestial architect, to construct a *nāṭyagṛha* or a theatre so that admission could be restricted. He immediately brought into being a theatre, acoustically perfect.[11]

In order to prevent any disturbance occurring again, various gods were entrusted with respective duties of guarding the actors and actresses, the production material and the theatre — the moon had overall charge of the theatre, the *lokapāla*s had to guard the sides, Mitra was in charge of the green rooms, Varuṇa the sky, Agni the stage, Megha the instruments, Brahmā the acting area, Indra the hero, Sarasvatī the heroine, Oṁkāra the clown, Hara the rest of the artistes, etc. Those gods were in respective charge of the various sections of the production and the theatre and were called *raṅgadevatā*s or the presiding deities of the theatre and held supreme charge of the different sections.[12] He, also, stated that the gods that guarded the production and the theatre should be worshipped before a production started. The worship was included in the *pūrvaraṅga vidhi* or pre-presentational rituals.[13]

Brahmā explained nature and purpose of *nāṭya* to demons and they were pacified and the production went on smoothly.[14]

When the production attained perfection, Brahmā took them to Kailāsa, the abode of Lord Śiva, and there presented two plays, out of the ten major forms of drama — *amṛta-manthana*, a Saṁvakāra and *tripuradaha*, a Dim. Lord Śiva, pleased with the production, addressed Brahmā

> O the high souled one, this drama (*nāṭya*) which is conductive to fame, welfare, merit and intellect, has been well-conceived by you. Now in the evening, while performing it, I remembered that dance made beautiful by

9. *NŚ*., I.64-66.
10. *Ibid*., I.69-70.
11. *Ibid*., I.79-81.
12. *Ibid*., I.82-100.
13. *Ibid*., I.126-31.
14. *Ibid*., I.101-6.

> *aṅgahāra*s consisting of different *karaṇa*s. You may utilise these in the preliminaries (*pūrvaraṅga*) of a play.[15]

This dance or *nṛtta* is called *tāṇḍava,* since it was first explained by saint Taṇḍu.[16]

Thus, according to *Nāṭyaśāstra,* Brahmā is responsible for the origin of *nāṭya*, Viṣṇu for *vṛtti* or modes of expression and Śiva for class dance.

---

15. *NŚ*, I.12-14.
16. *Ibid.*, IV.17-19.

Pl. I : Bharhut *stūpa* railing, south gate, corner pillar, bottom panel: four named *apsaras* dancing in heaven.

Pl. II : Bharhut *stūpa* railing, western gate, corner pillar, top panel, worship of Gautama's hair lock.

Pl. III : Bharhut rail pillar showing acrobatic scene.

Pl. IV : Bharhut *stūpa* railing, medallian depicting dancing couple.

Pl. V : Sāñcī *stūpa* 1 southern *toraṇa*, east face, north pillar, detail showing the worship of hair lock of Gautama.

Pl. VI : Sāñcī *stūpa* 1 western *toraṇa*, south pillar, detail showing the story of *Nāga* King Mucilinḍa.

Pls. VII & VIII : Sāñcī *stūpa* 1 eastern gateway, north pillar, east face — third to fourth panel depicting heavenly scenes.

Pl. IX : Sāñcī *stūpa* 1 eastern gateway, north pillar, east face — third to fourth panel depicting heavenly scenes.

Pl. X : Vidiśā, fragment of railpost with relief of musical scene.

Pl. XI : Udayagiri-Khaṇḍagiri (Orissa) Rānīgumphā verandah, lower storey, detail of freeze showing a dancing scene.

Pl. XII : Mathurā, architectural fragment depicting dance of *apsarā* Nīlāñjanā.

Pl. XIII : Mathurā, relief fragment with dancers and musicians.

Pl. XIV : Amarāvatī, coping stone, Buddha's descent from heaven in the form of an elephant being carried in a palanquin, depicted in the central part of the coping stone.

Pl. XV : Pakistan, the acrobats.

Pl. XVI : Pakistan, upright slab showing dancers in panels.

Pl. XVII : Pakistan, dancers and devotees.

Pl. XVIII : Pakistan, dancers in upper strip.

Pl. XIX : Pakistan, dancers and musicians worshipping *bodhi* tree.

Pl. XX : Pakistan, architectural fragment depicting acrobatic dancers.

Pl. XXI : Mathurā, relief panel to support bowl, carved on both sides. Side one showing a woman with parasol-bearer, a man and his attendant.

Pl. XXII : Mathurā, relief panel to support bowl, carved on both sides. Side two showing bacchanalion scene, courtesan with an elderly woman, a man and a child.

Pl. XXIII : Haddā (Afghanistan) danseuse and musicians worshipping Buddha's turban (Gāndhāra).

Pl. XXIV : Pakistan, lady playing on flute (Gāndhāra).

Pl. XXV : Mathurā, female acrobatic dancer, Sanghol.

Pl. XXVI : Pakistan, scene of harem.

Pl. XXVII : Mathurā, architectural fragment, depicting musician couple.

Pl. XXVIII : Pakistan, Buddha leaving asleep Yaśodharā (Gāndhāra).

Pl. XXIX : Pakistan, life in the palace (Gāndhāra).

Pl. XXX : Pakistan, life in the palace in upper strip and the renunciation in the lower (Gāndhāra).

Pl. XXXI : Udayagiri (Vidiśā) cave 19, doorframe, right jamb, detail showing theatrical scene.

Pl. XXXII : Devgarh relief panels showing female dancers and musicians.

Pl. XXXIII : Devgarh relief panels showing female dancers and musicians.

Pl. XXXIV : Devgarh relief panels showing female dancers and musicians.

Pl. XXXV : Udayagiri (Vidiśā) cave temple 5 Varāhāvatāra, wall to the left of the panel, detail showing heavenly dancers and musicians.

Pl. XXXVI : Auraṅgābād (Maharashra) cave 7 sanctum, panel on the left sanctum door, Buddhist goddesses with attendant.

Pl. XXXVII : Auraṅgābād (Maharashra) cave 7 sanctum, left wall, panel of dancing woman and female musicians.

Pl. XXXVIII : Ajantā, cave 26, left aisle, Māravijaya panel.

Pl. XXXIX : Chittor (Rajasthan), architectural fragment with dancing females.

Pl. XL : Chittor (Rajasthan), Architectural fragment showing dancing females.

Bibliography

General Works

Acharya, P.K., *An Encyclopaedia of Hindu Architecture*, Mānsāra Series; vol. VII, Oriental Book Reprint Corporation, New Delhi, 1979.

Agnihotri, Prabhudayal, *Patañjali Kālīna Bhārata*, Bihar Rāṣṭrabhāṣā Pariṣad, Patna, 1963.

Agrawala, V.S., *Bhāratīya Kalā*, Prithvi Prakashan, Varanasi, 1977.

———, *Gupta Art*, Prithivi Prakashan, Varanasi, 1977.

———, *Harṣacarita eka Sānskr̥tika Adhyayana*, Bihar Rāṣṭrabhāṣā Pariṣad, Patna, 1964.

———, *Kādambarī eka Sāṅskr̥tika Adhyayana*, Chowkhamba Vidya Bhavan, Varanasi, 1958.

———, *Pāṇini kālīna Bhāratavarṣa*, Chowkhamba Vidya Bhavan, Varanasi, 1969.

All India Kashiraj Trust, *Vārāṇasi* (An Introduction to the greatness of the city), Ramnagar Fort, Varanasi, 1981.

Altekar, A.S., *Corpus of Indian Coins*, vol. IV, 'The Coinage of the Gupta Empire', Numismatic Society of India, B.H.U.

———, *Education in Ancient India*, Manohar Prakashan, Jatanber, Varanasi, 1975.

———, *Position of Women in Hindu Civilization*, Motilal Banarsidass, rpt. Delhi, 1978.

———, *Rāṣṭrakūṭas and Their Times*, Oriental Book Agency, Poona, 1967.

Anand, Mulk Raj, *The Indian Theatre*, Hunt, Barnard & Co. Ltd., Aylesburg.

Appa Rao, P.S.R., *A Monograph on Bharata's Nāṭyaśāstra* (Indian Dramatology), A Naatya Maala Publication, 1967.

Archer, W.G., *The Hill of Flutes — Life, Love and Poetry in Tribal India — A Portrait of Santals*, S. Chand & Co. (P) Ltd., Ram Nagar, New Delhi, 1974.

Aschwin de Lippe, *Indian Medieval Sculptures*, North Holland Publishing Company, Amsterdam, New Oxford, 1978.

Auboyer, Jeannine, *Daily Life in Ancient India*, tr. Taylor, Simon Watson, Asia Publishing House, George Weidenfeld and Nicolson Ltd., 1965.

Bachhopher, Ludwig, *Early Indian Sculpture*, Munshiram Manoharlal Publishers Pvt. Ltd., Delhi, 1973.

Banerjee, J.N., *The Development of Hindu Iconography*, University of Calcutta, 1956.

Banerjee, P., *Apsara in Indian Dance*, Cosmo Publications, New Delhi, 1984.

Barkar, Harley Granville, *The Use of the Drama*, Sidgwick and Jackson, London, 1974.

Barua, B.M., *Bharhut*, vol. I-III, Indological Book Corporation, 1979.

Basak, Radha Govind, *Aśokan Inscriptions*, Calcutta, Progressive Publishers, 1959.

Bhandarkar, R.G., *Vaiṣṇavism Śaivism and Minor Religious Systems*, Indological Book House, Varanasi, 1965.

Bhat, G.K., *Sanskrit Drama* (Problem and Perspectives), Ajanta Publications, 1985.

Bhatt, S.C., *Drama in Ancient India*, Amrit Book Co., New Delhi, 1961.

Bongard Levin, G.M., *Some Problems of the Social Structure of ancient India*, History and Society Essays in honour of Prof. N.R. Roy, ed. Debi Prasad Chattopadhyay, Calcutta, 1976.

Bowers, Falbion, *Theatre in the East*, Thomos Nelson and Sons, Edinburg 1956, New York, Toronto.

Brockett, Oscar G., *History of the Theatre,* University of Texas-Austin, Allyn and Bacon, Inc. 470, Atlantic Avenue, Boston, Massachusetts 02210.

Brook, Donald, *The Romance of English Theatre*, Salisbury Square, London, Ec. 4, 1947.

Byrski, M. Christopher, *Concept of Ancient Indian Theatre*, Munshiram Manoharlal Publishers Pvt. Ltd., 1974.

Chakraborti, Haripada, *India as Reflected in the Inscriptions of Gupta Period*, Munshiram Manoharlal Publishers. Pvt. Ltd., Delhi, 1978.

Chaturvedi, Sitaram, *Bhāratīya Tathā Pāścātya Raṅgamañca*, Hindi Samiti, Suchana Vibhaga, Lucknow, U.P., 1964.

Cheney, Sheldon, *Theatre — Three Thousand Years of Drama, Acting and Stage*, Vision May Flower, 1952.

Chowdhary, Radhakrisna, *Sanskrit Drama in Mithila*, Reprinted from the *Journal of Bihar Research Society*, vol. XLIII Part I-2 , March-June, 1957.

Coomaraswamy, A.K., *History of Indian and Indonesian Art*, rpt. New Delhi, rpt., 1972.

———, *Yakṣa*, Part I & II, Munshiram Manoharlal, New Delhi, 1971.

Czuma, J. Stanislaw, *Kushan Sculptures: Images from Early India*, Cleveland Museum of Art, in co-operation with Indiana University Press, 1985.

Dasgupta, Hemendra Nath, *The Indian Stage*, Asiatic Society of Bengal, 1934.

Dawson, S.W., *Drama and the Dramatic*, Printed in Great Britain by Cox and Wyman Ltd.

Dean, Alexander & Carra L., *Fundamentals of Play Directing,* 3rd edn., Holt, Rinchart and Winston INC, U.S.A., 1974.

Desai, Devangana, *Erotic Sculpture of India: A Socio-Cultural Study*, Tata McGraw Hill Publishing Co., New Delhi, 1975.

———, 'Social Background of Ancient Indian Terracotta', *History and Society*, Essays in honour of Professor N.R. Ray, ed. Debi Prasad Chattopadhyaya, Calcutta, 1976.

Dikshit, R., *Women in Sanskrit Drama*, Mehar Chand Lachhman Das, Delhi-6, 1964.

Dikshit, Surendra Nath, *Bhārata aur Bhāratīya Nāṭyakalā*, Raj Kamal Prakashan, Delhi, 1970.

Diwakar, R.R. (Gen. ed.), *Bihar through the Ages*, Orient Longmans, Calcutta, 1959.

Donaldson, T., 'Development of the Naṭa-Mandira in Orissan temple Architecture', *Kalādarśana*, American Studies in the Art of India, ed. Johana G. Williams, Oxford & IBH Publishing Company, in collaboration with American Institute of Indian Studies, 1981.

Dwivedi, Shalagram, *Mṛcchakaṭika, Śāstrīya, Sāmājika evam Rājanītika Adhyayana*, Vishvavidyalaya Prakashan, Varanasi, 1982.

Dwivedi, Vachaspati, *Kathāsaritsāgara kā Sānskṛtika Adhyayana*, Prakashaka — Sushil Kumar Dwivedi, Patna, 1977.

Eck, Diana L., *Banaras — City of Light*, Alfred A. Knopf, New York, 1982.

Fabri, C.L., *History of the Art of Orissa*, Orient Longman Ltd., New Delhi, 1974.

Fick, R., *The Social Organisation in North East India in Buddha's Time*, tr. Shishir Kumar Maitra, Indological Book House, Varanasi, 1972.

Frederic, Louis, *Indian Temples and Sculptures*, Introduction by Jean Naudow, Thames & Hudson, London, 1959.

Gargi, Balwant, *Theatre in India*, Theatre Arts Books, New York.

Ghosh, Rai Sahib Manoranjan, *Memoirs of the Archaeological Survey of India no. 24*, Rock Paintings and other antiquities of Pre-historic and later times, Calcutta, Government of India, Central Publication Branch, 1932.

Ghosh, Manmohan, *Contribution to the History of the Hindu Drama*, (Its Origin, Development and Diffusion), Firm K.L. Mukhopadhyay, Calcutta, 1958.

———, *The Nāṭyaśāstra* (A Treatise of ancient Indian Dramaturgy and Histrionics) tr. in two volumes, Manisha Granthamala Pvt. Ltd., 1967, 2nd edn.

Gonda, J., 'The Indra Festival according to the Atharvavedins', *Select Studies*, vol. IV, 'History of Ancient Indian Religion', Leiden, 1975.

———, Sanskrit Utsava — Festival, *Select Studies*, vol. II Sanskrit Word Studies, Leiden, 1975.

Gordon, D.H., *Pre-Historic Background of Indian Culture*, tr. V.K. Sinha, Bihar Hindi Granth Akadami, Sammelan Bhawan, Patna, 1970.

Gupta, Jagdish, *Prāgaitihāsika Bhāratīya Citrakalā*, National Publishing House, Delhi.

Gupta, S.P. (ed.), *Kushan Sculptures from Sanghol* (1st-2nd century AD), vol. 1, National Museum, Janpath, New Delhi.

Harald Ingholt, *Gandhara Art in Pakistan*, Pantheon Books, New York, 1957.

Harle, J.C., *Gupta Sculpture*, Indian Sculpture of the fourth to sixth centuries AD, Clarendom Press, Oxford, 1974.

Herbert, Jean, *Banaras: A Guide to Panch Kroshi Yatra*, Saturday Mail Publication, Calcutta, 1957.

Hignet, Gilbert, *The Classical Tradition*, Clarendom Press, Oxford, 1949.

Horrowitz, E.P., *The Indian Theatre*, Benjamin Bloom, London WCI, 1967.

Jain, J.C., *Life in Ancient India as Depicted in the Jain Canons*, New Book Company, Ltd., 188-90, Hornby Road, 1947.

Jamkhedkar, A.P., *Vasudevahiṇḍī: A Cultural Study*, Agam Kala Prakashan, Delhi, 1984.

The Jātaka, ed. V. Fousball, Published by the Pali Text Society, Messrs. Luzac & Co. Ltd., London, 1962-64.

The Jātaka Stories, ed. and tr. E.B. Cowell, The Pali Text Society, London, 1973.

Joshi, N.P., *Life in Ancient Uttarāpath,* R.K. Berry, B.H.U. Press.

Kale, Manohar, *Bhāratīya Nāṭyasaundarya*, Megha Prakashan, Delhi.

Kane, P.V., *History of Dharmaśāstra*, vol. V, Part I and vol. II, Bhandarkar Oriental Research Institute, Poona, 1958.

Karambelkar, V.W., *The Atharvavedic Civilization*, Nagpur University, 1959.

Keith, A.B., *The Sanskrit Drama*, (Its origin, Development theory and practice), Oxford University Press, 1924.

Khosala, Sarala, *Aśvaghoṣa and his times*, Intellectual Publishing House, 1986.

Konow, Sten, *The Indian Drama*, tr. S.N. Ghoshal, General Printers & Publishers, Calcutta, 1969.

Kosambi, D.D., *The Culture and Civilization of Ancient India in Historical Outline*, Vikas Publishing House Pvt. Ltd., New Delhi, 1977.

———, *Myths and Reality*, Popular Prakashan, Bombay, 1962.

Kramrisch, Stella, *The Art of India*, The Phaidon Press, 1965.

Krishnadeva, *Khajuraho*, Brij Basi Printers, New Delhi, 1987.

Krishnamoorthy, K., 'Indra Dhvaja; A Historico-critical Study', *Kusumāñjali*, Intrepretation of Indian Art & Culture, vol. I, C. Sivarammurthy Commemorative Volume, Agam Kala Prakashan, Delhi, 1987.

Krishnamurthy, K., *Nāgārjunakoṇḍa: A Cultural Study*, Concept Publishing Company, Delhi, 1977.

Levi, Sylvain, *The Theatre of India*, vol. I, tr. from French by N. Mukerji, N. Writers Workshop Publication, Calcutta, 1978.

Lüders, H., *Corpus Inscriptionum Indicarum*, vol. II, Part II: 'Bharhut Inscription', Government Epigraphist for India, Ootacamund, 1963.

Macdonell, A.A., *A History of Sanskrit Literature*, William Heinnemann, London, 1917.

Macdonell, A.A. & Keith, A.B., *Vedic Index of Names and Subjects,* in 2 vols., Motilal Banarsidass, Varanasi, 1958.

Macgowan, Kenneth & Melnitz, William, *The Living Stage*, Prentice Hall, Inc, Englewood Cliffs, N.J. Fifth Printing, 1958.

Mackay, E.J.H., *Further Excavations at Mohenjodāro,* in two vols., Indological Book Corporation, vol. I, 1976; vol. II, 1978.

Mahapatra, R.P., *Jain Monuments of Orissa*, D.K. Publications, New Delhi, 1984.

Mankad, D.R., *The Types of Sanskrit Drama*, Urmi Prakashan Mandir, Karachi, 1936.

Marglin, F.A., *Wives of the God King — the Rituals of the Devadāsīs in Puri*, Oxford University Press, 1985.

Marshall, John, *The Buddhist Art of Gandhara*, *The story of the early school, its birth, growth and decline*, Oriental Books Reprint Corporation, New Delhi.

Marshall, J. & Foucher, A., *Monuments of Sāñcī,* with the texts of inscriptions ed., tr. and annot. by N.G. Majumdar, in 3 vols, Swati Publication, Delhi, 1982.

Mathues, Brander (tr. Induja Avasthi), *Nāṭaka Sāhitya Kā Adhyayana*, Atmaram and Sons, Delhi, 1964.

Mathur, J.C., *Drama in Rural India*, ICCR, Asia Publishing House, Bomaby, 1964.

Mehta, Rustam, J., *Masterpieces of Female Form in Indian Art*, D.B. Taraporevala Sons & Co. Pvt. Ltd., Bombay, 1972.

Mishra, Kamalakant, *Jātakamālā eka Adhyayana*, Ganganath Jha Kendriya Sanskrit Vidhyapitha, Allahabad, 1977.

Mishra, Urmila, *Prācīna Bhārata Men Nārī*, Madhya Pradesh Hindi Granth Akadami, Bhopal, 1987.

Mookerji, Radha Kumud, *Ashokan Inscriptions*, Progressive Publishers, Calcutta, 1959.

Motichandra, *Kāśī Kā Itihāsa*, Hindi Grantha Ratnakara Pvt. Ltd., Bombay, 1962.

Mukhopadhyaya, Mihir Mohan, *Sculptures of Ganga Yamuna Valley*, Abhinav Publication, New Delhi, 1984.

Nath, R., *The Art of Khajurāho*, Abhinav Publication, New Delhi, 1980.

Pal, Pratapaditya, *The Ideal Image*, The Asia Society in association with John Weather Hill, Inc., 1978.

Pandey, Kanti Chandra, *Indian Aesthetics*, The Chowkhamba Sanskrit Series, vol. II, Comparative Aesthetics, vol. I. The Chowkhamba Sanskrit Series Office, 1950.

Pandey, R.B., *Historical and Literary Inscriptions*, The Chowkhamba Sanskrit Series Office, Varanasi, 1962.

Priestley, J.B., *The Art of the Dramatist*, William Heinneman, 1957.

Puri, B.N., *India Under the Kushanas*, Bharatiya Vidya Bhavan, Bombay, 1965.

Raghuvansha, *Nāṭyakalā*, National Publishing House, Delhi, 1961.

Raja, C. Kunhan, *Survey of Sanskrit Literature*, Bharatiya Vidhya Bhavan, Bombay, 1962.

Randhawa, Mohinder Singh, *Indian Sculpture*, Vakils, Feger & Simons Limited, Bombay, 1985.

———, *Rare Sculptures*, Selections from some Indian Museums, Exhibited in Japan, National Museum, New Delhi, 1984.

Rangacharya, Adya, *Drama in Sanskrit Literature*, Popular Prakashan, Bombay, 2nd edn., 1967.

———, *The Indian Theatre*, National Book Trust, India, New Delhi, 1971.

Rao, S.R., *Lothal and the Indus Civilization*, Asia Publishing House, London, Printed in India by G.G. Pathare at Popular Press (Bombay), Pvt. Ltd., Bombay, 1973.

Rao, Uma, 'Samakālīna Sampreṣaṇa Aur Raṅgamañca', *Sarjan Aur Sampreṣaṇa*, ed. Sachchidananda Vatsyayana, Vatsalnidhi Prakashan Mala, Samvitti-1, National Publishing House, New Delhi, 1984.

Ray, Amita, *Life and Art of Early Āndhradeśa*, Agam Kala Prakashan, Delhi, 1983.

Ray, N.R., *Maurya and Śuṅga Art*, Indian Studies Past & Present, 1965.

Roy, Sarat Chandra, *Oraon Religion & Customs*, Printed and Published by K.M. Banerjee, Industry Press, Calcutta, 1928.

Sach, Curt, *World History of Dance*, tr. Dessie Schonberg, W.W. Norton & Company Inc Publishers, New York, 1937.

Saletore, B.A., *Ancient Karnataka*, vol. I, (History of Tuluva), Poona, 1936.

Saletore, R.N., *Life in the Gupta Age*, The Popular Book Depot, Bombay, 1943.

Sankaran, A., *Some Aspects of Literary Criticism in Sanskrit or Theories of Rasa and Dhvani*, The University of Madras, 1929.

Saraswati, S.K., *A Survey of Indian Sculptures*, Munshiram Manoharlal Publishers Pvt. Ltd., 1975.

Sarkar, H. and Misra, B.N., *Nagarjunakonda*, Archaeological Survey of India, Government of India, New Delhi, 1966.

Saskia, C., Kersenboom Strong, *Nityasumangali-Devadasi Tradition in South India*, Motilal Banarsidass.

Sastri, Hirananda, *The Aśokan Rock of Girnar*, Gaekwad's Archaeological Series no. II, Baroda State Press, 1936.

Shanti Kumar Nanooram Vyas, *India in the Age of Rāmāyaṇa*, Atma Ram & Sons. Delhi, 1967.

Sharma, H.V., *The Theatres of the Buddhists*, Raja Lakshmi Prakashan, Delhi. 1987.

Sharma, Rana Prasad, *Paurāṇika Kośa*, Varanasi Gyanamandala Ltd., Varanasi, Samvat, 2027. VI.

Shashtri, Ajaya Mitra, *India as seen in the Bṛhatsaṁhitā of Varāhamihira*, Motilal Banarsidass, 1969.

Shastri, Surendra Nath, *The Laws and Practice of Sanskrit Drama*, vol, I, Chowkhamba Sanskrit Studies, vol. XIV, Chowkhamba Sanskrit Series, Varanasi, 1961.

Sivarammurti, C., *Indian Sculpture*, Allied Publishers, Pvt. Ltd., Madras, 1961.

———, *The Masterpieces of Indian Sculpture in the National Museum*, National Museum, New Delhi, 1971.

———, *Some Aspects of Indian Culture*, National Museum, New Delhi, 1969.

———, *Sources of History Illuminated by Literature*, Kanak Publication, New Delhi, 1979.

———, & Bussagli, M., *5000 Years of the Art of India*, Harry N. Abrams, Inc., New York — The Tulsi Shah Enterprises, Bombay.

Subrahmanyam, Padma, 'The Temple as the Focal Centre of Dance Art', *Kusumāñjali*, vol. I, C. Sivarammurthy Commemorative Volume, Agam Kala Prakashan, Delhi, 1987.

Sukul, Kubernath, *Varanasi Down the Ages*, Bhargava Bhusan Press, 1974.

Thomas, E.J., *The Life of Buddha*, Routlodge & Kegan Paul Ltd., London, 1960.

Trivedi, K.H., *The Nāṭyadarpaṇa of Rāmachandra and Guṇa Chandra: A Critical Study*, L.D. Institute of Indology, Ahmedabad, 1966.

Varadpande, M.L., *Ancient Indian and Indo-Greek Theatre*, Abhinav Publication, New Delhi, 1st edn., 1981.

———, *History of Indian Theatre*, Abhinav Publication, New Delhi, 1987.

———, *Religion and Theatre*, Abhinav Publication, New Delhi, 1983.

———, *Traditions of Indian Theatre*, Abhinav Publication, New Delhi, 1979.

———, and Subhedar S., *The Critique of Indian Theatre*, Unique Publication, Delhi, 1981.

Vidya, Prakash, *Khajuraho: A Study in the Cultural Conditions of Chandela Society*, Taraporevala Sons & Co. Pvt. Ltd., Bombay, 1967.

Vidyarthi, L.P., *A Sacred Complex of Kashi, A Microcosm of Indian civilization*, Concept Publishing Company, Delhi, 1979.

Wakankar, V.S. & Robert Brooks, R.R.R., *Stone Age Painting in India*, D.B. Taraporevala Sons & Co. Pvt. Ltd., Bombay, 1976.

Wells, Henry W., *The Classical Drama of India*, Asia Publishing House, Bombay, 1963.

Wilson, Raghvan & Pisharoti, *Theatre of Hindus*, Susil Gupta (India), Ltd., Calcutta, 1955.

Winternitz, M., *History of Indian Literature*, vol. III, part I, Motilal Banarsidass, Delhi, 1963.

Yajnik, R.K., *The Indian Theatre*, George Allen & Unwin Ltd., London, 1933.

Yazdani, G., *Ajanta*, Part I, Swati Publication, Delhi, 1983.

———, *The Early History of the Deccan*, Part. I-XI, Oxford University Press, London, 1960.

Original Texts

Abhijñānaśākuntalam, 'Kālidāsagranthavali', ed. Sitaram Chaturvedi, Varanasi, V.S. 2001.

Abhinayadarpaṇa, ed. Vachaspati Garola, Samvartika Prakashan Allahabad, 1967.

Abhinavabhāratī, *Hindī Abhinavabhāratī*, Chief ed. Dr. Nagendra, (Abhinav Gupta) Department of Hindi, Delhi University, Delhi, 1972.

Abhiśekanāṭakam (Bhāsa) 'Bhāsanāṭakacakram', vol. I. Chowkhamba Vidya Bhavan, 1982.

Ādi Purāṇa (Ācārya Jinasena), ed. and tr. Pandit Pannalal Jain, Bharatiya Jnanapitha, Kashi, 1963.

Agni Purāṇa, Ancient Indian Tradition & Mythology, Motilal Banarsidass, Part I, 1984, Part II 1985, Part III 1986.

Amarakośa, Poona Orient Book Agency, 1941.

Anargharāghava, (Murari) Vidyabhavan Sanskrit Granth Mala 47, ed. Acharya Sri Ramchandra Mishra, Chowkhamba Vidya Bhavan, Varanasi, 1960.

Arthaśāstra (Kauṭilya), ed. Vachaspati Garola, Vidyabhavan Granthamala-75, Chowkamba Vidya Bhavan, Varanasi, 3rd edn., 1984.

Aśokāvadāna, Sanskrit text, Compared with Chinese Versions, ed. and annotated and partially tr. by Sujit Kumar Mukhopadhyaya, Cheena-Bhavan, Visvabharati Sahitya Akademi, New Delhi, 1963.

Aṣṭādhyāyī, ed. and tr. Shrisha Chandra Vasu, Motilal Banarsidass, Patna, 1962.

Atri-smṛti, 'The Smṛti Sandarbha; Collection of the Ten Dharmashastric texts by Maharshies', vol. I, Gurumandal Series no. IX, Calcutta, 1952.

Aupapātika Sūtra, Jinagam Granthamala, Granthāṅka-13, Chief. ed. Yuvacharya Sri Mishrimalji Maharaje, 'Madhukar', tr. Chhagan Lal Sastri, Agam Prakashan Samiti, Byavar, Rajasthan, 1982.

Avadānaśataka, ed. Vaidyopahvasriparasurama Sarma, Mithila Vidyapith Pradhana, 1958.

Avimārakam, (Bhāsa), 'Bhāsanāṭakacakraṁ', vol. II. Chowkhamba Vidya Bhavan, 1982.

Bālacarita (Bhāsa), 'Bhāsanāṭakacakram', vol. I, ed. Acharya Baladeva Upadhyaya, Chowkhamba Vidya Bhavan, Varanasi, 1982.

Bhāgavata Purāṇa, tr. and annot. by G.V. Tagare, Motilal Banarsidass, Part II to III, 1976, Part IV 1978.

Bhāvaprakāśana (Śāradātanaya), G.O.S. Baroda, 1930.

Brahmjālasutta, Nalanda Devanagari Pali Granthamala, Sutta Pitaka, Dighanikayapali (Silakkhandhavaggo) Padhanasansodhako Bhikkhu, Jagdisakassapo, Bihararajakiyena Pali Pakasanmandalen Pakasita, 1958.

Bṛhatkathāśloka Saṁgraha, A Study, ed. V.S. Agrawala, Prithvi Prakashan, Varanasi, 1974.

Bṛhatsaṁhitā (Varāhamihira), Vidyabhavan Sanskrit Granthamala-41, Chowkhamba Vidya Bhavan Varanasi, 1959.

Buddhacarita (Aśvaghoṣa), ed. E.B. Cowell, Oxford, Clarendon Press be Horng Hart.

Caraka Saṁhitā, vol. II, Shree Gulabkunverba Ayurvedic Society, Jamnagar, India, 1949.

Cārudattam (Bhāsa), 'Bhāsanāṭakacakram', vol. II, Chowkhamba Vidya Bhavan, 1982.

Caturbhāṇī (Gupta Kālīn Śṛṅgārahāṭa) tr. and ed. Motichandra, V.S. Agrawala, Hindi Granth Ratnakar Karyalaya Pvt. Ltd., Bombay, 1960.

Cullavagga, Gen. ed. Bhikku J. Kashyap, Pali Publication Board, (Bihar Government) 1956.

Daśarūpaka (Dhananjaya), Motilal Banarsidass, Varanasi, 1979.

Dhammakahāṇuyoga, Part I & II, Compilers, Anuyoga Pravartaka Muni Sri Kanhaiyalal

Dalsukhabhai Malvania, Managing editor Sri Chand Sarana 'Saras', Agam Anuyoga Trust, Ahmedabad, 1983.

Dīgha Nikāya, ed. Rahul Sankrityayan, Jagdish Kashyap, Bhartiya Baudha Śikṣā Pariṣada, Lucknow, 1979.

Divyāvadāna, ed. E.B. Cowell and R.A. Neil, Indological Book House, Delhi/Varanasi, 1987.

Dūtavākyam (Bhāsa), 'Bhāsanāṭakacakram', vol. I, Chowkhamba Vidya Bhavan, 3rd edn., 1982.

Dūtaghaṭotkacam (Bhāsa), 'Bhāsanāṭakacakram', vol. I, Chowkhamba Vidya Bhavan, 3rd edn, 1982.

Harivaṁśa, ed. Pandit Ramchandra Shastri Kinjawadekar, Chitrashala Press, 1st edn., Poona, 1936.

Harivaṁśa, Gita Press Gorakhapur, 4th edn., Samvat, 2044.

Harṣacarita, ed. Jagannath Pathak, Chowkhamba Vidya Bhavan, Varanasi, 1972.

Jātakamāla (Āryasūra), ed. Hendrik Kern, The Harvard University Press, Cambridge, Masachusetts, 1943.

Jātakaṭṭhakathā, vol. I, Jnana Pitha — Murtidevi Pali Granthamala, Pali Granth no. 1, Bharatiya Jnana Pith, Kashi, 1951.

Kāmasūtra (Vātsyāyana), tr. S.C. Upadhyaya, Taraporewala, Bombay, 1961.

Karpūramañjarī (Rājaśekhara), ed. Durga Prasad, Nirnaya Sagar Press, Bombay, 1927.

Karṇabhāram (Bhāsa), 'Bhāsanāṭakacakram', vol. I, Chowkhamba Vidya Bhavan, 1982.

Kātyāyana Śrauta Sūtra, Publisher, Jayakrishnadas Haridas Gupta, Chowkhamba Sanskrit Series Office, Vidya Bhavan Press, Varanasi, 1929 (Part I), 1940 (Part II).

Kāvyamīmāṁsā (Rājaśekhara), ed. C.D. Dalal and R.A. Sastry, Nirnaya Sagar Press, 1924.

Kāvyamīmāṁsā (Rājaśekhara), ed. & tr. Kedarnath Sharma Saraswat, Bihar Rashtrabhasa Parishad, Patna.

Kāvyamīmāṁsā of Rājaśekhara, Original text in Sanskrit and translation with explanatory notes, by Sadhana Parashar, New Delhi, D.K. Printworld (P) Ltd. 2000.

Kumārasambhavam (Kālidāsa), 'Kālidāsagranthāvalī', ed. Sitaram Chaturvedi, Varanasi, V.S. 2001.

Kuṭṭanīmatam (Dāmodar Gupta), tr. Atrideva Vidyalankara, Indological Book House, Varanasi, 1961.

Lalitavistara, ed. Shanti Bhiksu Sastri, Uttara Pradesh Hindi Sansthana, Lucknow, 1984.

Lalitavistara, ed. S. Lefmann, A.S. Halls, 1902.

Mādhyamvyāyoga (Bhāsa), 'Bhāsanāṭakcakram', vol. I. Chowkhamba Vidya Bhavan, Varanasi, 1982.

Mahābhārata (in six parts), Gita Press, Gorakhapur, 4th edn, Samvat, 2044.

The Mahābhārata (Ādi-Parva), ed. V.S. Sukthankar, Bhandarkar Oriental Research Institute, Poona, 1933.

The Mahābhāratam with commentary of Nilakantha (Ādi, Droṇa, Sabhā and Udyoga Parvas), ed. Ramchandra Shastri Kinjawadekar, Oriental Books Reprint Corporation, New Delhi, 2nd edn., 1979.

Mahābhāṣyam (Patañjali), (Parts I-III) Pyarelal Draksadevi Trust, Delhi, Part I, V.S. 2036; Part II, V.S. 2029; Part III, V.S. 2031.

Mahāparinibbāna Sutta, Mahasthavira Mahavira Granthmala, ed. Bhiksu Kittima, Publication U Chozan, 1st edn, Burma, V.S. 1988.

Mālatīmādhava (Bhavabhūti), ed. M.R. Kale, Gopal Narayan & Co., Bombay, 1928.

Mālavikāgnimitram (Kālidāsa), 'Kālidāsa Granthāvalī', ed. Sitaram Chaturvedi, Varanasi. V.S. 2001.

Mānasāra, Oxford University Press.

Mānava Dharma Śāstra, ed. B. Rev. P. Percival, Asian Education Services, New Delhi, 1982.

Manu-smṛti, Chowkhamba Sanskrit Pratishthan, Delhi, 1985.

Meghadūtam (Kālidāsa), 'Kālidasa Granthāvalī', ed. Sitaram Chaturvedi, Varanasi, V.S. 2001.

The Milinda's question (*Milindaprśna*), tr. I.B. Horner, Luzac & Corp. Ltd., London, 1963.

Mṛcchakaṭikam (Śūdraka), ed. M.R. Kale, Motilal Banarsidass, rev. edn., Delhi, 1972.

Mudrārākṣasa ed. M.R. Kale, Motilal Banarsidass, Delhi, 1965.

Nāgānanda (Śrī Harṣa), ed. Sansar Chandra, Motilal Banarsidass, 1970.

Nāṭakalakṣaṇaratnakośa (Sāgarnandī), tr. by Myles Dillion, Murray Fowler and V. Raghavan, The American Philosophical Society, Philadelphia, 1960.

Nāṭyadarpaṇa (Ramchandra & Gunachandra), G.O.S. Baroda, 1959.

Nāṭyaśāstra (Bharata), ed. Babulal Shukla Shastri, Chowkhamba Sanskrit Sansthan, Varanasi, 1978.

Nāṭyaśāstra (Bharata), tr. G.M. Ghosh, Manisha Granthalaya Pvt. Ltd., 1967, 2nd edn.

Pāñcarātram (Bhāsa), 'Bhāsanāṭakacakram', vol. II, Chowkhamba Vidya Bhavan, Varanasi, 1982.

Pratijñāyaugandharāyaṇa (Bhāsa), 'Bhāsanāṭakacakram', vol. II, Chowkhamba Vidya Bhavan, Varanasi, 1982.

Pratimānāṭakam (Bhāsa), 'Bhāsanāṭakacakram', vol. II. Chowkhamba Vidya Bhavan, Varanasi, 1982.

Priyadarśikā (Śrī Harṣa), tr. C.K. Nariman, A.V. Williams Jackson and Chales J. Ogden, AMS Press Inc., New York, 1965.

Raghuvaṁśa (Kālidāsa), 'Kālidāsa Granthāvalī', ed. Sitaram Chaturvedi, Varanasi, V.S. 2001.

Rājapraśneyī Sūtra, Chief ed. Yuvacharya Srimalji Maharaj 'Madhukara', Sri Agam Prakashan Samiti, Byavara (Rajasthan), 1982.

Rājataraṅgiṇī (Kalhaṇa), ed. Pandit Ranjit Sitaram, Sahitya Akademi, New Delhi, 1977.

Rāmāyaṇa (Vālmīki), Ramanarayana Lal, 3rd edn., Allahabad, Bāla-kāṇḍa, 1958, Ayodhyā to Uttara-kāṇḍa, 1950.

Rasārṇavasūtradhāra (Śiṅgabhūpāla), The Adyar Library Series, Adyar Library Research Centre, 1977.

Ratnāvalī (Śrī Harṣa), ed. Krishnarao Joglekar, Publisher Panduranga Javaji Sreshthi, 1959.

Ṛgveda, tr. R.T.H. Griffith, E.J. Lazarus and Co. Benares, 1989.

Ṛtusaṁhāra (Kālidāsa), 'Kālidāsa Granthāvalī', ed. Sitaram Chaturvedi,Varanasi, VS. 2001.

Saṅgītaratnākara, ed. & tr. R.K. Shringy, Motilal Banarsidass, Delhi, 1978.

Śatapatha Brāhmaṇa, Gaurishankar Goenka, Kashi, Part I, 1938, Part II, 1941.

Saundarānanda (Aśvaghoṣa), ed. and tr. E.H. Johnston, Motilal Banarsidass, Delhi, 1975.

Śiva Purāṇa, tr. by a Board of Scholars, ed. J.L. Shastry, Motilal Banarsidass, Delhi, vol. I-II, 1977, vol. III-IV, 1978.

Svapnavāsavadattam (Bhāsa), 'Bhāsanāṭakacakram', vol. II. Chowkhamba Vidya Bhavan, Varanasi, 1982.

Tiloya Paṇṇatti, vol. I, Jivaraj Jain Granthmala, Sholapur, V.S. 2000.

Theragāthā, ed. Bhikṣu Dharmaratha, Bhāratīya Buddha Śikṣā Pariṣad, Lucknow, 1988.

Urubhaṅga (Bhāsa), 'Bhāsanāṭakacakram', vol. I, Chowkhamba Vidya Bhavan, Varanasi, 1982.

Uttara-rāma-carita (Bhavabhūti), ed. M.R. Kale, Gopal Narayan & Co., Bombay, 1924.

Veṇīsaṁhāra, ed. Pandita Chhota Rama Tiwari, Benares, 1867.

Viddhaśālabhañjikā, ed. Babulal Shukla Shastri, Chowkhamba Orientalia, Varanasi, 1976.

Vikramorvaśīyam, 'Kālidāsa Granthāvalī', ed. Sitaram Chaturvedi, Varanasi, V.S. 2001.

Yājñavalkya-Smṛti, 'The Smṛti Sandarbha', Calcutta, 1852.

Articles and Journals

Acharya, P.K., 'The Playhouse of the Hindu Period', *S. Krishnaswami Aiyangar Commemorating Volume*, 15 April, 1936.

Agrawala, V.S., 'Games and Amusements in Aṣṭādhyāyī', *Indian Culture*, vol. XVI, July, Sept. 1949, no. 1.

———, 'A Survey of Gupta Art and some Sculptures from Numcna Kuthara', *Lalita Kala*, Lalita Kala Akademi no. 9, April 1961.

Anand, M.R., 'Rhythm of Dance and Music in the Bagh Caves', *Marg*, vol. XXV, June, 1972, no. 3.

Arjunwadkar, K.S., 'The Rasa Theory and the Darśana', *ABORI*, vol. LXV, Part I-IV, 1984.

Athavale, R.B., 'Ancient Sanskrit Drama and Music', *ABORI*, vol. XLV, 1964.

Ayyangar N., Ramadas, 'Curtain in Ancient Theatre', *ABORI*, vol. LIV, part I-IV.

Bajpai, K.D., 'The Kushan Art of Mathura', *Marg*, vol. XV, March, 1962, no. 2.

Banerji, Sastri, A., 'The Naṭī of Pataliputra', *IHQ*, vol. IX 1-2. part I.

Barua, B.M., 'Maskari Gosala's Early Life', *Calcutta Review*, 1927, April-June.

Belvalkar, S.K., 'Origin of Hindu Drama', *Calcutta Review* May, 1922.

Bhandarkar, D.R., 'Foreign Elements in the Hindu Population', *IA*, vol. XL, Jan. 1911.

Bhandarkar, D.R., 'Samaja', *JBBRS*, vol. XXI.

Bhat, G.K., 'Origin of Nāṭya: Role of Śiva', *ABORI*, vol. LVI, Part I-IV, 1975.

Bloch, T., *Archaeological Survey of India Annual Report*, 1903-4.

Bose, A.N., 'Hīnasippas', *Indian Culture*, vol. IX, Oct. 1942, March 1943, no. 2 & 3.

Bühler, G., 'New Jain Inscription from Mathura', *EI*, vol. I.

Coomaraswamy, A.K., 'Hindu Theatre', *IHQ*, vol. IX no. 1-2.

———, 'Picture Showmen', *IHQ*, vol. V.

Crook, W., 'Phallic Worship in the Himalayas', *IA*, vol. XXIX.

Deshpande, M.N., *Presidential Address, Indian History Congress, Proceedings of the Twenty-fifth Session,* Poona, 1963.

Dhavalikar, M.K., 'Sūtradhāra', *ABORI*, vol. LII, Part I-IV.

Divakar, H.R., 'Who First Introduced Nāṭya on Earth', *ABI*, 1923-4, vol. V, Part I.

Ghosh, M., 'The Hindu Theatre', *IHQ*, vol. IX, no. 1-2.

———, 'Indian Drama and its Vedic Affinity', *Our Heritage*, vol. XXVI, Part. I-II. Dec.-Jan. 1978.

———, 'On the Origin of the Hindu Drama', *IHQ*, vol. XXXI 1-4.

———, 'Problems of Nāṭyaśāstra', *IHQ*, VI. 1-2.

Gonda, J., 'Ascetics and Courtesans', *Adyar Library Bulletin*, vol. XXV, Part I-4.

Hardikar, A., 'Prekṣaka — A spectator', *ABORI*, vol. LXIV, Part I-IV.

Hazara, R.C., 'The Professional Jesters of the Vedic Age', *IHQ*, vol. XXXVIII, no. 2-3, 1962.

Indian Archaeology, 1954-55, A Review, Nāgārjunakoṇḍa.

Iyer, S., Venkitsubramonia, 'Siddhi in Bharata's Nāṭyaśāstra', *Annals of Oriental Research*, University of Madras, Silver Jubilee Volume, 1975.

Jayaswal, K.P., 'The Jogimara Cave Inscription', *IA*, vol. XLVIII, July 1919.

Krishnamacharya, K., 'On the Origin of Sanskrit Drama', *Quarterly Journal of Mystic Society*, Jan. 1934, vol. XXIV, no. 3.

Law, B.C., 'The Licchavis in Ancient India', *Journal and Proceedings, Asiatic Society of Bengal, New Series*, Vol. XVII. 1921.

Loman, J.R.A., 'The Comic Character of the Caturbhāṇī', *ALB*, XXV, p. 173.

Lüders, Heinrich, 'Indian Caves as Pleasure Resorts', *IA*, XXXIV, Sept. 1905.

Majumdar, N.B., 'Samāja', *IA*, vol. XLVII, Part DXCVIII, Aug. 1918.

Mankad, D.R., 'Hindu Theatre', *IHQ*, vol. VIII, no. 13.

———, 'Hindu Theatre', *IHQ*, vol. IX, no. 3-4.

Meere, S., 'Catharis and Rasa Realisation in Tragedy', *Annals of Oriental Research,* vol. XXIX, Part I & II.

Misra, G.S.P., 'The Vinaya Evidence on the Means of Entertainment in the Age of Buddha', *IA*, vol. 1 1964.

Ousley, J.R., 'Antiquities of Sarguja and its Neighbourhood', *JASB*, vol. XVII, Part 1948.

Puri, B.N., 'Some Aspects of Social Life in Kushana Period', *Indian Culture*, vol. XVI. July-Sept. 1949, no. 1.

Raghvan, V., 'Hindu Theatre', *IHQ*, vol. IX, no. 3-3.

———, 'On a Meaning of the Word Kauśika', *Journal of Oriental Research*, vol. XV, Madras.

———, 'Picture showmen', *IHQ*, vol. XII, no. 3, Sept. 1936.

Rai Govind Chandra & Vidya Prakash 'Varanasi at a Glance', *A Souvenir Issued on the Eve of XXIV Session of All India Oriental Conference*, Varanaseya Sanskrit Viśvavidyālaya, Varanasi, Oct. 1968.

Ramchandran, T.N., 'Cave Temple and Paintings of Sittannavasal', *Lalita Kala*, Lalit Kala Akademi, no. 9, April, 1961.

Ray, Amita, 'Sculptures in Aurangabad', *Marg*, XVI, June, 1963. no. 3.

Roychoudhuri, H.C., *IHQ*, vol. V.

Sankalia, H.D. & Dhavalikar, M.K., 'The Terracotta Art of India', *Marg*, vol. XXIII, no. 1, Dec. 1969.

Sastri, Kalikumar Dutta, 'Verses in the Bharata's Theatre', *Our Heritage*, special number, Sanskrit College, 150th Anniversary 1824-1974, Calcutta.

Sastry, R. Shama, *Mysore Archaeological Report*, 1926.

Singh, Madan Mohan, 'Ancient Popular Festivals in North-East India', *IHQ*, vol. XXIX, no. 4.

Srivastava, V.N., 'The Gupta Art of Mathura', *Marg*, vol. XV, March 1962, no. 2.

Sternbach, Ludwik, 'Second Supplement to Vaisya: Synonyms and Aphorism', *Bhāratiyā Vidyā*, vol. XI, no. 1 & 2, Jan-June, 1950.

Subbarao, D., 'A Critical Survey of the Ancient Theatre in Accordance with the Bharata's Nāṭyaśāstra and its Commentators', *Journals of Oriental Institute*, Baroda, vol. II, no. 2.

Subramaniam, A.V., 'Unity of Sentiment in Sanskrit Play', *Annals of Oriental Research*, vol. XXX, Part II.

Sundaram, S.S., 'Drama, Dance and Music in the Works of Bāṇa and Harṣa', *Saṁskrit Raṅga, Silver Jubilee Celebration*, 10-11 Sept. 1987, Souvenir.

Thomas, F.W., 'Notes on the Edicts of Aśoka', *JRAS*, 1914.

Vidya Prakash, 'Dance in Khajuraho Sculptures', *Bhāratī*, Bulletin of the College of Indology, 1963-64, no. 7, Parts I & II.

Wijesekera, O.H. De. A., 'Buddhist Evidence of Drama', *IHQ*, vol. XVII. no. 2, June, 1941.

Glossary

Abhyutthāncelā: Reaction of the spectators: Open admiration by standing up in their seats or fling clothes as present to the actors.

ācārya: the preceptor.

aho: Reaction of the spectator on something related to love, valour or wonder.

ālasya: Indolence.

amarṣa: Indignation.

aṅgas: Main divisions.

antaḥpura: Harem.

ardhahāsa: Subdued laughter.

aśru: tears.

asūya: Envy.

atihāsa: Loud laughter.

avahittha: Dissimulation.

āvega: Agitation.

autsūkya: Yearning.

bhāva: State.

bhaya: Terror.

bilva: The wood apple commonly known as '*Bel*' — a fruit with sticky pulp.

bodhi-tree: *Pīpal* tree under which Gautam Buddha was enlightened.

brahmacārī: Student practising sacred study before marriage, observing chastity.

Buddhist Nikāyas: Buddhist Scriptures.

capalatā: Inconstancy.

cintā: Anxiety.

danāṅgulikṣepa: Raising hands with outstreteched fingers in admiration of the actors.

Devapañho: Divine oracle.

dhr̥ti: contentment.

ghaṇṭā: Bell.

glāni: Depression or weakness.

gandharva vedabudha: One who has mastery over theatrical arts.

gāthās: Legends.

garva: Arrogance.

goṣṭhī: Gathering.

harṣa: Joy.

jaḍatā: Stupor.

jugupsā: Disgust.

kalpavr̥kṣa: Wishfulfilling tree of Hindu mythology.

kaṁpa: Vibration.

kārṣāpaṇa: Ancient Indian currency.

kathakas: Narrators.

krodha: Anger.

kinnaras: Semi-divine creatures, known for their knowledge of music.

kumārīpañho: Oracle by Virgin.

laya: Tempo.

mada: Intoxication.

mañcas: Dias or stage.

makaras: Crocodiles.

maraṇa: Death.

māra: Buddhist Version of Kāmadeva, the god of love and passion.

mati: assurance.

moha: Distraction.

nāgaraka: Citizen.

nakha: Finger nails.

nepathya: Back stage.

nidrā: Sleep.

nirveda: Despondency.

pralaya: fainting.

pulakaromāñca: Horripilation at the sight of something exciting and curious.

raṅgamgatā: Female artistes on the stage.

ratnin: One of courtiers of Vedic age.

sādhu: Exclamation at the sight of something Virtuous.

sahṛdaya: Refined and sympathetic audience.

śaṅkā: Apprehension.

śāstra: Scriptures.

sattva: Emotional response.

smṛti: Recollection.

śilāveśma: Cave house.

śrama: Weariness.

sveda: Perspiration.

tāla: Time (beats).

trāsa: Fright.

upāṅgas: Sub-divisions.

ugratā: Cruelty.

unmād: Insanity.

utsāh: Enthusiasm.

vīṇā: Flute.

vismaya: Surprise.

vuṇ or ṇvul: Suffix

vyādhi: Sickness

Index